The **2 0 0 0**

PRUNE
Book

The **2000**

PRUNE Book

HOW TO SUCCEED

IN WASHINGTON'S

TOP JOBS

JOHN H. TRATTNER

COUNCIL FOR EXCELLENCE IN GOVERNMENT

BROOKINGS INSTITUTION PRESS
Washington, D.C.

ABOUT BROOKINGS

The Brookings Institution is a private nonprofit organization devoted to research, education, and publication on important issues of domestic and foreign policy. Its principal purpose is to bring knowledge to bear on current and emerging policy problems. The Institution maintains a position of neutrality on issues of public policy. Interpretations or conclusions in Brookings publications should be understood to be solely those of the authors.

Library of Congress Cataloging-in-Publication data

Trattner, John H.
  The 2000 prune book : how to succeed in Washington's top
jobs / John H. Trattner.
      p.   cm.
Includes bibliographical references and index.
  ISBN 0-8157-8552-6 (cloth: alk. paper)
  1. Government executives—United States. I. Title: Prune book.
II. Title.
  JK723.E9 T715 2000   00-010584
  352.2'93—dc21   CIP

9 8 7 6 5 4 3 2 1

The paper used in this publication meets minimum requirements of the American National Standard for Information Sciences—Permanence of Paper for Printed Library Materials: ANSI Z39.48-1992.

Typeset in Sabon

Composition by Circle Graphics
Columbia, Maryland

Printed by R. R. Donnelley and Sons
Harrisonburg, Virginia

Contents

5 Positions in Foreign Policy, National Security, and Defense

6 Positions in Health, Safety, and Environmental Policy   207

Foreword

WITH THIS EDITION, the *Prune Book* concept is a dozen years old. Presidential appointees who came into plum jobs as 1989 began are now pretty wise prunes. So are those whom the ensuing two presidential elections brought into government. And a new generation is about to discover what *Prune Books* have been suggesting all along: that experience counts.

What else have we learned? That government can indeed improve its results when its people work smarter and better. The old tag line—better government through better people—may still be on the mark. It won't remain relevant, however, unless they are selected, trained, retained, led, motivated, and organized with vision and skill.

Conventional wisdom has it that politics rules substance in Washington. But in the selection of people for high-level positions, there are now signs of a greater effort to get the substance right, even at the expense of some political realities. *Prune Books* have encouraged that shift, while recognizing that tension between politics and substance will always exist.

We still contend with the perception that highly qualified people are those most likely to have backgrounds that present potential conflicts of interest. Perhaps the irony and paradox of that perception is beginning to be better understood. Joseph Kennedy earned a rough, tough reputation on Wall Street, but when he became chairman of the Securities and Exchange Commission, people said of him that "it takes one to know one." There are, of course, significant conflicts that are proper disqualifiers for public service. For the great majority of candidates for appointment, however, we must try to work our way back to a more balanced way of using experience and talent, allowing the best people to be tapped by reducing obstacles to their willingness to serve.

Reinventing government has its roots in programs like the *Prune* series. While success has not been as great as some optimists hoped, there has been progress. That cannot, should not, be measured by cost savings alone. By most surveys, the quality of most government services is better today than in 1988. Quality may be hard to measure, but it most surely is more valuable than all the money that is saved. We tend to forget the hidden and unmeasurable costs to society of coping with inefficient, low-quality government services.

Like the earlier *Prune* volumes, this book is designed to help sustain and build energy and momentum in the never-ending process of making government work better for all of its citizens.

Frank A. Weil
A founder of the *Prune Book* program
Former chairman, Council for Excellence in Government

Preface

THIS IS THE SIXTH BOOK in a series that began in the presidential year of 1988. Drawing directly on the experience of people who know government best, it attempts, first, to show what good leadership in the upper appointed ranks of the federal executive branch is really about. Then it discusses several dozen jobs and types of jobs at those levels in which such leadership is indispensable.

At the beginning, *Prune Books* confined themselves exclusively to profiles of high-level posts, mostly in the executive branch, selected for their central roles and accountability in guiding the most consequential work of the federal government. With the last volume, published at the start of the second Clinton administration, the scope of the books broadened. Beyond its examination of jobs, the 1997 book took a detailed look at the labyrinth through which presidential appointments—in the absence of overdue reform of the process—must continue to make their way. It also packaged insights gathered from a cross section of those who have served in these positions about the complicated demands of appointed service and how to weather them.

This 2000 edition continues the expanded reach of the *Prune* series that began four years ago. Its featured chapter on leadership in the executive branch finds a responsive chord in our conversations with more than sixty incumbent presidential appointees about the positions the book describes. We were struck by the number of them who, when asked about the necessary qualifications for the jobs they held, did not begin with conventional lists of specific professional credentials. Instead, they spoke first about personal qualities—skills with people and communications, accessibility, intellectual independence, objectivity, commitment, a sense of excitement, and a talent for reaching consensus, earning loyalty, and bringing employees to understand and adapt to necessary change.

Their emphasis on these elements of leadership competence affirms the basic ways in which people have to work together to advance toward any goal. It says that anyone attempting to lead a major enterprise in government must come to it in recognition of this fact of life and bring to the effort at least some of the personal—one could say human—attributes that it requires.

The job-profile section of the book contains discussions of two additional topics that deserve attention here. One addresses the special considerations involved in making cabinet and White House staff appointments. The other focuses on five senior management positions common to most federal agencies and integral to their effective operation. As for the fifty-six other profiled positions themselves, they are grouped by the areas of federal responsibility in which they operate: economy, technology, and trade; foreign policy, national security, and defense; health, safety, and environment; jobs, income security, and welfare; education, training, and lifelong learning; law enforcement; national infrastructure; and central management national infrastructure.

The narrative job descriptions are designed with a couple of main purposes in mind. First, to look at the issues that will engage these jobs in the administration elected in 2000—and beyond—and the substantive or operational problems their occupants are likely to face. Second, to supply a reasonably comprehensive idea of the scope of each job: what it's responsible for, how the work gets done, the variety and complexity of the task, and some recent history, where appropriate. Each profile also underlines the personal and professional credentials that serve the position best.

Rather than remind readers in each job discussion of activities, duties, and relationships that are common to all of these positions, let's stipulate them here. Most individuals in these jobs travel regularly to Capitol Hill, take part in annual rounds of budget development and defense, manage contacts with a bevy of constituent interest groups, pore over strategic plans and performance reports, struggle through the deliberations of interminable interagency working groups, talk daily or weekly with scores of colleagues in their agencies and elsewhere in government, deal with personnel matters, speak occasionally or frequently in public settings, and engage in varying amounts of contact with reporters, editors, and television interviewers. Unless these activities have a special meaning or importance for given positions, therefore, they don't get specific mention in the profiles. In most cases, however, you'll find such nuts and bolts data as the size of budgets and work forces.

Members of the Council for Excellence in Government, most of them veterans of service in senior appointed federal positions, chose the positions discussed in this edition. Their task was to peruse and discuss together the universe of some 700 jobs filled by presidential appointment, identify those they judged to be most critical, and select a manageable number for inclusion in the book. It has long been clear that many more jobs deserve attention of this kind than the number any one of these books can accommodate. Inevitably, those selected are the product of tough choices and close calls. Just as inevitably, some positions on the list this time have also been selected more than once over the years for earlier books. That's because the mandates of such jobs remain key to management of the country's public agenda, even as the nature of what they do evolves.

The information and comments the profiles present are derived mainly from lengthy interviews with individuals holding the jobs at the time the book was in preparation (January–June 2000). Since then, as normally happens in administrations nearing their close, a number of our interviewees have left their jobs. A departing official is usually replaced temporarily by someone serving in an acting capacity while the job awaits its next confirmed appointee. In any case, the subsequent departure of some of those we talked with does not lessen the value of what they told us or change to any real degree the substance or character of the jobs they recently held.

Firsthand research with job occupants present and past has been basic to all books in the *Prune* series. These volumes gain additional authority from the opportunity given each interviewee to read the draft profile in order to corroborate and sanction the information and direct quotes drawn from the interviews. From time to time in the cases of jobs previously described, this book's profiles borrow fragments of still-valid comment from those interviewed for earlier volumes. Continuing past practice, each profile also appends a biographic sketch of the job's incumbent and lists those who held the job earlier—in this case, since 1989—and their present positions or status. Inevitably, in a handful of cases we were unable to assemble complete biographical data or identify the current activities of some previous occupants.

Now and then a reader has expressed surprise that a position considered noteworthy was not covered. Indeed, a great number of the several hundred *Prune* jobs merit attention in these books. And, while no single volume can discuss them all in the kind of detail provided here, those positions that almost won places in this one are listed in appendix 2. Moreover, occupants of several jobs chosen for inclusion in the book declined to be interviewed. It is virtually meaningless to portray jobs in any detail without the central contributions or fresh, authoritative insights of the individuals who currently hold them. In the absence or unavailability of predecessors whose service was of very recent date, therefore, the inaccessibility of these few incumbents effectively eliminated discussion of their positions from the book.

For one or two other positions the book does include, we did not interview the current occupants but relied on appointees who had just departed the jobs and were available for interview. That was because the incumbents either felt they were too new to be able to talk meaningfully about their positions or were in an acting status.

The Council adheres to the simple truth that relevant experience is a critical credential in finding the right person for a job with a high degree of responsibility and trust in the conduct of public business. Experience is by no means the only necessary ingredient. But it deserves as much consideration by presidents, cabinet officers, and White House personnel officials as any of the others. To emphasize this point, we chose the *Prune* title to contrast the content of *Prune* books with that of a sought-after congressional publication—*Policy and Supporting Positions*—issued at the end of each presidential election year. Known more widely as the "plum book" (explanations for this vary), it is basically a list of several thousand executive branch positions filled by presidential appointment, among them the several hundred requiring Senate confirmation.

Plum books say nothing—that is not their purpose—about the experience that informed observers might deem necessary to handle the jobs effectively. In creating a resource that would do this and more, the Council wanted to remind readers and users of the inestimable value of experience: the quality developed through work, study, observation, practice, and the accumulation of on-site knowledge. A plum may look good on the outside but offers no guarantee that its content will satisfy. A prune wins no beauty prizes, but it has been around a while and has, as they say, the scars to prove it. It leaves no doubt that you will get what you see. That's what experience will do for you. And that's what *Prune Books* try to reflect.

Acknowledgments

MANY PEOPLE AND SEVERAL ORGANIZATIONS deserve lasting thanks for their singular contributions in bringing the 2000 *Prune Book* into existence. Two individuals head the list. Frank Weil, a former chairman of the Council for Excellence in Government, is a founder and leading benefactor of the *Prune* project. As with all of the previous volumes, he supplied substantial personal funds for the 2000 effort, sought resources for it elsewhere—an effort also joined by Council chairman John Macomber—and was helpful in many other ways. John C. Whitehead, like Frank a member of the Council's Board of Trustees, continued the generous support he has steadily provided for the book and other Council activities.

The Carnegie Corporation of New York has been a mainstay of these books since they began a dozen years ago. We greatly appreciate its ample grant for the 2000 effort and the personal role and interest of Geraldine Manion, chairperson for democracy and special projects. Joining Carnegie this time was PricewaterhouseCooper's energetic new Endowment for the Business of Government under the leadership of Mark Abramson. In addition to its financial support, the endowment is publishing as part of its Grant Reports series versions of this book's chapters 2 and 3. We would like to recognize the endowment for its interest and support.

As president and CEO of the Council, Pat McGinnis invested considerable time and thoughtful effort in many phases of this book's editorial production: fundraising, selecting jobs the book would cover, reviewing the drafting. Her guidance and reliable instincts were great assets throughout. Further, she played the central role in organizing three conferences with the White House, 1997–99, to orient new appointees and nominees to the nature of governing. Those sessions, the first of their kind and well managed by Council vice presidents Sally Sachar and, later, Heather Weston, were the basis for the book's special chapter on leadership.

Particular thanks go also to the dozens of individuals whose experience in matters of leadership and appointed service in government is the backbone of the book. Conveyed in panel discussions and lengthy individual conversations, their observations form the only reservoir of information available to new presidential appointees in the detail presented here. We are deeply grateful to them—current and past appointees, other executive branch officials, former members of the Congress, senior congressional and White House staff members, authors, journalists, political consultants—for sharing their accumulated wisdom so readily and enthusiastically.

We would like to recognize the Council Principals, whom we convened in the fall of 1999 to debate the choices for positions to be included in the book and to reach consensus: Donald Alexander, Walter Broadnax, Allan Burman, Christopher Chapin, Edward DeSeve, Aurelius Fernandez, Leslie Francis, William Hansen, Helen Kanovsky, Wallace Keene, Morgan Kinghorn, Cynthia Metzler, Nancy Rohrbach, Heather Ross, Jill Schuker, Michael B. Smith, Virginia Thomas, and Edwin Williamson. We are obliged to the many others who responded to our faxed request for input on the same subject. Our gratitude goes also to Katherine Higgins, who talked with us about appointments to the cabinet and to the White House staff.

I am especially grateful personally for the strong support of Laura Skaff and Sean D'Souza of the Council staff and of consultant Margaret Cerrato. Laura wrote chapter 3 of the book—"Key Positions in Strengthening Federal Management"—and did most of the individual interviews for the 2000 *Prune Book*. She brought to those assignments extensive experience in the field of government performance as well as a useful proficiency in research, developed in her previous work in federal and state government. We are indebted to her for the skill and poise with which she braced sixty-odd senior federal executives about their jobs—about the issues, challenges, and problems associated with them—and about their outlook and advice. Margaret Cerrato managed the administrative demands of the interview schedule, pursuing, arranging, and following up appointments and tracking the evolution of the schedule—all with refreshing grace and reliability. She was equally efficient in performing a number of research tasks and handling a voluminous correspondence. Sean D'Souza handled a hundred and one formatting chores and computer problems associated with producing the manuscript. His technical knowledge was admirable and his patience endless. It was an unusual pleasure to work as a team with three such capable, committed people.

A number of other people, beyond the immediate Council periphery, supported this effort in ways too diverse to mention. We appreciate the specific help in this respect of Stuart Eizenstat, Steven Kelman, Michael Messinger, Michael B. Smith, James Northup, and Jan Verrey (who transcribed dozens of interviews). Prominent in this category are our friends at the Brookings Institution Press—Director Robert Faherty, Acquisitions Editor Christopher Kelaher, Marketing Manager Becky Clark, and Art Coordinator Susan Woollen, as well as Gary Kessler, and who edited, proofread, and indexed the pages, in that order. "Critical" is an overused word, but the only one that can describe their flexibility, understanding, expertise, and ideas. All were indispensable.

There was, finally, the great support and thoughtfulness of still other members of the Council staff, especially Najia Aziz-Arsalayee, Shuron Coleman, Sue Ducat, Melissa Hardin, Ramiro Inguanzo, Janice Johnson, Anthony Shelborne, Dave Sheldon, Paulson Tharapatla, Ellen Weiss, Heather Weston, Barry White, and Joiwind Williams. Their help was plentiful and its value beyond estimating.

Introduction

THE "CHANGING OF THE GUARD" that occurs when a new president is elected is unparalleled in the rest of the world. The breadth and
depth of the turnover in leaders is breathtaking. Not only the White House
staff and cabinet, but also more than 7,400 other jobs are available for the
new president to fill. Though the obstacles in the appointments process
are daunting, it is amazing that so much change takes place in a reasonably orderly way.

Presidential appointments have been characterized in the past as
"plum" jobs, available to reward loyal supporters. Our image of a
"prune," that is, a plum seasoned with experience and wisdom, seems
more apt these days. Long gone are the perquisites of higher office and,
unfortunately to a large degree, even the prestige and respect once
afforded to public servants.

The challenge for the new administration is to lead in a way that not
only achieves important results in the public interest but also connects
with and inspires the trust of the American people and others around the
world.

We know from opinion research conducted for the Council by Peter
Hart and Bob Teeter that most Americans, especially young Americans,
no longer think of government as of, by, and for the people. They think
of it as "the" government, rather than "our" government. This should
be regarded as a wake-up call for the new leaders, not only in the executive branch but in Congress as well. Skill and effectiveness operating

"inside the beltway" will not alone be enough to inspire people around the country to participate in governing or to persuade young people to choose careers in government.

Elliot Richardson, a founding member of the Council for Excellence in Government, said in his last speech at the Council, "Trust is not just a cornerstone, but *the* foundation of representative self-government."

In a discussion at the Council a month before his death on the eve of the twenty-first century, Elliot spoke eloquently about the most important qualities of the next president. A president, he said, needs a strong sense of history and an intelligent and searching imagination—to understand the needs of people everywhere, to see how a president's actions will affect their lives, to learn how to translate the complexity of a modern, fast-changing society into policies that encourage balanced change beneficial to society, and to grasp how foreign leaders, opposing political personalities, powerful opinion makers, and others think and respond to political imperatives as the president sees them.

His advice applies not only to the president, but also to the cabinet, the White House, and the subcabinet appointees who are the subject of this book. All must have a sense of history and the imagination to look around the corner and envision the future they want to help create.

A sense of history comes from studying the lessons of the past and understanding the context and nuances that contributed both to successes and failures. Besides reading this book and others about past administrations, the new team should take the time to talk and really listen to their predecessors and others who have been players in the process. Most who have held these positions regard their service as a public trust and are more than willing to offer insights about their experience in an honest and constructive way.

Beyond understanding the past, the new president and his team must have the imagination to think imaginatively about the future and how to engage the American people in creating it. Technology has tremendous potential not only to improve the performance of government but also to connect it to the citizens it serves. Unusual allies and innovative partnerships undoubtedly will play a larger role in strategies to achieve excellence in government and excellence in our society.

The American people, especially young people, are optimistic about the future of government and its potential to make a positive difference in their lives and those of their fellow Americans. Leaders with a sense of history and the imagination to look ahead creatively have the potential to build broad ownership of our democracy and to make us proud of its accomplishments.

Patricia McGinnis
President and CEO, Council for Excellence in Government

The 2000
PRUNE
Book

1

White House Staff and Cabinet Appointments

It would be pretentious to offer an incoming administration extensive advice on what kinds of individuals should be considered for senior White House staff positions or as potential heads of cabinet departments. These appointments, or most of them, are some of the most personal that a president makes. They are at the same time among the most politically sensitive. Presidents usually know their own minds on recruitment at this level; they aren't noticeably receptive to suggestions launched from outside the circle of their political intimates.

But some general points can be made—and here are some notable ones, offered by well-known veterans of the campaign and transition wars and of high-level service close to the presidency:

—**Put the White House chief of staff in place on the day after the inauguration.** Do the same for other key staff members—at a minimum, the personnel director, general counsel, and legislative assistant. This means knowing well ahead of time who will take these jobs. It's a serious mistake to put them or other important staff choices off until a cabinet is chosen.

—**So-called cabinet government is not a good or a workable idea.** But an overly aggressive White House staff, so domineering that it drowns out the cabinet and other voices, won't fly, either.

—**Avoid loading the White House staff with purely political people from the campaign.** The task now is to create and run a government.

—**Consult outgoing White House staff people.** They have an unmatched store of valuable advice to pass on.

—**Avoid creating new White House positions or restructuring the staff at the beginning.** Save this for later and do it with the benefit of experience.

The chief of staff is, of course, the pivot of an efficient, focused White House. One of the closest to the president in frequency of contact, the job is central to the processes of formulating decision options and regulating the flow of information to the president. It is responsible for overseeing the work and handling the individual concerns of several hundred substantive, operational, and administrative people on a staff of high turnover. A chief of staff must know the Congress, understand politics, function as a key presidential confidante, motivate and cheerlead the staff, and generally make the place run.

That's why this individual must be chosen early and be prepared and operating on the administration's first day. Former Bush White House counsel Boyden Gray made that point effectively at the third workshop for journalists convened in June 2000 by the Council for Excellence in Government in its *Government from the Inside* series. "President Bush got an early start before he was even nominated," Gray recalled. The candidate "ran a sort of bake-off" among people he was considering as potential chiefs of staff, giving each of them a significant piece of responsibility for Bush's activities at the nominating convention and ensuing campaign. As a result, Gray said, the future president knew who his chief of staff would be well before the person himself knew.

Moreover, says Katherine Higgins, who served as cabinet secretary in the Clinton White House, "you've got to have a chief of staff who really understands the importance of building a team." What happens, Higgins told us, "is that people are so busy doing their jobs that it's easy to get disconnected or not know what's going on. If there is no regular way to manage the affairs of the White House so that everyone feels a part of it and knows what's happening, people will go off on their own and try to figure it out as best they can. That's very dangerous and counterproductive."

White House staff and the people who process cabinet-level appointments "have to be in place early on," Gray said at the Council workshop for journalists. It's a point on which there is virtual unanimity. "Carter and Clinton got around to appointing the White House staff very late," said Harrison Wellford, a Carter appointee who served in the transitions of both presidents, "and it hurt them badly in the first hundred days." Leon Panetta, Clinton's second chief of staff, underscored this urgency in comments at a Heritage Foundation roundtable discussion in 1999, "Running the White House" (part of the foundation's Mandate for Leadership series entitled *Keys to a Successful Presidency*). Panetta noted a "natural tendency" to wait until after the cabinet appointments to focus on staff at the White House. He called that a mistake. "Appoint the key staff as soon as the president is elected," he advised. "I can't tell you how important it is to try to learn that lesson." This should be as high on a new president's agenda as cabinet selection, Panetta said, "because you need to have your personal team in place as you move forward."

Accomplishing this, said former Reagan chief of staff Edwin Meese at a later Heritage session in May 2000, is "a sign of confidence and sure-footedness." In fact, Harvard professor emeritus Richard Neustadt argued in that discussion that staff appointments should actually precede those to the cabinet. Not only does the president need immediate support, Neustadt said, but some staff and cabinet appointments also should be "positioned" to provide a perspective almost as broad as the president's will need to be. Should a new president and chief of staff establish new staff jobs or revise the White House staff structure? "Start filling the central positions pretty much as you find them," Neustadt counseled. "Do your innovating in terms of restructuring toward the end of the first term."

On Panetta's recommended list for early appointment were the chief of staff and deputies (in order to get the core management operation under way); the senior foreign and economic policy teams; the legal counsel; and the people who will run domestic policy, the budget, the press office, communications, and legislative affairs. There's no indefinite honeymoon period for these appointments, he warned. A president who isn't setting policy within the White House from Inauguration Day forward, who is not taking the offensive, will find out that others are. "It's just the nature of this town," he said.

Observers of White House operations agree that to reward political and other campaign staffers with jobs in the White House to any significant degree is unwise. The point has been made many times, but it bears exploring because the mistake in question seems to recur at regular intervals. Understandably, the instinct to stick with those who have brought you this far can be difficult to resist, and at least some campaign staffers can advance legitimate claims to jobs in the West Wing. Reflecting on this, Katherine Higgins says "the campaign model is that you want to have the ear of the boss. It's all about proximity. So everybody thinks the way to do it is to work in the White House—the closer you are to the Oval Office, ostensibly the more power you have. When in fact it can be argued that it's the agencies, what happens outside the White House, that's just as important, at least in terms of getting the work done." But former Kennedy White House counsel Theodore Sorensen put his finger on reality at the Heritage discussion in May. "Forget about putting campaign staff in the White House," he said. "You now have to govern."

Margaret Tutwiler, a former Bush White House staff member, spoke tellingly to this at the Council's workshop:

> I had worked in the Bush campaign and was now working with Jim Baker who had been named chief of staff. And all these strange people began coming into my life, who had never worked in the campaign. I had slaved in the campaign for two and half years and remember asking Jim Baker one day who these people were. What have they done? How did they help get us here? And he said something I did not understand at the time: He chose these people to go into responsible positions at the White House in large measure because they had previous executive branch, preferably White House, experience. The [campaign] group were still finding their way around

the machinery of the executive branch nine months after we'd been there. The people Baker put into key positions already knew the machinery of the executive branch. It is something that definitely serves any president well—to have people who know how this massive machine works in reality.

The responsibilities of core senior staff positions imply the kinds of professional backgrounds they require. At the personal level, these should be individuals who already have generous amounts of experience with political, governmental, and media Washington. This is a different mix than is found elsewhere, even in state capitals. Candidates for the senior jobs should also demonstrate a high comfort level on the public platform and in media settings. They are just as essential as cabinet chiefs as spokesmen for and defenders of policy and, like them, just as reflective of the president's judgment in choosing them.

"Being bright helps," says Higgins. "It's not just your everyday people who can stay afloat. But it's also being agile. Things happen because you're operating in the real world, whether it's a plane crash or natural disaster or a foreign policy emergency or a crisis on Capitol Hill." Many very bright people "get overwhelmed" in White House jobs, she says, "because it is not linear."

In the realm of appointments to the cabinet, it's useful to recall for a moment the once-lively debate over the merits of what is called cabinet government as opposed to policy authority centralized in the White House. Definitions of cabinet government vary. Generally, the concept calls for department secretaries to enjoy wider discretion in choosing the people the president will appoint to high-level political management positions in their agencies, and somewhat greater control of decisionmaking within their own domains, with less command-and-control scrutiny from the White House. Whatever the precise definition of cabinet government, however, most observers agree that it doesn't work as a general operating approach or over the long term. "If the president says he wants cabinet government and wants to appoint the cabinet first and worry about the White House staff second," Wellford told journalists at the Council's June 2000 workshop, "that's a clear sign that he's on the road to perdition."

Cabinet government is "neither a good idea nor a workable idea in our system," said Theodore Sorensen at that meeting.

From time to time, presidential candidates have said they would want to make the cabinet very important and we'll have regular meetings and the cabinet will vote on decisions. The truth of the matter is, none of them have done so. Why, when you're going to decide on agriculture policy, do you want the secretary of defense or the secretary of the treasury or other very busy people sitting around the table when they have little or nothing to contribute? There are a few issues, such as the civil service or the upcoming budget, that are of interest to and involve every member of the cabinet. And for those purposes, cabinet meetings are worthwhile. Other than that, most cabinet meetings are usually quite boring and not all that useful.

In his 1996 book, *Reflections of a Radical Moderate*, the late Elliot Richardson asserted that the cabinet as presently structured "is incapable of being the kind of deliberative body to which presidents can usefully submit key issues." Virtually all the cabinet meetings he attended under three presidents, he wrote, "focused on bland common denominators like the economic outlook, displays of budgetary breakdowns, or the status of the administration's legislative proposals."

On the other hand, Sorensen said at the workshop for journalists, "if the only alternative to cabinet government is an aggressive White House staff, I would flash at least an amber light. Of course, the president needs people who see the government as he sees it—that is, governmentwide. He needs people who can help coordinate the views that come in from the departments. He certainly needs the best and the brightest. But let's not have too many of these aggressive types; let's not have purely political instead of substantive types in the White House."

The trend to centralizing core policy and decisionmaking in the White House has been clear for at least a generation. One major reason is that events have simply overtaken theory, as George Mason University's James Pfiffner reminded the Heritage audience in 1999. "Many things that used to be done outside of the White House" by cabinet departments and agencies "are now done inside," Pfiffner said. Among them are domestic policy, foreign policy, international trade policy, national security, legal advice to the president, outreach to interest groups, and personnel recruitment. Over the years, these functions and more have come to be coordinated, if not ordained, in the White House or by agencies in the president's executive office—the Office of Management and Budget, the National Economic Council, the National Security Council, the Office of the Legal Counsel, the Office of Presidential Personnel.

Several related developments spurred that migration of authority. The process of governing has faced growing complexities posed by rapid social change at home, by economic globalization abroad, by the rise of commerce by Internet, by seismic corporate integration across national boundaries, by ever-faster advances in biosciences and information technology, by the emergence of new protagonists on the international scene, and by new kinds of threats to global stability. On a different level, administrations have had to develop new strategies for pursuing their objectives during recurring bouts of unusually partisan conflict with the Congress. The emergence of financial surpluses challenges administrations to redefine the shaping and management of the federal budget.

Inevitably, under the press of factors like these, the White House has tightened the reins and reached instinctively for greater policy control of departments and agencies. Almost gone are the days of assertive, quasi-independent cabinet figures in the tradition of Harold Ickes Sr., Henry Morgenthau, Dean Acheson, or Henry Kissinger. It was in recognition of this evolution that Richard Neustadt, in the Heritage Foundation session in May 2000, offered some advice to incoming presidents. "Cushion cabinet members," he said, "against the shock of discovering that they are not going to be the president's chief policy advisers." The fact is that cabinet departments have been gradually relegated to the implementation, not the design, of key policy and key decisions.

But exceptionally important roles remain to cabinet officers and heads of agency today, roles that suggest the personal qualities to look for in making appointments at this level. "People who are good at these jobs have a sense of vision, a sense of mission, and know what they want to accomplish," says Katherine Higgins. "They care about the mission of the department, they can lead, they can put together an agenda and get people to endorse it and implement it." Higgins—who was also chief of staff to the secretary of labor before she went to the White House and returned to Labor later as deputy secretary of the department—adds that effective cabinet officers are "pretty quick studies in figuring out how Washington works. They've got political common sense and are not tone deaf in terms of the press and politics. They are effective communicators and high-energy, driven people."

As internal and external communicators, cabinet and agency heads are spokespersons—proponents and defenders of policy. To a very significant degree, they tend an administration's relations and advocate its goals with the Congress. They travel tirelessly around this country and to others, as necessary. Ideally, they are innovative, smart about information technology, and sensitive to government's work force deficiencies, especially in attracting capable young adults.

Constance Horner, who ran the White House personnel office for the last year and a half of the Bush administration, observed to us in 1996 that cabinet secretaries are chosen partly because they meet certain political needs of the president—partly because they send certain policy signals. As veterans of careers in fields like state or national politics, business, or law, cabinet leaders have political constituencies of their own. Some of those constituents support the administration; some of them don't. But both are important to the president. With these groups, cabinet members need leeway to sustain the relationships that are part of the reason they find themselves at the top of the government.

An effective cabinet team in today's circumstances should demonstrate the readiness and skill to operate as part of an integrated, collaborative group. Its members should be prepared to cooperate fully in advancing the president's goals, to communicate usefully—upward, downward, and with one another—and to subordinate their own agendas to that of the president. On the last point, Higgins says the issue is "not so much diverse opinions or divergence of opinions. It's how they get conveyed. No president can afford to have them aired in the press, as opposed to in the family. This is part of the conversation that any president and/or chief of staff has to have with the senior people from day one—the rules of the game."

As she also points out, "all knowledge doesn't rest at the White House." Cabinet members do have to be able to run their departments and service their customers. They do have some opportunity to come up with policy ideas that work. At the same time, "people have to be loyal to the president. He's the one who ran for office. He's taken the political risks. It's his agenda that people voted for. And everybody in the cabinet has got to know whom they work for."

2

Presidential Appointees and the Leadership Challenge

Many men and women who take appointed leadership jobs in a new ad-ministration have managed enterprises of one kind or another in their ear-lier careers. But most have not done it in the federal government. While there are some similarities between the two, the differences are far more important.

In fact, an administration's high-level political leaders inhabit a bracing landscape unlike any other. At their home base, appointees operate in the equivalent of a vast forest that echoes with the multiple tasks of governing—issues and goals, policy and action. On the upcountry slopes of the Con-gress, they negotiate the sometimes-fierce crosswinds of money, prerogative, and politics that deeply affect what they can achieve. Meanwhile, waves of watchful media beat steadily against the shores of this domain, now and again flooding the forest or sweeping an appointee (or an administration) out to sea. Surrounding the entire region lie the great plains of the people, who view what they see and hear with a mixture of hope and doubt.

Each main feature of this world—the executive branch, the legislature, the press, the public—tests the management skills of presidential appointees in distinctive ways. Those who can hack it are best equipped to lead the way to what every administration prizes most—the results it is setting out to get. Those who can't or don't want to play in that league will have a harder time achieving anything notable—and may even fail.

This chapter focuses the firsthand insights of dozens of qualified people on these leadership challenges and the management issues that are in-volved. Nothing they have to say makes any claim on original truth—no secret gospels, no revelations, no strokes of genius. Rather, theirs are the collected nonpartisan voices of common sense, realism, and experience. They have all been around the track; they speak usefully and with author-ity. They are cabinet secretaries, other veterans of executive branch ap-pointment, former members of the Congress, professional congressional staffers, journalists who cover government and individuals who teach or write about it, and knowledgeable political hands. Some have labored in more than one of these areas. (For the sake of easier reading, we are not at-taching names to what they impart here, although sometimes their present or former positions are indicated. You'll find all the information on sources in appendix 1.)

What follows draws liberally from what these seasoned individuals said at leadership conferences for new presidential appointees that were con-vened jointly by the White House and the Council for Excellence in Gov-ernment in 1997, 1998, and 1999; and from interviews with the occupants of the appointive jobs profiled elsewhere in this book. Largely through their eyes, we'll look at each sector of that diversified terrain where appointees toil. But first, brief comments from five of them that suggest the basic leadership tasks involved.

Former presidential appointee, about the executive branch:

It's hard for people in the private sector and even academia to understand how hard it is to get things done in Washington, how dense a thicket of constraints surrounds you. Constraints put in place by Congress, by budgetary limits, by campaign promises, constituency groups, the administrative procedures act, the Constitution, all kinds of reasons why you can't do something you need to do, why you can't advance a perfectly reasonable piece of your agenda.

Former member of the House of Representatives, about the Congress:

All legislative powers are vested in Congress. Not most, not some, not domestic, but all legislative power is vested in Congress, and members of Congress take that seriously. Congress is much more ideological than the public generally is, and much more ideological than most members of the executive branch. Members of Congress are political. They are expected to be political. The role of Congress is to be the forum in which differing points of view are debated, thought out, and one or the other prevails.

Head of an agency, about the media:

You've got to understand that almost nobody in Washington is paying attention to your issue, regardless of how essential it is. You've got to break through the background clutter. You have to educate the media about your agency and its objectives. As a starter, better you invest an hour educating a reporter than try to get a story out.

Senior White House staffer, about the public:

It's really important nowadays that you explain why what you do in government is relevant to people's lives. It used to be self-evident, because there were a lot more tensions and everything "the government" did was seen as relevant. Generally now it's seen as irrelevant, and you have to make your case.

Political consultant, about the public:

What is truly lacking in so many people in government is that they don't bother to develop an understanding of where the public is. I've always believed that almost nothing in government is do-able if the public doesn't want it. There are times when members of congress or presidents actually lead for a while. But in the main, what gets done here is done because there's a reasonable group of people out there that think it's important.

Leadership in the Executive Branch

What is successful leadership in an administration in Washington? Is it designing policy? Making decisions? Issuing instructions? Giving a speech? Spending money?

Hardly. Such activities are essential; they're what most political managers routinely do. By themselves, they don't amount to strong, productive management. A lot of people in government today recognize that, but it's useful to make the point for each new administration. Leading successfully really means getting something tangible, something visible, for the money and effort invested. In a word, results.

In private business, as is so often repeated, the bottom line—profit or loss—makes it relatively easy to judge results. In government, it's harder. Much that looks like a result really isn't. When public leaders think they've gone the last hard mile, crossed the finish line, they often haven't.

Suppose the Federal Aviation Administration is investing millions to protect the health of air travelers by developing a climate control system for passenger jets that doesn't distribute airborne bacteria around the cabin. It plans the project, puts the job out to bid, spends the funds, convenes a lot of interagency consultation, tells the media about it. But those aren't results, only steps along the way. Not until the prototype is built, tested successfully, and demonstrated to airframe builders and airline executives is any real result in hand. Not until airlines are convinced they should install the new system—or are required to by regulation—has the FAA gone the full route by ensuring that passengers benefit from it.

Or take the actual decision by the Internal Revenue Service to allow electronic filing of tax returns. Announcing the plan, getting the technology designed, hiring the personnel—again, those were just way stations. Certainly, they added up to a lot more than just a visible intention to make the change. But they were not yet a real result. That came when people could actually go on line, send their returns to the IRS, and see them accepted, safe and sound, as advertised.

The first lesson of leading within an agency, then, is to pursue ends, not means. It's not how much money you spend, how many meetings you call, how many policy papers you put out, how many times you testify on Capitol Hill. It is not input, or even output. It is what the professionals like to call desired outcomes. It's results.

> Focus on outcomes, not on input. It's so easy to get caught up in getting the process right and getting the regulations just perfect and anticipating everything that might go wrong, but failing to notice that no real people were touched by what you did.

Part of the problem in going after results is the understandable attraction for appointees of the world of policymaking. Policy, after all, is what guides most of their work. It seems like the most important aspect of a leadership position. It requires creativity, design skill, the art of negotiating—loftier assets, to some, than the ability to run things, and it seemingly is more likely to earn recognition and prestige. Again, however, policymaking alone doesn't bring results.

> A lot of us come to Washington and want to be engaged in high policy. If we just get the policy right, everything will be different. I would suggest just the opposite. We spend much more time on policy than is needed, and so little on implementation. In the end you're going to be judged on what actually happens, not on whether there is a new declaration of direction and a nice event at the White House.

Why are better results the executive branch's most critical assignment? It is not just their enormous intrinsic value for the national well-being. It is also because there are increasingly workable ways to measure results—that is, to measure performance. The Government Performance and Results Act, passed in 1993, was only the beginning. Tools to measure are becoming more precise. They are beginning to find more acceptance among the decisionmakers who appropriate money for government programs. That means executive branch managers will be facing ever-strengthening mandates from the Congress to get better results for the resources they use.

Yet the most convincing reason why results matter can be found in national opinion surveys. Just about every poll in sight shows persistent, widespread public disenchantment with government (though not with government's potential). Government today turns large numbers of Americans off. A majority thinks of it, not as our government, but as the government; According to a June 1999 Council for Excellence in Government

Hart/Teeter national poll, only one in four believes Washington works for the public interest. But most people continue to believe that it can. They want better results from government. And that, in the end, is probably the most urgent mandate of all.

The Customer Question

Private business learned some time back that long-term survival and profit are possible only if an enterprise is making those who use its product or service happy. Satisfy your customers on a sustained basis, it can be fairly be argued, and you have achieved a supremely important objective (a point suggested by Xerox in a 1993 publication, *A World of Quality: The Timeless Passport*). The federal government, too, is paying increasing attention to the customer challenge. Exhorted by presidential orders, aided by polls and surveys, agencies are cranking customer focus and satisfaction into their strategies. The American people, it is often alleged, are government's ultimate customers. No doubt about it, happy customers are a major calibration on an agency's results barometer.

But let's also be realistic. Public agencies face realities not encountered in a corporate setting. First, their customers and the sources of their funding are usually not one and the same. Second, they work under constraints and oversight that don't impede private companies or nonprofits. Third, in government, satisfied customers are not invariably the best measure of results or of what is best for the country.

> We can easily have very happy customers in programs that efficiently put out money and place few demands on recipients. But that may be the worst possible result for the effectiveness of the resources. A happy customer is not always what the taxpayer should want.

A case in point, cited by the author of that quote, is the disability benefits distributed by the Social Security Administration. It would be nice to support beneficiaries to the limits of what each of them claims is necessary. But that would hardly be practical in a society where many interests compete for the available public resources (and it would violate fiduciary norms for which SSA also has a responsibility). The right result here—the one that best responds to both individual and national interests—is the optimum balance between the requirements of the claimant and of good financial stewardship of a public resource.

Put another way, customers are a key element in seeking the right result, and it's great if what you're doing makes them jump up and down with pleasure. But, for government managers, customer satisfaction is not the sole or final objective. In this democracy, Americans want results from government not only as individual customers of its services, but also as citizens intent on shaping a more peaceful, educated, compassionate, healthy, just, and creative society.

Tools: Change

There was once a federal agency charged with helping people hit by natural and other kinds of disasters. But it had big problems that kept it from doing an effective job. For one thing, it was an organizational jungle—or, in the words of its newly appointed leader: "This was an agency with a lot of little agencies inside of it. None were working together. There was no customer service. There was no support for one another or one another's programs."

This agency also had operated on the assumption that it was statutorily unable to aid disaster victims until requested by state governments. Further, well after the cold war had ended, the media discovered the agency was spending most of its budget to maintain communications for government leaders after a nuclear attack. Successive administrations had loaded the agency with their least-capable political appointees. It was the butt of jokes within government circles and of congressional criticism; legislation was in the works to abolish it. A survey showed that half its workers would take new jobs if offered them.

There is still a federal agency responsible for helping the victims of disaster. But the problems of the Federal Emergency Management Agency are behind it. Fresh leadership reorganized its structure, giving career officials a leading voice in the crucial decisions. A reinterpretation of legislation governing its actions now allows the agency to put resources at the locations of predictable natural disasters before they strike. Much of the money that once funded nuclear war communications now goes to disaster preparedness, training, and up-to-date relief techniques. FEMA speeded the various ways it responds to victims' needs, expanded its communications to the public, reached out to the many congressional committees with jurisdiction. Its success in all this has drawn raves everywhere—from the Congress, state disaster relief agencies, the media, the people it has helped.

Another federal agency—the Labor Department's Occupational Safety and Health Administration—once found itself in a different kind of difficulty. Its job was to set and enforce rules that protected employees in six million American workplaces. But employers had long seen agency inspectors as more interested in paperwork infractions than real dangers to health and safety. They charged that inspectors cared only about enforcement quotas and that the agency failed to heed the costs levied on smaller enterprises. While an industry spokesperson labeled OSHA "our least-loved agency," organized labor alleged it was slow to modernize its health and safety standards and lax in nailing employers who violated them. The steady cross fire led a widely read magazine to call it the most reviled agency in government. A drop in budget and staff had meanwhile weakened OSHA's inspection capacity—leaving only enough to visit a given factory floor, assembly plant, or repair shop once every eighty years. Various pieces of proposed legislation tried to undermine or abolish its authority and further cut back its funding.

Again, the turnaround for this agency came under new leadership unafraid to change things. It sought to alter the image of the agency from ineffective nitpicker to strategic, smart operator. It set up an internal team to redesign OSHA's work in the field—a team that was the agency in microcosm, with field and headquarters people, managers, and frontline employees working together full time. They came up with a plan to get measurable results by using data that defined local safety and health problems. OSHA would then attack those problems not only with traditional enforcement but with partnerships, education, and outreach. The extra resources to do it would come from gains in efficiency, to be achieved by improved quality processes and better use of information technology. At the same time, the team approach would help convert the agency's stiff, top-down culture to one of innovation and risk taking.

OSHA took many steps meanwhile to make sure the Congress got its message of redesign and transformation.

> It pursued an agreement with the Congress not to have to do everything, but to be able to concentrate on a relatively small number of things that will turn out to be particularly valuable. So that lesson is one of limiting as well as focusing liability.

The results? OSHA became an agency able to survive an entire congressional session without any further reduction of its mandate. After four years, its budget had increased by about 7 percent. It won a prestigious award for innovation. An association of employers participating in the agency's voluntary protection program testified against a House bill that would have restricted OSHA's enforcement powers. An industry journal called the new era "one of the more promising periods" in the agency's history and hoped its reforms would not disappear. Looking back, OSHA's boss said:

Once you set a course of change, you have to stick with it. You don't have to stick with every detail, but you can't waver on fundamentals. You have to show people that you mean it. You have to hype the results and protect your pioneers. Gradually, if things really are better, the change will take hold. You've got to experiment, trust yourself, ask for help, be prepared to make mistakes, and just hope your big mistake doesn't happen on a slow news day.

Books enough to fill the average library have addressed the idea of organizational change: how to bring it about, how to manage it. For our purposes here, the major point is not how well the changes in these two agencies succeeded. Nor does every federal agency by definition need change, especially of that kind or scope. The point is that good leaders everywhere, public or private, have to know the value of change and how to act on it when necessary.

When you begin managing a new entity, it's important to ask whether things will get better if you work harder at doing the same things you're doing now. Will results improve, will satisfaction be higher, will reputation increase, if you work harder at what you're doing now? If the answer is not obviously yes, then you have to answer the question what you need to do differently in order to make it happen. Simply working harder on a path that goes nowhere is not going to produce change or indicate whether change is necessary. FEMA is viewed as successful now because it made sure disaster relief worked for victims of disasters—not for governors, not for federal agencies, not for the photo opportunity.

In the end, when change is necessary, fear can't be allowed to block it. The prevailing conviction—and assurance—should be that:

Risk is acceptable and failure does not mean you lose your job or your career.

▨ Tools: Electronic Government

Begun with the emergence of the personal computer in the 1980s, exploded by the Internet into a radical, ongoing transformation of society in the late 1990s, the information technology revolution will by the middle of the current decade largely transfigure government as well.

The Paperwork Reduction Act of 1998 ordered the federal government to put all its services and transactions online by 2003. Responding, the

Clinton administration in December 1999 issued a series of presidential executive orders. In the language of these directives, the aim was to harness IT as "a powerful tool for tackling some of our toughest social challenges as well as fostering economic growth." They assigned a number of general tasks to the federal government as a whole and particular responsibilities to specific agencies. The intended scope of the orders is evident in some of their language—for example, in making public access to government information and services easier:

> *Access* organized not by agency, but by the type of service or information that people may be seeking. Data identified and organized in a way that makes it easier for the public to find. . . . Each agency shall permit greater access to its officials by creating a public electronic mail address through which citizens can contact the agency with questions, comments, or concerns. . . . The secretaries of Health and Human Services, Education, Veterans Affairs, and Agriculture, the Commissioner of Social Security, and the Director of the Federal Emergency Management Agency, working closely with other federal agencies that provide benefit assistance to citizens, shall make a broad range of benefits and services available though private and secure electronic use of the Internet. . . . To the maximum extent possible, departments and agencies to make available online, by December 2000, the forms needed for the top government services used by the public.

> . . . in government's purchasing functions:

> Promote the use of electronic commerce for faster, cheaper ordering on federal procurements that will result in savings to the taxpayer.

> . . . and in protecting privacy:

> Agencies shall continue to build good privacy practices into their web sites by posting privacy policies.

To be sure, elements of local, state, and federal government are already doing some of this. The Department of Agriculture used the Internet to get public comments on organic food standards. Though it cost several hundred thousand dollars, this exercise opened up the rule-making process. It drew 400,000 hits on the department's web site, whose creative design allowed people everywhere to comment, see other comments, and build on the comments without having to come to Washington and plow through all the paperwork.

Again, the director of a large organization within an agency reports that "information technology and especially web technology are extremely powerful ways to reach various constituency groups and get information out. It's really paid off for us."

The under secretary of commerce who runs the National Oceanic and Atmospheric Administration describes IT as "probably the biggest thing affecting us." His agency has about a thousand web pages—like weather.gov and climate.gov—where anyone interested can find the latest information on everything from solar flares to global warming. The more NOAA puts on its web site, he says, the more people are interested in it. For this senior appointee, information technology is "the big growth area of the future. The electronic world is the one that's going to drive us the most."

A former high-level official in the federal procurement community points out that many agencies are putting their requests for bid proposals on the net. An increasing exchange of information between government and vendors is taking place on the net, he adds, and it's a place "where the folks on the front lines—particularly the eighteen-year-olds—are coming up with a lot of interesting ideas." His advice: "Ask your human resources people for the names of the ten, fifteen, or one hundred youngest employees in the organization. Send them all an e-mail, invite them to a brown-bag lunch. The purpose is for them to give you ideas about how you can use the web better in your agency."

Despite encouraging examples of what's already being achieved, most newly arriving presidential appointees will find their agencies up to their elbows in the job of moving toward those e-government objectives mandated in 1999. It is a tough road to travel, one for which executive branch agencies are not now technically well prepared. In a speech in March 2000, David Walker, comptroller general of the United States and boss of the General Accounting Office, noted that government "is no longer the primary innovator in the area of information technology" (as it was, for example, in developing the Internet's precursors). "Many current government IT systems are outdated and not integrated," Walker said. "In addition, we have an overload of information and a lack of knowledge. Government faces a number of internal skills gaps as well as a lack of effective contractor oversight."

A major effort has been under way, meanwhile, aimed at drawing an organized, disciplined, across-the-board blueprint to help the federal government achieve the objectives set out by the paperwork reduction legislation and the executive orders that followed. Those mandates created an exceptionally strong framework for this initiative, which began in late 1999 under the auspices of the Council for Excellence in Government and the National Partnership for Reinventing Government.

Both organizations recognized that the multilayered complexity of the transformation to e-government poses formidable questions of scope, scale, philosophy, and technology, to name but a few. They saw clearly that the best answers lay with the public and private players who will drive the change—business, government, civic groups, and the research community. These groups, they believed, were best equipped to produce the expertly designed, comprehensive, collaborative approach that a task of these dimensions demands. It was abundantly clear that other advantages for government could accrue from an effective move to full electronic capability: for example, a reinvigoration of the federal civil service, fueled by the development of an IT work force of high quality. Many additional potential benefits were visible in a government that could commune directly, instantly, and continuously with individual people, with business, with government at other levels, and with itself.

In November 1999 the Council's Intergovernmental Technology Leadership Consortium and NPR convened a cross-sector symposium of electronic commerce and information technology leaders from government, industry, academic institutions, and the research sector. Examining with experienced eyes the nature of the e-government challenge and how to meet it, they set out four areas—transformation, roles, infrastructure, and information—in which the design should proceed. In March, joined now by the National Science Foundation, the initiative formed four corresponding working groups to set objectives, identify barriers, and shape specific options for the action recommendations, to be offered by the Council publicly in the fall of 2000 to the country's newly elected presidential and congressional leadership.

It's useful to look briefly at what these groups think e-government should look like. It would be citizen driven and user friendly, organized according to how people use it, not how agencies manage it. Full e-government would not merely supply information online, but also allow users to complete transactions and interact with their government. It would be accessible to everybody, anywhere, and at any time, and not just to people on the near side of the well-named digital divide. E-government would be designed, created, and maintained through cooperation between the public and private sectors. It would be innovative, encouraging the advance of new technology and applications, and cost effective, secure, and private. Finally, e-government offers a clear opportunity to close in on two goals that are as elusive as they are crucial. First, to rekindle the interest of young Americans in government and public service by making government completely accessible to them—expanding their understanding and appreciation of it and making it more meaningful and real. Second, to revitalize American democracy by narrowing the factual and psychological gaps between government and people and engaging millions more of them in the democratic process. To underscore the urgency here, the government blueprint outlined above will include recommendations for top executive leadership that is strongly attuned to these goals and for the selection of cabinet and agency chiefs who are able and ready to lead the charge toward full e-government within their organizations.

No matter which route government follows toward these objectives, agency chief information officers will be among the key figures charged with stewarding the change at the leadership and policy levels, not just at the technical level. Their jobs are examined in detail in another section of this book. But make no mistake: it is agency political leadership that, besides overseeing the problem solving, will have to spearhead the charge, cutting through the barriers of turf and entrenched attitudes and habits to make electronic government the full-fledged reality that the country, its economy, and its people need.

Tools: Performance Management

By its very name and nature, the idea of measuring public-sector performance doesn't fire most people's imaginations. Government has had a hard time embracing it, too. Starting in the mid-1960s, various presidential edicts tried to get a handle on federal government performance by trying to measure it. They laid down complicated formulas centered on programs, planning, and budgeting; zero-based systems; and the like. No doubt these excited the financial managers and budgeteers of the time. None made much of an impression on the government's work force as a whole or on its executive ranks. Mostly, these systems just melted down.

In the early 1990s came the first statutory attempts at performance measurement—to some degree with the Chief Financial Officers Act, more extensively with the Government Performance and Results Act. The Results Act, in particular, doesn't merely tell agencies what to do—to plan strategically, set goals, devise measures, and report performance annually—it compels them by force of law. It poses these requirements only in broad outline in a few pages, leaving agencies to fill in the blanks with their own structures, formats, and procedures. And there have been some successes.

One of the reasons Congress was impressed with our plan was that we put forth a measure that didn't just say we'll work harder at something. We will be measured and held accountable for those results. That means everybody really has to sign on to pieces of it.

Still, the executive branch's response so far to the Results Act's requirements gets mixed reviews. The federal executive branch remains huge, its moving parts numerous and tangled, its tasks many, and its time for any one of them in short supply. It's hard to abandon old habits—to switch the focus from process to results. Even the Congress, which created the act, has divided views. Performance and reform enthusiasts on the Hill propelled the act into being, but what it is producing so far has gotten a chillier reception among other legislators, especially appropriators. And inevitably, in various quarters of government at both ends of Pennsylvania Avenue, lurks concern about the possible use of performance information as a weapon, not a tool. Finally, as suggested by Donald F. Kettl, who directs the LaFollette Institute of Public Affairs at the University of Wisconsin, performance first needs to be understood for what it really is. It's usually presented in terms of measurement, he says, when it's really about communication.

The ultimate problem doesn't lie in designing ways to measure performance or proving that they work. It lies in getting people, whether in the executive branch or the Congress, to value the information generated by measurement—and to use it constructively as a fundamental element in managing and governing.

> If you were a CEO or a senior executive in any important private business, you would be using performance numbers to manage your organization on a day-in, day-out basis. Probably anywhere between 25 and 50 percent of your time would be involved looking at numbers, often on a daily basis.

That's because good—repeat, good—performance measures are management's signals of the results it expects and a highly useful way to drive performance. But in government, most presidential appointees are only marginally involved in managing to such numbers.

> The culture of the senior political levels in the executive branch is total obsession with Congress, the legislative stuff. But it's not by any means the whole job. Even getting good laws passed is only the first step towards improving the lives of the folks we are serving. And that involves things happening inside your organization. In government agencies, if they're really doing performance management, senior ex-

ecutives are looking at those numbers, asking for direct reports about what's going on. This is not a staff exercise. It is an executive exercise. The challenge is to move from those little documents, those annual performance plans, to making it part of managing your organization.

Out of all this, we can distill a couple of simple truths for senior appointees. First, no government organization should lack some sort of system that will show how well or badly it is doing what it is funded to do. Second, no political manager in such an organization should ignore the information that system produces. To do so is to invite trouble, perhaps major trouble, that—count on it—will jump up and bite hard where it hurts.

▪ Career Work Force

As a new presidential appointee moving into your agency job, do you value institutional knowledge and memory? Look to the career service. What about sheer ability and commitment? The best career people can match anyone in the private sector. Ability to change, adapt, learn? For many in your work force, it's as good as anywhere. But how about entrenched attitudes, dug-in positions? No question, some career public servants have them—and not always for the wrong reasons. Loyalty and support for the new appointed boss? Usually not a problem if the boss meets them half way.

There is one certainty here. Political managers can't really run their jobs or get results without the cooperation and help of their senior professionals—whatever they may think of them.

> The assumption of every new political group coming in is that career civil servants are captives of the previous administration. It's easy to believe that only the folks who walked inthe door with you care about accomplishing the mission of your administration. But the message to political appointees is that they are not going to get their jobs done if they don't work closely with the senior career people—and that they shouldn't assume they are the enemy within.

Okay, but isn't the government's work force still basically different from those in other sectors? The answer is mixed. In the collective, career government people have much the same profile as any other large group of employees. Skilled, ambitious achievers at one end, less gifted or imaginative stragglers at the other, most of the rest somewhere in the middle. The rules do make it considerably harder to hire, fire, or move them around. There is less mobility, certainly less turnover, in government than many appointed newcomers are accustomed to. A fast-track program is available to talented entrants, and a bonus system operates for senior careerists. But for most other people, merit cuts less ice than it does outside government when it comes to promotions, pay raises, or moves to more desirable jobs. In most cases, that means making the best of the career work force that is in place.

> If all your people are extraordinary, getting extraordinary results is a lot easier. But extraordinary people are not bunched together in most organizations. You have to produce extraordinary results with ordinary people. FEMA and OSHA did it. That's what the most successful organizations in America do every day. That's the management task.

Talent does exist, however, at every level in federal agencies. These professionals know what's going on, what has to be done, what needs fixing—and they're ready to follow good leadership. The trick is to find them, enlist them, and make a habit of listening to them.

> There was a guy who controlled budget, personnel, space, and computers. He was great—the exemplar of professional executives in the federal service. And the organization came to know that he knew how to push my buttons. If I really had a bad idea and they had to talk me out of it, they'd send him in to do it. He saved me from some gross errors. There were other days when I said "Nope, we're going to do it this way." Every once in a while I was right. But it's tricky, because some people who resist and obstruct are doing it for good reason.

An ability to hear what career colleagues and subordinates are saying depends on open, not closed, doors.

> My predecessor said to me, "Be careful in the elevator. Everybody will try to talk to you about stuff. Don't talk to them." It seemed to me that was exactly the wrong advice—the kind your mother used to give you that was always wrong. When I first came into the agency, people had never even been on the floor where our offices were. They had to use key cards to go up and down the elevators, as if it was an armed camp. I dispensed with the key cards and invited everybody to come on up with their ideas. I said we would take them seriously, that there wouldn't be repercussions for ideas we didn't like. People took me at my word.

▨ A Joint Endeavor

The political versus career relationship in government works well only as a two-way proposition. An effective political manager will share as well as control, give as well as take. This has great value inside an agency . . .

> They want to be part of what you're trying to do and provide their best input to make that happen. I can tell you this: they work very hard, and some very long hours. I think they're all scared of change. Sharing information with them makes a big difference.

. . . and outside it:

> There is a temptation in a political process like this to move to sort of a legislative gag rule—make sure nobody talks to the Hill but the political executives. Don't kid yourselves. There is an enormous value to including career people in the process of deciding on your positions, deciding on the language, deciding how to communicate them. By the time you get to a conference committee, if you don't have the kind of trusting relationship with your career staff in which they understand the administration's priorities and you understand their implementation of them, it is not their failure, it is yours.

Working with the Congress

If you're a presidential appointee who deals regularly with the Congress, you may already recognize some of the striking contrasts, obvious and not so obvious, between the Hill and your own branch of government.

Unlike the executive branch, with defined, stated objectives set by its political leadership, the Congress is an arena where two parties push legislative agendas that are often in direct, open conflict. Further, a political party running the executive branch normally has no problem controlling it or getting its various elements to pull in the same general direction. In the Congress, however, neither party—whether in the majority or minority—can always count on such order within its ranks. A majority's ability to control the decision on a given bill may only be nominal.

The congressional operating schedule offers another useful comparison. Increasingly hostage to the demands of fund-raising and fence mending, the Congress's work on substance is nowhere near as orderly, nor its progress as straight-line, as that of the executive branch. Its irregular pace and rhythm, its fractionated processes, can skew the timing and legislative hopes of any administration.

> The Congress is now basically a Tuesday-to-Thursday club. What you have is a lot of members of the House and Senate who come in Tuesday morning, leave Thursday night, and are not here a lot.

Over time, factors like those have widened the inherent differences in approach and attitude between the two branches. That makes it harder for people in either place to understand, and allow for, the work habits, tactics, strategy, and outlook typical of the other. It's true as much of relationships between career staffs as between executive branch appointees and members of Congress. How well you can manage across these divides has a lot to do with the impact you can make in your job—how far you can go toward your objectives.

▨ A Few Critical Generalities

You shouldn't plunge into the congressional dimension of your job without some overall appreciation of the Congress as probably the strongest, certainly the most contentious, power center in a city with several of them. A sense of this emerges from several comments by veteran observers, first about the job of the Congress:

> The framers really had in mind making Congress a formidable power, the first branch of government, giving it powers to legislate, appropriate, investigate; giving them their own single constituencies to pay attention to; terms of office distinct from the president; a bicameral legislature that ensures substantial conflict between the House and the Senate—a natural tension that develops between politicians' need to represent their constituents and to engage in serious deliberation and policymaking. It's a body remarkable for its division of labor and specialization and the importance of congressional staff. Remember the framers had in mind to make it a complex, personal, explicitly political process.

> The source of its prerogative . . .

> Article I of the Constitution is the Congress. It is not the executive branch, it is not the judicial branch, it is the Congress. The founding fathers felt that was the seminal force for democracy—where the

people had the direct authority to influence their lives in a pluralistic system. The fact is, regardless of what we think about individual members, everything emanates from that source of power.

Its personality . . .

People from Will Rogers on have tried to diagnose and explain Congress. Some see it as an august deliberative body. One woman member of the House of Representatives referred to it as an unruly day-care center. Let me suggest another option: it suffers from attention deficit disorder.

The way it operates . . .

Simple majorities don't matter any more. You either have unanimous consent to get something done, or you need a committed super majority of sixty or more. That puts a big burden on anybody doing business from the White House or from the agencies—the burden either to build unanimous consent for your issue or to activate a very committed super majority. The power the Constitution gives to the minority is still very evident. There are continued attempts to take away that power but it's still a very important one in that it protects the minority.

. . . and its members' sense of independence within their own parties:

People in the executive branch make the mistake, in terms of what they expect of the Congress, to assume that members of their own party there are supposed to carry out the president's will. Supposed to be the floor leaders for the president, supposed to be the point men and women for the president's programs. It is important to remember that members of Congress, even of your party, are only loosely part of the same team. And the reason is that they are part of a separate branch of government that takes its role as a separate branch of government very seriously.

Nor can you expect to work well with the Hill without mastering at least a few other fundamentals. It helps to know something about the House and Senate rules and about parliamentary procedures. It's almost mandatory to be familiar with structure and function—especially in the design and funding of executive branch programs.

On that front, a senior White House staffer with congressional experience recommends that appointees "know the difference between the appropriations and authorization committees." That may sound pretty elementary. But "those are different processes on the Hill that people sometimes don't distinguish from each other."

Decisions on Money and Programs

So let's look at that for a minute. According to House and Senate rules, here's basically how the Congress is supposed to provide money for government programs. The power to authorize funds belongs to legislative committees that have jurisdiction over the various areas of government responsibility—health, labor, science, defense, and so on—and over executive branch agencies and programs in those areas. They are the authorizing committees. The power actually to make the money available resides with the appropriations committees and their various subcommittees. As they move toward these decisions, committees conduct hearings where executive branch agency leaders or senior political managers make their cases for the new or existing programs and money requests laid out in the president's annual budget message to the Congress.

Each year, the Congress divides its funding task into thirteen regular money bills that cover all government agencies and functions (plus the District of Columbia). The rules prescribe an annual two-step procedure. In step one, an authorizing committee enacts a measure that can create, continue, or modify a program (or an agency) for a set or indefinite amount of time and okay the appropriation of money for it. The measure may specify the duties and functions of the program, its structure, and the responsibilities of the executive branch officials involved.

In step two, the appropriations committees, after getting the recommendations of their thirteen subcommittees, allocate funds to the programs that have been authorized. These decisions then come to the floor of each house for approval. Differences between House and Senate versions of these decisions go to joint conference committees for resolution; the results of that go back to each floor for approval. Once that is in hand—and the president signs the measure—the programs or agencies affected finally have budget authority to incur obligations and spend the money. If unanticipated needs arise within a program during the fiscal year, the Congress can and often does provide supplemental funding in a separate measure.

Keep firmly in mind that there are two kinds of spending for federal programs—discretionary and direct. Generally, discretionary funding takes the two-step route outlined above. But direct spending is funded by the authorizing process alone and today accounts for about two-thirds of all outlays. Most direct spending goes into entitlement programs, where the level of funding is already fixed by previously enacted law. Social Security, for example, gets its funding through permanent appropriations in the program's authorizing law. Other direct spending, like that for Medicaid, is an "appropriated entitlement;" it is funded each year by the appropriations committees, but the authorizing legislation controls the amount.

Those are the rules. How do they work in practice?

As individual appropriations, the thirteen money bills are supposed to go through the painstaking process outlined above and be adopted by October 1, the beginning of the fiscal year in which they apply. These years, it rarely happens. The reality is that a handful of bills might get through on time and the Congress, with the deadline looming, hastily wraps the rest into one large "omnibus" bill for quick passage that critics say is also largely unexamined passage. For any bills that still don't make it, legislators must enact what is called a continuing resolution. This makes stopgap funding available for the affected agencies and programs until the appropriations can be made. (Sometimes agencies have gone through an entire fiscal year on continuing resolutions.) In cases of extensive deadlock, where agreement on most appropriations is still absent at the October 1 mark, the Congress has been known simply to stop the clock, postponing the deadline for a few days.

▦ Appropriators versus Authorizer

Further, many observers believe the whip hand in making funding decisions for executive branch agencies increasingly belongs to the appropriators.

> There are three political parties in Washington: the Republicans, the Democrats, and the appropriators. And the appropriators operate at a different beat from everybody else.

"My own experience," says a political consultant with a lot of it, "is that the appropriations committees are quickly becoming the only committees in the sense that more and more stuff is getting done at the last minute." That refers to the habit in both houses over the last decade or more to put off most individual funding for agencies or groups of agencies during a legislative session, then fold them all into monster "omnibus" bills enacted in the last few days. As this consultant points out, "the number of what would ordinarily be called authorizing pieces of legislation that are rolled into the omnibus bills is quite long."

"The authorizers do have a lot of impact on appropriations committee language," adds a former congressman. "They are by no means irrelevant to the process. But if you look over the last several decades, you've seen a very sharp decline in the power of the authorizing committees and a very sharp increase in the power of the appropriations committees." It's understandable, he says, that the executive branch might think it is wasting time dealing with authorizing committees and decide to "just focus on the appropriations committee, where the decision is probably going to be made that will really count." He notes the development of a new science—drafting language that is really authorizing language to put into an appropriations bill.

Why is this happening? It shouldn't, according to the House and Senate rules that enforce the separation of the authorization and appropriations processes. Among other transgressions, they forbid the inclusion of legislative language in appropriations bills. Yet to enforce these provisions, it's necessary to raise a point of order—formally invoke the rules. And the rules can also be waived by suspending them.

"If I had a scale of whom you should pay attention to, I would clearly start with the appropriators," is the realistic advice of another onetime member of the House. "If you're going to spend time and effort getting to know people, it's those in the appropriations process. You try to build a leadership program that involves the White House, that is bipartisan, that involves the appropriators, that plays off the authorizers. Usually, lesson number one, the appropriators are going to win. So take that to the bank, regardless of the issue."

Or, as a former congressional staffer puts it: "When there's a fight between the appropriators and the authorizers, stick with the appropriators. They get a shot at you every single year."

Don't let this advice unbalance your approach too much, however. The same people who offer it also warn against neglecting the authorizing committees. This is where the day-to-day oversight of what you do resides. Authorizing committees are "your champions," says one, "who have invested a lot in your bureaucracy. Don't ignore them." Make certain you don't "screw around with your authorizing committee," says another, since they "can make your life miserable. Don't work on your appropriators without letting the people you really work with, the subcommittee chairs, the ranking members, know what you're doing and why you're doing it. Don't think the appropriators are where the only action is and you can forget these other guys."

Legislators and Their Constituencies

Another factor not to overlook is the relationship between members of Congress and the people they represent. They are not just those whose votes sent the member to Congress last time around. They are individuals and groups with businesses, economic interests, issues, causes, and special situations the member is expected to look out for. Some of them may not necessarily be confined to the member's home district or state. Together, all these constituencies come first in every member's daily thoughts—not least because they matter decisively in an objective that preoccupies every member: reelection.

"People who deal with Congress deal in peril if they don't recognize the incredible interconnection that members of Congress have with their constituents," observes a former member. "It tends to be the way they learn about a lot of what they know. They learn by anecdote, by the individual case of what went wrong in a business, what went wrong for an individual, what went right at the Social Security Administration." A former colleague from the other side of the aisle agrees: "The most significant driving force for any member of the House or Senate is his or her origins—the district or the state."

Recognizing the many differences between House and Senate, smart political appointees will tailor their approaches accordingly. House members are "better prepared," but "more provincial," according to a veteran of service in that chamber. Senators are less prepared, which means their personal and committee staffers swing greater weight. "But senators have a broader view. You may have a quicker, more positive decision on your behalf with a member of the Senate because of the more reflective nature of that body." Depending on where they are in the election cycle, senators also have far more time to deal with the issues. A good rule of thumb is to think of House and Senate as almost separate entities, while never considering one more important than the other.

Relationships

"If you keep the Congress involved, there are no surprises," says an agency head. "They may not always like what you do, but at least they're not surprised. They don't read it in the paper and think, gee, I didn't know anything about that." A senior White House official makes the same point. "They feel worse about reading it in the paper than if you call and tell them that they can't get what they want. No surprises."

If you're trying to develop or strengthen relationships on the Hill, she suggests finding ways for members of the Congress "to share the credit for what you're doing." For example, invite them to events, to tour facilities, to visit programs. If you're having a press conference about something they are concerned with, ask them to join you. In other words, "give them some ownership of the issues, bring them into the process." Be sure in this that you are being bipartisan about it. Don't limit it to just members of your own party. And "look to the members of your committee and then members beyond that. Get them to help you with their expertise."

A lawyer and lobbyist who also served in the Congress recommends being proactive.

> Initiate contact with them. Say "I'm working on these topics and I know they are of concern to you, your district, your committee, you personally." Say you've got scientists or engineers, social workers or nurses or doctors, whatever it is, you have people that can answer some of their questions on those subjects and they should put you down as a resource. Ultimately they need information from you about the topics that you deal with, so why not make it an open-ended offer to begin with? It's much better to offer the help than have somebody serve a Freedom of Information Act subpoena on you.

You can also make the same offer to staff people who work on given issues for members or committees. Do the same thing with chairs and ranking members of committees. This can have a variety of payoffs. For instance:

> It could be in the waning days of one of these omnibus bills that you get a phone call and your input makes the difference in somebody being stuck or willing to bend a little bit. In the final hours of congressional sessions, bending a little bit is what it's all about.

"That doesn't mean you have to co-opt the policy of your department," says this same experienced Hill observer. "It doesn't mean that you have to turn your policy inside out. In a great many instances, it means having information available in which to make a reasoned choice. You have the key to much of the information." If you don't choose to give that key to decisionmakers in the Congress to use now and then, they may see you as "hiding something or unwilling to help—and that's not good for anybody."

Recently, when a big agency published certain information as required by law, it put some people on the Hill into a serious snit. Here's what happened, related by the chief of the agency:

When we first implemented that by the date required, there was a huge uproar about the way we were doing it. Some on the committees were very upset. We went over and said, "Look, we know, we see, we hear, this is not the way it should be, let's work and try to figure out how we can fix this." If we had responded very defensively, and taken sort of an arms- length approach, I think we would have been in some kind of a war. But that wasn't our point of view. We were not trying to make this thing work badly, we just didn't quite figure it out right. So we said, "Come in and help us." And they did, and we've made it better. So I think the approach is not to be defensive when things go wrong, and to solicit help from all quarters. When you can't accommodate somebody's specific desire, be very up front about why that is. By and large, that has worked pretty well so far.

Oversight

Very few high-level administration appointees in the last fifty years have not felt the thrust (some would call it the sting) of congressional oversight. A less polite term, one you'll encounter frequently, is micromanagement. Oversight means the Congress's responsibility to supervise federal agencies in their program and budget management, their progress toward stated goals, their problems and prospects, and much else. In the process, legislators are supposed to gather information to assist its decisions on designing and paying for government's efforts to run the country's public business. Onerous though it can be, federal agency political managers must learn to work in businesslike fashion with congressional exercise of the oversight function.

The oversight role normally resides in the congressional authorizing committees. It can take the form of committee hearings, field trips, official requests for information, informal inquiries, simple phone calls, and a variety of other mechanisms. Legislators quite naturally use the opportunity for related purposes—to speak for their constituents, promote a point of view, commend or criticize, uphold or undermine. Oversight is a necessary but imperfect function that depends for effectiveness on the willingness of the executive branch and the Congress to work together. Here's how a past House member views it:

There can be too much oversight, without any doubt—too much demand for information and documentation that is not looked at. But a lot of this demand arises from frustration. A member will ask an executive branch official to do this or that. The official says, yes, that's absolutely right, Congressman, I agree with you wholeheartedly, and walks out the door and nothing ever happens. This gets very frustrating and members feel the executive branch is not paying any attention, not consulting, not taking them seriously.

The inevitable result?

The only way to get the attention of the executive branch is [something incisive like] dropping in an amendment they don't like. In their view, that's micromanaging, and it probably is. It arises out of a frustration over the lack of serious dialogue between the two branches and the feeling that the executive branch often looks upon the Congress as an obstacle to be overcome, not as a partner in the process. If you have that frame of mind, you're in deep trouble with the Congress.

On the level of personal attitude and behavior on the Hill, a former congressman cautions executive branch managers not to "get personal at any time with arguments or issues." That watchword advice is one of the fundamental truths about the Congress—universally recognized and applicable as much to relationships between members themselves as between members and administration officials:

Remember that today's adversary may be tomorrow's ally.

And some related advice:

Don't be put off by an initial hostile attitude. Sometimes it seems hostile on the surface, but dealing with Congress and the staff is a very personal thing. Call up the staff person of the member that appears hostile and try to have a meeting. You're sure not going to get anywhere if you don't try to have the meeting.

One of the former congressmen quoted earlier takes this further. "Don't grovel," he says. "State your case, but don't be submissive or appear to be weak. Don't be in a situation where members think you're their vassal." Members are interested in you, just as you are in them, and for the same reason: because you can do something for them. "You're part of a legislative process that's important to them. Don't feel that you're the supplicant in the relationship."

The final word on personal behavior is the old maxim, a cliché but a useful one, quoted by an agency assistant secretary, suggesting that one can "catch more flies with honey than vinegar."

▦ Getting Things Done

Whatever your objective with the Congress, immediate or longer term, achieving it will need a variety of strategies, tactics, or combinations of each. On this question, the best take comes from people who have been the targets of these various approaches while serving in the House and Senate.

One direct approach is lobbying—personal contact with members to enlist their support of a program, a funding request, or other desired action. Depending on what you're seeking, this can be a tough, often frustrating, mission. Yet a former congressman of long service thinks the executive branch puts too few resources into it. "An administration cannot do an effective job if it only trusts three or four people to come to the Hill and lobby, or starts too late," he says. He views the 1999 failure to ratify the comprehensive test ban treaty as a "classic example" of that. "You've got to start early and you've got to stay with it. You have to be flexible according to the members' level of understanding of the issue. You have to consult very broadly, not just with a few." In his experience, the executive branch often makes the "big-time" mistake of confining its lobbying to members of the committee with jurisdiction over the issue.

Naturally, executive branch lobbying has to fight for congressional time and attention with legions of lobbyists for commercial and other nongovernment interest groups ranged along a very long spectrum. These people are specialists in what they do, devote full time to it, and can call on experience, resources, and techniques not available to the executive branch. They are also far better paid. Comparing their objectives on the Hill with those of the executive branch risks distortion or oversimplification; often, it's an apples-and-oranges comparison. But there are times when the interests of both coincide to a point where some form of alliance can be useful.

Among a number of indirect approaches to desired action in the Congress are those endorsed by a cabinet secretary with prior service in the House. "How do you get members' attention? Ask their colleagues to talk to them. That is probably the best way to get their support—a neglected way, but critically important. Next best is editorials in their home state newspapers. Generate those through your public affairs office. That has strong impact. Be careful that it isn't obvious that you're doing it. Third: phone calls rather than written material. Phone calls from live people in interest and stakeholders groups make more of an impact than letters, computer e-mail, telegrams, or faxes."

Also recommended is a continuous process of educating members on your issue or objective.

Go to the power centers outside of your committee, the whips, the Hispanic caucus, black caucus. If it's a children's issue, there are a lot of caucuses that deal with children. Go to members who belong to informal groups that might be responsive to your issue. Be creative, tenacious and persistent.

Many agencies have congressional liaison offices, sometimes headed by an official at the assistant secretary level. It's their job to shepherd an agency's legislative requests, track the progress of bills through the committee and floor processes, maintain the agency's relationships on the Hill, assist preparations for testimony by agency officials, spot opportunities to negotiate deals or compromises, do some hand-holding with individual members—committee chairs, ranking members, others with power or influence over the fate of a given issue. "Generally, they're very good," says this agency head about congressional liaison operations. "On the whole, very competent people." However, he cautions, they tend to get too tight with their key congressional contacts, to develop what in other realms might be called clientitis. "Many of them have good instincts," he says, "but if you have to err when taking their advice, be a little bolder than what they recommended."

Another cabinet secretary and onetime congressman says an appointee's job "is to carry out the policy of the president. Not to do it blindly, but with good judgment." Presidents, he observes, don't need "sycophants who just parrot everything without thinking through what will help get the message and the policy through." What they do need is the use of independent judgment and wisdom in working with the Congress. "Don't be afraid to use those qualities in the process as long as you're not working at cross purposes with what the policy objectives are." From that flows a further point: assets like integrity, insight, and discretion in an executive branch leader earn trust on the Hill and are likely to carry that individual further.

▨ Dealing with Individual Members

From the wealth of comment and counsel tendered by those who have served in the Congress, some common keynotes emerge when it comes to individual legislators and the do's and don't's of working with them.

Members today, says one of their colleagues, have several roles. They are legislators, politicians, and educators. They are students who must learn quickly. They are advocates for their constituents and communities, dignitaries invited to every function in their states or districts, to say nothing of many events in Washington and abroad. They are traveling fact finders. They are dealmakers.

And, we can add, never forget they are fund-raisers, driven to invest disproportionate time in the effort to be reelected.

To get the most out of your one-on-one contacts with them while sidestepping the pitfalls, the following points can help:

—Find out who individual members are, what they did before they got into Congress, what they care about, what their roles are on the Hill. Some members are more engaged in legislation, some are more service and advocacy oriented for their own states. Get to know how their offices function, not just in Washington but in their states and districts. Don't just look to the members. Get to know their staffs in Washington and back home.

—Understand members' relevance to your concerns. Are they on the committees that you deal with? Are they particularly involved in your issues? Have they written anything or spoken out on them? Especially when you're planning to call on a member, explore the political framework of what you are seeking. Think out whether the issue you're talking about is a plus or a minus for the member. Is it a problem to be on your side, or is it a layup—an easy issue to help you with? How well will it play back in their districts? Does it have a significant bearing on their political futures?

—For you, the most important person in a member's office is not the chief of staff, the legislative assistant, the appropriations person, or the substantive foreign policy expert. It's the scheduler. A former congressman says, "Things got so busy for me in latter years that I had to schedule an appointment with my scheduler in order to see what I was doing."

—Basic rules when you visit a member: State why you're there. Put it right up front. Be succinct, professional, and utterly candid about what is in your interest. Get to the point. Don't ramble. Don't be caught off guard. Think about what tough questions might be thrown at you. Leave before your welcome runs out.

—Don't try to make the member an expert on the subject. Members survive on one-pagers. Make succinct, direct points that zero in so the member understands what you're talking about. The member's relevant staffer is much more informed. You'll want to talk at length with that staffer, probably provide some briefing materials. Don't give it all to the member, who isn't going to read it. At the same time, some members will know more about the issue than you do. Be prepared, therefore, to deal with various members at various levels of comprehension.

—Members won't always object if your response to something they want is nonresponsive. This is especially true if a member's request is something outrageous like, "My constituent Dolly Jackson was in Paris for three days and wants to be ambassador to France." Members often try to deal with such problems by bucking them to the executive branch. In this case, if you answer that the lady isn't likely to get the job because she doesn't sound qualified for it, you've resolved that member's problem.

—Don't assume that because a member is going toe to toe with another member, there's some antipathy between them. Public differences don't necessarily mean there are private differences as well. Quite often, members of different parties, or those who are adversaries in public, are good friends privately.

—Don't be afraid to tell a member that what the member said about you or your issue was unfair and you want to explain why. Don't appear to be totally submissive, as if you've been whacked and must make amends. Remember that you're all in a political process, and in the executive branch you are dealing with the Congress on a very professional basis. Don't be afraid sometimes to put a little edge in what you need to get done.

The Media

There was once a court jester, a man who liked to live dangerously. He couldn't resist making bad puns. The king hated them. The more bad puns the jester came up with, the angrier the king became—to the point where he threatened the jester with dire punishment if it continued. It did, of course, and the jester was sentenced to hang. As the rope tightened around the jester's neck, however, the king relented. He offered a reprieve if the jester promised never again to crack an outrageously awful pun. The jester agreed. "Have you anything else you want to say?" the king asked. "Well, sire," came the instant reply, "no noose is good noose." (They hanged him, naturally.)

In today's Washington, good news is usually less interesting to media covering the federal government than bad news. It probably always will be—for all kinds of reasons, people simply pay more attention to bad news and, therefore, so do the media. It's just human nature. Bad news concerning your agency doesn't have to be a hanging offense, however. Yet, afraid of generating bad news, people who run federal agencies sometimes fall into the mistake of trying to make no news at all. And there you have the essence of the media challenge for federal leaders.

A federal agency with a good media operation has several things going for it. First, an agency that doesn't wait to be asked—that finds creative ways to attract objective, positive coverage and tells its story honestly and factually—can make and keep a favorable impression among people everywhere. That will boost the agency's ability to perform well across the board. Reporters and editors respect an institution that is accessible and helps them do their jobs. Implicitly or explicitly, that gets reflected in what they report. The results are not lost on that agency's citizen customers, congressional overseers, other government agencies, and the public at large.

Example: When the Defense Department prepared to deploy U.S. troops to peacekeeping duties in Bosnia in1996, it knew all too well that a lot of public opinion in this country opposed the move. Already skeptical about the need for a U.S. peacekeeping role, Americans also worried about combat casualties in a distant war. To turn the situation around, the Pentagon adopted an assertive, consistent communications strategy on Bosnia that portrayed the troop deployment as a mission to help others help themselves, not to take sides or dictate terms. As part of their assignment, American troops got media training to help them convey that message. Given easy access to American soldiers in Bosnia, journalists reported to American audiences on their lives and work there. About a month into the mission, a major opinion poll showed that more than half the American public supported U.S. policy in Bosnia. Later, the American military presence was stretched beyond its original one year—and U.S. troops remain there today. Almost no one has argued, then or since, that they should come home. It was a classic example of how to take your case to the public via the media and win.

▪ Handling Bad News

Second, since bad news is inevitable in the life of any institution, an agency that knows what to do at such times can minimize the impact.

> Bad news is not like wine or cheese—it does not improve with age. You have a choice. Do you want to have a one-day story that says you screwed up? Or a three- or four-day story that says you screwed up and lied about how you screwed up and you tried to make it go away and it didn't go away? Better to just get it over with.

"The other day," a television correspondent notes, "the FBI announced the arrest of a veteran employee of the Drug Enforcement Administration, an auditor who had been skimming thousands of dollars for years from the DEA. The DEA put out a press release saying, here's who the person is, here's what the FBI said he did, here's what we've done to try to fix it. Boom—the story just absolutely vanished like paint thinner. Because they stepped up to the plate and said the guy's a bum and he's out. That's exactly the right way to handle it."

Or take the story of costly Mars Polar Lander mission in late 1999. It failed because, despite repeated attempts, no contact was ever established with the spacecraft after it was to touch down. The National Aeronautics and Space Administration was on the front pages for days, with much of the coverage unfavorable. But the agency kept putting out whatever news and comment it could about the mission. "Every time we learn something about what's happening on Mars or isn't happening, we have told the media as we learn it," a NASA official told a network anchorman at the time. But he wondered whether it was worth it, "since it seems to me we're just going to continue to get the bad news over and over again." He wanted to know how the anchorman saw the situation.

"I think NASA took a very candid approach," was the reply. "You handled it the way it should have been handled." Maybe there was no way to put a good face on the story, he said, "but every step along the way, the audience and I were being informed of what was going on. I think NASA is to be congratulated." He went on to say that "We all have our share of bad news, personal, professional, agency. You get the story out there, in my view, you're going to be a lot better off trying to cut your losses early and getting your case out than you are in delay, delay, delay."

There is also a third point here. The assets an agency builds in its proactive mode are often just as useful when it must adopt a reactive stance. A federal agency official tells a story about tainted milk that broke when she was an adviser to a state governor. The milk had been contaminated by bad dairy feed. Reporters were demanding to know immediately when the state was going to pull all milk.

> We just invited a group of them in to talk. We told them it was easy to think the big issue was when were we going to pull the milk. But you also had to think through a lot of other things. If you pulled all the milk, what were you going to do with it? You can't just go pour it out because it seeps into ground water. And what about the years spent getting people to drink milk because of the things in it that are good for them? We said, let's talk through this domino effect and the fact that a lot of careful thinking has to be done. And the reason we were able to say those things, at a time when the national press was really pouring in, was because we had offered proactive briefings, try-

ing to make sure there would be a real dialogue going on when something's happening. They were people that we had built good relationships with. I know that's what helped us through that.

Offense or Defense?

"There are generally two kinds of agencies," says the network television anchorman. "One has an agency head or press chief who, when the press calls, says 'let's see what we can do.' The other is the 'oh my God, it's the media, now what?' kind. Chances are the first kind of agency is going to get a lot better treatment, because there's going to be more cooperation there. I think it takes a sea change in mentality."

No question—spending less time in a reactive crouch and more on advance planning, effective public communications, and outreach is the best investment for working with the media. We've already seen the value of proactivity. What are the other specific elements of that strategy?

COMMUNICATORS ■ A former agency public affairs official who was also a television reporter and anchor says, "Get your communication people in on things early, not when decisions and actions are fully formed." Communicators "think differently" than their policy colleagues. Indeed, government public affairs people have been suggesting since forever that they be on hand when policy is taking shape, not after the fact. That allows them to understand what the policy is to be and ask all the tough questions now that the press will ask later. It allows them to see to the vital, but often neglected, task of coordinating an agency's public communication with other relevant government institutions and—above all—with the White House. Sometimes their participation can help improve the policy decision itself. Sometimes it will alter the way policy is to be presented publicly. Listen to the advice of a leading national public opinion expert: "In government, you need to spend a lot more time figuring out this is going to be the story, this is how we're going to do it, this is how we're going to use the secretary or the under secretary, this is the position."

So—one fundamental of good media strategy—communications people have to be there "both on offense and defense," as the former public affairs official puts it. It is promotion and damage control, all wrapped into one. Years ago, another government communicator put it into words for all time: Public affairs people want to be there "at the takeoffs as well as the landings" (when it will also be their job to pick up the pieces if things don't go well).

This is not a question of policy wonks versus communication people. The question is: What's the mission? If you're going to put together a good program, you've got to think of what all the down sides are. Somebody has to be at the table seeing it from that other perspective.

Here's how one head of agency operates: "In my office, we don't ever have any meetings with media unless two people are in the room in addition to the substantive expert—my lawyer and the public affairs person. They sit in on the development of all of our policy. If they're not into it, if it's not part of your strategy from step one, you'll be behind the eight ball."

TECHNIQUE ■ Next, agency seniors who deal personally with journalists in individual contacts should have one or two rules of thumb in mind. A game plan, for example. "Go in with an agenda," says a White House official. "That takes some skill so that you don't simply ignore the question on the table. You need to answer the question asked. But, as quickly as you can in the construct of that question, get to what it is that you want to say." Don't give a journalist total control of the agenda. "If you have something to say, make sure you say it. Don't have to offer the excuse later that, 'Well, she never really asked me about X.'"

An agency assistant secretary who meets fairly often with reporters says he usually starts by speaking on a background basis for a while (meaning that what he says cannot be attributed to him by name or position). That's "just to get a feel for what the reporter is about and what the questions are." He thinks it's important to "get a sense of what role you're being cast in for the interview. You have to figure out where the reporter's coming from, what kind of a story is being written, and then you can decide how you can write your own part. If they're just casting you as the dumb government bureaucrat, chances are you want to avoid saying anything that will confirm the impression."

By responding promptly to calls from journalists, you give yourself the opportunity to add the administration's or your own personal point of view to the story and supply information that expands its scope or meaning. "To get the administration side is just so invaluable," a reporter points out. "It's a small thing to remember, but if you get a call from a press person, especially someone working for a wire service, TV, or cable, you have to try to get back to them in a timely fashion. If you don't call back until the next day, it's probably over." A colleague puts it a different way: "Reporters are the distant early warning system of Washington, so you should return their telephone calls. Otherwise, when you see it in the paper the next morning you'll think, "If I had just called him back."

When possible, especially on policy issues, work both sides of a newspaper—the editorial board as well as the reporters. "Sometimes an editorial board takes wrongheaded or uninformed positions," a correspondent observes frankly. "They do their thing and they don't usually share it with the reporting staff. Sometimes they like to scoop reporters by writing about an issue the reporting staff hasn't done anything with. That's embarrassing, especially when they get it wrong. You need to work both sides. An agency leader agrees: "Talk to editorial boards. They are the heart and soul of it."

Use the specialized media, the "trade press," in addition to the mainline media. These publications and television channels can make a big difference on particular issues on which they focus. Find out which such media are relevant to your agency's mission; there may be dozens. As one reporter joked, "I'm sure, if you work in the Department of Housing and Urban Development, there's a *Modern Bricks Magazine*. Or *Food Stamp Monthly* if you're at Agriculture."

QUALITY ▪ The third element of a media operation that works is the quality of what's being said. Journalists are often in a hurry, driven by deadlines and competition. Government leaders don't face those particular kinds of pressures. They have less excuse for being inaccurate in what they convey publicly.

> The news cycle today is constant. It's not just the evening paper and the evening news. There is talk radio and the net and the cable channels. So there is terrible tension between getting the story right and getting it right away. You need to do both, but it's more important to get it right. The press puts a higher priority on getting it right away. Their biggest fear is they will be in a lot more trouble for being late than for being wrong. You have to have a higher priority on getting it right. You've got to have your credibility. It's the most important thing, it's why you were brought into this government, in part, and it's what you need to take out of this government with you when you leave.

Never lie in speaking with journalists in any official capacity. Sooner or later, but inevitably, you'll be caught out and your credibility—assuming there's any left—will never be the same. It's also bad for the people you work with, your agency, and your administration. Be as factual and accurate as possible.

But also remember the story about the witness being sworn in at court who, when asked to tell the truth, the whole truth, and nothing but the truth, asked, "Which one do you prefer, judge?"

In other words, you don't have to volunteer information that isn't being asked for, but what you do say should be the truth.

Make sure people can understand what you are saying. If a government communication is unintelligible, a university media expert argues, people assume the agency or office that put it out is trying to hide something. "I'm a big advocate of simple English that is straightforward and comprehensible because I think it suggests honesty," she says. Here's a perfect example of what she's talking about, offered by the television reporter cited earlier:

> The deputy assistant secretary is there, in all of his deputy assistant secretary-hood, trying to explain this and he's not speaking English. He's saying that "the share of the youth cohort that has sustainable exposure to illicit substances has been trending downward," when what he really means is fewer kids are using drugs. So speak English. Ask yourself if your next- door neighbor will understand what you're saying. How would you say it on the telephone to your mother? Write it down that way.

Even in a crisis or emergency situation, don't let it destroy the quality of what you say publicly or of how you handle the media. "Take a breath and tell them you have to get back to them," says the former senior White House executive—"you have to track it down, round it up, find out." If it's a serious crisis focused on your agency or area of responsibility, you'll almost certainly have things to say to the press. But don't jump out with statements or position papers before you know what's actually happening. "It's just a question of experience and judgment," as the White House official sees it. "Sometimes, if you just let it go, it turns out not as big a crisis as you thought it might be." You might not need to respond right away, or perhaps ever. In any case, you can tailor what you want to say accordingly.

Capable press spokesmen and spokeswomen are critical. Maybe they have been journalists themselves, maybe not, but they have to be people who can talk with calm confidence to the press in any setting, on any basis, individually or in formal briefings. Good spokesmen are articulate, informed, and up-to-date on the institutions they represent, their policies, and their actions. In some larger agencies, you'll find an individual handling the spokesman function as a full-time assignment, presiding at a daily or semiweekly press briefing, supported by a small staff. Elsewhere, the job is part time or ad hoc.

Whatever the case, spokesmen are only as good as the quality of their information and access to policymakers. Deny them either of these and you cripple their ability to advance or defend the interests of their agencies or the administration. Make them mouthpieces only, without reasonable latitude to think, inquire, or speak on their own, and the media will ignore them. Take them into your confidence and trust and they will help you get the results you're looking for.

SURVIVING IN THE GOVERNMENT-MEDIA CULTURE ▪ The fourth important component in a good media strategy is productive working relationships with journalists, in which each side has reasonable confidence and can expect reasonable treatment. Right, you might well say—and, in the current Washington climate, about as likely as the sun rising in the west.

True, government and media coexist in a wary relationship too often characterized by mutual suspicion. True, there are certain mind-sets on both sides—among them, that government executives are obfuscating, overloyal, condescending, usually ready to run for protective cover; that reporters are imperious, self-important, poorly informed, vulnerable to the instincts of the herd.

No one would deny that there is more than a little justification for these sentiments. But they shouldn't dominate the scene. Instead, consider the following excerpts from the comments of three of the print and television journalists quoted earlier as they focused on this question of attitude:

Newspaper correspondent:

Reporters don't expect you to make yourself look bad or your agency look bad. In fact, a lot of times, part of our mission is to present a balanced story, whatever it is. To be fair, we try to let each side make its very best argument. We'll sort through a lot of listening to try to get the kernel of what your case is. Don't presume that someone is coming at you with any particular agenda or ideological bias or even to make you look bad. We're probably just a little frantic and a little harried and just need some good solid information from a credible source and want a good story. Our credibility is very important to us. It's as simple as that.

Television anchor:

Credibility is all we have. Without it we have no reason to do what we do. Why should we risk our credibility by misrepresenting the information that is given us? We may test the information. But it would be foolhardy of us, whose livelihood depends on credibility, to try to manipulate the facts until they become nonfacts.

Newspaper correspondent:

I expect people to tell me the truth and deal with me in good faith and they only get one chance. If they don't, then I know where they are and can never trust them again. That doesn't mean I would never talk to them again. It's just that I have a sense of what their ethics are.

Television correspondent:

Ninety percent of people in government think the media only care when they screw up. Wrong. Yes, the media are fascinated when government screws up. Bad news is interesting. But the media love it when people in government win, when they succeed. Help them help you tell your own story.

Newspaper correspondent:

It's a really delicate human relationship. In the end we're just all people and we don't want to burn our sources. We want to be able to come back to you on another day and have you take our phone calls and give us information. But we don't want to be in the bag for somebody either. It's a delicate line to walk.

Consider also the experience of the chief of a large federal agency that deals with the public, down on the ground, every day. Soon after his arrival, he overhauled the agency's general approach to its citizen customers, which had been increasingly criticized by the Congress and the public. The controversy and the resulting change had generated considerable press coverage. "People report on anything that happens here," he says. "And we try to be very, very open. We've published lots of information that's never been published before. We try to respond to people, give them accurate information. If somebody publishes something we don't think is particularly accurate, we'll try to call it to their attention. We try to do it more in terms of giving them additional information, rather than just criticizing what they've said." The result?

On the whole, it's been pretty good. I don't think there have been more than a couple of stories I can remember of any significance that I really considered to be hatchet jobs. There have been a couple, but not very many, considering the total number. I'm not saying we always think the coverage is wonderful. But it's basically fair, accurate, within the limits of what you have to expect.

And here's how the head of an agency in the foreign policy field views his own relationships with the media:

I found the press generally understands when there are things you can't answer. It's better just to say, "I just can't get into that" than try to split hairs, be cute, and end up saying something that will make them feel you didn't quite level with them. We deal a lot in sensitive information. The press always wants to know, "What did you tell them last week or what did they tell you?" I answer that I'll talk about what our position is, but not about what the back and forth of our negotiation is, because I can't work if I negotiate in public. People generally respect that.

Leaks

At some point most political leaders, appointed as well as elected, find themselves dealing with the consequences of anonymously disclosed information, or leaks. Typically, a leak is the product of a one-on-one contact with a journalist initiated by an individual with the intention of exerting a specific effect. Because of its total lack of sourcing, the reliability of any information that gets into the media in this way needs extra scrutiny.

How do you know a leak when you see one? While it's not always simple, one frequent clue is the complete anonymity of the source—though that by itself is not conclusive. Second, since they are agenda driven, leaked stories usually have some kind of target: a policy, a cause, an action, an individual. Third, now and then a story based on a leak will claim to reveal confidential or surprising information, previously undivulged, perhaps with a whiff of the sensational.

Don't get the idea, however, that every leak by definition occurs for some sinister or nefarious reason. In fact, leaks are motivated by a variety of objectives, the main ones catalogued by political scientist and commentator Stephen Hess in his 1984 book, *The Government-Press Connection:*

Ego leak:	To flatter a sense of personal importance.
Goodwill leak:	A play for positive treatment of the leaker by the reporter.
Policy leak:	To promote or hinder a proposed course of action.

Animus leak: To attack an individual or voice resentment.

Trial balloon: To test public opinion before making a policy decision.

Whistle-blowing: To correct a perceived wrong.

▨ Bottom line

The evidence suggests that an objective, outgoing stance with the media over the long term is likely to produce similar treatment in return. Will there be exceptions and aberrations? Of course. Can a federal department or agency afford to relax when its relations with the media are in good shape? Of course not. It should carefully think out its media operation and carefully manage it—all the time. There's no such thing as a free ride with the media. Whatever the degree of pain or pleasure you think you are deriving from media coverage of your agency, however, the coverage isn't going to go away. It only makes sense, therefore, to invest the extra effort that makes it as positive and beneficial as possible.

The Public and Government

Americans have always been skeptical of government. It's written in their history, engraved in the founding documents of the republic. It's part of the political culture. Though never immune from twisting negatively toward cynicism, skepticism has helped powerfully to leaven and renew American democracy.

Skepticism doesn't exert that kind of impact, however, unless accompanied by a reasonably high, sustained level of public confidence in government. In that situation, people can turn a critical eye on government and still believe it will mostly do the right thing as a positive force in their lives. That's healthy. It is when public trust heads downward, and remains down, that skepticism edges into cynicism. That's unhealthy.

Reliable opinion polls, briefly cited earlier, agree that only about a quarter of the American public today has substantial confidence in the federal government. That compares with levels of 40 to 50 percent a generation ago—just after Vietnam and Watergate—and is far below those of the 1950s and 1960s. Specifically, the 1999 national Hart/Teeter poll of the nonpartisan Council for Excellence in Government found that people who felt disconnected from the federal government outnumbered those with a sense of connection by more than two to one. It discovered a majority belief that government is no longer "of, by, and for the people." While confidence in government was slightly higher in 1999 than five years earlier, it remained, and remains, low. The federal government, more remote from the public than state and municipal governments, consistently gets the lowest confidence rating in the biennial Hart/Teeter poll.

Note at the same time, however, that Americans also saw important tasks for government in this century, especially in fields like education, defense, medical research, reducing violence, and protecting the environment. They think government will remain an important institution, one they hope will respond better to their needs. They look at themselves, the public, as potentially a more potent factor in improving government than any other group or institution. People don't want government to go away. They care relatively little about making it smaller or bigger. What they want is better quality.

The consequences of current public attitudes are predictable. In the long term, they're serious, not to say ominous. Americans recognize government's role and potential but feel little ownership of it. In their turnoff, half of those eligible to vote in the 1996 presidential election did not vote. Most don't involve themselves in other forms of governing—communicating with elected politicians, engaging in or following the course of public debate, participating in political campaigns, teaching their children. Young adults, drawn more strongly than any others to the idea of community service, don't think of government as a channel for that service and feel even more disconnected than their elders.

A leading national opinion expert reminds us at the same time that distrust isn't only about government and the workings of government:

> It's about how people feel about the country, how they feel about Washington, and how they feel about the country's ability to deal with major problems people feel are not being solved. Today those problems are moral and ethical problems. Distrust of politicians is a leading cause of distrust of government, and the perceptions of the honesty and ethics of politicians is one of the principal culprits in the public's view of Washington and the federal government.

Public confidence and trust, the Government Accounting Office's David Walker reflects, are "arguably the most prized commodity in a democracy— very easy to lose and tough to earn." Many groups in the public, private, and nonprofit sectors have for some years been waging a carefully designed, often very creative campaign to win it back. (The annual Innovations in

American Government Awards and the broad-based Partnership for Trust in Government, both established and supported by the Ford Foundation, are two of the best-known efforts.) As executive branch managers, people in presidentially appointed jobs are directly implicated in this struggle and, of course, are well positioned to help lead it. For them, it all comes back to—you guessed it—results.

Again, results the country wants, and can see, are the best evidence that government is doing its job. They respond directly to the concerns and hopes evident in the poll data cited above. There is no better fuel for the enterprise called restoring public trust in government. Almost as vital as results themselves is making certain that people know about them.

> I can't emphasize enough how important telling your story is. If there's a difference between government and private industry, it is in the ability to tell one's story. In government there is a sense that if you put out a press release once, it's enough. There isn't necessarily a sense of reinforcing it, of going back. There are great stories to be told.

A media expert with high-level White House experience suggests that taking the results story where it counts the most means reaching beyond those who already have an opinion or a stake.

> That applies in general terms to almost any issue, whether it's the NBA playoffs or national drug policy. Draw a little pyramid. At the top of it is the 1 percent who are the key decisionmakers. Below them there are about 5 percent who are key influencers—the people who cover it, the people who know, the people who advise. Below that, about 15 percent who are the informed citizenry. Below that, 79 percent of general, mass public opinion. Those are the people you've got to reach in a democracy. Those are the people who run the country. If all you do is talk to that 1 or 5 or even 21 percent at the top of the pyramid, you're not reaching the vast majority of this country.

We have argued here that results are what matter most in taking on a presidential appointment in Washington. We've provided real-life, first-hand wisdom from experienced people about major leadership and management tasks that, along with policy and politics, most appointees must handle with reasonable success if they expect to get results.

These are not, of course, the only such issues that demand the time and attention of an administration's high-level political leaders. Others—budget development, financial management, questions of personal integrity—will also enmesh presidential appointees to varying degrees. Though they are not within the scope of this chapter, we have addressed such issues in other *Prune* volumes.

Final point: If results come first, the reasons that bring talented people to seek selection by a chief of state for high office also demand intense focus. The last burden any administration needs is someone who has joined up primarily to enhance a career. Personal goals are important; they clearly have a place; an effective stint in government will serve them. But almost without exception, people whose careers need little boost from public service make the best appointees—among other reasons, because personal ambition is unlikely to interfere with clear thinking or clear judgment.

Here, therefore, are the thoughts of a former White House official who had a broader opportunity than most to see this principle in operation: "Motivation is very important for the mission of your agency. If you don't believe in it, if you don't believe it will make a difference in the lives of ordinary people, stop doing it. Go do something else. Because if you don't believe in it, it's going to show to everybody. Everybody will notice that you're there more for the ride than for the goal."

3

Strengthening Federal Agency Management

Laura F. Skaff

During the 1990s, the push toward a more businesslike federal government through management reform took several approaches. Among them was the National Partnership for Reinventing Government (as it is now known), with its measures to increase efficiency, notably via work force streamlining. The Congress produced the 1993 Government Performance and Results Act plus landmark legislation to reform federal procurement and other operations. Private sector tools, like total quality management, were brought in.

Amid those undertakings, three new senior management positions made their appearance at the agency level: chief operating officer (COO), chief information officer (CIO), and chief financial officer (CFO)—sometimes collectively called the C-suite jobs. Together with two other long-established management posts—inspector general and general counsel—they were designed not only to elevate and strengthen agency management but, as with the CIO position, to speed government's full entry into the information age.

These five positions, common to most major departments and agencies, deserve special attention. Beyond their fundamental roles in agency management and in the general move to boost performance, it is instructive to examine the forces behind their emergence and the problems each has encountered. This chapter will also discuss each of them in terms of their history and operating environment, their impact as change agents, and their place in the transformation that technology is bringing to government.

For fresh knowledge, insight, and comment about these jobs, we talked individually and at length with two former deputy directors for management of the Office of Management and Budget, and to occupants of these positions at half of the fourteen federal cabinet departments, including some of the largest—the departments of Agriculture, Commerce, Defense, Health and Human Services, Housing and Urban Development, Transportation, and Treasury, as well as the Federal Deposit Insurance Corporation.

John Koskinen, who oversaw the federal government's massive Y2K preparations, thinks the Government Performance and Results Act has—critically—"caused people to focus on what difference programs are making. And a big part of the answer to what difference we are making with a program is how well it is organized and managed." That's precisely where these new functions ultimately exert their impact. The combination of CFO, COO, and CIO positions, Koskinen says, means "that we now have a series of positions in the government where good managers—people who are not necessarily policy experts—can be recruited and retained. I think that sends a very important signal to the public that we care about management. But it also helps the departments by providing management leadership at senior levels of the organization."

In 1990 the Congress created the CFO position, because, among other factors, certain legislators believed federal financial management needed the teeth that a century of earlier reform legislation had failed to provide. Similarly, the Clinton administration in 1993 designated some twenty deputy secretaries as the chief operating officers of their agencies. With an eye on the roughly comparable COO position in private industry, administration management strategists reasoned that agencies would operate better under senior executives who would also keep their second-in-command roles in policy and representation. And the CIO position, as suggested above, emerged on the rising tide of the information technology revolution. As the federal executive now moves toward e-government via the Internet, this job seems likely to take on greater weight and reach. To varying degrees and for other, comparable reasons, that is true of the general counsel and inspector general positions as well.

Additional underlying changes within the federal government have fueled the need for the new positions. Agencies in the last decade made a major shift from reliance on compliance management, dominated by heavy regulation, to an increased focus on results. Along with this went an emphasis on the flattening of organizational structure and a resulting reduction in the layers of review. In this environment, the C-suite jobs are supposed to perform the vital functions of improving and coordinating management across diverse agency functions.

Yet, despite convincing arguments supporting establishment of these three posts, their creation has generated a degree of controversy. First, there is the issue voiced by Edward DeSeve, like Koskinen a former deputy director for management at the Office of Management and Budget. He worries that the jobs, as they function over time, might tend to separate agency management and policy functions, a split he regards as artificial. "You can't divorce management and policy," he says. "I don't think that's possible, and I feel it's been a real detriment to public administration, as it was called. I believe it should be called public management, which is not only managing the work government does, but managing the policymaking function at the same time."

Other debate continues to surround the question of how centralized federal agency management should be. Part of this dates to the early 1990s, when the White House established the President's Management Council, under the OMB deputy director for management, to guide and coordinate agency management efforts. According to Koskinen, some members of the Congress felt the White House had not gone far enough. They wanted a separate office of federal management at the senior level. Such a structure,

Koskinen says, would have represented a "throwback to a command and control approach" unsuited to current reality in the federal government. Today, as pointed out by OMB director Jack Lew elsewhere in this book, virtually no support exists for a separate office of management.

On this point, Koskinen refers to his experience during the Y2K episode. "I've managed the Y2K issue for the government, for the country, and the world with a staff of ten people. That's because there is no way, when you start to talk about organizations of the size of federal agencies, that you can really manage them from a single point. All you can do is provide leadership, guidance, and coordination. The work has to be done by the people who are, in fact, living with the systems and with the problems. And those are the people in the agencies."

Chief Operating Officer

Brought into being in tandem with the reinvention effort, the COO position was intended in part as a centralizing influence, responding to the impact of efforts to flatten agencies and shift decisionmaking downward. Establishment of the position also recognized that heads of agencies have broad-based chief executive officer responsibilities that leave them little time to focus on management.

Historically, senior career service staff have overseen agency management. But they have often been unable to gain the support of the political leadership for major changes. That is why Koskinen sees the COO job "in many ways as the most important new management position, because it sends a signal that the number two, politically appointed position in each of these departments is going to be someone who is concerned with management issues—how to deal with thousands of employees and billions of dollars in expenditures. Yet, at the same time, the COO is the most fragile of these positions since it doesn't exist by statute."

This, of course, leaves the effectiveness of a COO vulnerable to the chemistry, or lack of it, between the occupant of the job and the head of the agency. A deputy secretary-COO is not always the choice of the secretary-CEO; the choice may be dictated by the White House, leading to resentment or perception of the COO as a threat. Dave Barram, a former COO at the Department of Commerce, thinks the administration taking office in 2001 should have the option of deciding whether to continue the position. Should the position be dropped, however, he believes there will be some hard questions to answer from both sides of the aisle in the Congress.

In an environment where the background of many political appointees is law, the Congress, the nonprofit and academic worlds, and government at other levels, those who established the COO position had a range of expectations for it. They hoped, first, that it would bring more managerial expertise to the mix. Specifically, they wanted the COO function to reduce fragmentation within federal agencies coordinating diverse operations, gain better coordination between agency policy and functions, give the deputy secretary position more clout and definition, and bring more high-level attention to agency management issues. With these factors in mind, they looked in their early deputy secretary nominations for people who would not be merely policy mirrors of their secretaries. Instead, they sought individuals who could bring to the office strong managerial expertise, preferably gained within large conglomerates, similar to the environment within most federal departments.

But some see another dimension to selecting COOs. For Barram, the old adage that a manager is a manager is a manager does not ring true. A good COO, in his view, should know the business of the agency in question. "If you're the deputy secretary of Commerce, it's important to understand about NOAA, trade technology, minority business, census, a lot of different parts of your business."

Barram does believe the COO strengthens agency management. But he warns against viewing the secretary-CEO position as purely a policy job and the deputy secretary-COO position as solely a management job. "You can't separate management and policy," he says. "I think the presumption was that secretaries were going to be politically oriented, policy oriented, and maybe not as management oriented, and that some people were needed in there who were focused on management. That doesn't really work very well. If, as a COO, you don't understand and work on the policy issues, you won't be effective in your management role. By the same token, a secretary who completely abdicates the management part of it won't be successful as a secretary."

The same principle applies to the reporting function. Barram feels that all department heads, including the CFO and CIO, should report through the COO to the secretary on policy as well as management issues—and suspects that some agencies don't follow this procedure. Similarly to Koskinen's views above, he believes separating reporting lines makes an artificial and unnecessary distinction. "It gets back to the secretary and the deputy having no light between them," he says—"when someone reports in to one of them, she or he should speak for the other." "The value of the COO to me," Barram says, "was that you end up with two strong people at the top with some specific responsibilities, but sharing the fundamental management responsibility." He acknowledges, however, that the real answer as to how these two positions should be mutually structured in these ways depends almost totally on the individual secretary and deputy secretary.

A sharp dissent to the view of management from a single senior position was voiced to us four years ago by Paul O'Neill, a former deputy director of OMB who is now chairman of Alcoa. The COO concept, he said, assumes a "uniformity of activity" in federal agencies that he doesn't think exists. He rejected the notion that a single individual can be the senior managing official in an agency as complex as most federal agencies are.

But COO Richard Rominger at the Department of Agriculture sees a major part of his job as bringing greater cohesiveness to the department's numerous programs. He believes the historical lack of coordination at Agriculture was intentionally created by congressional committees that preferred more direct influence over the individual programs to working through the secretary. In 1993 the department was a loosely joined group of forty-five distinct agencies, each with its own budget and information technology systems. With the COO in place, a more corporate way of doing business emerged. The focus has increasingly become the department's priorities, not those of the Forest Service or the Office of Food, Nutrition, and Consumer Services. Assisted by the creation of CFO and CIO positions, Agriculture's budget and technology systems are coordinated for the first time. A further major value of the COO, according to Rominger, flows from the position's capacity to bring under secretaries and assistant secretaries together when intramural disputes need resolution.

Rominger and Barram think the President's Management Council has given federal government COOs powerful reinforcement. For Barram, the PMC has been a place for COOs to share their struggles and successes, as well as a forum where they can unite their efforts to gain attention for, and work toward solutions for, their issues. It has, he says, been a valuable mechanism in recognizing and dealing with duplicative activities. The PMC, adds Rominger, has also been useful in resolving disputes between agencies.

While he sees many similarities between the public- and private-sector versions of the COO job, Rominger thinks the government COO clearly faces more constraints. Chief among these, he says, are limitations created by personnel systems and by congressional oversight—in effect, a 535-

member board of directors. "When you see the dramatic changes taking place in the corporate world—the downsizing, the mergers—you know there is more freedom in the private sector."

Barram identifies other primary challenges for the federal COO. Some are those faced by any enterprise—people, technology, and budget. Of these, he also feels that personnel issues are the most problematic. "You don't have the same flexibility you have in the private sector and yet you're only as good as the people and structure you have in place for them to function." Redundancy is another major issue. "There's no company this big and even companies have a difficult time making sure they are not redundant from one division to another. If we're going to do more with fewer resources, we need to be less redundant"

What are the qualifications of an effective COO? Beyond general management ability, Rominger mentions personnel and human relations skills, budget acumen, and experience in shaping policy. He comes back to the relationship between the COO and the agency chief as the most essential factor in a COO's success. "I think, when you're coming into this job, you should make sure you're going to be able to do something in the position, not just take it because it's offered to you. To do that, you must be able to work comfortably and compatibly with the person who's the secretary in the department."

A number of outstanding questions remain about the COO position. Should it be institutionalized by statute? Is there an inherent conflict between this and the chief of staff positions? Should a basic set of managerial competencies be required for COOs?

Raised public expectations is the most difficult challenge that lies ahead for COOs, in Barram's view. "I think that the country is going to increasingly expect us to get the most out of our resources and to have only those resources that we need," he comments. "We have to be willing to make tough decisions around people and structure, something that has not been in the culture here in the government." He looks at technology as the most critical of these resources and believes the chief responsibility for ensuring that the work of the CIO and the rest of the organization are closely aligned falls on the COO. "You have to wake up every day figuring out what does technology mean for our business today."

Rominger thinks budget pressures will increasingly plague federal agencies as the need to fix Medicare and Social Security intensifies, squeezing funding for discretionary programs. He predicts that human resource issues will also come to the fore under continuing pressure for agencies to do more with less. Among them will be such questions as the removal of under-performers and keeping staff training abreast of rapid changes in technology. All these are prime subjects for central COO attention.

Beyond the structural and specific management issues, says Koskinen, "the major challenge for COOs will be integrating the major management efforts now under way—information technology and its better use, strategic planning, performance measurement—and monitoring where programs are going to make sure they are spending money as effectively as possible while accomplishing goals that people can understand."

Chief Information Officer

By now it's a well-known story. At the dawn of the information age, the federal government was the leader in the development and use of information technology in this country. Then came a series of mistakes—unwise early investment, a lack of coordination across agencies and programs, negligence in recruiting and retaining technological expertise and talent. These put government behind the curve, in its own internal information technology competence as in its still-limited capacity to use IT in serving the public. Now, with the help of legislation, a couple of important recent presidential directives, and the contribution of business and nonprofit organizations, it is trying to catch up.

Creation of the CIO job was the work of two groundbreaking legislative reforms in federal information management—the Paperwork Reduction Act of 1995 and the Clinger-Cohen Act of 1996 (formerly the Information Technology Management Reform Act of 1996). By way of overall goals, they require agencies to use greater discipline in controlling their investments in information technology, develop an overall information architecture, and define measures to see whether and how information technology is contributing to improved program performance. Specifically, Subdivision A of Clinger-Cohen requires three tasks of agencies before they invest in new information technology. First, to ask what IT functions are being performed and whether they are consistent with the agency's mission. Second, to see whether functions could be carried out more effectively and cheaply by the private sector. Third, for functions consistent with mission, to examine and redesign or reengineer such functions before applying new technology to them.

Effective information management leadership at each agency, of course, is central to effective implementation of these reforms. While the two pieces of legislation conventionally hold agency heads responsible for doing this, part of their real significance is the directive that CIOs be appointed to play the major role at the working level.

As deputy director for management at OMB, John Koskinen was partially responsible for the emergence of the CIO position. He points to the notorious failures of information technology efforts within federal agencies as the chief factor driving passage of Clinger-Cohen. According to Koskinen, repeated questioning from members of Congress produced formation of a task force, led by OMB, whose job was to identify the common problems behind the phenomenal cost overruns, delays, and failures plaguing so many agency information technology projects.

Fortunately, a timely report by the General Accounting Office, reviewing effective practices in the private sector, helped point the way to critical improvements that government agencies could adapt. Among the lessons guiding business in its IT efforts, the GAO identified the rule that no new technology installation works if it doesn't produce a deliverable within twelve to eighteen months. By contrast, most federal IT projects were being operated with five- to seven-year time frames. Yet without intermediate deliverables, there was no way to test systems along the way and make needed corrections. Further, almost by definition, systems completed seven years out are obsolete on delivery. Federal agencies also differed markedly from the private sector in their propensity to disconnect IT decisions from policy and program managers. Thickening this isolation was the federal requirement that all IT projects of any size be approved by the General Services Administration.

Clinger-Cohen set out the principle that an agency's top policy and management leadership should be integrally involved in, and ultimately responsible for, the development and direction of IT systems. On the heels of this new legislation, the onset of year 2000 preparations helped direct the attention of top agency management to IT issues, especially when the White House made clear its intention to hold the leadership accountable for system failures. Under Clinger-Cohen, moreover, IT projects were to be developed in short-term modules and measured against preestablished performance goals for system deliverables.

An early result is the most recent attempt to automate the Internal Revenue Service—an IT modernization project, says Treasury Department CIO Jim Flyzik, that is probably unmatched in the world for size and complexity. The task is not made easier by the constant flow of new and modified tax laws and regulations. Yet Flyzik feels quite confident that the present effort will be successful. There are several reasons for his optimism: substantial up-front planning has occurred, the system is being built in small, incremental stages, and measures are in place to determine success at critical stages throughout development. Results in other agencies also illustrate the effect of Clinger-Cohen:

—At the Department of Housing and Urban Development, CIO Gloria Parker points to improvements in capital planning and IT investment processes as a major accomplishment. Before Clinger-Cohen, she says, "there was not a coordinated effort to involve HUD leadership in capitol planning and IT investment strategies. Great strides have been made to align IT resource spending with the mission of the department."

—Through the efforts of CIOs, agencies have been able to integrate many of the data quality and data access projects across their organizations, bringing an enterprisewide perspective to these activities. From the CIO's centralized focus have come greater interoperability across systems and open architecture capable of supporting the agency's mission.

—To facilitate wise IT investments, the Treasury Department has set up an investment review board with an agencywide membership. Initially, this group focused on IT investments; more recently, it has broadened its scope to cover all major investment and budget initiatives. The CFO chairs the group; the CIO steps in as cochair for IT issues.

—A closer linking is evident between IT investments and agency missions and goals. At Treasury, all proposed investments must show an impact on the agency mission and specify performance measures. (Often, however, performance targets are still developed after the fact.)

But the initial challenges faced by agency CIOs were numerous and tough. Foremost was the assignment to ensure that the potential Y2K problem would not disrupt federal operations. In most cases, CIOs stepped into their new jobs to find that efforts to address Y2K were seriously behind schedule. Koskinen credits the CIO Council with enabling the kind of government-wide coordinated effort needed to deal with the Y2K challenge. (Although Clinger-Cohen did not call for establishment of such a body, the Clinton administration created it by executive order in mid-1996. Like the CFO Council in its domain, the CIO Council provides an arena for creating goals, discussing common problems and solutions, exchanging notes, and building a professional community among specialists. The CIO Council got a head start with OMB and GAO guidance on capital investment in IT and information security, and the GAO review of best management practices referred to above.)

Just as critical was, and is, the poor management of information security in many federal agencies that is putting assets worth billions of dollars at risk and vast amounts of sensitive data in danger of unauthorized disclosure. Underscoring this extreme vulnerability have been presidential commission reports on the growing exposure of U.S. computer networks to exploitation and terrorism. Other typical issues facing agency CIOs are rooted in the need to:

—develop integrated systems architectures,

—establish sound information management investment review processes,

—integrate strategic information planning with overall agency strategic plans,

—build the staff skills and capabilities agencies need to navigate rapid technology advances.

Making these changes means strengthening the core IT competencies of federal staff at all levels. HUD's Gloria Parker has led CIO Council efforts to identify these and to give strong attention to what she views as the critical area of IT project management. What government really needs, she says, is good, strong project management skills. "Contractors are used extensively; however, we must have government project managers who understand the technology and are able to assess the impact of this technology on the mission and functions of the agency." Accordingly, the STAR (Strategic and Tactical Advocates for Results) Program, an initiative spearheaded by GSA with strong backing of the federal CIO Council, stresses project management skills and strategic planning. The CIO Council has also established a virtual "CIO University" for prospective CIOs. At HUD, training in IT skills is geared to all levels—support staff through the executive level.

What has made her job difficult, Parker reflects, is that many of the processes HUD is using today vary greatly from approaches used in past years. "It hasn't been difficult in terms of our knowing what we need to do. The difficulty comes in when hard decisions must be made and, due to the limited dollars available, funding is not available to cover all of the important initiatives."

One highly promising sign that the CIO concept has gained broader acceptance is the proliferation of CIO positions at the bureau and program level within agencies, supported by internal department CIO councils. At Treasury, a CIO has been appointed for each of the agency's fourteen operating bureaus, and the department's CIO Council acts as a corporate decisionmaking body, overseeing IT applications in areas ranging from telephone systems to Internet firewall services. But effective as all this is, it doesn't change the departmental CIO's ultimate responsibility, under Clinger-Cohen, for the success of IT systems throughout Treasury.

What skills and experience, coming in, qualify an individual for CIO responsibilities? The list generally includes leadership ability, technical skills, an understanding of business operations, and good communications and negotiation skills. It's worth noting that a GAO review of initial agency CIO appointments raised concerns in a number of agencies that the people in these jobs were technically not qualified, held other major management responsibilities simultaneously, or did not report directly to the head of the agency. Part of the reason for this traces to timing: creation of the CIO position midway through an administration made it more difficult to sell departments on the importance of well-qualified and highly placed CFOs.

Treasury's Flyzik thinks recent appointments have put better-qualified people into CIO jobs, a development that should increase the position's clout. A good CIO needs to know "not only where technology is going but understand how IT fits into the mission of the organization." Perhaps most important, however, is a CIO's ability to establish credibility across the organization. In essence, the CIO must "sell the job as a set of skills" increasingly important to program managers. Parker expresses similar thoughts. She believes a CIO must be both a change agent and a visionary. "You've got to be able to see across the board where your organization should be going and then be able to have the drive and the wherewithal to market that vision to all the other executives and get them on board."

In some agencies, like Treasury, senior IT positions existed before Clinger-Cohen. That legislation set up a direct line of access between the CIO and the agency head, embodying Flyzik's view that "the CIO must be able to get to the secretary and subagency heads whenever needed. If you don't have that level of visibility and the ability to get to the senior officials, you're going to have a very difficult time being effective." In other agencies, CIO responsibilities were tacked on to those of the existing CFO—in effect, a dual role. But Flyzik asserts that one individual doing both jobs faces an impossible assignment. "I know what the CFO does here and her schedule is like mine—it's absolutely packed."

Regardless of the particular structure or placement of the CIO position, Flyzik believes the toughest problems arise when the CIO lacks authority over resources. "If there's a place where CIOs are struggling, it would be in those agencies where the CIO has certain responsibility and accountability for program results, but no authority whatsoever on resources."

DeSeve and others believe that keeping up with an astonishingly rapid pace of technological and other kinds of change is the number one challenge ahead for federal agencies. Survival in such an environment will require that CIOs adopt a much more strategic approach while continuing to deal with existing operational issues. As DeSeve puts it, "it isn't just running the boiler room, it is engineering how the ship should go forward." He also sees a difficult problem just ahead in the area of computer security. Solving it will, he says, "take the concerted effort of the CIOs to get the support needed from Congress and the administration for the necessary upgrades in hardware and software, along with additional personnel and training."

As federal agencies grapple with this environment, their efforts are marked by increased outreach to the private sector. The CIO Council has created a liaison group with industry to help feed private sector ideas into the government on a continuing basis. In any case, the increased visibility of the CIO position, thanks to Y2K, is likely to continue with the high-level federal attention now focusing on the Internet and electronic commerce. With presidential executive orders stating explicit goals and deadlines for electronic government (for more on this, see chapter 2, "Presidential Appointees and the Leadership Challenge"), agency heads are putting substantial pressure on their CIOs.

Private industry has also developed a management position known as "chief knowledge officer" to complement the CIO position. In effect, the CIO fills the policy function for information technology. The advantage for the federal government, says John Koskinen, is "the focus this person would bring to policy and program issues, working with agency heads to think about where the department is going and how information technology can be used to move the organization into the twenty-first century."

Parker sees herself as a radical in terms of how she perceives federal efforts to date in the area of e-government. "We have put a lot of information out on the web from which our business partners and the public are benefiting. However, I think we can go a lot further in this area and actually use the Internet to truly change the way we do business," she says. Before federal agencies can go much further, she believes, changes in legislation will be necessary. But she thinks the move in the direction of e-government will bring significant reductions in administrative workload and a more user-friendly government.

Looking at the future, Flyzik believes much more needs to be done on an interagency, intergovernmental, and global basis. "I think citizens are going to demand it. Today there is still too much stove piping, too much dealing with different agencies for different things. Technology will allow us do a lot more to make life easier for people if we do a better job collaborating across localities, agencies and governments. It's a global economy and we need to think of global kinds of information technology approaches."

Chief Financial Officer

Before passage of the Chief Financial Officers Act of 1990, only two federal agencies produced audited financial statements each year. Today, all agencies with CFOs do so. Even more noteworthy, the majority of them receive what are known as clean opinions—the information presented is accurate and truthful, and not misleading in any material respect.

That is probably the most fundamental and important impact that CFOs have exerted to date on federal financial management. According to Edward DeSeve, a recent deputy director for management at OMB, the significance of audited statements lies in "the discipline agencies have developed to be able to properly account for the funds, for the property, for the plant and equipment, and for the other budgetary resources they're given." At the Department of Health and Human Services, CFO John Callahan adds an important point: audits help provide a road map to the areas in which agencies can make more progress below the clean-opinion level.

What the CFO Act and subsequent amendments have essentially done, in the view of CFO Sally Thompson at the Department of Agriculture, is to define federal financial management to reflect private sector practice. "I think that it has brought financial management out of the closet, and out of the dark ages."

DeSeve also believes that the involvement of CFOs in the construction of their agency strategic and performance plans—and in many cases, in the consolidation of performance and budget documents—has been a significant accomplishment. And for Callahan, the integration of performance goals with budgets has given his department much more credibility with Hill appropriators.

William Lynn is CFO and comptroller at the Department of Defense. He sees the primary value of the CFO position in the balanced, objective advice it gives the secretary on budget allocation decisions. "In defense," he says, "you're always going to be able to get more money; the key is to spend the money on the highest priorities so that you end up with a strategy-driven budget." At the same time, he sees a fundamental gap: his appropriators do not work along the lines of the department's performance goals and show no interest in doing so. Thompson at Agriculture has encountered the same attitude. Program managers who depend on congressional appropriators for their funding, and who see that the appropriators aren't sold on performance goals, think of financial management as an "afterthought," she says. She thinks the growing attention given by appropriators to performance and financial management is critical to getting internal agency support for solid financial management.

Establishment of the CFO position marked the first attempt by the Congress to institutionalize financial management in federal agencies. Some called the CFO Act the most significant financial management legislation in forty years. Agencies in which a CFO function was to be created were required, in addition to audited financial statements, to do long-range financial planning, integrate budget and accounting data, standardize their systems for managing and accounting for cash and credit, and develop cost information. The act also mandated central leadership for financial management within OMB, creating the positions of deputy director for management and U.S. comptroller and setting up the Office of Federal Financial Management

It further initiated the CFO Council to convene CFOs in regular dialogue under the tutelage of the OMB deputy director, the comptroller, and the fiscal assistant secretary of the Treasury Department. Early in its life, says DeSeve, the CFO Council transitioned from a group led by OMB to an organization directed primarily by its members—"from being a site receiving a broadcast to a network of mutually reinforcing individuals with their own agenda."

The act envisioned the CFO as an agency's principal financial officer, reporting directly to the head of the organization and responsible for all financial management activities. Typically, these would include finance, accounting, budget, and financial information systems. But OMB directives outlining the functions that should ideally report to the CFO did not include budgeting and set no requirements for CFO office structure or functions. Given those circumstances, interpretations of who and what actually report to the CFO has varied among agencies, which have also adopted widely divergent ways of organizing the CFO function itself.

One example is the combined management office used by the Department of Health and Human Services. John Callahan has held the titles of CFO, CIO, and assistant secretary for management and budget. These multiple roles have been made more manageable by the establishment of several deputy positions reporting to Callahan—a deputy CFO, a deputy CIO, and deputies for budget, grants, acquisition, and human resources.

Callahan says the breadth of his responsibility and his direct access to the secretary have given him substantial positional influence. A strong management office has also proved a better way to coordinate department management after the decentralization of most program operations. A further advantage to this model in Callahan's view is that career staffers are involved at a higher level in primary management functions, ensuring greater stability in these critical areas.

At the Department of Defense, the shaping of the CFO position has also been faithful to the CFO Act, with the sole focus of the position being a full range of financial activities consolidated into the CFO's job. The CFO-comptroller carries responsibility for overseeing the budget justification before the Congress, for internal budget programming and planning, and for all the department's finance and accounting. Further, the position was elevated from an assistant secretary to an under secretary. Lynn describes the change: "it used to be that the internal program budget and the congressional budget justification weren't linked completely, and that is a linkage that has to be made. So putting it together—it's a little bit of wear and tear on the occupant of this office, but it's definitely worth it in terms of the integration we get."

The Department of Agriculture is one of the few largest CFO agencies that doesn't place budget responsibilities under the CFO. According to Sally Thompson, this arrangement has, however, succeeded because of her close working relationship with the budget director. The separation from budget has also allowed her to concentrate on modernizing financial systems in a very big and diverse organization, a task she likens to turning the Titanic around. But she feels that, in the long run, the budget functions should be placed with the CFO.

What about financial systems? Increasing the timeliness of financial reporting is a goal common to most federal agencies. Ideally, reconciliation of accounts should be done on a month-to-month basis. But few agencies have achieved that level of timeliness. Improvements to agency automated systems promise to increase data timeliness while reducing the labor intensity of the process. Yet new systems development has been costly and raises issues of data security.

At the Department of Agriculture, for example, development of new financial systems often poses the dilemma whether it is more critical to have funding to staff services or to have financial systems in place to manage a program more effectively. Thompson offers the statistic that over the past few years, while program dollars have increased by more than 50 percent, funds to administer these programs have dropped by 28 percent. Replacing the department's antiquated financial systems could actually save money and staff resources in the long run, but short-term financial pressures make such an investment impossible. Defense now uses an all-electronic process to put its budget together internally and transmit it to the Congress. While automation has improved speed and efficiency, Lynn believes more could be done to rethink the process.

The CFO Act's authors set high standards for the CFO, calling for "individuals who possess demonstrated ability in general management of, and knowledge of and extensive practical experience in, financial management practices in large governmental or business entities." In fact, however, initial appointees to CFO posts were by and large people already in place. In many cases, CFO responsibilities were added as collateral duties to the jobs of assistant secretaries for management or administration.

Subsequent appointments have come under the scrutiny of OMB, with an eye to beefing up the level of financial expertise. To wield the kind of influence necessary for true effectiveness, Callahan at HHS suggests that CFO appointees be individuals with a substantial level of experience in government, preferably including experience with the Congress. Thompson feels the CFO should also be a certified public accountant, one with broader experience than mere number crunching. In addition, she believes strong interpersonal skills are key in bringing decisionmakers together and building an effective financial management team.

Recent appointees better reflect the level of experience called for in the act. To ensure that the level of experience of financial management employees also keeps pace with the changing requirements of financial management, the CFO Council has placed primary attention on identifying necessary competencies and developing an innovative array of recruiting, training, and retention options. A total of 58 percent of federal financial management employees received twenty or more hours of continuing professional training during calendar year 1999, and 21 percent had one or more professional certifications as of May 2000. OMB and the Council have set targets for further improvements in future years.

Callahan cites the Presidential Management Intern program as a model for bringing in bright entry-level staff. He also believes there should be less concern with possible conflict-of-interest situations arising after people leave government. Postemployment restrictions designed to prevent this, he notes, can deter talented individuals from considering government service. "We should create some situations where good midlevel people from these firms can come in, work for the government for a period of time, and then go back out."

Just as procurement and grants management staff are certified, there is some advocacy for the certification of financial personnel. In fact, the need for well-qualified people has led the Department of Defense to institute a certification process for its financial management staff. It has worked to up-grade both its internal training programs and its external measurement of the programs. To address training needs for financial staff, some agencies are exploring the use of distributed learning systems, which bring desktop training to professionals within agencies.

The Congress and OMB are critical partners for CFOs. The link with OMB provided by the CFO Council has been instrumental in pushing forward many financial management changes that all federal agencies need. As for Capitol Hill, CFOs, with their key involvement in developing and defending agency budgets, typically spend a lot of their time there. For Thompson, this means developing partnerships with key congressional staffs. "I always feel that people don't agree with me because they just don't understand. So I work really hard on the education process and try to act as a go-between for the people here and up there." A strong, direct relationship with the agency's secretary and deputy secretary-COO are the most vital internal relationships for a CFO, in the opinion of those with whom we talked. Some also stress the importance of a strong career team working with the CFO.

As for the future, DeSeve feels the biggest task for CFOs is "to continue to embed ever better performance metrics and financial metrics in budgets, going beyond activity-based costing and better understanding cost drivers." He also believes that agencies will continue to try to cut costs, particularly the cost of administering procurement contracts wherever possible.

It's clear that further automation of financial systems is coming as most agencies try to improve the timeliness, accuracy, and accessibility of information. But Callahan warns that government agencies are prone to believing they need customized applications when ready-to-buy programs could be used instead. As he puts it, "we should use basic, robust, off-the-shelf programs rather than trying to create the most elegant information technology program that maybe only three people know how to use." Thompson sees a need for a critical change in focus by CFO offices from transactional processing—a chore that technology will soon take over—to analysis of what the numbers mean. In essence, this is a shift to strategic and outcome-based thinking, centered on what the agency is trying to accomplish and how well it is moving toward that goal.

The increased reliance on automated financial systems brings with it the need for improved security for these systems. Callahan believes CFOs could do more, in close cooperation with agency inspectors general, to raise program integrity by working not just to identify the problems but also to find solutions.

Further collaboration with private sector companies also seems likely. According to Callahan, to understand how progress is made in the financial management field, "public sector people should get a better understanding of CFO operations in the private sector." Some of this bridging between sectors has already occurred through the CFO Council's effort to identify ways of dealing with an increasingly fast-paced and dynamic environment.

Yet Thompson, who has spent much of her career in the private sector, does not believe that privatization of federal financial functions is a viable option. She uses payroll systems as an example. "There are a lot of companies that process payroll," she says. "So I thought, well let's just go get one of the Fortune 500 payroll systems. It doesn't work. There's just too much difference between a federal payroll system and the private sector. I see a lot of room for the private sector, but I see it more in partnerships and in tandem with the federal government, not in lieu of it."

What keeps Thompson in the public sector, despite long hours and low salary, is the belief that she can make a real difference in the delivery of services to people who need them. Sadly, she points out that many of her department's employees have better equipment at home than in their offices. "That's not the way to run government. We're going to change that. We're going to educate people. I'm sure they'll understand and give us the money once they understand."

General Counsel

Many federal general counsels—GCs—will tell you that their chief concern is the rising tide of litigation involving their agencies. At the Department of Health and Human Services, General Counsel Harriet Rabb identifies efforts to increase the quality of agency service as a primary factor in this problem. Initiatives to improve the quality of nursing homes and Head

Start centers, for instance, have meant that those unable to meet new quality standards often end up bringing actions against the department.

Next is the huge agenda of legal work plaguing most federal agencies. As Rabb describes it, the hardest issues are being comfortable with the responsibility for the legal work of "an incredibly diverse set of clients and an extraordinarily complex set of issues." Both she and Nancy McFadden, GC at the Department of Transportation, say the extraordinary caliber of their career legal staffs is the major factor in managing this kind of workload. And they believe this most essential resource—capable staff—will soon be in jeopardy. Most of these people are nearing retirement. With little to offer by way of competitive salaries and other incentives like frequent training, Rabb and McFadden see maintaining the quality of legal representation from which most agencies now benefit as difficult.

Within federal agencies, the stated role of the Office of the General Counsel (OGC) is to provide advice on legal matters to management. General counsels are pivotal players in the clearance, or vetting, process inside agencies and hold dual, sometimes conflicting roles in interpreting the law and representing their clients' interests. While they don't typically testify before the Congress, they do play a key role in the legislative process. An OGC is heavily involved in the preparation of legislation and comments on it to OMB. In addition, the office typically helps draft agency testimony and briefs those who deliver it.

Unlike the other positions examined in this chapter, general counsels lack a coordinating body where they can discuss and resolve common issues. In 1979 the Carter administration established an entity called the Federal Legal Council, but it became inactive after a few years in the absence of support from subsequent administrations.

Franklin Roosevelt's solicitor general, Oscar Cox, once described general counsels as either "cold" or "hot" lawyers. The terms stuck. Cold lawyers are seen as satisfied with telling management a proposal is unacceptable because there are no specific provisions that allow management to implement it. They tend not to offer any options or specify the legal risks of a proposed action. Hot lawyers ask management what it wants to do and work with it to devise plans that will achieve the objective, identifying risks and developing options.

It seems evident that today's environment, where federal managers struggle for the flexibility to improve their operations, provide better customer service and cut costs, needs more hot lawyers. McFadden believes that appointing a political appointee to head an OGC facilitates the hot approach.

"I often find that someone who has been in a job for twenty years feels they know the stuff and will say 'no, you can't do that. While it is usually somebody in a position like mine who says, 'well, I want to know more, I want a little more analysis and options, how do we get to yes?'"

Identifying their customers is a central issue for general counsels. Customers might be the president, the agency, the agency head, the midlevel manager posing the issue, or the public at large. The reality is that multiple customers, internal and external to government, exist and present various, often competing needs that the GC must balance. One by-product of this, however, is a lack of congruence that can intrude between the expectations of agency managers and OGC performance. To avoid that, the National Partnership for Reinventing Government developed the idea of exposing OGCs to quasi-market forces. This approach would separate OGC service and control functions and allow line managers to select which they want to consult for advice. The General Accounting Office has adapted this approach by assigning legal staff to serve specific line managers and soliciting those managers' input into attorneys' performance evaluations.

Rabb believes a holistic approach to customer service is most effective. "I don't understand how a person who's looking at the litigation coming forward would have any sense at all that she really understood what a program was trying to accomplish—how to decide whether this is worth fighting for, settling, or taking to the Supreme Court." What is needed is "a shared sense of enterprise" among people who have ownership of a program, she says. "Someone who is there with the client when the policy is made, when the regulation is written, when the implementation guidance is sent out, and when the litigation happens."

OGC effectiveness has been limited in many agencies by management's failure to involve the office at an early point. Managers may see this as a way of avoiding cumbersome and lengthy approval processes. But general counsels believe such delays render their advice ineffective and that their engagement at the outset of strategic planning and decisionmaking can save significant time and resources. To encourage early consultation, the National Partnership for Reinventing Government has suggested that OGCs offer managers a streamlined approval process.

At HHS, Rabb felt more than comfortable with the timing and level of involvement. Policymaking meetings, she says, were inclusive and collaborative. Such meetings typically were attended by the heads of all operating and staff divisions, including the general counsel. Still, while this early, deep involvement was ultimately beneficial, Rabb also felt the strain of attempting to cover many areas of policy formation in addition to attending to litigation-related tasks.

Within complex, multiagency departments, the role of the general counsel is particularly challenging. Where a number of modes with highly specialized operations exist, as in the Department of Transportation, individual legal counsels are the norm: consolidating numerous legal staff members into a direct reporting relationship with the OGC may be neither practical nor desirable for effective operations. The OGC operations at Transportation and Health and Human Services illustrate the contrast between unified and balkanized office setups. Despite the large program size and complex structure within HHS, the OGC is centralized under the office of the secretary. Rabb supervises all three hundred lawyers within the department's headquarters and those in ten regional offices. Headquarters staff are organized primarily along functional lines related to particular programs like the Food and Drug Administration or the Health Care Financing Administration. In addition, some of the lawyers are generalists and cover the areas of ethics, business, administration, and legislation.

Rabb finds the chief advantage of this unified structure in its maximum value to the secretary and independence for the legal staff. "Lawyers don't have to worry that their budgets are at the mercy of judgments by subagency administrators whom they advise. Just as valuable is the confidence such an arrangement tends to give the secretary. As Rabb explains it, the secretary knows—and the rest of the department knows—that the views of the OGC "are not filtered through or in any respect affected by the fact that lawyers are actually on the payroll" of any of the subagencies. "So it provides independence and protection for the lawyers and also for the department." Less positive has been the effect on the OGC budget. "The Hill is not very enthusiastic about spending money on the secretary's budget, which is where lawyers appear," Rabb says. "It turns out the world doesn't think lawyers are as necessary as our clients do."

Has the reinvention movement influenced the work of federal GCs? Those interviewed for this chapter felt that efforts to reduce regulations and create greater flexibility within their departments had created heavier workloads. McFadden and Rabb both also said the recent adversarial relationship between the Congress and the administration vastly complicated their jobs. According to McFadden, her office had to spend an undue amount of time responding to congressional oversight requests. One required the identification of every piece of guidance the department had issued in the previous three years. Rabb says "there is such acrimony and partisanship that the department gets pulled from pillar to post. It's a mean season and I don't see it going away."

The general counsel position needs an experienced lawyer with a background in litigation. A knowledge of federal regulatory policy and a familiarity with the Congress are also highly desirable. But a specific area of expertise relevant to the agency seems much less critical then flexibility and the capacity to juggle multiple priorities. McFadden defines a successful general counsel as "someone able to learn quickly, who can rely on the folks who really know the areas, and who can see the big picture while responding to crises." Rabb emphasizes the value of flexibility in moving quickly from one priority to another amid an intricate and ever-changing workload.

Internally, the most important relationships for a GC are those with the head of agency and the deputy or chief operating officer. Rabb and Mc-Fadden attribute most of their success to strong ties with the top leadership that give them a place at the table when all major decisions are made. In Rabb's case, a close relationship with the secretary meant her advice was seen as unbiased and in the best interest of the department, with no hidden agendas. In large agencies, particularly those with decentralized operations, it is imperative to develop good working associations with regional and associate general counsels. And in any agency, a wise general counsel will also see to effective collaboration with the inspector general.

Externally, the Department of Justice looms large in the work of GCs as a clearance point for interdepartmental litigation and legal policy. In sidetracking a number of potential problems, McFadden also depended on her relationships with congressional staffers and their willingness to consult her. In addition, relationships with the outside bar can be useful in gaining broader perspectives on given issues.

OGC use of more advanced technology could mitigate the loss of capable staff but not offset it. Many offices have tended to use whatever additional resources become available to hire new legal staff to handle always-rising workloads. As a result, they have not kept pace with private-sector counterparts in using the most advanced technology. Among the tools that should help improve the efficiency of OGCs in the near future are electronic dockets and online libraries. Solutions like these, combined with intensified campaigns for additional resources, will be necessary if federal general counsels are to stay even with their increasingly complicated responsibilities.

Inspector General

Tracing the history of this position, the 1993 *Prune Book* on financial management positions pointed out that, until 1978, the development of inspection, audit, and investigatory functions within the federal government had progressed in fits and starts. They were fragmented, weak, obscure, and lacked independence and scope. Even within a single agency, they had proved to be isolated from top management and from each other. Inspector general positions existed in a couple of agencies in the 1950s and 1960s, but they were toothless. What tenure and authority they had were unprotected by statute.

When legislation advancing the notion of a presidentially appointed, statutory IG position was introduced in the early 1970s, every affected department opposed it, as did OMB. A key objection was based on unconstitutionality: the proposed IG position would work with the executive branch but report directly to the Congress. In 1976 the Congress nonetheless created a statutory IG job at the former Department of Health, Education, and Welfare. Later, supporters of the statutory position drafted another bill to add such IGs at about a dozen more agencies. Despite the hostility of these and other agencies, this legislation became law in 1978. For the first time, it brought audit and investigative operations together in the same IG operation. It mandated the IG to report twice yearly to the Congress. By 1988 there were nineteen statutory IG positions; that year the Congress added five more under presidential appointment and another thirty-three at "designated federal entities," where IG appointments are made by the heads of the organizations.

Inspectors general have the broad mission of detecting fraud, waste, and mismanagement in agency programs and operations; conducting audits and investigations; and recommending policies to promote economy, efficiency, and effectiveness. Currently, the fifty-seven IG offices employ nearly 10,000 audit and investigative staffers and spend about $1.1 billion annually.

In 1981 the President's Council on Integrity and Efficiency came into being, with the assignment of encouraging cross communication among IGs. In this, of course, it closely parallels the work of the CIO and CFO councils discussed earlier and, like them, operates under the guidance of OMB's deputy director for management.

To date, the success of the IG function can be measured in one respect by what the General Accounting Office says are billions of dollars in agency savings and cost recoveries and thousands of criminal case prosecutions. Fiscal year 1996, for example, saw investigative recoveries totaling about $1 billion and successful prosecution of more than 12,500 cases.

As the largest such operation in the federal government, the IG office at the Department of Health and Human Services has secured a large part of these savings. Perhaps one of the best examples of the IG impact on federal operations can be found in the Medicare program. On taking the IG post in 1993, June Gibbs Brown found little being done to combat fraud, waste, and abuse in Medicare. For years, the inflation factor used to calculate Medicare payments had considerably exceeded the general inflation rate (and estimates at the time showed that the program would go broke by 2001). Substantially increased IG investigations into program payments and the creation of compliance partnerships with states, practitioners, and medical facilities subsequently produced a negative inflation rate.

Under the influence of congressional requirements and attention, IG efforts have traditionally focused to a substantial degree on compliance audits. This emphasis has generated what some see as a vicious cycle: negative compliance findings lead to additional regulation, followed by increasingly detailed audits and compliance reviews. An institutional culture thereby arises that discourages entrepreneurship and innovation—precisely the desirable characteristics of a reinvented government.

In 1993 the National Performance Review (now the National Partnership for Reinventing Government) recommended a change. Federal inspectors general, it suggested, should move away from a concentration on compliance auditing in favor of evaluating management control systems. Further, they should recast their operating style into a more collaborative, less adversarial approach. Responding to this, the IG corps wrote a "vision statement," which described their new role as agents of positive change, working for constant improvement in the management and program activities of their agencies "and in our own offices."

This revision reflected the increasing responsibility placed on inspectors general by management reform legislation. The 1990 Chief Financial Officers Act, as expanded by the Government Management Reform Act of 1994, gave IGs the task of annually auditing their agencies' financial statements and bolstered their ability to identify weaknesses in internal controls and breakdowns in financial management systems. Finally, passage of the Paperwork Reduction Act of 1995 and the Clinger-Cohen Act of 1996 gave IGs an important additional role in protecting federal assets from fraud and misuse as agencies begin modernization and improvement efforts in such areas as information technology.

But the NPR-inspired change in IG focus has been slow. Brown acknowledges that audits have gotten a bad name and that in the past they were at times too narrowly focused. She has pushed to broaden audits and investigations where possible to cover entire programs and look for patterns of misconduct, rather than individual instances. "I know that what I do, and I think most of the other IGs do as well, is take a more global approach, so that we're looking at big picture items, not over somebody's shoulder to see if the timekeeping is right. The products we provide give senior people the whole picture. I consider it a failure if we give them one incident rather than identify all the factors that will allow them to make a decision."

The key to a number of very positive gains against fraud, abuse and waste, Brown says, has been adoption of a more preventive, partnership approach. Underlying this is a philosophy of bringing all those with responsibility for a program into efforts to control misspending. Medicare uses doctors, nurses, and other professionals in analyzing medical records to determine whether payment amounts appear appropriate. This approach has also meant entering into partnerships with states in working through Medicaid cases. The most important health-care fraud and abuse partnership is one based on the Health Insurance Portability and Accountability Act. The act required the attorney general and the inspector general to coordinate federal, state, and local law enforcement activities in the Health Care Fraud and Abuse Control Program. As a result of this program, the federal government collected $1.873 billion in connection with health-care fraud cases and matters in the last three years.

Another aspect of the prevention approach used at HHS is the voluntary compliance program. For a Medicare provider, a ruling based on an IG investigation and excluding it from all future work in federal health-care programs was the kiss of death. But until the HHS compliance program came along, providers never knew what an upcoming review might cover. Now, participants in the program get a checklist of areas to be covered in an investigation. Although not a total guarantee against exclusion, a provider that has followed the compliance requirements and taken preventive measures where necessary is likely to get permission to continue operating in Medicare even with a determination that an error has occurred.

Establishment of audit committees has helped some agencies to gain support of audit recommendations and reduce program risks and vulnerabilities. Gaston Gianni, the IG at the Federal Deposit Insurance Corporation, says most heads of agencies lack the time to review audits and look into the recommended solutions for problems they uncover. He thinks that audit boards furnish a mechanism to take care of this—to be sure that the results of audits are vetted at a high level and considered from an agencywide perspective. "If we make a recommendation," he explains, "and the program people say they don't want to follow it, the audit committee determines what is in the agency's best interest."

Most IGs are preoccupied by keeping up with the growth in the programs they are charged with monitoring. Some find themselves in a catch-22 situation. If they had additional resources, they could more than offset the cost of those resources by the increase in recoveries and prevention of misspent funding that would result. The difficulty is obtaining the upfront funding. At HHS, the Office of the Inspector General resolved this dilemma with a direct allocation from the Medicare Trust Fund to fund audit inspection and investigation. Recovered funds go directly back into the fund and the office estimates that it recovers between 98 and 99 cents of every dollar spent.

The Government Performance and Results Act of 1993, or GPRA, also provides a potential new role for the IG. While the act does not give IGs explicit responsibilities, its emphasis on managing for results and identifying opportunities for increased accountability falls within the expanded vision that IGs drafted into their mission. In a growing number of federal agencies, IGs are providing valuable advice in the preparation of the strategic and performance plans required by the act, in evaluating performance measures, and in supporting data sources. Listing the actions needed to strengthen OIGs, the GAO has urged that more IGs help in the development of agency strategic plans as a way of better assessing their organizations' risks and problems and identifying solutions that use performance measures to evaluate progress.

At HHS and the FDIC, inspector general offices don't participate significantly in the review of agency efforts to measure performance under the GPRA. Brown and Gianni justify this by the need to devote their limited resources to areas where the potential for huge dollar losses resulting from fraud and abuse or program inefficiencies are greatest. Indeed, OIGs are not currently required to evaluate agency performance measures. But Gianni believes his office will eventually get more involved in helping programs increase their use of quantifiable data and verify the accuracy of supporting data. "If OIGs are going to be out there looking at our agencies," he says, "we had better participate in the ball game."

Impartiality is the key to IG effectiveness, and several unusual features protect it from politicization. An inspector general cannot be dismissed without a presidential explanation of the reasons to the Congress. OIGs enjoy their own personnel authority, separate from that of their agencies, and their budgets are independent line items in their agencies' budget requests. Probably most important, the inspector general is the only official in an agency or department who can communicate directly with the Congress without first being cleared by OMB. IG independence often comes as a surprise to new agency bosses. Although it is not required, Brown makes a practice of sharing relevant testimony with agency heads and hearing any comments they may have. "We don't want to play 'gotcha' or surprise them with something they can't respond to because they don't even know it's going to be brought up."

While she agrees that independence is crucial, particularly in the direction and sharing of investigation findings, Brown also believes that a good relationship with the secretary and program leaders is equally important. "If you really can work in sync," she says, "and they have an appreciation for what you're doing, they are going to use the products you produce and you will be more effective. If they don't respect your office and what you're producing, you may as well forget it, because you're not going to get changes as the result of your work."

This is a view that Gianni shares. He sees the OIG as a kind of shadow administration for a chief of agency. "We oversee to ensure that the goals of agencies are accomplished in an efficient manner and that no laws are broken. And that's certainly the objective of all heads of agencies. I think they should look to their IGs as assets rather than, as some do, as enemies."

Though twenty-eight IG positions are presidentially appointed, before each of the last three presidential elections, the Congress has requested that incoming administrations treat the occupants they find in place as careerists. Respecting this support for nonpartisan OIG leadership, the Bush and Clinton administrations replaced IGs only as vacancies occurred. Further on this theme, the practice of awarding performance bonuses to IGs who are members of the career Senior Executive Service has stirred concern. Conveyed by agency heads, the awards create in some perceptions the appearance of a conflict of interest and potentially compromise OIG impartiality. Brown agrees but sees the more critical issue as the disparity in the pay of IGs and senior career OIG staff. She notes that some of her top staffers, with bonuses, make up to $40,000 more a year than she does. As a result, it has been increasingly difficult to recruit inspectors general for many agencies.

Those most qualified for the posts are experienced IG staffers, who are, however, unwilling to take the pay cut involved. Instead, the most frequent recruits are retired Secret Service staffers, who, under current law, can collect retirement pay while employed in the federal service.

Ideally, candidates for IG positions should combine two or more credentials such as investigative experience; a knowledge of auditing procedures, government auditing standards, and accounting; and substantial background in the conduct of program evaluations. Since auditing standards for government are unique and complex, candidates with prior government service are best suited to the job. Experience with the Congress and in law enforcement is an additionally helpful qualification. Beyond the requirement that IGs report to the Congress, Gianni notes an increasing congressional interest in more efficient executive branch management, in the legislated reform measures that interest has produced, and in the work of the inspector general. To him, that means an IG should be able to interact comfortably with legislators. Brown particularly underscores the need to work closely with the Department of Justice and OMB, citing the number of cases where joint reviews are required and overlapping responsibilities exist. She also believes a variety of financial, legal, or business skills are useful.

The dual accountability that inspectors general must maintain with the Congress and their agencies is a special consideration. As Brown describes her role, "You're walking a fine line. To be successful with Congress, you have to make sure your work is respected on both sides of the aisle. To satisfy the agency, you have to be accurate and thorough—it only takes one bad product to sour people. In many other positions, you know who your comrades are and who you can call on. We don't and can't. We really have to maintain our independence."

A key external relationship for the IG is that with the Department of Justice, which, as Gianni explains, must accept cases the IG wishes to be prosecuted. If Justice declines to prosecute, the case in question becomes a matter for administrative action. And, for the greater success of their efforts to identify and correct risks and vulnerabilities within their agencies, Gianni and Brown agree that IGs must work closely with their CIO and CFO colleagues.

Of the total federal IG work force, about half are auditors, a quarter are investigators, and the remaining are evaluators and administrative staffers. Investigations vary widely, depending on the mission, programs, and operations of the agency involved. Within the Department of Defense, for example, the bulk of investigations concern frauds by individual contractors and health-care providers. And, as is evident from earlier discussion, external misconduct or fraud are also the main targets for the OIG of the Department of Health and Human Services in its monitoring of the Medicare program. In other agencies, internal administrative investigations—cases of alleged noncriminal misconduct by agency employees—are the principal activity.

Brown sees rapid growth in the use of information technology as the biggest current and future issue for IGs. Auditing systems and overseeing the strengthening of systems security, IG offices must compete with many other agencies in the tight marketplace for technically competent staff. Many experienced OIG staff members are nearing retirement age, another problem future IGs will have to meet and resolve. In matters of personnel, Brown says the President's Council on Integrity and Efficiency has been beneficial to the IG community. Many positions in the IG organization require specialized training and certification. Through the PCIE, a training academy and a web site have been set up, resources that the smaller OIGs could not have afforded on their own. The PCIE has also provided a mechanism for the sharing of legal interpretations and case files on common issues.

In general, the OIGs have far to go in reshaping their roles to give better support to line managers in supplying information on best practices and judging these managers' oversight activities. Given the continuing gap between responsibilities and resources, the more efficient use of people on the line will become more vital.

For an inspector general, Gianni observes, "the power to investigate is at the same time critical and sensitive. You're dealing with people's lives. It has to be done very carefully. You have to make sure you're protecting individual rights while you're trying to achieve your mission." He calls inspectors general the unsung heroes of government. "The good they accomplish isn't highlighted enough and public and administration appreciation is certainly not there."

Conclusions

The five positions examined in this chapter are clearly about more than simply good management. They represent an almost inevitable response to the rapid changes taking place in the world, in society, and in government and the need to secure the continued success of federal agencies within that environment. Whether it's the fast march of technology, the litigious inclinations of the American people, stronger pressures for government accountability and efficiency, or the need for better coordination among and within levels of government, the leadership these positions are designed to offer is increasingly indispensable.

While one might argue for or against the various approaches taken to structure or operate these jobs, there is little doubt that they have had a positive and significant impact on federal management. Agencies can better account for their resources, make greater use of technology, provide enterprisewide responses to critical public needs, and build the efficacy and integrity of their programs.

Yet an increasing vulnerability threatens these advances. The more interchangeable public and private management positions become, the greater the temptation for private companies to lure away the best talent in these posts. One of the greatest challenges for future administrations will be to find and keep highly qualified people in these slots and in the staff positions that support them.

Most of the individuals we interviewed say the opportunity their work affords to serve the public and make a difference is the reason they stay in government. But continuing to expect experienced, talented people to sacrifice so much in order to serve is not merely unfair. It is unrealistic. Like quality anywhere, good management requires an investment. Without it, the public will pay far more in the long term for lost efficiency, mismanagement, and duplication.

4

Positions in Economic Policy, Technology, and Trade

▨ U.S. Trade Representative

EXECUTIVE LEVEL I—Presidential appointment with
Senate confirmation

RECOMMENDED SKILLS AND EXPERIENCE ■ Several kinds of
background are valid preparation for this position. Ideally, candidates
should combine at least two of them: law practice in the field of international trade, substantial work with the Congress in the trade area, demonstrated success as a negotiator inside or outside government, a thorough
exposure to U.S. international economic and foreign policy. Charlene
Barshefsky, who has led her agency since 1996, adds that she knows of no
one ever considered for the job who did not already have "significant congressional experience."

She herself was the deputy U.S. trade representative for three years before moving to the top position and, in her first year as the USTR, negotiated three central, global market-opening trade agreements in information
technology, financial services, and telecommunications. In all, nearly 300
trade agreements have been concluded during her time at the agency. Before coming into government, she was for eighteen years associated with a
Washington law firm, specializing in international trade law.

The trade representative should have a keen, far-ranging sense of the role
of foreign trade in the U.S. economy and its place in the development and
conduct of U.S. foreign policy. Across the range of the USTR's responsibility, a strong relationship with the president is highly important.

INSIGHT ■ The USTR—the acronym stands both for the trade representative and the agency itself—pursues objectives that have characterized U.S.
trade policy since the end, in the early 1930s, of the ruinous era of high protective tariffs and low levels of international trade. Those goals are opening
world markets, expanding trade, and enforcing trade laws and agreements.
In stating them in House testimony on the USTR budget and agenda in the
spring of 2000, Barshefsky reminded legislators that ten administrations
since Franklin Roosevelt "have worked toward an open world economy
under the rule of law."

Beginning in 1963, the Office of the Special Trade Representative, created by the Trade Expansion Act of the previous year, was in the vanguard
of that effort. In 1974 the Congress made it a cabinet-level agency in the executive office of the president and gave it responsibility for coordinating
trade policy. Six years later, the agency chief acquired a new title—the U.S.
Trade Representative, with the rank of ambassador—and was assigned re-

sponsibility to set and administer overall trade policy as the country's head trade negotiator, chief trade policy adviser to the president, and U.S. representative in the principal international trade bodies.

To coordinate and set policy on trade and trade-related issues, one of USTR's key instruments is a structured interagency mechanism similar to that employed in foreign policy decisionmaking. It gathers the input of seventeen federal agencies and entities, resolving differences of view and readying trade issues for presidential decision. The process starts with the Trade Policy Staff Committee at the senior civil servant level, supported by several dozen subcommittees and task forces. It sends issues of critical importance, and those on which agreement has not been reached, to the Trade Policy Review Group, at the under secretary and deputy USTR level. The third, most senior, interagency trade echelon is the National Economic Council, in which agency deputies address decision options prepared for the president, trade-related issues of special importance, and those still unresolved.

In trade negotiations themselves, the USTR brings in private-sector views and counsel through an advisory system that supplies guidance and consultation on policy development as well as help in monitoring compliance with the agreements negotiated. The presidentially appointed Advisory Committee on Trade Policy and Negotiation, with forty-five members representing all sectors of the U.S. economy with a stake in international trade, gives USTR general policy guidance on trade issues. Specific guidance comes from policy advisory committees organized in the areas of industry, agriculture, services, labor, defense, environment, investment, and intergovernmental affairs. Expert sectoral, technical, and functional committees also furnish advice on trade-relevant matters that range from government procurement to intellectual property issues.

What are the major trade issues that will be on the table in 2001 and beyond? "By and large," Barshefsky says, "the kind of aggressive market-opening agenda we have pursued will be pursued by the next administration. As an economic and substantive matter, this is vital for the United States." Far from being a matter of ideology, she asserts, it's a question of making certain that U.S. exports continue to expand—a big factor in the growth of the U.S. gross domestic product since 1993. "The key countries with which we've dealt will remain the key countries," she says. In Asia, these are Japan, China, and Korea. Barshefsky also foresees expanded trade relationships with India and the members of the Association of Southeast Asian Nations and predicts complete normalization of trade relations with Vietnam, Laos, and Cambodia.

She thinks those taking office in 2001 should work to strengthen ties with Europe, a very important trade and investment partner with which the United States has "a number of conflicts, and they are not small. There is a range of initiatives that could be pursued." Probably the most pressing of these is Europe's agricultural subsidies, which continue to hamper U.S. and other agricultural exports to that area and to third countries despite decades of effort to lower or remove them. If there is a solution to this, Barshefsky thinks it must come through the collective pressure that can be organized via the World Trade Organization (created by the Uruguay round of trade negotiations in which the USTR figured prominently).

Elsewhere, she believes Russia will be "a fertile ground" for the new administration and that development of the new Free Trade Area of the Americas—expected to be the world's biggest such zone at its targeted completion date in 2005—"will heat up very substantially." On Capitol Hill, Barshefsky says one of the biggest questions will be whether to pursue renewal of the administration's authority for fast-track trade negotiations that the Congress allowed to expire in 1999. Finally, there will be the expected launch of a new global round of trade negotiations.

How broad is public support in this country for international trade? "I think it actually has a far broader base than polling tends to uncover," Barshefsky says, "because of the way poll questions are asked. Do you believe in free trade? The majority will say no. Do you believe in fair trade? The majority will say yes." But, in fact, they are one and the same—because "you would never do a free trade agreement" if it didn't also promote fair trade. "Do you believe in trade agreements?" she continues. "The majority says no. Do you believe in agreements that enhance U.S. exports? The majority says yes."

Americans are under no illusion about their link to the global economy, she says, or the reality that, without it, this would be a poorer country. "Americans are also in love with imports, no question. They want lower prices, competition, the best products, the broadest possible choice." The American people "can be and, I think, are" quite receptive to the notion of trade, "particularly when you present them with specific trade initiatives. Fast track is a bit nebulous as a concept; it's a procedural issue. But present people with an actual agreement and show the benefits that will arise, and their attitude changes." Editorial opinion, Barshefsky adds, is "quite pro-trade" and she finds it significant that resolutions from associations of mayors and governors constantly evidence the pro-trade views of the great majority of their members. The trade missions sent abroad by states and cities is a further indication. "These local officials know exactly where the jobs are coming from," she says: "from our ability to export."

Our conversation with Barshefsky took place not long before the House of Representatives voted to approve the comprehensive market access agreement the Clinton administration had reached with China as a basis for permanent normal trade relations. Senate approval was widely expected to follow. Her comments at the time show what—from the administration's standpoint—would have been the consequences of congressional failure to support the move. It would, she said, have denied the United States the benefits of the agreement, forced the United States to stand by while China entered the World Trade Organization and opened Chinese markets to the rest of the world, badly damaged the cause of economic reformers in China, and increased tensions in the Asia Pacific region. "No U.S. interest would be served," she said.

Clearly, there were, and are, other legitimate points of view on this issue that will continue to bear on the evolution of the new trade relationship with China. Putting that relationship in place and moving it forward will be a major preoccupation for the USTR in the years ahead. But if that is to be done successfully, it goes almost without saying that the USTR will have to take into account and be responsive to all quarters with a stake in the outcome.

When the Congress, in the Trade Act of 1974, elevated the USTR and strengthened its authority, it also set up a close advisory and oversight connection with the agency. Under the law, five members from each house are appointed as advisers on trade policy; others can be added for given negotiations or issues. In fact, the USTR has worked closely with the Congress since its beginning. On matters like the China trade agreement, Barshefsky discerns a partly ideological, partly substantive debate in the Congress as to whether questions like labor standards or environmental protection should be "ancillary to or integrally related to" trade agreements. For her part, she thinks it's a matter of working, "as we've been doing with both sides, to try to move the two sides of this debate closer together. It will require flexibility. And it is critical for anyone holding this job to have very, very good relations on both sides of the aisle."

Another reason for this is that "resources are always an issue. We're a very small agency and the demands are very high. No one comes in at nine in the morning and nobody leaves at five. People work all the time and the travel demands are extraordinary." For fiscal 2001, Barshefsky asked the Congress for an appropriation of just under $30 million and a rise in full-time staff to 203 (from 178). "It's a tiny budget—somewhere between a quark and a nutrino," she says, "because you're looking at an agency that has within its purview two trillion dollars in trade." (USTR figures show that U.S. two-way trade rose from about $1.3 trillion in 1993 to more than $2 trillion in 1999, with the possibility of reaching $2.5 trillion in 2000.)

"This is not a job," Barshefsky says, "for someone with no fundamental interest in the work of the agency. And by work, I mean not only the high-profile things, not only the Chinas, but all the other agreements and investment treaties that must be negotiated to make the global playing field level and keep it that way." This is not a job whose occupant need only "skim the surface." Every country and every agreement is important in Barshefsky's concept. The intellectual property rights issue is just as important to U.S. relations with Ukraine as the trade agreement is to U.S. relations with China.

The job, she says, "requires exceptional commitment, very heavy travel, a desire to work, and a nonhierarchical mentality." The USTR must be "completely accessible to the building. My door is always open. I've never known a successful USTR who preferred to be surrounded by one or two key people and keep everyone else at bay."

PROFILE

Current U.S. Trade Representative
Charlene Barshefsky, 1997–

Career summary
Acting U.S. trade representative, 1996–97
Deputy U.S. trade representative, 1993–96
Private practice of law, ending as partner, Steptoe and Johnson, 1975–93

Education
B.A., University of Wisconsin, 1972; J.D., Columbus School of Law, Catholic University, 1975

U.S. Trade Representatives since 1989
Clinton administration
Michael Kantor, 1993–96 (currently partner, Mayer, Brown, and Platt)
Bush administration
Carla Hills, 1989–93 (currently chief operating officer, Baylock and Partners)

Department of Commerce

▓ **Under Secretary for Export Administration**

▓ **Assistant Secretary for Export Administration (Licensing)**

▓ **Assistant Secretary for Trade Development**

▓ **Executive Levels III (under secretary) and IV (assistant secretaries)—Presidential appointments with Senate confirmation**

RECOMMENDED SKILLS AND EXPERIENCE ▪ The necessary personal qualifications for these positions are similar in two notable respects. The first is a background in the Congress. Both William Reinsch, who in 1994 became the under secretary running the Bureau of Export Administration (BXA), and Michael Copps, assistant secretary for trade development since 1998, underscore the value of experience on the Hill and knowledge of how the institution works. Roger Majak, who took over as assistant secretary for export administration in 1997, thinks a familiarity with "the Hill view" is useful. All three served substantial congressional tours, on members' staffs or on committee staff—or both. Two also held other positions closely related to the work of the Congress.

The second essential qualification common to these three jobs is the ability to manage. Reinsch: "The biggest thing that hit me in the face when I got here, and continues to hit me in the face, is the management skills that are required and the time you have to spend managing. I wasn't trained to do that, and nobody on the Hill is trained to do that." Majak: "It's a big management job. We have a thousand requests a month for licenses and advisory opinions on whether a product is subject to controls or not and how it's to be treated. It's like a factory, the product that comes out of here. There are ingredients coming in and something that has to go out the door, or you stall out, get overloaded, and companies start to complain." Copps: "Managing a government agency is different than managing a private-sector operation. You probably can't know that until you're here and faced with it. You have to have management capacity to deal with that."

These positions also have individual needs, of course—and they tell you something about the nature of the jobs themselves. When the late former secretary of commerce Ron Brown interviewed him as a potential under secretary for export administration, says Reinsch, "he wanted to know what the business community would say if I got the job. I said they probably would be happy because they think I agree with them. He asked me the same thing about these other people (generally, critics of U.S. export control policy). I said they also would probably be happy because they think I agree with them. And Brown said it sounded like I was the person he was looking for." Reinsch says that "having a reasonably blank or neutral slate, in terms of public perception, is important." But "you need somebody in this job whom the business community is not going to write off from day one as either an enemy or an idiot. The biggest mistake would be to put in a political hack."

Majak says his job—as assistant secretary administering the licensing function for U.S. exports in the BXA—is best served by "a technical knowledge of the export control system. It's a workhorse sort of job. You have to know, or quickly learn, a very complicated decisionmaking system, thousands of pages of regulations. And a long history of cases, since this is essentially a case-by-case review. There are guidelines, policies, and parameters, but every case is looked at individually. And they vary immensely— the technologies vary, destinations and end users vary, and the rules we apply vary." In addition to the technical background, Majak thinks some grounding in national security and foreign policy is an asset. Lastly, because the decisionmaking on licensing has become a multiagency exercise requiring consensus, he believes negotiating skills are "really important."

For Copps, private sector ties are valuable for the credibility they bring to the intricate business of trade development. "My bag is putting together public/private partnerships," he says. "That's why I really came to this job, as an ideal place to do that. Because our main constituency is the private sector." He knows the private sector alone can't get the trade development job done "in a world where so many procurement decisions are made by government and investment decisions dictated by government." Nor can the public sector do it alone "without the input, experience, good judgment, and perspective" of the private sector. "If you're going to be successful in the global economy, it will only be because we find innovative ways to work together." A commitment to outreach is also on Copps's list. "If you don't want to spend a lot of time in interagency discussion, on Capitol Hill, with the media, in travel to explain why trade is important to communities across the country, then you shouldn't be in this particular assignment."

INSIGHT ■ These three positions—two on the export control side, one concerned with trade development—exemplify the distinction drawn by legislation in the late 1980s between controls and promotion. Until then, all foreign trade functions were the province of the Commerce Department's International Trade Administration. In 1987, persuaded that a single individual could not manage export controls while trying to boost U.S. sales in foreign markets, the Congress established the Bureau of Export Administration. The BXA was assigned the task, in Reinsch's words, "of controlling exports in a way that protects the country's national security and foreign policy objectives."

But in making the distinction, the Congress did not take it all the way. Logically, in the view of some, the BXA should have the import controls portfolio as well—defending U.S. industry against unfair trade practices on the import side. Instead, that function remains with the International Trade Administration. "If you really want to do it right," Reinsch comments, "there should be a bureau of trade promotion and a bureau of trade regulation."

Be that as it may, the BXA's national security mandate has ramifications in several directions. For one thing, the bureau is responsible for safeguarding the health of the defense industrial base and its ability to produce for defense needs when necessary—a responsibility it wields under the Defense Production Act. The act gives the president authority to override the civilian contracts that private companies may be working on and order them to produce for the military. "People think the DPA is a relic of the Korean War," Reinsch says, but it was used during the Persian Gulf war of 1991 and in the 1999 action in Kosovo.

For similar reasons, the BXA can order plants to remain open. This happened with a Michigan company, for example, that made flat-panel displays of a particular size and configuration for a number of military uses, including the Apache helicopter. Although it was the only producer of the screens in the country, the company announced in the fall of 1998 that it was going to close. "It wasn't a commercially viable operation," Reinsch relates. "We ordered them to stay open to fulfill their contracts and spent a lot of time, with the Department of Defense, trying to find a buyer. The goal wasn't to keep them in business per se, but to maintain production."

Second, protecting the viability of the defense industry means performing many studies of various industry elements. "We tend to do micro things," Reinsch says—fighter plane ejection seats, ceramic packaging for microprocessors, heat collection devices within computers, metallic tape. "Mostly we look for situations with a critical component that is not being produced here and could make our whole production chain vulnerable. When that happens, we don't have any money to step in and do anything ourselves. Mostly what we can do is ring an alarm bell, let the Pentagon know."

Third, the control of exports in a national security context, far from being a static, mechanical function, must take account of rapid technological advance that affects thinking in the Defense Department about its approach to certain kinds of acquisition and alters the relationship between the Pentagon and its defense industry suppliers. Reinsch explains: "This administration has changed the process and, beyond that, we've thought about the subject in a different way, driven really by changes in the information technology sector." The F-22 aircraft, for example, is being designed to carry three high-performance computers "just to fly the plane, do the avionics." And the Defense Department's conventional processes of acquiring such technology was simply taking too long—in some cases, longer than the life cycle of the equipment in question. Like much other defense acquisition, therefore, the Pentagon turned to faster, commercial purchasing off the shelf on the outside.

"What that does, though," Reinsch continues, "is make Defense reliant on a commercial sector for which its purchases are peanuts. The reality now is that the Pentagon needs IBM more than IBM needs the Pentagon. What IBM needs for its survival is exports. Fifty percent of computer company sales are exports." And here's the crux of this situation: The Defense Department figured out that, if it wants these critical defense suppliers "to survive, be healthy, make money, invest research and development money in next-generation products, it will have to tolerate fairly high levels of exports from these companies. Because that's the only way the companies will stay on the cutting edge."

For the BXA, that has meant shrinking the number of items it controls and going to a system based more on who the end user of a product is likely to be. Majak, the BXA assistant secretary who runs its licensing half, calls his job "a kind of risk management operation: a complicated effort to balance national security risks—and to some extent foreign policy risks—against the benefits of trade. It's a matter of drawing the fine line between where you can sell valuable or militarily useful technologies and where you shouldn't." Since the cold war, when this effort covered a broad waterfront, the goal has been to narrow and refocus the controls.

"The beauty of bipolarism and the cold war," Reinsch reflects, "is that you didn't have to do a lot of end user analysis. If it was going to the Soviet Union or the Soviet bloc, you assumed it would end up in the hands of the Russian army. Now you can't assume that anymore." The "enemy" today,

Majak notes, "tends more to be terrorist groups, even individuals. It's less country-oriented and requires a lot more judgment." Majak is frequently asked why the money and people devoted to the licensing activity have not dropped in light of the fewer number of export license applications (down from 150,000 at their peak in the Reagan administration to 12,000 a year in the Clinton administration). The answer is that these cases are "much more complicated than they were" when it was easy to say no if any doubt existed.

"We'll ship a high-performance computer to a bank or a phone company in China," Reinsch explains, "because we know where it's going and what it's going to be used for, and we have a high level of confidence that it will stay there and be used for that purpose. But we won't ship the same machine to somebody 100 kilometers down the road because it's an institution that does military research and we don't have a high level of confidence, despite what they might tell us." Decisionmaking in the new era means using more varieties of information, such as that from companies about their customers overseas.

All these considerations have also led the BXA into sharing more decisionmaking with other agencies than it ever has, particularly with the Defense and State departments. And the challenge, Majak says, is to "make the process work and not slip back into broader controls, unless the security situation were to fundamentally change."

The real problem, Reinsch says, one that hasn't changed for twenty years, is "the extreme susceptibility of this issue to political exploitation." As he elaborates it, it's easy to charge an administration with selling something to the Chinese or another potential military opponent that will help that opponent later in a possible armed conflict. In fact, "every administration makes its mistakes." During the Reagan administration, he recalls, sensitive computer technology was sold to South Africa but made its way to the Soviet Union by way of Hungary. The Bush administration "had all this stuff that went to Iraq. And I was one of the Democrats pounding the administration over the head in 1989 and 1990." And now, "Clinton has China and we're being pounded for shipping things to China."

What's more, this debate takes place in a climate where even the experts sometimes disagree. "You can talk to somebody at the Pentagon and get one answer," Reinsch points out, "and to one of my engineers and get another." However, 95 percent of the time licensing decisions are reached by consensus. "What drives you crazy is the other 5 percent, which end up being exploited by one party or the other." Leaks from within an administration to the Congress occur regularly, says Reinsch, who remembers experiencing them when he was on the Hill. "This is a small pond. There aren't many people who do this. And they mostly know each other. Some of them are essentially still fighting the cold war. They've objected to the policies of the last three administrations and I have no doubt they'll object to those of the next."

No administration, Reinsch says, "has had policies of giving away the country's security. We don't license things we think will have an adverse impact. Nor do we have rogue people merrily stamping 'approved' on licenses that the Defense Department doesn't know about." The point he makes is that "the system follows the policy." Whether it's the goal of rapprochement with Iraq, as in the 1980s, or expanded trade with China, administrations tend to license exports that support their policies. "Sending the licensing function to some other agency isn't going to change that," he asserts. You need to change the policy." The Congress can change budgets, people, and processes. "But if a president wants to have closer commercial relations with a country, that's what he's going to do."

For the future, Majak says, China will continue to be "a big question mark." That doesn't mean that current U.S. policy isn't clear. "But it's a mixed policy. We have engagement but we also have caution and verification. I think that's good. But it makes decisions on specific exports very difficult." As for the major areas of streamlining controls, which has been a major objective for him, he believes the list is now down to a much more reasonable, manageable scope, but "it has to be kept up to date because the technology is always changing." Then there are new products or new ways of disseminating them—biological and chemical weapons that the BXA has always kept an eye on but that become more important as potential threats in the hands of terrorists. "So I certainly don't see the export control function disappearing."

Reinsch says the BXA staff is "pushing 400," and worries that, competent as many of them are, their skills "are not all appropriate to what we're doing now." While they remain, the bureau can't hire people who do have the skills. In the Congress, the BXA's formal committees of jurisdiction are the Senate Banking Committee and House International Relations Committee—a situation Majak calls "rather strange" in that "we don't have corresponding committees in both houses." He reports "rather cordial and constructive relations on the Senate side," where the banking committee has "shown an interest" in renewing the Export Administration Act, the BXA's basic authority and in "responding to some of the characteristics we think are essential in this kind of legislation." On the House side, the relationship is "somewhat more distant." There is a significant amount of inter-action with committee staff in their oversight role, but Majak says the com-mittee has shown relatively little interest in legislation. The armed services committees in both houses, Reinsch notes, have been playing an increasing oversight role in BXA affairs.

As for the assistant secretary for trade development, Copps outlines these major elements of his portfolio:

—Conduct of export promotion activities—seminars, trade missions, conferences—with what Copps calls a new emphasis. "We try to put gov-ernment proactively on the side of business, something that for one rea-son or another hasn't happened in the last thirty years. Maybe it was the exigencies of the cold war, when we were preoccupied with national se-curity. But we have now understood that security also means economic security and we've become more serious about competing around the world. We've really tried to be strategic about it and advocate U.S. busi-nesses and workers."

There are at least two features of this that should be noted. The first is turning substantially more small businesses into exporters. "Some people act as if we have to debate whether or not we're going to be part of the global economy," Copps comments. "But that decision was made long ago. It's a question of whether we participate well or poorly. And one measure of our success will be the extent to which small- and medium-size enter-prises, which are a real engine for our economy, are participating." On this front, he notes some progress. From 112,000 total U.S. companies in the export arena in 1992, the figure has climbed to 209,000, of which 97 per-cent are small- and medium-size firms. "A big increase," Copps says, "but still very small compared to the universe out there." There are a lot more small- and medium-size companies that should be exporting." To push fur-ther, the Office of Trade Development operates the Trade Information Cen-ter at the Department of Commerce; offers a toll-free telephone service on which would-be exporters can find out what they need to know and where to go for financing, if necessary; and reaches out around the country through the 105 U.S. offices of the U.S. Foreign Commercial Service. Copps also mentions plans to work with the manufacturing extension partnerships run by Commerce's Technology Administration to commercialize new tech-nologies (see also this chapter's profile of the director's job at the National Institute of Standards and Technology).

Second is the idea that advanced information technology has added a highly effective resource to trade promotion. "Many of the traditional tools of promotion, like trade missions, are still good," Copps says. "Sometimes there's no substitute for going out to develop that personal relationship. But if it's a seminar mission or a technical mission and you're trying to get experts together to explain something, you can often do it by videoconference. You don't need to take that many trade missions when you can hook people together like that."

—Assistance to the U.S. Trade Representative, including participating in and analyzing trade negotiations. One of the reasons why the trade representative's office gets a lot done with fewer than 200 people, Copps says, is that his office supplies sector knowledge and resources on which the USTR regularly draws. "More often than not," he says, "they require the help of our experts."

—Management of the advisory process through which U.S. representatives in any significant set of trade negotiations draw on the experience and hear the views and objectives of the private industry sectors involved. "Any kind of trade agreement can go before our private sector advisers," Copps says.

The trade development staff numbers about 400, and the office has an annual budget of nearly $60 million. About 20 percent of it comes as "earmarked grants" designated by the Congress for specific purposes. A typical grant Copps cites has for several years supported the development of innovative technologies in textiles manufacturing—an industry, he points out, "that was written off by many people as labor intensive" and one the United States was losing to other countries. "It turns out the situation isn't quite that simple," Copps says. "There's a tremendous future for a capital-intensive textile industry, an area where we can and should be competitive."

He describes two kinds of challenges for his successor. One is internal and goes beyond the usual need to deal with resource constraints and handle the work generated by congressional oversight. "There are more and more things to do in areas like biotechnology, the new information technologies, and e-commerce," he says. "But you can't do everything and so prioritizing becomes more and more serious." The second challenge lies overseas, "where you're faced with what other governments are doing to extend their sphere and influence in the global economy." Many of them, says Copps, "are spending considerably more for export promotion on a per capita basis and have more people working on it."

PROFILE

Current Under Secretary of Commerce for Export Administration
William A. Reinsch, 1994–

Career summary
Senior legislative assistant to Sen. John D. Rockefeller IV (D-W.Va.), 1991–93
Chief legislative assistant to Sen. John Heinz (R-Pa.), 1977–91
Before 1977: Legislative assistant to Reps. Richard Ottinger (D-N.Y.) and
   Gilbert Gude (R-Md.); acting staff director, House Environmental Study
   Conference; teacher in Maryland

Education
B.A., Johns Hopkins University, 1968; M.A., Johns Hopkins School of
   Advanced International Studies, 1969

Under Secretaries for Export Administration since 1989

Bush administration
Position vacant, 1991–94
Dennis Kloske, 1989–91 (current position unavailable)

PROFILE

Current Assistant Secretary of Commerce for Export Administration
Roger Majak, 1997–

Career summary
Legislative director, Powell, Gold, Goldstein, Frazer, and Murphy, 1990–96
Manager, federal government affairs office, Tektronix, 1985–90
Staff director, House Foreign Affairs Subcommittee on International Economic
   Policy and Trade, 1975–85
Staff member, Commission on the Organization of Government for the
   Conduct of Foreign Policy (Murphy Commission), 1973–74
Chief of staff, Rep. Jonathan Bingham (D-N.Y.); legislative intern, office of
   Senator Bingham; legislative intern, office of Sen. Joseph Tydings (D-Md.),
   1968–73

Education
B.S., Northwestern University, 1964; M.A. and all requirements for Ph.D.
   except dissertation, Ohio State University, 1964–67

Assistant Secretaries for Export Administration since 1989

Clinton administration
Susan E. Eckert, 1993–97 (currently senior fellow, Institute for International
    Economics, and Brown University, Watson Institute for International Studies

Bush administration
Michael Galvin, 1991–93 (currently president, Galvin Enterprises)
Position vacant, 1989–90

PROFILE

Current Assistant Secretary of Commerce for Trade Development
Michael J. Copps, 1998–

Career summary
Deputy assistant secretary for basic industries, Office of Trade Development,
    Department of Commerce, 1993–98
Senior vice president for legislative affairs, American Meat Institute, 1989–93
Director, government affairs, Collins and Aikman Corporation, 1985–89
Administrative assistant and chief of staff, Sen. Fritz Hollings (D-S.C.)

Education
B.A., Wofford College, 1963; Ph.D., University of North Carolina, 1967

Assistant Secretaries for Trade Development since 1989

Clinton administration
Ellis R. Mottur (acting), 1997–98 (currently deputy assistant secretary for
    technology, Department of Commerce)
Raymond E. Vickery, 1994–97 (currently president, Vickery International)
Position vacant, 1993–94
James C. Lake (acting), 1992–93 (current position unavailable)

Bush administration
Timothy J. McBride, 1990–91 (currently executive, Daimler-Chrysler
    Corporation)
Michael P. Skarzynski, 1989–90 (currently vice president and general manager,
    Lucent Inferno Network Solutions)

■ Under Secretary of Commerce for Intellectual Property and Director, U.S. Patent and Trademark Office

EXECUTIVE LEVEL IV—Presidential appointment with
Senate confirmation

RECOMMENDED SKILLS AND EXPERIENCE ■ Besides running the U.S. Patent and Trademark Office—PTO—this under secretary is the chief policy adviser to the president and the Congress on domestic and international intellectual property matters and also cochairs the National Intellectual Property Law Enforcement Coordination Council. Q. Todd Dickinson, who took over the job in late 1999 (and held it in an acting capacity for nearly a year before that), thinks the key credential is experience in the intellectual property system. He himself was a patent lawyer for twenty-five years. "I don't think you necessarily have to be a lawyer," he says, "although most people in the patent and trademark bar would probably say this job ought to be held by an intellectual property lawyer." In any case, he recommends a thorough grounding in the policy and technical aspects of what the PTO does. Management ability is valuable, although Dickinson recognizes it is tough to combine that with the particular background he's talking about.

INSIGHT ■ At the end of 1999, the Congress included in its fiscal 2000 omnibus appropriations a set of decisions that will be landmarks in the history of the U.S. Patent and Trademark Office:

The legislation transformed the PTO into what is known as a performance-based organization, an action intended to free it from bureaucratic, one-size-fits-all rules in a number of management areas—procurement, hiring, compensation. Instead, the PTO is using techniques like performance plans, performance measurement, flexible personnel policies, and bonuses to drive its operations toward greater efficiency and productivity. It is one of only two entities in the federal government, as of April 2000, to acquire this substantial degree of independence (the other is the Student Financial Assistance Office in the Department of Education).

To Dickinson, performance-based organizations are not so much policymaking or regulatory agencies as operational units. "We turn out product—patents and trademarks," he explains. Yes, the PTO does have the responsibility for administration policy on intellectual property issues, an important and growing field. "But mostly, we turn out a product. Ninety-five percent of our work is focused on that." The PTO gets 300,000 patent applications a year; at the end of 1999, it awarded its sixth millionth patent.

Partly to underscore the independent management approach the PTO was to take, the legislation put some significant distance between it and its parent Department of Commerce. In the 1990s and earlier, several proposals in the Congress to turn the PTO into an entirely independent government corporation died under the opposition of the patent examiners union and independent small inventors, among others. It was favored, however, by the PTO's major constituency groups—among them large corporations and intellectual property lawyers. The 1999 bill is a compromise on this point. The PTO remained at Commerce, but as an independent agency.

Concomitant with that, what had been the position of commissioner for patents and trademarks was elevated to its current under secretary level. The job will continue to be filled by presidential appointment. The assistant commissioners who run the office's patent and trademark divisions will be appointed by the secretary of commerce, with performance-based contracts and bonus potentials dependent on reaching agreed-on objectives. The new appointment structure, Dickinson says, enables the PTO "to get more regular, less politicized management of the two functions."

The legislation created two advisory boards for the PTO, one each for patents and trademarks. The Patent Advisory Board will encompass independent inventors and representatives of large companies and the PTO unions.

Dickinson also established an office addressing the interests and problems of independent inventors—problems such as the risk of being conned by firms that cheat independent inventors while pretending to help them market their ideas.

The Patent and Trademark Office is one of the world's big three, along with that in Japan and the European Patent Office. A total of 85 percent of all patent applications in the world go through those three. Reflecting on history, Dickinson notes that patent law developed individually in different countries, based on varying traditions and, in the Anglo-Saxon context, on common law. With globalization has come an intensified need for cooperation in patent-granting operations. One way to do that, he says, is to develop a "one world system." Another, perhaps more practical, way is to harmonize the domestic patent and trademark laws of various countries.

The United States "has tried to do some of that harmonization, some by rules, some by statute." For example, "we are the only country on earth that awards priority to the first person to invent an invention. The rest of the world awards it to the first person to file a patent application." The latter, he says, is a simpler system, but lacks the "judgmental questions that arise as to who was first and based on what evidence."

But the U.S. system is one of long tradition—the first to invent. One of the most vocal PTO constituencies on this issue is the small inventor community, the source of only 14 percent of patent applications. In person and using the Internet, Dickinson says, this group has learned to communicate to the Congress its fears for the U.S. system if, as the world community would like, the United States moves toward the first-to-file regime. Nonetheless, the 1999 legislation modified the U.S. system "to make it a little more global, a little more user friendly and, frankly according to most of its advocates, to improve the quality of the work as well."

Another traditional candidate for change—a change that has now occurred as a result of the 1999 legislation—was the U.S. position as the only country in the world that did not publish patent applications at some point while they were pending. "Almost every country publishes eighteen months after they've been filed; we keep them secret throughout the entire process," Dickinson says. But there are good reasons to publish, especially where fast-moving technologies are concerned. "You don't want people making substantial research investments and then find they are locked away from getting a patent because someone else has beaten them to the punch. Eighteen months gives applicants enough lead time to get going without having to worry about competition right off the bat."

The first U.S. patent was granted in 1790. Numbering of patents began some forty-five years later. Today, one of the PTO's biggest challenges is managing growth. During the Clinton administration, patent applications rose by 60 percent. In addition to the current 300,000-a-year rate of patent applications, trademark applications were up 25 percent in 1999 alone. For much of the last decade, PTO hiring was frozen and the time an applicant had to wait for decision—called pendency—moved up from nineteen months in 1993 to what Dickinson says was thirty-six months or more. (The time during which an application is actually in process by a patent examiner—cycle time—was 12.9 months when we talked with Dickinson in early 2000. The PTO hopes to cut that to twelve months or under by 2003.)

With 6,500 employees and an annual operating budget of about $900 million, the PTO is also the only agency in the federal government that is fully funded by fees, according to Dickinson. Patent application fees, maintenance fees from patent holders, and renewal fees from trademark owners are "the only money we get." In 2001 he expects total revenue to be about $1 billion. But there's a hitch. Each year a significant fraction of this income is designated for non-PTO purposes. In 1990, Dickinson says, the earmark came to about $2 million. In 1999 it was $116 million; in the fiscal 2001 budget, it will exceed $368 million. The reorganizing legislation of that year permits this practice to continue, but requires that the money must be returned to the PTO later. Some doubt exists that this will actually happen over time. But Dickinson takes a reasonably philosophic attitude. "You've got to look at all revenue sources to manage and balance the federal budget," he says. But if future budgets don't address the problem, he says, it will have a "serious impact" on the PTO mission.

There's no question that the lost revenue hurts in an era of steadily rising patent applications. If the PTO can hire only enough new examiners to replace those lost through attrition, Dickinson says, pendency will rise. "The issue is the quality of work we do versus the pendency."

It's a tough balance, he adds, for another important reason. The term for a patent is twenty years from the time the application was filed, a worldwide standard the U.S. adopted as a member of the World Trade Organization. Recent legislation provides that, when certain administrative delays occur in the processing of applications by the PTO, successful applicants get "term back." That means that the period of delay is added to the term of the patent.

"If we don't get the revenue we need to process applications in a timely manner," Dickinson points out, "we're giving term back." "Each day I've got to give back on a drug that's delayed because I don't have the money to process the application for it may mean $50 million on the health-care bill seniors have to pay fifteen or twenty years from now." That's because, once a patent on a drug expires, it can be manufactured as a generic drug, usually with a dramatic fall in price.

A similar system, framed by the Hatch-Waxman Act, affects the operations of the Food and Drug Administration. It provides for giving back term on patents granted to pharmaceutical manufacturers whose marketing efforts can be held up by delays in FDA drug approvals. Dickinson thinks this was a direct factor in FDA reform of its approval process.

However you approach it, patent search and examination is not a simple or quick process. A trained examiner must decide whether an invention meets the statutory criteria: Is it new? Is it statutory subject matter? Does it have utility? And there's a lot more. "It requires almost two years of work, unfortunately, for a patent to get through that," Dickinson points out. The PTO has responded in several ways. One is a hiring program begun in 1998 that added 1,500 patent examiners to a base of 2,000. Another approach is to reengineer the system, chiefly through automation and electronics. And that presents a special management concern, Dickinson says. "This system has been around for 200 years. We are overseen, if you will, by a 20,000-strong cadre of lawyers whose own life work is very much dependent on our rules and regulations. They're not always eager to see a lot of change."

But the PTO has been able to do some substantial reengineering, he says. Automation has been in progress for ten years, and in the 1990s the PTO spent a billion dollars on it. "We're moving as rapidly as we can toward a system where we can manage the entire process electronically, online," Dickinson says. Another automation issue for examiners and constituents was the capacity to search PTO databases electronically. "We've put half our database, back to 1976—the most important part of it—and all our trademarks on the Internet. It's freely searchable, and anyone can do it." The first online filing of a patent application came in December 1999. The first for a trademark was received in October 1998.

As his agency moves through the complicated processes of sweeping change, Dickinson sees other challenges in the areas of quality and of policy leadership on intellectual property matters. The first of these, given huge growth in the office's workload, is partly a question of maintaining the quality of the patent examination process. Hundreds of new examiners coming in need training and equipping. Sustaining quality has also involved steps like installing new systems for quality measurement—for example, of a statistically valid sample of patents about to be issued; and establishing a group of senior examiners to review and analyze the handling of applications. On intellectual property, Dickinson believes it "becomes much more important as economic development shifts from manufacturing to information." The concept of intellectual property is "a key way to protect assets in the information age—and another reason why we're seeing this huge increase in applications."

Still, Dickinson considers the biggest issue for the PTO in the future to be the annual skim-off of fee revenue for budget purposes elsewhere in government. Beyond its acute need for additional examiners, the office must make other investments, such as continued automation training, that will keep it from being overwhelmed by the rising tide of applications. The PTO has worked with the Office of Management and Budget, Dickinson says, "to try to find a solution to the question of how we can more permanently and regularly retain the fee revenue. If we can solve that, a lot of other things start to fall in place."

PROFILE

Current Under Secretary of Commerce for Intellectual Property and Director, U.S. Patent and Trademark Office
Q. Todd Dickinson, November 1999–

Career summary
Acting assistant secretary, acting commissioner of patents and trademarks,
    January–November 1999
Deputy assistant secretary, deputy commissioner, 1998–99
Counsel, Dechert, Price, and Rhoads, Philadelphia, 1995–97
Chief counsel, intellectual property and technology, Sun Company, 1990–95
Counsel, Chevron Corporation, 1981–90

Education
B.S., Allegheny College, 1974; J.D., University of Pittsburgh School of Law, 1977

Commissioners of Patents and Trademarks since 1989

Clinton administration
Bruce A. Lehman, 1992–98 (currently president and CEO, International
    Intellectual Institute)
Harry F. Manbeck Jr., 1990–92 (currently partner, Rothwell, Figg, Ernst,
    and Manbeck)

Bush administration
Donald James Quigg, 1985–89 (currently partner, Roper and Quigg)

▓ Director, National Institute of Standards and Technology

**EXECUTIVE LEVEL IV—Presidential appointment with
Senate confirmation**

RECOMMENDED SKILLS AND EXPERIENCE ■ NIST's director typically should have an engineering or scientific background and the seasoning to run a sophisticated R&D operation. Experience in the public sector at some level is a plus. To these, Director Raymond Kammer adds the ability and interest to stay current on technical developments and opportunities and to "carry a vision for the staff." He also thinks the director needs the instinct and flair to present science and technology in ways that nonscientists can understand and feel comfortable with—"even be excited about from time to time."

INSIGHT ■ NIST is this country's oldest multiprogram national laboratory—and, says Kammer, "the best measurement and standards laboratory in the world." Its basic focus on measurement technology and standards research helps American industry improve the quality of its products and boosts competitiveness overseas. Thus NIST performs its central mission: supporting U.S. economic growth. It does this in four ways:

—Its research laboratories generate measurement and standards data, evaluation, and test methods crucial to the technology infrastructure of American industry. The most important areas of this work are electronics, electrical and manufacturing engineering, building and fire research, information technology, physics, chemistry, and materials science.

—Its Advanced Technology Program gives competitive seed-money awards to innovative and collaborative private-sector enterprises pursuing development of high-risk advanced technology with far-reaching economic promise.

—Its Manufacturing Extension Partnership supplies expert assistance to smaller companies in technology and business methods.

—It manages an outreach program, linked to the annual Malcolm Baldrige National Quality Award, that offers guidelines on organizational improvement to business firms and educational and health-care organizations.

Kammer sees two major challenges. First is what he calls creating a strategy for the agency that takes into account the relentless, quickening advance of technology. The fast pace is steadily shortening the time between successive generations of product. When he was in his twenties, "lasers leisurely unfolded into existence." Today, new generations of software evolve in six to eight months, microprocessors in eighteen. "A jet turbine engine from design to delivery is now twenty-nine months. That's about the most complicated thing mankind makes, also the most regulated," he says—someone at the Federal Aviation Administration has to agree to every step in its assembly. "And they're still doing it in twenty-nine months. So if you miss the boat, if you don't see a trend, you can be playing catch-up for five or six months after that. It's very hard."

Keeping up with the technology means the director must continually question "the assumptions of the staff and the technical leadership of the agency," Kammer believes. This is a good example of what it takes these days to manage the dynamics of a leading-edge scientific agency. While Kammer knows most people are more comfortable staying in what they're are familiar with than going after change, he also recognizes that scientific and engineering history is marked by alternating periods of incremental and extraordinary change. "You can trust the practitioners in a particular technology to make an incremental change. You can't expect them to make the discontinuous change. They need to be challenged to do that. Sometimes the technology and science changes so dramatically we have to get different staff to stop what they're doing and start something different."

Another strategic, and related, issue for the director is the multidisciplinary nature of the most interesting opportunities in technology today. The response to this is not continual reorganization of NIST to stay abreast of the times. It is to shape the agency and work force so that it's relatively easy for people to range across specialized fields or organizations when they deal with tasks requiring the application of several kinds of knowledge. Doing that is "very hard," Kammer says, and part of the problem might be labeled overspecialization. "Our education system turns out, not just physicists, but atomic physicists who don't really think they have anything to do with optical physicists or nuclear physicists, for example."

The second main challenge in this job is resources. Getting them, Kammer says, means "getting buy-in" from the people in the Congress and elsewhere who make resources available. This sometimes depends on simply giving them a technical understanding of how something works. "But a lot of it is getting them to understand what the opportunity is, what the consequences of not doing it are." It is difficult work requiring a lot of "relationship building" on the Hill but also within the Department of Commerce and at the White House.

NIST's Advanced Technology Program exemplifies the kind of initiative for which relationship building is especially critical. It is among the agency's most successful undertakings and certainly the most controversial. Authorized near the end of the Reagan administration, begun in the Bush administration, ATP initially spent some $10 million to spur progress in esoteric endeavors like manufacturing technology for low-cost flat panel displays and precision optics for soft X-ray projection lithography. The ensuing years have seen significant expansion in the benefits ATP pumps into the economy. One of these—soon en route to the market place—is a small analytical device, installed on a computer card, that will allow genetic testing for disease across the board, instead of only for the half dozen ailments, such as cancer, for which such tests are now performed. Because the current testing technology is expensive (about $1,200), it is normally used only when family history suggests that it is advisable. The new device, according to Kammer, will only cost "a couple of bucks a pop. And it will change everybody's life."

Over the years, he reports, the government and the private sector have each invested $1.4 billion for ATP projects. "So the total program has spent $2.8 billion, conferred a competitive advantage on the manufacturers involved, and kept jobs inside the country, which is probably more important." The "analytical reality, not just by economists in my employ but by independent economists who have studied the program, is that this works extraordinarily well," Kammer asserts. Yet in the Congress, ATP has been a bitterly contentious issue, the object of "polarized debate" sparked by differing philosophies about what it is and where it should go. But "if you made an analytical decision, based on the economic results and the investment, you would not only keep the program, you'd probably grow it."

NIST operates on a budget of about $800 million that, Kammer says, is rising. (The Advanced Technology Program's share of the fiscal year 2000 budget was $142 million, about $61 million down from 1999, but money carried over from previous years just about made up the shortfall.) More than half the agency's staff of 3,300 are scientists and engineers, working on its campuses in suburban Maryland and Boulder, Colorado. NIST's congressional authorizing committees are the House Science Committee and the Senate Commerce, Science, and Transportation Committee; its appropriations panels are the State, Justice, and Commerce Appropriations subcommittees of each chamber.

While its programs have grown through the 1990s, NIST's staff has not increased since 1980. "When the possibility of growth and funding was presented to us, we made a fundamental decision not to let the staff grow," says Kammer, who since 1980 served more than once as deputy director of the agency. "We're still what we were then. And we're forming strategic alliances with others." He calls his staff "a very inner-directed group of people," working in a culture "that values excellence above everything else." That kind of objective integrity is critical, right to the top of the agency.

How hard is it to recruit staff? NIST is "far from competitive from the standpoint of compensation," Kammer says. At the working level, laboratory scientists other than those in information technology get about 80 percent of their market value. Information technology scientists get 40 to 50 percent. But NIST provides countervailing advantages—it buys its scientists the best equipment available, trains them, urges them to publish, pushes them to follow their research wherever it takes them, does not require them to teach.

Still, the agency over the years has been able to cut its work force when necessary and use the money to hire different kinds of staff. Yet "we're not so ruthless that we don't give people the chance to change," Kammer says, "and many people have been able to." Nor does NIST partake in traditional personnel and performance management aspects of the civil service system. When in the 1980s the agency saw that it was taking too long (seven months) to make offers to doctoral candidates using the conventional civil service list, it used its influence on the Hill to set up its own arrangement. Kammer says, "In principle, I can be walking across the campus, see what I imagine to be the light of intelligence in somebody's eyes, take out a business card, write, 'you're hired' on it, make the salary number up, and the person's on board. We designed the system ourselves. It has a lot going for it in terms in staying a competitive laboratory."

Established in 1901 as the independent National Bureau of Standards, NIST used to sell a considerable share of its services to a number of other federal agencies. It still earns some funding that way. The Environmental Protection Agency, for example, sometimes needs "sophisticated analytical chemistry that they're not really capable of mounting for themselves," Kammer notes. As a regulatory agency, EPA prefers not to go outside government for such services, because private laboratories that have the talent to provide them "probably also have some stake in the game," as Kammer puts it.

Today, however, having mostly recovered its ability to set its own priorities, NIST in Kammer's view is a much healthier laboratory than it was ten years ago. " I don't say we are the best measurement and standards laboratory in the world lightly. I say it because I have benchmarked us against the world, attribute by attribute. You don't have to be bad to get better, and one of the commitments we have made is to continue to get better."

PROFILE

Current Director of the National Institute of Standards and Technology
Raymond Kammer,1997–

Career summary
Chief financial officer, assistant secretary for administration, and chief
   Information officer, Department of Commerce (acting)
Deputy under secretary of commerce, oceans and atmosphere, 1991–93
Deputy director, NIST, 1980–91 and 1993–97

Education
B.A., University of Maryland, 1969

Directors of the National Institute of Standards and Technology since 1989

Clinton administration
Arati Prabhakar, 1993–97 (currently vice president, Interval Research
· Corporation)

Bush administration
John W. Lyons, 1990–93 (retired)
Raymond Kammer (acting), 1989–90 (incumbent)

Department of Defense

■ **Director, Defense Advanced Projects Research Agency**
■ **Noncareer appointment, Senior Executive Service**

RECOMMENDED SKILLS AND EXPERIENCE ■ Given this agency's highly advanced exploration of technology's outer reaches, a professional engineering or scientific background is essential—not merely as a passport to get through the front door but as a knowledge base on which to build. DARPA's breadth is such that any incoming director will feel "like a post-doc, learning from scratch," according to Fernando Fernandez, who assumed direction of the agency in May 1998. He says the position particularly calls for prior work in innovative processes and a familiarity with "how people who do that kind of work think." Especially where the agency's future is concerned, he thinks its director should have experience in running an operation with extremely creative technical people. "The dynamics of this place are exactly those of a small research and development company, all very bright people, all looking over one another's shoulders." To keep it that way, the director needs another skill: the ability to attract exceptionally talented people with the promise of working on extraordinary issues in advanced technology.

Candidates for the job should have a meaningful background in defense-related research and development, preferably in or associated with the Defense Department. And while solid credentials are a must, it's worth repeating here a comment noted in an earlier *Prune Book* profile of this job: the frontiers of military technology are pushing out so quickly that they can outdate even the best personal qualifications. As suggested above, a DARPA director must therefore be able to move quickly along the learning curve.

INSIGHT　■　DARPA's job is to deal U.S. armed forces a winning hand in the effective use of advanced technology. That effort—shaped by DARPA but implemented elsewhere—focuses especially on weapons systems, combat equipment, and communications, but it reaches into many other requirements of military readiness and operations. In everything it does, this agency is staring hard not just at the future but also at the far future, trying to make intelligent guesses about what avenues of inquiry and exploration are likely to be the most fruitful. This often means looking into potentially promising areas where the risk is also great enough to deter others from venturing. For years, that singular mission has distinguished DARPA from most other federal agencies in several notable respects.

Work force is probably the most critical of these. Fernandez calls his agency "one of the few places where smart people can be given resources to make a difference in some really important problems." Like those who have preceded him, he thinks the director's most crucial assignment is to establish an atmosphere where such individuals want to come to DARPA to do that kind of work—"where more want to come than we have room for, where that is a signature of the agency." Today, this goal, and the agency's work generally, encounter a challenge that didn't exist a decade ago. As Fernandez sees it, "We're not in a time now where defense is felt to be that big a deal." Compared to other national problems, he thinks defense is viewed as less important than it once was, "and research for defense is even smaller," making it tougher to get the talented people he's talking about.

Indeed, the major requirement for nurturing an innovative environment at DARPA, Fernandez says, is "bringing in new people constantly. Moving people and moving projects. If you don't refresh your gene pool, after a while you start talking to each other about the same things." To keep new blood flowing in, he tries "to have a balance of things they can work on that will give them something to do once they leave. They come here always for a short time and they want to do better for themselves when they leave." Since DARPA holds no financial rewards, it has to be able to offer professional career enhancement that includes outside networking for post-DARPA opportunities. Fortunately, to streamline and speed its recruiting, the agency has what is called "experimental personnel hiring authority" to bring accomplished scientists and engineers from the outside into term appointments.

Another feature that sets DARPA apart is how it operates. Fernandez calls his agency an investment management firm because, it contracts for just about everything it does. "Virtually all of it is done out of house. Our projects are all over the world. We have no laboratory, own no facilities of any consequence. We never make products here. Everything is done by other people—in industry, academia, government laboratories. DARPA's philosophy is to go outside. We subsidize groups of people in particular places to learn how to do something, how to build something." This, he says, is really making markets for new ideas: getting something to "where a DARPA customer says, Gosh, I want to buy this, and picks up the contractors and pays them to build the real, engineered version."

And who are the agency's customers? Unlike his predecessors, Fernandez makes a sharp distinction between the commanders in chief in the field (the "CINCs"), who are the "consumers" of the technology products that DARPA spurs into existence, and the military services, which are the real customers for those products. "The services are the people who hire the contractors and take things to the operational level. The commanders in chief operate everything and command everybody. But if you don't buy the right things, it makes no difference what happens," which is why he urges the CINCs to talk to their services and ensure the right decisions. DARPA's market, then, is a two-step proposition—consumer and customer. "In Washington," Fernandez notes, "a lot of people don't understand that."

Again, DARPA differs from other federal entities in the nature of its mission. Where other agencies usually pursue identified goals along defined paths, this one has few road maps and often little guidance. One of his hardest assignments, Fernandez reflects, is trying to explain that innovation is always about the unexpected, and rarely about a long-term plan. "Innovation is setting up a structure that lets you seize opportunities and exploit them. You don't exactly know when they're going to happen or how. But you've got to be able to move very quickly." That's very different from the top-down approach found elsewhere in government, where the requirement is generated first and the technology to produce it follows. This is okay for a mature market, he says, but in areas marked by fast change, it doesn't work.

That's why DARPA was created. The agency's role is "unique," Fernandez says, because it can work in areas "still so new that no one is clear how any products might be used, only that it could solve a problem." Thus the agency might be "building the prototype of a big system for one of the military services and at the same time be funding a professor and a graduate student on something with the potential of being revolutionary." He worries that senior technical people are not as much involved in policy as they were twenty or thirty years ago. Yet "there are some serious issues"— he cites informational warfare and biological defense as examples—"where senior technical input at the policy table will be important." This has implications for the market-making concept outlined above.

The biggest problems arise, paradoxically, when DARPA is successful. "I can prototype something that's uniquely military, that's so new they hadn't thought about it four years ago," Fernandez says. "But it's very difficult for the military to put into rapid development something that really looks good but that wasn't part of a previous plan." That's because the budgeting process is not designed that way. So, in this example, Fernandez's new prototype may get approving nods from the generals today, but money for it must be cranked into a budget memorandum that won't make it available for, say, another eighteen months. "The question meanwhile is, what do you do with your people who have been working on this?" he says. The answer is that they get reassigned. When the money does come in a year and a half later, "we end up doing the problem all over again."

But failures are okay, Fernandez points out. "DARPA is supposed to fail. We set the bar too high, we failed." It's the successes that can cost time and money, and he says the agency is trying to solve this problem by working with individual military service leaders on ways to get around it.

DARPA tries to spin the products of the research it has generated to existing commercial companies first. For certain military needs, however, there are no parallel commercial markets for the products involved. An example is completely mobile telephone systems not requiring links to landlines. "The commercial world will say it doesn't want to solve that problem," Fernandez explains, "because they have no need for it. There is problem after problem where we have to find ways to get new ideas inserted while technology is rapidly changing" but where the commercial sector sometimes has no interest.

Another ongoing and critical problem he identifies is preserving DARPA's access to ideas that belong to others. The agency must maintain an understanding with its program managers on dealing with contractors "in ways that protect their intellectual property, which companies value much more than in the past," he says. DARPA's challenge is to make sure it has entreé to those ideas. "You've got to keep telling people that, if we're not trusted by people who come in with ideas, they'll stop coming and we lose our access to their ideas."

DARPA's budget, currently at about $1.8 billion, has slowly decreased since the mid-1990s. V. Larry Lynn, an earlier director, once commented that increasing budgets bring a demand to increase the size of the organization, something he termed anathema to DARPA's structure and objectives. It's better to be small and highly entrepreneurial than be large enough to do everything people want done, he said. Today, concerned that the budget does not drop further, Fernandez has been talking to the Congress and the Defense Department about holding the budget at an agreed level.

The agency's staff level has remained steady. "We still have about 120 people that run everything," Fernandez says. "It's a very flat organization— on purpose. Anybody who comes here from a huge organization is going to feel a little funny when they find out how DARPA depends on just a few people." His work force wants to be treated like individuals, like the small creative R&D group that it is. "They'll challenge anything that comes from the front office and you better know why you're doing it," he says. "In my opinion, this is the most alive place in the entire defense research and development community. It's exciting people who are coming through with good ideas."

PROFILE

Current Director of Defense Advanced Research Projects Agency
Fernando L. Fernandez, May 1998

Career summary
President and chairman, Board of Directors, AETC, San Diego, 1994–98
President and chairman, Board of Directors, Areté Associates, Los Angeles, 1976–94
Vice president, Physical Dynamics, Santa Monica, 1975–76
Program manager, R&D Associates, Santa Monica, 1972–75
Researcher, department manager, and associate group director, Aerospace Corporation, 1963–72

Education
B.S., mechanical engineering, M.S., applied mechanics, Stevens Institute of Technology, 1960–61; Ph.D., aeronautics, California Institute of Technology, 1969

Directors of the Defense Advanced Research Projects Agency since 1989

Clinton administration
V. Larry Lynn, 1995–98 (retired, consultant)

Clinton and Bush administrations
Gary Denman, 1992–95 (currently president and CEO, GRC International Bush administration)
Victor H. Reis, 1990–92 (currently director, Center for Nuclear Strategies, Science Applications International Corporation)
Craig I. Fields, 1989–90 (currently chairman, Defense Science Board)

Department of Energy

▨ Chairman, Federal Energy Regulatory Commission

EXECUTIVE LEVEL III—Presidential appointment with
Senate confirmation

RECOMMENDED SKILLS AND EXPERIENCE ■ Although this
agency's chief has historically come from outside the commission, one of
the best credentials for this position is prior service as a member of the Federal Energy Regulatory Commission itself. In the 1990s two sitting members moved to the chairmanship. Since no more than three commissioners
can belong to the same party at any one time, promotion of a commissioner
to the top job is a convenient option to looking for the requisite credentials
on the outside and one that virtually guarantees an experienced choice. It's
important to understand also that the industries that FERC regulates divide
into components—producers and pipeline companies within the natural gas
industry, for example—that compete vigorously in cases the commission
considers. It matters to these factions that their interests are adequately represented among the commission's membership. This is a factor to consider
not just when naming a FERC chairman but also in choosing other members. The chairman of FERC should clearly be familiar with the energy
industry or at least have background in a regulated industry. Just as important, as the current chairman puts it, is an understanding of "modern organizational behavior." Finally, the right candidate should possess
"diplomatic and interpersonal skills" that can coalesce a sometimes divided
five-member commission around policy initiatives that advance the agency's
objectives.

INSIGHT ■ The Federal Energy Regulatory Commission is an independent, five-member agency within the Department of Energy. (The organization charts show a dotted-line relationship between FERC and the
department's top leadership.) FERC sets rates or charges for the transportation of natural gas that is resold to consumers—and for the transmission and sale of electric power that is resold at wholesale—in interstate
commerce. It establishes rates for the interstate commercial transmission
of oil by pipeline and licenses and inspects all state, city, and private (nonfederal) hydroelectric enterprises. It deals with environmental questions
associated with the activities under its regulatory authority.

FERC chairman James Hoecker, who has held the post since 1997, sees the far-reaching changes taking place in the natural gas and electric power industries as a major issue for his agency in the next few years. For FERC, it's a transformation that has meant big internal shifts as well. In his message to the Congress accompanying the agency's budget request for fiscal 2001, Hoecker noted that the markets for natural gas and electric power "have become closely intertwined, raising many new regulatory challenges." What's more, the dramatic changes occurring are the result of competition the commission had long encouraged. "Regulated monopolies have given way to open networks that support change and competition," he said, "and energy commodities and service markets move much faster than ever before." Industry creates new services and entities as fast as it sees new market opportunities, Hoecker's message added, and regulated energy companies "restructure themselves frequently, acquiring new assets and divesting old ones." All this means that FERC must "understand the market much more fully and respond to new issues much more quickly," while continuing to meet its traditional responsibilities.

The big changes have obliged the commission to update its regulatory model, Hoecker says. "We have worked hard to promote competition, but have been forced to do it with an organization that was designed for cost-of-service rate regulation. So we've been through a two-and-a-half-year reengineering process that has reconfigured the way our staff works, and the way our organization is structured." At the staff level, new organizations have emerged, many processes are now driven by teams, and processing time has dropped. Because the agency gets "a million pieces of paper a month and that's too much," Hoecker says it has invested more heavily in information technology that permits it to do business electronically and has cut down on "transfers of paper from one office to another." An especially difficult element of the internal adjustment, he says, has been "the converging of our electric and natural gas staffs that have been separate for sixty years."

Several factors underlie the narrowing divide between the natural gas and electric power industries, Hoecker explains. One is the efficiency of gas turbines developed in the past two decades that makes them more attractive as generators of electric power than most other means of doing so. "Their technology can be sited more easily than a big electric plant, and they take less time to build, are cheaper, and can produce power at far lower cost than anything except some of the old coal-fired plants," he says. The electric power companies also like gas generated power because they improve the reliability and efficiency of the transmission system. That places new strain on pipeline delivery systems, however, and will generate new competition for the commodity.

In fifteen years of trying to bring competition to the respective interstate marketplaces of the two industries, Hoecker says, the commission has found state regulators less eager to move in that direction than FERC itself. "Resistance from state government," he says, "is much more intense on the electric power side, because that industry has always been a highly regulated local business." Even though FERC's electric power regulation is only at the wholesale level, "it's just more important than it used to be." The problem has ruffled communication between FERC and the states, and jurisdictional turf wars and policy debates have marked the relationship. "What we're trying to do is create markets where markets have never really existed before," Hoecker says. While that has now been largely achieved for the interstate natural gas trade, he thinks it will take "another five to seven years to get this far on the electric side."

In the area of environmental impact, FERC has a task familiar to many another regulatory agency: seeking a balance between economic benefit and the risk of degrading the environment, often while being reproached from both sides. "This agency has a reputation in the environmental community of having never seen a project it didn't like," Hoecker comments. "It has a reputation in some parts of the industry as being a little too green. Kind of ironic, but that's the way it works out." In the last two years, FERC has revised its processes for finding a public need for building new natural gas pipelines while seeing at the same time "a lot more resistance" to building them from landowners and even state and local politicians. "We think natural gas is environmentally more benign than burning coal," he says. "But the land disturbance involved in building these delivery systems is getting much more attention than it used to. I think we've been pretty successful in working with the pipeline industry to improve its processes, its outreach to landowners, and its environmental work."

Among the five FERC commissioners, Hoecker says, "we all share equal decisionmaking authority, in the sense that each of us has one vote on any particular item that comes before us. In that sense, it's a majority rule situation." Substantively, the chairman has primary responsibility for setting the commission's agenda. By statute, some items require action by a date certain. "We don't have any discretion about that," notes Hoecker, "but on a large number of other things filed before the agency, the priority in which those are taken up and the nature of other kinds of policy initiatives is heavily influenced by the chairman." Although the chairman doesn't establish this alone, what goes on the commission's twice monthly agenda and circulated for notational voting "is governed largely from the chairman's office. The progress of the agenda and the emphasis in particular areas or policies are the two things that separate this office from those of the other commissioners."

The chairman, in addition, is the administrative head of the agency, authorizes the budget, approves the funding levels for agency offices, and makes senior personnel appointments and other decisions. For fiscal 2001, FERC submitted a budget of $175.2 million and asked for 1,250 full time employees—a slight increase over its existing staffing level. Hoecker's budget message stated that the commission would "recover the full costs of its operations through annual charges and filing fees," which it would return to the Treasury "as a direct offset to its appropriation, resulting in a net appropriation of zero dollars."

Hoecker says the agency has cut its size by 8 percent during his chairmanship, something that could not have been done unless it had reengineered itself. "The difficult challenge for the future is that we're going to be asked to take on more responsibility. There's major federal energy legislation pending that will give us much more to do, particularly in the electricity area. Even without legislation, the agency is being drawn into new areas like bulk power reliability. In any case, we've reached a point where we're as lean as we can be and still do our current work. Our reductions, which have been achieved to date entirely through attrition, would have to be reversed, or at least halted, if this legislation passes."

FERC was created by the Department of Energy Organization Act of 1977. Reflecting on its position and work, Hoecker says that, like other independent regulatory agencies, this one has historically been viewed "as more of an arm of Congress than of the administration." He values that independence as the means by which FERC can bring technical judgments, not ideology, to bear on its decisions. "There may be people on both sides of the aisle who disagree with our decisions, but I think they largely respect the expertise we bring to the process and the fact that we call things as we see them and don't pursue any political agenda."

He sees the chairmanship as "a critically important job" in moving the commission's "regulatory and pro-competitive market agenda" forward. This work, he says, "involves such a balance of diverse and conflicting interests and values that it takes someone with some intellectual and small-p political dexterity to make those balances work." The FERC chairman, Hoecker says, "is ultimately the main lubricator of the process here. If he or she has trouble bringing the other commissioners on board for the major initiatives, the agenda here will stall and federal policy will create uncertainty in the market."

PROFILE

Current Chairman of the Federal Energy Regulatory Commission
James J. Hoecker, 1997–

Career summary
Commissioner, Federal Energy Regulatory Commission, 1993–97
Of counsel, Jones, Day, Reavis and Pogue, 1990–93
Partner, Keck, Mahin and Cate, 1988–90
Various staff positions, FERC, including assistant general counsel for gas and
    oil litigation and assistant general counsel for rulemaking and legislative
    analysis, 1993–97

Education
B.A., Northland College, 1967; M.A., Ph.D., University of Kentucky, 1975;
    J.D., University of Wisconsin, 1978

Chairmen of the Federal Energy Regulatory Commission since 1989

Clinton administration
Elizabeth Anne Moler, 1993–97 (currently senior vice president, Unicom)

Bush administration
Martin L. Allday, 1989–93 (currently partner, Scott, Douglass, and
    McConnico)

Department of Justice

▓ Assistant Attorney General, Antitrust Division

**EXECUTIVE LEVEL IV—Presidential appointment with
Senate confirmation**

RECOMMENDED SKILLS AND EXPERIENCE ■ First, the conventional attributes. This assistant attorney general should have a background in the practice of law, specifically as a litigator and preferably in the antitrust area. Experience with the federal judicial system is a strong asset; as

Assistant Attorney General Joel Klein puts it, "the engagement of the federal courts has always been critical to the long- and even medium-term legitimacy and integrity of antitrust enforcement." Occupants of the job need a familiarity with the complex evolution of commercial competition at home and around the world. Beyond these basics, Klein thinks there must be strong commitment to global antitrust enforcement, which he sees as a "major issue" in the new century. Just as important as any of the above is intellectual and personal independence. As Klein makes clear, "this is a law enforcement job, not a political job. You have to understand that politics has no role to play in antitrust enforcement."

INSIGHT ▪ Say "Microsoft" and you'll have identified a major focus of this job over the past several years. The government's antitrust case against the software giant also attracted unusual media attention to the individual in charge of prosecuting it. As Klein points out, however, "we try our cases in the courtroom," not in the media. An action with the impact and ramifications of the Microsoft case is clearly going to invite heavy media scrutiny "and even the odd characterization," he says. "But I came to this job from the White House and it's a night-and-day difference in terms of interaction with the media." While the individual in his position does need some media savvy, "you really do want to try your cases in court. It's what keeps our law enforcement powerful."

Promoting and maintaining competitive markets is the name of the game here. Two venerable statutes—the Sherman and Clayton antitrust acts a century and more ago—define the antitrust responsibilities of the federal government. Klein calls them "the critical legal framework in which we act." Responding to a business environment then imprinted with the philosophy of the robber baron, the two acts shield trade—basically, the sale and purchase of goods and services—from conspiracies and other actions designed to restrain or limit it. That means price fixing, corporate mergers that reduce competition in a given market, the use of market power to maintain or extend monopolies, and similar activities. The statutes affect just about every industry and phase of business, including manufacturing, transportation, distribution, and marketing.

"The Sherman Act in particular," Klein says, "but to some degree the Clayton Act as well, are thought of as the Magna Carta of our free economy." And their mandates have come down, mostly unchanged, to the present time, reflected in the specific antitrust responsibilities of the division Klein took over in the mid-1990s.

What especially distinguishes the acts is the continual application of changing circumstances to the bedrock principles embodied in the law. They truly are common law statutes evolved by the courts, Klein says. They allow for the growth of the case law as it is applied over time, based on an increasing understanding of economics, practical experience, the lessons of deregulation, globalization, and much else. It's considerably different from, say, a health and safety statute where, as Klein says, "the courts have already got the words of the law." In the judicial nature of things, he adds, Sherman and Clayton "are much more like constitutional provisions than statutes."

Klein's division investigates potential antitrust violations, conducts grand jury proceedings, develops cases, and prosecutes them. It argues appeals from initial decisions, negotiates final judgments that can include fines and prison sentences, and enforces them. All together, these efforts fall into three categories of cases—criminal violations, civil nonmerger cases like that brought against Microsoft, and mergers.

In the civil and merger areas, the Antitrust Division shares jurisdiction with the Federal Trade Commission, which was established by the Clayton antitrust legislation. The division and the FTC divide this work, Klein says, by areas of expertise. "It's not always a precise dividing line but, as examples, we've been doing telephones and air transport cases for years and they've done pharmaceutical companies and retail stores." Some history exists of dispute between the two organizations on matters of jurisdiction, but this seems largely a matter of the past. "Sure," Klein says, "human nature being what it is, that will arise on rare occasions. But we have a very smooth working relationship. As markets move, as products converge, we occasionally find ourselves questioning who has better jurisdiction. But it's a tiny fraction of the time."

His division is also responsible for advocating competition within the federal government. That involves formal appearances in federal administrative proceedings, development of legislative initiatives to promote deregulation, and elimination of unwarranted exemptions from the antitrust laws. The responsibility is one of two that Klein sees as policy functions of the job. The other is acting as a "spokesperson around the globe on issues of deregulation, enhanced free trade, and effective competition policy."

How does the Internet economy intersect with the responsibilities of this job? "In two respects," Klein says. "First, there's no question that the infrastructure of electronic commerce presents issues—who has control of access to bandwidth, the operating system in the browser—of the kind we've been litigating with Microsoft. So there will be a series of questions about whether the infrastructure is open in a way that allows for meaningful competition." Second are the antitrust considerations that operate everywhere else. "If you were to see a merger of two major Internet players in commerce, we would analyze that; just as we would a merger of two major bricks-and-mortar players or, for that matter, a mixture of both."

Does the antitrust division interest itself in potential mergers ahead of time? It's usually the other way around, Klein says. If the value of a proposed merger exceeds $15 million, "which is almost anything worth paying attention to," the proposal must be filed with the division and cleared there or by the Federal Trade Commission before it can be carried out. "So you don't need to run ahead of the process. There may be specific reasons for doing so, a handful of times a year. But not generally."

Klein views his organization as underfunded, "really stretched well beyond the limit." The range of merger activity has gone up substantially in the last ten years, and the division's international enforcement program on cartels has risen "by leaps and bounds." In the years ahead, it will need significantly greater resources. For fiscal year 1999, the division's budget amounted to about $100 million. In the same year, it brought in fines from criminal cases in the range of $1.1 to $1.2 billion—some twelve times its budget level. Fees from merger filings earned another $100 million. "We are not only self-funding, but many times over," Klein comments.

In a steadily more deregulated, globalized economy, what are the big antitrust issues of the immediate future? Klein thinks merger review has become "paramount" in the global economy where, for example, "digital convergence" in industries like cable and telephone is a prominent feature. "The second major area of enforcement will be the international cartel business," he says. Globalization is generating rising pressure on "a handful of major producers" to seek wider profit margins through cooperation in cartel-like fashion. Finally, Klein predicts that the twenty-first-century economy will see "major concentrations in single-firm power." When that becomes a major "bottleneck problem," he says, "there will be a role for monopoly enforcement."

PROFILE

Current Assistant Attorney General of the Antitrust Division
Joel I. Klein, 1997–

Career summary
Acting assistant attorney general, Antitrust Division, 1996–97
Principal deputy assistant attorney general, Antitrust Division, 1995–97

Deputy counsel to the president, 1993–95
Partner, Onek, Klein and Farr, 1981–93
Associate and partner, Rogovin, Stern and Huge, 1976–81
Mental Health Law Project, 1975–76
Law clerk to Justice Lewis Powell, U.S. Supreme Court, 1974–75
Law clerk to Judge David Bazelon, U.S. Circuit Court of Appeals for the D.C.
　　Circuit, 1973–74

Education
B.A., Columbia University, 1967; J.D., Harvard Law School, 1971

Assistant Attorneys General of the Antitrust Division since 1989

Clinton administration
Anne K. Bingaman, 1993–96 (currently chairman CEO,
　　Valo Telecommunications)

Bush administration
James F. Rill, 1989–93 (currently head, antitrust, and trade regulation practice,
　　Collier, Shannon, Rill, and Scott)

Department of the Treasury

▓ Commissioner, Internal Revenue Service

**EXECUTIVE LEVEL III—Presidential appointment with
Senate confirmation**

RECOMMENDED SKILLS AND EXPERIENCE ■ "This is much
more a management and administrative position than a policy job," says
Commissioner Charles Rossotti. "We don't say anything about what the
tax law ought to be or what the Congress should do" with respect to the
Internal Revenue Service. But what the IRS does exerts an impact on everyone in the U.S. economy. Rossotti believes candidates for this position
should demonstrate a solid management background. Preferably, it would
include success in managing extensive organizational change. Former
commissioners have also listed accounting and financial management
skills, familiarity with information systems, and expertise in tax law as
valuable assets.

INSIGHT ■ The first, and main, thing to know about this position is that its current occupant is driving agencywide change of extraordinary complexity. That will also be the preoccupying task of his successors for the foreseeable future.

Here are some of the reasons why. As the country's primary tax collector, the Internal Revenue Service currently gathers in some $1.8 trillion each year—at a cost of less than half a cent on the dollar—and hands back about $185 billion in refunds. To do so, the agency relies on ancient computers (some more than thirty years old), a telephone system that still keeps many taxpayer calls from getting through, and a work force contending not just with agency reorganization but with new measurements of their own effectiveness. And those are only the systemic problems.

More critically, the IRS is struggling to comply with the mandates of 1998 legislation spurred in part by the angry testimony of taxpayers in Senate hearings in 1997 and 1998. Leading the complaints were charges of abuse by IRS agents that included bullying, threats, and raids (in April 2000, a General Accounting Office report in April 2000 said the charges were mostly unfounded). In response, the Congress told the IRS to reduce its emphasis on aggressive tax collection and pay more attention to customer service. It gave the agency authority for sweeping redesign to achieve these and other reforms. Accordingly, the IRS developed a simplified structure to serve four main categories of taxpayers—ninety million high-compliance individuals; twenty-five million to thirty-five million small businesses and self-employed people; mid-sized and large businesses; and the tax-exempt sector. The plan reorganized the IRS into four major lines, each dedicated to one of the four major groups. As of December 1999, the first of the new divisions was in place; the other three were to be formed in the following twelve to eighteen months.

In further response to the 1998 reform law, many agents were switched from tax collection to helping taxpayers. Audited tax returns—always a tiny fraction of total returns—dropped by 70 percent below the levels of the early 1980s, and in 1999 there were actually more audits of returns reporting income of $25,000 or less than of those showing income above $100,000. Between September 1998 and September 1999, property seizures from delinquent taxpayers declined by 99 percent. "We don't collect taxes anymore," an IRS agent told the *New York Times* in 1999. "We're not allowed to."

Inevitably, the agency now finds itself dealing with the potential fallout of the changes it has instituted. The stronger focus on taxpayers, the less aggressive approach to collection, the increased resources invested in internal change, the level-funded IRS budget for fiscal 2000—all these have fueled concern in the Senate and elsewhere about an open season for tax cheating. "It's quite unrealistic to expect people not to take advantage of the opportunity that's been presented to them," former IRS commissioner Donald Alexander was quoted as saying in early 2000. If compliance with the tax laws should drop by 5 percent, he pointed out, it would pretty well eliminate the current budget surplus.

In February of 2000, the General Accounting Office (the congressional bureau that tracks the performance and financial management of executive branch agencies) said its annual audit of the IRS showed that billions of taxes still go uncollected, some honest taxpayers remain the target of unjustified actions, and the IRS should be more forceful with those who underpay. Other assessments of the agency run in a similar vein. In their Government Performance Project, *Government Executive* magazine and Syracuse's Maxwell School of Citizenship and Public Affairs in 1999 and 2000 examined the management performance of twenty federal agencies, giving the IRS an overall rating of C. The agency got a score of 57 out of a possible 100 in the Clinton administration's 1999 American Customer Satisfaction survey of thirty agencies. That compared with an overall federal score of 68.6. But in the same survey, the IRS got a rating of 71 among those filing their returns electronically.

Remember also that enforcement and regulatory agencies, by the nature of their work, understandably rank lowest with the American public, a fact evident in a Roper Survey on the IRS's own web site. Since late 1985, it shows, the IRS has consistently been lower in favorability than what Roper calls "most agencies." The agency hit its all-time low of about 32 percent in 1998—the year of the IRS Restructuring and Reform Act.

It is early days yet in a reform of the magnitude Rossotti is managing. Since 1998 the IRS has risen in Roper's favorability index, while other agencies have dropped. In the downbeat February 2000 audit report cited above, the GAO nonetheless gave the IRS a clean bill of health, its third in three years, on its handling of the vast amounts of money flowing on and off its books. And in a *Washington Post* interview a month later, Rossotti–who took charge of the agency in 1998 with the mission of overseeing its reorganization—said "we're right about where we thought we'd be." He said he measures progress in "inchstones," not milestones.

"It isn't that we're just trying to become more of this or less of that," Rossotti told us. "What we're really trying to do is improve the overall effectiveness of the agency. No businesses and very few government agencies today have the luxury of doing just one thing and ignoring everything else. You have multiple objectives, multiple stakeholders."

Since most taxpayers are compliant and try to pay their tax bills, "we think they deserve good service and not have life made any harder for them than is necessary. But they also expect us to collect the taxes that are due. Those are the two objectives we have to reach. We have an opportunity to do better on both of those than we are doing now. That's what we're trying to do."

Implementation, not visioning, is the way Rossotti is trying to get there. Setting priorities is his biggest problem. "There are just a thousand things we really need to do. People are telling us they want us to fix this or that broken thing. If we try to do them all, we won't do any of them. And if we try to do them one at a time, we won't get there, either." An exceptionally tough balancing act is therefore required. "It is how we deal with fixing specific problems that really affect people today, immediately, versus how we deal with the underlying problems. That is really the excruciating dilemma that we face all the time. And we will continue to face it." One of the immediate tasks he refers to is the more than 800 changes in the tax code that were part of the 1998 reform legislation. The agency had to work the changes into its operations—they included seventy-one provisions on taxpayer rights—even as it was preparing for a potential Y2K computer crisis.

Also established by the 1998 restructuring act is a nine-member oversight board for the IRS. Six of these members are appointed by the president from the private sector. The commissioner, the secretary of the Treasury, and an employee representative are the other three. Among the duties of this unusually powerful body are approval of the IRS budget before it goes to the Treasury Department and the choice of senior managers, their evaluation, and their pay.

For internal operations in fiscal 2000, the IRS's budget was $8.2 billion. Its work force remains at 98,000, down by about 10,000 from the level of a few years ago. Rossotti says far-reaching change at the agency does not mean "getting rid of people." He has tried with some success, and in partnership with the National Treasury Employees Union, "to get across the idea that, yes, it's a lot of change, but we're going to work with the people we have here." While that has helped, he says the reorganization is still a cause of employee anxiety. "In any large organization, the natural tendency is caution. It's 'I don't know what to do, so I won't do anything, I'll just wait until somebody tells me.'" Especially in some compliance activities, "people have been cautious to the point of not taking action sometimes where it's required."

In establishing new measures of employee performance, the IRS has put customer satisfaction, employee satisfaction, and business results at stage center. Frontline workers, for example, are no longer judged mainly by the tax dollars they produce, but also by the quality of results—results that in some cases depend on how well employees know their own jobs.

"Since this is a management job primarily, that means dealing with people, communicating, listening to people, trying to reconcile priorities," Rossotti says. "You have to be willing to engage with a lot of detail and a lot of people. There's no substitute for really trying to find out what's going on."

PROFILE

Current Commissioner of the Internal Revenue Service
Charles O. Rossotti, November 1997–

Career summary
Chairman of the board and founder, American Management Systems, 1970–97
Various positions in the Office of Systems Analysis, Office of the Secretary of
    Defense, 1965–69
Consultant with Boston Consulting Group, 1964–65

Education
B.A., magna cum laude, Georgetown University (1962); M.B.A, Harvard
    Business School (1974)

Commissioners of the Internal Revenue Service since 1989

Clinton administration
Margaret M. Richardson, 1993–97 (currently with Ernst and Young)

Bush administration
Shirley D. Peterson, 1992–93 (currently president, Hood College)
Fred T. Goldberg Jr., 1989–92 (currently partner, Scadden, Arps, Slate,
    Meagher, and Flom)

▒ **Assistant Secretary for Economic Policy**

▒ **Assistant Secretary for Tax Policy**

▒ **Assistant Secretary for Financial Markets**

▒ **Assistant Secretary for Financial Institutions**

EXECUTIVE LEVEL IV—Presidential appointments with
Senate confirmation

RECOMMENDED SKILLS AND EXPERIENCE ▪ The best qualifications for these positions can be found among professionals who, by training and background, share a common body of expertise, interest, and experience even if they require different backgrounds and skill sets. Desirable candidates might be lawyers specialized in taxation (particularly for the tax position) or other fields with an economics orientation. They might be seasoned senior staff members of relevant congressional committees, especially those that oversee the work of these four Treasury offices. They might be highly trained, experienced economists who have taken a part in shaping federal policy, macro or micro, in such areas as taxation or interest rates; some have helped write legislation in these areas. Still others are people who have been at the receiving end of government policymaking and understand its impact on markets and on investment and business decisions.

Beyond those kinds of professional competence required by the jobs, their occupants stress broader, personal capacities. An ability to spot emerging issues and pursue them aggressively, for example. An inclination to find any public policy issue interesting from an economic perspective and explore its implications for policy. A tactical sense of how to achieve a desired outcome. Finally, recognition that far-ranging, fast-moving changes characteristic of market economies everywhere should not obscure, or alter, the principles of fairness, balance, and integrity basic to economic policymaking and regulation.

▒ **Assistant Secretary for Economic Policy**

David Wilcox, who came to this job in 1997, says his work falls into two categories. On the microeconomic side, as he outlines it, the Office of Economic Policy (OEP) advises Treasury's secretary and deputy secretary on domestic issues not covered elsewhere in the department. He thinks of this as the "all other" portfolio. "We don't have lead responsibility for most international issues. We don't sell the national debt to the public, because there's another assistant secretary who handles that. I don't keep the nation's checkbook, because Treasury has a fiscal assistant secretary. I don't have responsibility for regulating the banks, because there's an assistant secretary for financial institutions."

So what's left? "In my view," Wilcox says, "the best portfolio in the department, a rich mix of mainly domestic economic issues" that notably focuses on policy surrounding Social Security and Medicare. That's important for two reasons. First, the secretary of the treasury is managing trustee of the trust funds of Social Security and Medicare and is staffed in that role by this assistant secretary. Second and more consequential, Wilcox's office analyzes the current flow of proposals to reform both programs—aimed at securing their long-term solvency—and develops the Treasury Department's position. Lead responsibility for that task has always centered on this position, Wilcox notes, and has consumed half to two-thirds of the time he has been at the department. The solvency issue, he is certain, will continue to be a very active one for the next administration.

Still in the microeconomic category, the OEP (with a staff of thirty-five) has been very active in "formulating the administration's overall budget strategy," including debt reduction, spending proposals, and the implications of alternative tax cut approaches. There is a long spectrum of other issues. To illustrate, Wilcox mentions two. One is proposed legislation that would put the federal government into the business of reinsuring private companies hit by catastrophic natural disaster. This is a typical proposal on which the OEP counsels the department's leadership; in this case, the fundamental question is whether it is a good idea for the federal government to take on what Wilcox calls a significant contingent liability. Second is a Treasury initiative to "promote personal financial literacy"—an effort to get Americans to prepare more carefully for their own retirement. On this subject, Wilson explains, "economic incentives have been historically inadequate. They don't seem to be enough to induce people to engage in careful financial planning." Something more is needed, "perhaps like the social marketing campaigns that have encouraged more people to fasten their seat belts or reduce their smoking."

As for the macroeconomic dimension, Wilcox says his office is responsible for analyzing the current overall economic situation—such as employment and gross domestic product data and wage and inflation information—and "trying to synthesize all that into a coherent picture for the secretary and deputy secretary." Here there is a "tricky" division of labor between his office and the international side of the department. Exchange rate issues, for example, are the province of the international side. But the implications of exchange rates for the U.S. economy, in such areas as output, employment, and inflation, belong to the OEP.

"One enormous challenge I face every day is figuring out what my priority that day needs to be," Wilcox says. "And that's a mix of how important the issue is, per se, and how big an impact I think I can have on it." Some issues with less significance on the national agenda are those where he thinks he can have a disproportionately positive influence, and he tries to make room for them. "There are other issues of just a surpassing importance, in my realm anyway," like Social Security and Medicare or budget strategy, and these "obviously have a huge claim" on his time.

"There is clearly ten times more that could be done than can be done," he says. Given the time constraints, that presents a second challenge, and one that faces most federal managers at this level. Wilcox expresses it as "gaining maximum leverage on the outcome, since for any significant issue, a number of people are interested in influencing it. How do you most effectively integrate into the process and figure out where the leverage points are?"

Perhaps more than for some other positions, Wilcox predicts that "the portfolio of the next occupant of this office will be very dependent on the agenda of the next administration." It will, he says, be driven by what is happening in the Congress and by the objectives of the president and secretary of the treasury. "There are a thousand constructive things yet to do in government and there are big challenges waiting for this job," Wilcox says.

He thinks his position requires a Ph.D. economist. But, he says, "you have to be prepared in a way that a doctoral education doesn't ingrain in you. You have to think about tactical issues to a much greater degree. How do I think about accomplishing my objectives within the administration? How do I think about positioning the administration vis-à-vis the various blocs that may be active on these issues on Capitol Hill? What are the outside interests in industry or state government or elsewhere that may have a bearing on them?"

▨ Assistant Secretary for Tax Policy

Helping to design the tax policies that an administration wants to pursue is the central mission of this job. From it derive other closely related tasks, outlined by Donald Lubick, who held the position from 1996 to 1999.

First, to present administration tax policies to the Congress and seek their adoption, defending them meanwhile against proposals that would dilute, defeat, or otherwise alter their objectives. Second, to stay in constant touch with the concerns of major stakeholders in U.S tax policy and the professional associations and to lobby groups that represent them—taxpayers, business and industry, lawyers, accountants, investors, and more.

Third, to work with international organizations and individual countries in negotiating tax treaties and, equally vital, to reconcile conflicts in international tax policy and resolve situations that jeopardize fiscal management in developed economies. Lubick says the Office of Tax Policy plays an important role in the Organization for Economic Policy and Development, now moving much more energetically than in the past to establish international principles of tax policy.

Fourth, to support technical assistance in tax matters to nascent market economies in the former Soviet bloc and to developing countries elsewhere. Fifth, to analyze economic and legal policy involved in domestic and international tax decisions and supply revenue estimates for development of the annual federal budget.

The OTP (with a staff of about one hundred and thirty that includes twenty-five to thirty lawyers and forty economists) also has a key function with respect to the Internal Revenue Code. It sets policy criteria that underlie administration of the code and, with the Internal Revenue Service, prepares the applicable regulations. In fact, says Lubick, an important part of the OTP job is the maintenance of good relationships with the IRS, with which the OTP has always been a close partner. The OTP is the IRS's chief spokesman in the Congress on any matters of law, "including the procedural tools available to them to enforce the tax laws."

Lubick, who has served several tours at Treasury, is concerned by what he saw during his most recent stint as a tendency to "substitute tax policy for what otherwise would be expenditure programs." This, he says, was an administration break with traditional tax reform views held by occupants of this job under both parties, "which were to try to reduce the role played by taxation." He traces the change partly to the legacy of budget crises in the past ten or twelve years, "when spending programs were taboo." As a result, he says, "people tend to use the tax system to accomplish the same thing. They propose very appealing-sounding tax credits, or deductions, going for things that are inherently good, whether in education or housing or health. That plays havoc with the ability to administer the tax code and the efficiency of delivering programs." While no one could argue that such moves aim at desirable goals, "in most cases it's dubious that they are efficient in accomplishing those purposes. The Internal Revenue Service is not the agency to run policy in health, housing, mineral exploration policy, or whatever."

Lubick identifies several other major issues engaging this job:

—Harmful tax competition stemming from unfair practices by other countries. Typically, this involves "problems of bank secrecy," where a lot of potential tax revenue disappears in schemes to shift the tax base from developed countries into no-tax haven countries around the world. Lubick says the Organization for Economic Cooperation and Development is making a U.S.-led effort to remedy this. It's slow going, he adds, because "everything is voluntary and you can't pass a law."

—The impact of electronic commerce on the tax base. "A lot of the tax base may be disappearing into cyberspace," Lubick fears. Offshore operations to evade taxes are not new. But he says "it's very hard to figure out where profits are earned if you conduct your transactions in the Cayman Islands or someplace similar through electronic communication." He calls this a very serious problem which, again, the United States leads other OECD members in investigating.

—Tax revenue losses to the states in Internet-based commerce. "There has been a lot of talk about not killing the Internet with taxation," says Lubick. "I think everyone agrees there should not be discriminatory taxation." The OTP tries to sustain the principle that taxes "should be as neutral as possible. But that doesn't mean there shouldn't be any. The idea is to help the states protect their revenues on a nondiscriminatory basis." The OTP therefore has stepped in as a broker between the business community and the states and localities "to develop a system that would prevent discrimination against either way of doing business, whether it's e-commerce or bricks-and-mortar sales."

—Proposed revisions to the Social Security System. "It's financed by payroll taxes," Lubick points out. The OTP is not necessarily the lead player here. But on the question of partially privatizing the system, it has developed proposals "that don't change basic Social Security benefits but do set up broad-based individual savings accounts that we think are a middling approach to much of what has been suggested."

—The "proliferation of corporate tax shelters, which are seriously eroding the base" and proposals to repeal the estate tax or the income tax itself. At this writing, the House of Representatives has voted to eliminate the tax on personal estates over a period of about nine years. Lubick thinks that "assaults on the progressive nature of the income tax" are a matter nearly certain to confront the next administration as well.

He sees two chief issues for the future, however. Whether there should be tax cuts, or whether the federal budget surplus should be used instead for spending or debt reduction, "is going to be number one." Number two is "what is going to be done about Social Security taxes" as part of the overall resolution of the problem of continued solvency.

"I think the notion of the neutral tax system really means that the OTC is the ultimate protector of the free market, because it is trying to prevent the tax code from regulating the economy," Lubick reflects. "That's the role it has taken."

■ Assistant Secretary for Financial Markets

This is primarily a policy position. Its occupant focuses on management of the federal debt, federal policy for the regulation of capital markets, and federal responses to events in those markets. The latter two responsibilities are exerted mainly through the President's Working Group on Financial Markets, whose steering committee is chaired by this assistant secretary.

Included in these duties, says Lee Sachs, who came to the job in 1999, is that of advising the secretary on "basically anything to do with financial markets, which can span a pretty broad range." At the moment, that mostly means U.S. domestic markets. Whether it may one day also take on an international dimension depends, Sachs thinks, "on who's in this office and who's in some of the positions on the international side" of the Treasury Department in the next administration. There is, of course, an inherent interaction between the two and Sachs has taken an active part in international market discussions.

"This job is really split into two parts," Sachs says. "There's the market side—financing the government, the President's Working Group on Financial Markets, the financial markets. The other is the government financial policy side, which is essentially the lending side of the Treasury." In the financial policy area, "we oversee such entities as the Federal Financing Bank, which lends to other government agencies, and the Community Adjustment and Investment Program" (part of the North American Development Bank, which is concerned with the impact of changing trade patterns resulting from the North American Free Trade Agreement).

On the debt management front, Sachs says much of his office's work has related to "the welcome task of financing the government in an era of surplus as opposed to an era of deficit"—a different set of strategies than what has been required in the past.

In that connection, some observers note the recent odd juncture between the Treasury Department's plan to reduce the federal debt and efforts of the Federal Reserve to forestall inflation by raising short-term interest rates. The Treasury operation has involved buying back billions of dollars' worth of previously issued long-term bonds and cutting back on issuing new ones. That drove up the price of long terms, at least in the first half of 2000, dropping their yields below the short-term rates the Fed was raising. This unusual inverted yield curve meant that borrowers—who normally go to the short-term markets and whom the Fed was trying to restrain by raising short-term rates—could simply turn to the long-term market for lower rates, adding fuel to the economy.

Some bond market observers worried during 2000 that this could weaken the effect of Federal Reserve interest rate changes on the economy. Depending on how the situation has evolved by early 2001, these seeming cross-purposes of Treasury and the Fed would clearly be on the agenda of the newly elected administration and specifically, of course, as a policy challenge on the desk of the next assistant secretary in this job.

Sachs notes projections that the publicly held national debt will be paid off by 2015. "There are real challenges associated with that," he says. We have to figure out how to do it in a way that minimizes the impact on the capital markets and minimizes the cost to the taxpayer." Meanwhile, he notes, the acceleration in technology development is sweeping through U.S. and international markets and significantly altering their structure. "The changes are coming very quickly. We must be in a position to address the policy issues arising from that and assure that our markets remain the most competitive in the world. The pace at which some overseas markets are catching the U.S. market in terms of efficiency is apparent."

Treasury, of course, does not regulate financial markets (that's the job of the Securities and Exchange Commission, discussed elsewhere in this chapter, and the Commodities Futures Trading Commission). As a policymaker, however, Sachs recommends legislative, regulatory, and other measures and says there are implications for his office in much of what takes place in securities markets and how they develop. Treasury has pushed, for example, for legislation on market development aimed at preventing other markets from surpassing those in the United States. "You wouldn't want to cause one of the fastest-growing markets in the world to be based in London or Frankfurt, as opposed to New York or Chicago, just because we have an inefficient regulatory structure," he says. "While the current framework here in the United States remains outdated, markets overseas are developing in a legal and regulatory environment that allows greater efficiency, transparency, and liquidity. This is the result of a more rational regulation and an environment of legal certainty."

The potential systemic risk posed by out-of-control hedge funds and by the derivatives market, as demonstrated by events in the fall of 1998, offers another example. There were many calls, Sachs says, for regulation of hedge funds and derivatives. Among others, the question was taken up by the President's Working Group on Financial Markets, producing two sets of recommendations in 1999 for legislative and other measures to counter the problem (no regulation of hedge funds, a change in regulatory structure for over-the-counter derivatives). Sachs and his colleagues spent considerable time in 2000 trying to get these measures put into place.

"Much of the follow-up to those recommendations is something my successor will have to handle," he says. "We're doing everything we can to implement as much of it as possible this year. But these issues don't go away. The challenge is to establish a regulatory framework that will strike a balance between allowing the economy to realize more fully the benefits of innovation, transparency, and efficiency and, at the same time, ensuring the integrity of the underlying markets, providing appropriate protection for retail customers and, where possible, taking steps to mitigate systemic risk."

Assistant Secretary for Financial Institutions

"This office spends a lot more time on Capitol Hill than most," says Gregory Baer, assistant secretary since late 1999. "We're congressionally focused. We're sort of unique within Treasury in that we're almost purely a legislative policy office."

An excellent case in point is the huge effort invested by Baer and his office in passage of the Financial Services Modernization Act, which became law in late 1999. It permits affiliations between banks and companies engaged in the full range of financial activities—brokering, dealing in securities, merchant banking, sponsorship of mutual funds, and selling and underwriting insurance. It was the first financial services reform since 1933, superseding the much-criticized, much-debated Glass-Steagall Act as the governing statute in this domain. The new law, Baer says, "allows greater synergies by letting banks, investment banks, and insurance companies merge and provide a financial supermarket." Passing it had been "the primary mission of this office for twenty years."

The law added new scope to Baer's office: regulatory authority—a role the office did not have before. "Along with the Federal Reserve," Baer says, "we now decide what new financial activities will be permitted for U.S. financial institutions." While the new statute already sets out a long list of these, requests for additional kinds of operations "come to us and the Fed and we jointly decide." His office also has a policy (but not a regulatory) responsibility for government-sponsored enterprises such as Fannie Mae and Freddie Mac.

It is doing increasing work in the area of electronic commerce, a good deal of which, says Baer, "is really financial services online—how payments are made; and on the security of online payments. Clearly, the move of the financial services industry online is going to create a whole new set of issues," he predicts, "around safety, soundness, and consumer protection." A lot of the issues that were resolved earlier with laws to deal with them "are now going to be reopened as we go online. Bank supervisors obviously have a bigger job, looking at the big picture, and so do we." When we talked with him, Baer's office had just spent considerable time on digital signature legislation that was then working its way through the Congress. In June the Electronic Signatures in Global and National Commerce Act—what Baer calls "the first real e-commerce financial services bill"—passed the House and Senate and was signed by the president. "We're pretty heavily focused on financial privacy and consumer protection issues," Baer also points out. Where privacy is concerned, the imperative that individuals should control the use of personal information must be balanced against the need to allow financial entities to serve their customers. "There's pretty strong tension," Baer says of this question, "and it's not going away."

Another major concern, one Baer says might be his favorite project, is "critical infrastructure protection"—defense against computer hackers. Mandated by a presidential directive on protecting civilian infrastructures, the Treasury Department and his office lead the effort to help the financial services sector defend its computer systems.

"We work closely with information security people in all the large financial service firms," Baer says. One product of this is establishment of a computer defense center for the industry. According to Baer, about thirty of the largest firms have formed a limited liability company "to share computer attack information with each other on a real-time basis" through the center (exact location not disclosed). If Bank X gets broken into or experiences a new virus, he says, it messages the center with technology that protects the bank's identity; the center then redistributes the information to each member. "What the center is really about is giving them a heads-up, some time, and advice," Baer points out. "Time is just as important as technology."

He hopes the center will extend to include medium-sized and small banks. "We think the value is even better for a medium-sized bank because it doesn't cost very much and they'll be able to get advice virtually free. They'll have somebody to call and get analysis." If hacker and virus penetration on the Internet continue at the same pace, Baer says, "we'll be spending more and more time on it." With funding he has received for the purpose, he plans to add a member to his small staff of about thirty, who will specialize in electronic security issues.

In his position, Baer says, "you have to be willing to work fantastically hard. You have things you have to do. But at Treasury there really is a kind of free marketplace for ideas. So if you want to be effective in this job, you've got to imagine new issues and go after them. The great thing is that there is a never-ending series of things to do. You just have to realize their importance and work hard on them."

PROFILE

Current Assistant Secretary for Economic Policy
David W. Wilcox, 1997–

Career summary
Senior economist, Division of Monetary Affairs, Federal Reserve Board, 1986–97
Senior economist, President's Council of Economic Advisers

Education
B.A., Williams College, 1980; Ph.D., Massachusetts Institute of Technology, 1987

Assistant Secretaries for Economic Policy since 1989

Clinton administration
Joshua Gotbaum, 1995–97 (currently executive associate director and controller, Office of Management and Budget)
Alicia Munell, 1993–95 (currently Peter F. Drucker Chair in Management Series, Finance Department, Boston College)

Bush administration
Sidney L. Jones, 1989–93 (currently adjunct faculty, Brookings Institution)

PROFILE

Current Assistant Secretary for Tax Policy
Jonathan Talisman (acting), 1999–*

Career summary
Deputy assistant secretary for tax policy, 1997–99
Chief minority tax counsel, Senate Finance Committee, 1994–97
Legislation counsel, Joint Committee on Taxation, U.S. Congress, 1992–94
Akin, Gump, Strauss, Hauer, and Feld, 1984–92

Education
B.S., University of Virginia, 1981; J.D., University of Virginia School of Law,
    1984
*Not interviewed for this profile

Assistant Secretaries for Tax Policy since 1989

Clinton administration
Donald Lubick, 1996–99 (currently consultant)
Leslie B. Samuels, 1993–96 (currently partner, Cleary, Gottlieb, Steen,
    and Hamilton)
Fred T. Goldberg Jr., 1992–93 (currently partner, Skadden, Arps, Slater,
    Meagher, and Flom)

Bush administration
Kenneth W. Gideon, 1989–92 (currently partner, Wilmer, Cutler,
    and Pickering)

PROFILE

Current Secretary for Financial Markets
Lee Sachs, 1999–

Career summary
Deputy assistant secretary for government financial policy, U.S. Treasury,
    1998–99
Bear, Stearns, and Company, 1985–98: senior managing director, 1991–98;
    senior managing director, head of global capital markets, 1993–98;
    board of directors, 1994–98

Education
B.A., Denison University, 1985

Assistant Secretaries for Financial Markets since 1997

Clinton administration

Gary Gensler, 1997–99 (currently under secretary for domestic finance,
 U.S. Department of Treasury)

Darcy Bradbury, 1995–97 (currently affiliated with Bankers Trust Company)

PROFILE

Current Assistant Secretary for Financial Institutions
Gregory A. Baer, 1999–

Career summary

Deputy assistant secretary for financial institutions policy, U.S. Treasury,
 1997–99

Managing senior counsel, Board of Governors, Federal Reserve
 System,1990–97

Associate, Williams, and Connolly, 1987–90

Education

B.A., University of North Carolina, 1984; J.D., Harvard University Law
 School, 1987

Assistant Secretaries for Financial Institutions since 1989

Clinton administration

Richard Scott Carnell, 1993–99 (currently Associate Professor of Law,
 Fordham University School of Law)

Deborah J. Danker (acting), 1992–93 (current position not available)*

Jerome H. Powell, 1991–93 (currently managing director, Carlyle Group)*

Bush administration

David W. Mullins Jr., 1988–90 (currently partner, Long Term Capital
 Management)*

*Served in the function before creation of assistant secretary position

Comptroller of the Currency

EXECUTIVE LEVEL III—Presidential appointment with
Senate confirmation

RECOMMENDED SKILLS AND EXPERIENCE ■ Significant experience in finance is the first consideration. But Eugene Ludwig, comptroller from 1993 to 1998, attaches a warning: "If you take someone who is is rooted in Wall Street but has no sense of how Washington works, it would be pretty tough sledding." Sensitivity for "the political complexity of the federal system," he emphasizes, is just about mandatory. By similar logic, choosing an individual who knows the capital but lacks a "feel and touch for finance" would be an equally bad move.

Both Ludwig and John Hawke Jr., the current comptroller, are lawyers— the next most critical background to look for in filling this job. Ludwig spent two decades in banking law and financial transactions. Hawke, who held the position on a recess appointment for nearly a year before beginning a full five-year term in 1999, was previously the Treasury under secretary for domestic finance. Among earlier posts, he headed the financial practice of a leading Washington law firm, later becoming its chairman, and served as general counsel to the Federal Reserve's Board of Governors.

One further point: another former comptroller once described this position as "something of an anomaly," because it is "largely free of executive branch control and accountable to the Congress to some degree." While the job is distinctive in those respects, Ludwig says, it is also a part of the administration. In it, he felt free to express his own views, act on them, and "if we disagreed, just go my own way, but try to give honest advice and help." It seems clear that potential nominees should be assessed for their skill in handling these intricacies, bringing what Ludwig calls "an independent and forceful voice" to federal management of the U.S. financial system.

INSIGHT ■ Comptroller appointments run five years, a fact that primarily reflects the job's function as a regulator, but also its importance to the health of a major national industry and its semiautonomy within the executive branch. The comptroller's chief mission is to maintain a sound, competitive national banking system through regulation of 2,600 federally chartered commercial banks (but not state-chartered institutions) and nearly seventy U.S.-based based branches or agencies of banks overseas.

That domain represents nearly 60 percent of the assets of the U.S. commercial banking system. Mandated to see that national banks serve the best interests of their customers, comply with the law, and don't endanger the security of the U.S. banking system, the Office of the Comptroller of the Currency—OCC—employs a nationwide examiner staff of 1,900. The OCC exerts its authority through annual, on-site examination of national banks and their trust activities and operations abroad. That, the OCC says, covers a bank's loans and investments, capital earnings, funds management, liquidity, sensitivity to market risk, and compliance with such consumer banking laws as the Community Reinvestment Act of 1977.

The agency also brings enforcement action against those not in compliance with regulations and the law; approves or denies applications for new bank charters, branches, or mergers; and issues rules or decisions governing banking practices such as investments, lending, or community development activities. Under the Community Reinvestment Act, for example, the OCC every two years evaluates a bank's record in helping meet the credit requirements of its community, including low- and moderate- income areas, and uses that information in considering any future requests by the bank to expand, merge, or relocate.

Beyond oversight of the OCC, the comptroller serves a concurrent term as a director of the Federal Deposit Insurance Corporation and of two other lesser-known entities—the Federal Financial Institutions Examinations Council and the Neighborhood Reinvestment Corporation—and is a member of the Basel international committee that sets worldwide bank supervision standards. Created in 1863 by the National Currency Act (later reenacted as the National Bank Act), the OCC is independently funded through assessments on the assets of national banks. The banks also pay for OCC processing of their corporate applications and for its yearly examinations that are supervised through six OCC district offices. Revenue also comes to the agency from its investments, mostly in U.S. Treasury bonds.

In a development familiar to many federal agencies, the Internet is briskly changing the sector on which the OCC focuses, revising at the same time some of the factors the comptroller must take into account. It's an experience familiar to many other federal agencies. "Financial institutions are, at their core, information businesses," says Ludwig, "and what's going on worldwide is a revolution in information technology. Of all businesses, financial services are the most affected." Among individuals, he explains, finance is really "a trading of claims." While claims are physically represented by cash and checks from time to time, "they're fundamentally virtual." The lightning advance of information technology, therefore, is also a major development for finance and banking. In fact, the OCC created the first Internet bank—"just another step in the modernization of banking," says Ludwig, one that for his organization changes the kind of examination it conducts and requires different examiner skills. "Thus far," he says, Internet banking "is more about a new means of distribution, as opposed to a new set of products. Ultimately, there will be a new product set as well. But we're not quite there yet."

Does he think that providing banking services online will present uncontrollable risks over time? "The answer is no. There have been some minuscule hiccups to date and there may be some minor ones along the way, viewed over the course of history. But provided that proper encryption is maintained, "it's not an area that should cause immense concern." Ludwig does think, however, that those involved in federal management of the financial system should do some hard thinking about the impact of increased volatility in financial markets, which is a product of globalization and the very fast speed at which information now moves.

Historically, bank examiners operated with a checklist and tended, especially if time was short, to give equal weight to all of its items. While the items were far from nonsensical, Ludwig relates, they were not organized—triaged—in any particular way. Since the value of supervising a bank is to lower its risk of failure, he felt examiners should really be looking first at the areas that seemed riskiest, while continuing to spot- check the others. As comptroller, he set up a system for large banks that begins by identifying what looks risky and establishes an examination schedule for a given bank for the following year. Based on experience, data from the bank in question and from the home office, and the perceived risk in the bank's various activities, the planned examination is fine-tuned and cleared in Washington, then shared with the bank.

"Very frequently," Ludwig recalls, "a bank would tell us it thought our third priority should really be our first priority and wanted us to take a hard look at it. The very good banks actually view examination as a symbiotic relationship because it's a double check on what they're doing." He says this "supervision by risk" approach "has been adopted by every federal agency and became a model, through the Basel committee, for adoption worldwide." The English Financial Supervisory Authority, he adds, is currently using it.

Interaction between the OCC and the Congress is intense. Ludwig thinks he probably testified twenty to thirty times a year. "I always assumed that if you were successful from a policy perspective, regardless of partisanship, everyone would cheer. But I found there were some who did not view success as necessarily a good thing. When banks fail, and there will always be failures irrespective of how much better the OCC does, the natural re-action is to point fingers and claim that the regulatory mechanism was asleep on the job. But the whole nature of the insurance mechanism we have and of a dynamic market economy, which we want to have, bespeaks of some limited failures from time to time."

Some of those who have held this job have portrayed it as confidential and apolitical in nature, such that a comptroller seen to favor one party over another will destroy its credibility. Ludwig agrees, but says "the apo-litical notion is often thrown around by those who would like you to be apolitical as long as it means apolitical for someone else." The comptrol-ler's office is a particularly unusual federal regulator, he reminds us—"the one financial supervisor that is actually part of the administration." On one hand for the comptroller's consideration are what might be called the general policy responsibilities of the administration. On the other, the "specific individual institutional responsibilities that must have absolutely nothing to do with any kind of view expressed by the administration." For the comptroller, that's "an important balancing act, and not an easy one."

The history of the job reveals, says Ludwig, a record of attempts more often than not to put the comptroller at the service of the Treasury Depart-ment or the president. He believes that is "a very bad thing." There is usu-ally tension, in fact, between the comptroller and the secretary or deputy secretary of the Treasury. "That's always been true." But he emphasizes that the comptroller's role within the community that manages federal responsibilities for the national financial system, plus the job's close super-vision of the examining function, contribute "experience and vision that is tremendously valuable." Happily, he says, during his time in the job, no one in the administration tried "in the least way" to influence an OCC exami-nation of, or policies directly related to, an individual institution.

What's on the OCC agenda for the future? Ludwig notes that the finan-cial modernization legislation of 1999, which allows banks to expand their traditional activities to areas like brokerage services, "puts the congressional stamp of approval on what financial institutions can offer and how they offer them." What it did not do, he says, is "remake the regulatory mecha-nism." Instead, "it tried to make a patchwork on the regulatory mechanism that exists." He therefore thinks the next administration, of whatever party, will face many of the same issues the OCC has been dealing with, "but in sort of a different way. They'll be dealing with a somewhat changed landscape"—the extended operating sphere for banks—with largely un-changed regulatory authority, a task he says will be "quite challenging."

The next comptroller, he suggests, should "be prepared to have an agenda, a program within the bounds of the law, and should try to carry it out and fulfill the responsibilities of the job. That doesn't always make you popular; it's most likely to make you unpopular at any given moment with almost everybody, including, at times, the people who put you in office. But as long as you're doing that in a straightforward way with some sensitivity for others' duties, the right thing, and the issue is not you but what you think your own responsibilities are, I think you can pretty well execute without blowing yourself up."

To illustrate the point, Ludwig tells the story of an encounter with a member of Congress who "had been egged on to investigate some minor thing related to what the office was doing." When the investigation concluded, he called the member up and said, "Look, I'm proud of what we did. I think we did the right thing here. This was a good program." At the end of the conversation, the member said he thought the OCC had done the right thing, too. "And, Ludwig says, "that's the way I think you have to proceed."

PROFILE

Current Comptroller of the Currency
John D. Hawke Jr., December 1998 (recess appointment); October 1999
   (five-year appointment)

Career Summary
Under secretary of the Treasury for domestic finance, 1995–98
Various positions–chairman, senior partner, head of financial institutions
   practice, associate–at Arnold and Porter, 1962–75 and 1978–95
General counsel, Board of Governors of the Federal Reserve System, 1975–78
Counsel, House Select Subcommittee on Education, 1961–62

Education
B.A., Yale University, 1954; J.D., Columbia University School of Law, 1960
*Not interviewed for this profile

Comptrollers of the Currency since 1989

Clinton administration
Eugene Ludwig, 1993–98 (currently managing partner, Promontory
   Capital Group)

Bush administration
Robert L. Clarke, 1985–92 (current position not available)

Federal Emergency Management Agency

▨ Director

EXECUTIVE LEVEL II—Presidential appointment with
Senate confirmation

RECOMMENDED SKILLS AND EXPERIENCE ■ The only person
to head the Federal Emergency Management Agency with any prior experience in this field is James Lee Witt, who led the Arkansas Office of
Emergency Services before becoming FEMA's director in the spring of
1993. That might partly explain the agency's reputation before he arrived
as a backwater institution incapable of effective performance. It stands to
reason, in any case, that Witt's successor should be an excellent manager
with significant firsthand exposure to the requirements of emergency preparedness and response to natural and manmade disaster.

For that background, it hardly needs pointing out, the best places to look
are clearly the offices of emergency response in the states and localities,
which run the bulk of such efforts in this country. Candidates for the job
should have at least some of the specific expertise (budget management,
flood insurance, intergovernment coordination) and skills (political sensitivity, community and media relations) that will allow them to get a running start. More than usually, this is a job where it pays handsomely to have
direct experience, not just political compatibility, in the driver's seat.

INSIGHT ■ What is "emergency management?" As redefined by today's
FEMA, it is a four-part process that begins with preparedness for emergencies and disasters and continues through response and recovery to mitigation—easing or eliminating the long-term effects on people and property. It
is the director's job to coordinate these elements, including the work that
up to thirty federal agencies may contribute as well as activities in any given
emergency of the American Red Cross and other voluntary agencies. The
agency's chief also supervises the National Flood Insurance Program and
the U.S. Fire Administration.

FEMA's turnaround, from laughing stock in 1993 to frontline success
(outlined elsewhere in this book), has often been set out as an example of
creative leadership, of reinvention, of outreach to customers, of sheer resolve to make things work on the part of an agency in the process of rebirth.
It was, in fact, all of those things. It was a question of replacing "very

serious stove piping" with "a flatter, more functional organization," Witt says. It was identifying those parts of the agency that needed elimination, "reestablishing" areas we felt would be the focal point for where we wanted to go." It was bringing together senior career managers for three days at the beginning to set new priorities and "rework our mission statement." It was telling highly skeptical members of the Congress, governors, county officials, and mayors—one by one—that FEMA now meant business. And, over time, it was a question of providing the evidence.

There was a lot more. What Witt expresses now is the hope that "when I leave, we'll have institutionalized a lot of the changes we've made and that they will be continued for some time." An example of what he means is the appointment of disaster assistance employees, nonpermanent workers as-signed to FEMA headquarters and regions who are temporarily activated to meet surge requirements during emergencies. Another, with broad im-plications, is a new approach to reducing disaster damage that bases pre-ventive actions largely on local decision, brings in the private sector, and involves long-range planning and investment in prevention steps. Known as Project Impact, it is a nationwide public and private prevention partnership that, Witt says, has aroused substantial congressional support. In ten years, he predicts, it will make "a significant difference in lives saved, jobs saved, and reduction of the devastation we normally see in communities."

When the impact of a calamity—a flood, say, or an earthquake—outruns the ability of local and state governments to cope, presidents declare a major disaster and FEMA takes over. It activates its own response and coordinates it with all other federal, state, local, and nongovernment enti-ties that, depending on the nature of the emergency, may have pieces of the action. The range of immediate response activity is great: the provision of food, water, shelter, and electric power and the operation of fire, evacua-tion, and medical services. Later come the early steps to help individuals and institutions recover and rebuild and, in the case of flood disaster, the management of insurance claims in the 18,000 communities that partici-pate in the federal flood insurance program. FEMA also runs an extensive public communications program, one of whose key purposes is to keep people abreast of situations that pose real or potential threats, advise them of what is being done on their behalf, and tell them where to get help.

Perhaps even more important—in the context of Project Impact—are FEMA's preparation and prevention responsibilities before emergencies occur. Again, the scope is extensive—running a variety of training or edu-cation programs for citizens and emergency professionals alike, promoting the use of land and of smart building codes to minimize damage, helping communities develop plans for continuation of essential government services, urging businesses to design their own emergency management plans and showing them how, and furnishing research support for local fire and medical teams.

For added understanding of FEMA's world, consider the following FEMA-supplied facts and figures:

—As of May 2000, close to 180 presidentially declared disasters had occurred during Witt's time at the agency. They affected 3,655 counties in fifty states. Among these episodes were the country's most costly flood, the most costly earthquake, and a dozen hurricanes that inflicted damage. Since the late 1980s, more than 500 people were killed in events of this kind.

—All fifty states and eight U.S. territories are vulnerable to floods. Even though hard-to-predict chance floods occur only 1 percent of the time every year, FEMA estimates that better than nine million homes and other properties are at risk.

—U.S. coasts are hit by an average of five hurricanes every three years. Eighteen states on the east and gulf coasts are at greatest risk.

—Tornadoes, which affect nearly all states, are responsible for the greatest property damage in the central part of the country. Overall, severe windstorms are a major cause of U.S. fatalities and property loss.

—The United States has about sixty-five volcanoes, active or potentially active. When Mount St. Helens blew in 1980, it took sixty people and $1.5 billion in damage with it.

—This country has one of the highest rates of loss from fire among industrialized countries, in terms of both death and financial loss. In many areas, valuable real estate is exposed to frequent urban and forest fires.

—To these can be added landslides that occur in every state and endanger 40 percent of the population and the rapidly expanding threat of man-made incidents like the release of toxic materials. The worrying possibility of terrorist attacks poses problems of another order of magnitude.

At its headquarters and ten regional offices, FEMA's employs a full-time staff of 2,400 and about 7,000 disaster assistance employees. For fiscal year 2001, the agency asked the Congress for budget authority of $971 million and $2.6 billion in emergency contingency funds. Looking back, Witt thinks his work on the Hill in the early days was a central factor in revitalizing FEMA. "The one-on-one meetings with different committee members were the most critical factor. We basically said, this is what we have done to reorganize, these are the priorities we've set, and these are our goals and the drivers of our budget. They had that blueprint of what we wanted to do and where we were going. They could see it and their staffs could see it." Witt adds, however, that the twenty-six congressional committees to which FEMA reports represent a heavy burden in time and effort. He favors "refocusing" the committees and cutting the multiplicity of oversight.

In media relations, Witt resolved early to "be up front and truthful. If they request something, we're going to give it to them, whether it's good or bad. We're going to be flat honest with them." The improvement in press coverage of FEMA, in fact, was one of the notable features of the agency's comeback. "The media has been very, very good," Witt says today. "We've had some negative stories. But they've been fair."

At the outset of his tenure, he recalls, "I don't think Congress knew what mitigation and prevention were. Now they talk about it, want to do more of it. I don't think they or state and local officials will let it slow down. And that's really going to increase what we can do in that area." He identifies key future tasks for FEMA as (1) better preparation for the impacts of terrorist activity and (2) "dramatically" cutting the costs of disasters—getting people, communities, and states to assume more responsibility for how they build and where they develop." The job of protecting the environment will be "huge" as U.S. population shifts in the direction of the coasts. Many people don't understand that, if they protect the environment and "build better and safer," then the environment in turn will protect them. "There's a lot more to FEMA," Witt adds, "than just emergency management."

P R O F I L E

Current Director of the Federal Emergency Management Agency
James Lee Witt, 1993–

Career summary
Director, Arkansas Office of Emergency Services
County Judge, Yell County, Arkansas
Witt Construction Company, Arkansas

Directors of the Federal Emergency Management Agency since 1989

Bush administration
William C. Tidball, 1993 (retired)
Wallace E. Stickney, 1990–93 (retired)
Robert H. Morris (acting), 1989–90 (current position unavailable)

National Science Foundation

▓ Director

EXECUTIVE LEVEL II—Presidential appointment with
Senate confirmation

RECOMMENDED SKILLS AND EXPERIENCE ■ The NSF chief
should be a scientist or engineer of distinctive achievement, widely recognized in the science and technology communities. Direct experience in an academic environment as a teacher or basic researcher at the graduate level and the ability to manage a large organization are requisites. Beyond that, the individual selected for this job must understand the basics of emerging, fast-moving scientific disciplines as well as their actual or potential implications for society and U.S. scientific leadership. Rita Colwell, who took the NSF helm in 1998, has made this point more simply, quoting former professional hockey star Wayne Gretzky's maxim that "I skate to where the puck is going, not to where it's been."

INSIGHT ■ Colwell calls this job "one of the very best in government if you're a scientist or engineer." It's not difficult to imagine some of the reasons. First is the distinctive way in which the National Science Foundation operates, rooted in its history. As originally proposed, the NSF was to be an independent nongovernment foundation, operating with federal funding to support research and education in science and engineering. With President Truman maintaining that it could not be completely independent if it ran on federal money, the Congress created it in 1950 as an independent federal agency. A National Science Board, with twenty-four part-time members, representing science, engineering, industry, and the campuses, sets policy; the director runs the foundation. All are presidential appointees with six-year terms.

A second reason concerns the nature of the NSF's work. In 1999 Colwell called the foundation "a unique agency" in the federal research and development structure. Comparing her organization with other agencies that support R&D, she pointed out that the NSF does not have a mission-oriented research objective such as energy, oceans, biomedicine, agriculture, or space. "Instead, we have the mission to support and fund the underpinnings for all research disciplines and the connections between and among research disciplines."

Third is the NSF's approach to evaluating the 30,000 new or renewal proposals it receives each year for research, graduate and postdoctoral fellowships, and education projects in mathematics, science, and engineering. The foundation not only makes no attempt to dictate or specify the kinds of research it will support; it relies extensively on outside evaluators across the scientific, engineering, and education communities for peer review of proposals. Colwell says the NSF performs 250,000 reviews a year, using 50,000 reviewers. In the federal government, the National Institutes of Health is virtually the only other agency that takes this exterior approach to the proposal review responsibility.

According to the NSF, it makes about 9,000 new awards each year. They take the form of contracts, grants, and cooperative agreements with more than 2,000 colleges, universities, other kinds of education and research organizations, and small businesses everywhere in the country. That amounts to 20 percent of all federal support to academic institutions for basic research. "The responsibility is a very serious one," says Colwell. "The NSF funds 70 percent of the mathematics research done in the United States and a significant amount of engineering research. In some disciplines, it supplies perhaps all the available funding." While she says the White House Office of Science and Technology Policy sets the science and engineering agenda for the country, the NSF's funding decisions have a significant influence on the direction that agenda takes.

The NSF director works with the senior staff of seven NSF directorates, sits ex officio on the National Science Board and chairs its executive committee, represents the U.S. government in international science councils like that of the Group of Eight, and serves on a number of senior-level interagency committees. Interaction with the Congress is important, Colwell says, because legislators "need to understand what is being done, and why, and be a partner in the process." The country is at a juncture, she comments, where the value of basic research in science and technology and its linkage to national economic health "is probably the best understood" in recent history. "The NSF enjoys bipartisan support, strongly positive from both sides of the aisle. Our initiatives are recognized as truly national and not partisan." But she says the foundation must do a better job of informing some members of the Congress who "innately" understand that basic research is important but lack a fuller grasp.

For fiscal 2001, the NSF's budget submission asked for $4.57 billion, a 17.3 increase from fiscal 2000. For Colwell, resources are her major challenge. She puts first priority on "building a budget with strong rationale, fully justified, that is visionary and anticipatory of future needs and directions—and at the same time thoroughly grounded in good business practices." The foundation has developed "strong justification for the investments we propose in the budget. It's been a tough effort but a worthy one, and I think we've risen to it."

But she also thinks "we are dangerously underfunding basic research in this country." The NSF budget "absolutely has to be increased. We have a $1.8 trillion federal budget and yet we're the only agency whose mission is basic research across all disciplines." The NSF budget, she asserts, "really needs to be at least ten, if not twelve billion dollars, to be able to fund all the very good research we can't support now." The agency has underscored that its average grant in 1999 was $1,000 less in constant dollars than in 1963. While an average NSF grant falls somewhere between $75,000 and $90,000, Colwell says, National Institutes of Health grants average $250,000. "And an NSF grant runs about 2.8 years," she adds, "not long enough to graduate a Ph.D. student." Other issues that concern Colwell:

—Responding to all the opportunities. "You have to be sure you're hearing the voices of all the people who need to do, or benefit from, basic research in science, math, and engineering. We must craft our initiatives and budget in ways that allow us to pursue the opportunities fully and effectively, especially these unmet needs."

—Taking into account the increasing role of industry in basic research "and the connectedness with universities." Ensuring the ethical conduct of science—that research meets the highest standards and that taxpayer dollars, when assigned to institutions in the form of grants and contracts, are properly spent and not wastefully or wrongfully used."

—Greater "interdisciplinarity" of research. "Traditionally, until a decade or so ago, research was pretty much chemistry, physics, and math. Now it's biochemistry, nanotechnology, biocomplexity that involves physics, chemistry, math, biology, ecology, space science, and more. We have to find ways to evaluate proposals that rise above disciplinary segregation, break down the stove pipes, and bring integration."

—Education. "We're working hard on the best use of a billion dollars of the four billion we have to enhance science, math, and engineering education and performance of children in K-12. When you consider that $300 billion a year is spent on K-12 education, our $1 billion is not significant in terms of numbers. So we have to make sure it's very significant in its investment."

—Technology. "The NSF is at the forefront of change. We're the change makers. We took the Internet from the DARPA (Defense Advance

Projects Research Agency) net, expanded it to universities, and introduced it to the public at large. The NSF is responsible for Doppler radar and for magnetic resonance imaging." But this has also meant internal change—for example, the NSF became fully electronic. Within a year, "we expect to have all of our proposals and reviews done electronically, externally and internally."

The director of the NSF, Colwell says, "is responsible for somewhere between 1,100 and 1,500 employees," a number that includes contract employees. About a third of its scientists rotate in, typically from universities or under the Intergovernmental Personnel Act, to spend from two to six years at the foundation before returning to their institutions. They are generally people between thirty and fifty—an age range in which such tours of service away from their home bases can be disruptive of careers and families. But the cross-fertilizing effect of their work at the NSF may be another reason why Colwell likes her job. "It's like having a constantly young community, always addressing the cutting edge of science," she says.

Still, she repeats, returning to the resources theme, "the way we're doing the science is wasteful of people's time and effort." She would like to be able to support longer grants at a funding level equivalent to that of the NIH. As it now stands, "a young scientist is either writing a proposal or trying to write a paper to justify the renewal of a grant he or she has just received—because it takes a year to start up and the grant only runs for 2.8 years." That means that they are spending large amounts of time "chained to their PCs" that could be used for research. "And we, in turn, are spending a lot of time reviewing and handling the proposals here. That money could be spent funding more proposals," Colwell says. "To me, it's wasteful and even abusive of our young scientists. Congress can certainly stop this by increasing funding for the grants."

PROFILE

Current Director of the National Science Foundation
Rita R. Colwell, 1998–

Career summary
President, University of Maryland Biotechnology Institute, 1991–97
Professor of Microbiology, University of Maryland, 1972–97
Vice president for academic affairs, University of Maryland, 1983–87
Member, biology faculty, Georgetown University, 1963–72

Education

B.S. and M.S., Purdue University (1956; 1958); Ph.D., University of
Washington (1961)

Directors of the National Science Foundation since 1989

Clinton administration

Neal F. Lane, 1993–98 (currently assistant to the president for science and
technology policy)

Frederick M. Bernthal (acting), 1993 (currently president, Universities
Research) Association

Bush administration

Walter E. Massey, 1991–93 (currently president, Morehouse College)

Frederick M. Bernthal (acting), 1990–91 (currently president, Universities
Research Association)

Bush and Reagan administrations

Erich Bloch, 1984–90 (currently principal, Washington Advisory Group)

Securities and Exchange Commission

▨ Chairman

**EXECUTIVE LEVEL III—Presidential appointment with
Senate confirmation**

RECOMMENDED SKILLS AND EXPERIENCE ■ It's difficult to
imagine that anyone could perform effectively in this position without relatively close exposure over a significant period of time to the nature and
operation of U.S. securities markets. Among the first places to look for
potential SEC chairs is among the senior officers of major domestic stock
exchanges. Individuals with long experience, substantial track records, and
high-level responsibilities in established brokerage houses represent another
pool of possible candidates. But those who make the choice would do well
to look for one or more additional qualifications: a general familiarity with
the current U.S. regulatory environment; a grasp of how domestic and international market developments, the economy, and economic policy bear on
one another; experience with the Congress.

An understanding of accounting and auditing principles doesn't hurt, nor does media skill or legal training or practice. In fact, Arthur Levitt, whose second consecutive appointment as SEC chairman ends in mid-2003, says he is the second nonlawyer to hold the job. But Levitt's own background includes an eleven-year stint as chairman of the American Stock Exchange and many prior years on Wall Street. Note also that an SEC chair must be, and must be seen to be, completely nonpartisan and to act with impartiality and—need it be said?—total integrity.

INSIGHT ▪ Investing is not like banking. Unlike deposits in a checking or savings account, which up to a point are guaranteed by the federal government, nothing assures the future value of even the best-rated stocks and bonds. Nonetheless, in the late twentieth and early twenty-first centuries, vigorous economic growth and the longest stock market run-up in American history (and lately the most volatile) have persuaded more people than ever to invest in U.S. securities markets.

If they invest badly, or if the markets fall or fail, no government or other mechanism in this market economy will automatically restore investors to grace. What they do expect, however, is a chance to take their best shot— with the benefit of full information, truthfulness on the part of the securities industry, and a shield against outright fraud. That's, of course, where the Securities and Exchange Commission comes in. Protecting the interests of American investors, says Levitt, is his main job. After that, he says, "everything else falls into place."

Born in 1934 out of the hard lessons of the 1929 crash, the SEC is the primary overseer and regulator of U.S. securities markets. Its legislative mandates—the Securities Act of 1933 and the Securities Exchange Act a year later—embody two ideas. First, that the basic facts about a security, about who is offering it, and about the risks involved should be available to any investor, large or small, before purchase. Second, that brokers, dealers, and exchanges—those who sell and trade—must do it fairly and honestly and put investors' interests first.

Under the rules enforced by the SEC, public companies must disclose significant financial and other information about themselves and the securities they are offering. The commission also regulates the other important players: stock exchanges, brokers, advisers, public utility holding companies, and mutual funds, using its enforcement authority to sustain the integrity of the markets. Providing false information about a security or its issuer, using inside information to gain advantage in a purchase or sale, cooking the books to mislead or defraud investors—these are examples of violations that the commission routinely runs to earth. In a given year, it brings four or five hundred enforcement actions. SEC protective efforts focus not just on average American investors who put their money into stocks, mutual funds, or the occasional bond. They extend also to the sophisticated professionals attracted to the hedge funds, derivatives, futures, and other investment instruments whose values derive indirectly from the ebb and flow of markets and the interaction of changes in individual securities prices.

But since no agency of government, as Levitt reminds us, can by itself protect investors or consumers against fraud, enforcement activities have always been based on what he calls a "trilogy." These are the authority of the SEC itself, the powers of the self-regulating organizations—the various national stock exchanges and other markets—and the actions that private individuals can bring against alleged violators. "We believe those three elements give investors the best kind of protection possible," Levitt says. In this context, he mentions the commission's additional emphasis on educating investors "to be able to spot the kinds of problems that have hurt them in the past" and states that the current SEC is the first to give significant time and effort to educate investors to protect themselves. The effort has included about thirty-five town meetings around the country, in addition to a steady stream of investor alerts and educational materials.

The SEC has five commissioners, about 2,850 staff members around the country, including 1,500 in Washington, and eleven regional or district offices. Commissioners are appointed by the president and confirmed by the Senate to staggered five-year terms, with one commissioner's term ending each June 5. As is the case with certain other federal regulatory bodies, no more than three of the five can belong to the same political party. The president designates one of the five as chair. Commissioners meet regularly, in sessions normally open to the public and the press, to consider matters brought to them by the staff and to make decisions. Typically, they interpret the basic security laws as they apply to current issues, take enforcement measures, and engage in rule making—amending existing rules or proposing new ones to take account of developments in the securities markets.

One such development has been the impact of technology. "We're now dealing with electronic markets and international markets," Levitt says, "and we're determined to see that America's markets take advantage of this technology." He believes that a global stock exchange and twenty-four-hour-a-day trading are on their way. In this fast-moving environment, the commission "believes passionately in bringing about the best results for investors by stimulating and nurturing maximum competitive pressures to create efficiencies that will benefit investors." That may sound easy, "but it's very, very complex, particularly because technology has made things possible that could never have occurred before. The nature of the competition is no longer just the New York Stock Exchange, NASDAQ, and the bond market. So market structure is a critically important challenge."

And market structure is changing in ways that will dramatically redesign U.S. capital markets. As related in a *Washington Post* article, the directors of the New York Stock Exchange were persuaded by the NYSE's chairman late in 1999 to drop a rule that for generations had prevented the exchange's competitors from trading stocks that were central to the NYSE's own operations. In its place, the NYSE asked the SEC to forbid securities dealers from trading outside the auspices of a stock exchange unless they can offer better prices. Meanwhile, NASDAQ's chief was working on a plan to split NASDAQ from its parent National Association of Securities Dealers and turn it into a profit-making organization. Spurring both of these moves was the transforming influence of the Internet and electronic markets but, equally, the bully pulpit influence of the SEC chairman (about which more later). Levitt had made it clear in a public speech that the NYSE should drop the rule in question and followed that up with less-visible prompting. He had also made clear that, in the interest of their greater competitiveness, the NYSE and the NASDAQ should become for-profit enterprises. Further, Levitt has stated plainly—in an interview on the public television program *Wall Street Week,* for example—that the decimalization of stock prices would benefit investors.

Beyond the key mission to protect investors, Levitt sees his other chief duties as setting the agenda for the work of the commission ("making sure we're working on the right things at the right time") and acting as the SEC's "principal emissary to the outside world"—investors, the securities industry, other private-sector groups, the Congress, agencies in the federal government with which the commission works closely, state securities regulators, and foreign securities regulators and exchanges. In the international arena, the SEC makes a particular effort to get other countries where Americans invest to bring their disclosure and oversight requirements closer to those of the United States.

Reflecting on particular issues that the commission has faced, Levitt says American companies "are so competitive that when one of them begins to stretch the envelope in reporting their results, all their competitors do the same." So the SEC has put a particularly high priority on "seeing that the numbers investors are exposed to are accurate and reliable." One of its prime tactics on this front has been to go public when necessary—"speaking about it, even using humiliation, if you will." The commission also established a blue-ribbon committee that developed "standards for audit committees to monitor the reporting of numbers by publicly owned companies." It has done it by working with the accounting profession itself and, of course, through enforcement when companies have simply gone over the line.

"And I think the quality of reporting has improved considerably," Levitt says. "This is a cultural change and not one we can just attend to and forget about. It's one that future commissions will constantly have to review, to see that U.S. corporations develop the kind of cultural adherence to standards that benefit the public interest and capital formation."

Concerned for some time that compensation standards for brokers were "largely quantitative and not at all qualitative," the commission has encouraged brokerage firms to find different ways to reward their executives and move away from entirely quantitative compensation "that creates conflicts between the interests of investors and those of brokers." Again, it has done this "by speaking about it, writing about it." As a result, he asserts, increasing numbers of brokerage firms are using fee-based compensation.

A third SEC priority, Levitt says, has been the municipal bond markets—"kind of an oriental bazaar where investors weren't able adequately to determine what they were buying or how much they were paying." To deal with this, the commission set up an office of municipal affairs, enacted rules requiring more disclosure, and is urging the industry to go further "to bring the debt markets more in line with the disclosure standards of our equity markets."

He stresses the need for the SEC chairman to have broad and regular contact within American society generally, and especially with business and investor groups, labor, and the media. Different strategies exist to maintain these relationships. For example, "I call a dozen companies every week," he says, to ask them "how our service has been, if we processed their filings on time, are the questions we ask reasonable. That astonishes them. They aren't used to government being user friendly." The town meetings mentioned earlier, he says, "are intended to persuade investors that this is a government agency that doesn't just sit in Washington behind some barrier, but cares about bringing Pennsylvania Avenue to Main Street. We ask them if they have problems, if they have complaints, how can we help?"

Thinking about this kind of outreach, Levitt confesses that "the bully pulpit has surprised even me. It's an extraordinarily effective way of getting our message across."

PROFILE

Current Chairman of the Securities and Exchange Commission
Arthur Levitt, 1993–

Career summary
Chairman, New York City Economic Development Corporation, 1989–93
Chairman, American Stock Exchange, 1979–89
Various positions in the investment industry, 1963–79

Education
Williams College, B.A., 1952
Chairmen of the Securities and Exchange Commission since 1989

Bush administration
Richard C. Breeden, 1989–93 (currently president and CEO, Richard Breeden and Company)

5

Positions in Foreign Policy, National Security, and Defense

Agency for International Development

■ Administrator

EXECUTIVE LEVEL II—Presidential appointment with
Senate confirmation

RECOMMENDED SKILLS AND EXPERIENCE ■ Extended resi-
dence in the still-developing world is the single best qualification to lead
an agency that administers nonmilitary economic assistance and humanitarian help to dozens of them. USAID's current chief thinks the eight years
he lived in east Africa (Kenya and Tanzania) went a long way in helping
him understand the problems facing "powerless people" as well as what
it takes to help such countries stabilize themselves. But other kinds of experience are also important. The foremost is familiarity with the folkways
of Capitol Hill, where some legislators continue to question the utility of
foreign assistance, joining colleagues who have various other reasons to
restrain real growth in USAID funding. A USAID administrator who lacks
the background to make the agency's case in the Congress will need guidance from well-versed senior staffers. A close understanding of how and
where this agency fits into the official foreign policy community is especially valuable in light of the structural shifts of 1999, when USAID almost
went the way of the formerly independent Arms Control and Disarmament Agency and U.S. Information Agency. Diplomatic skill is an asset,
since the USAID administrator must lead the U.S. role in international crisis management, work with nongovernment assistance organizations, and
deal with counterpart foreign officials and agencies.

INSIGHT ■ Anyone running this agency needs to recognize that developing countries are this country's fastest growing export markets, expanding at the rate of 13 percent a year over the last decade and a half.
That compares with 9 percent U.S. market growth in the industrialized
world. USAID reports that in 1997 U.S. exports to developing countries
were $275 billion, up from $239 billion in the previous year. Six years
ago, the annual report of the U.S. Export-Import Bank showed that exports represented more than 25 percent of the U.S. gross domestic product. It estimated also that emerging markets in ten developing countries
would, by 2000, absorb 75 percent of the exports of all countries. A continuation of this phenomenon will, of course, depend on the continuing

advance of the developing world toward enduring economic health, mature democracy, and political stability.

The fact is that USAID is much more than a token of U.S. philosophical concern for the economic or political progress of less fortunate peoples. It directly serves the interests of the United States in a global economy on which this country heavily depends. Yet U.S. foreign assistance has for some years amounted to a bit less than half of 1 percent of total annual federal outlays—the lowest foreign USAID spending of any industrialized country. Former USAID director Brian Atwood made the point very succinctly: "Poor people can't buy American products."

The agency's origin traces to the U.S. role in the 1945–60 period in rebuilding western Europe and then buttressing it against the potential encroachment of Soviet communism. It came into official existence with the Foreign Assistance Act of 1961. While USAID functioned as an instrument of American cold war policy across the ensuing three decades, the agency today operates in a changing world, with a mission that is very different but even more urgent. To achieve what is termed sustainable development and assist U.S. foreign policy objectives, USAID works to support and protect the growth of market economies and agricultural development; population, health and nutrition; the environment; democracy and governance; education and training; and humanitarian assistance. The agency focuses on four areas—Africa, Asia and the Near East, Latin America and the Caribbean, Europe and Eurasia—including countries of the former Soviet bloc.

J. Brady Anderson, who took over this job in August 1999, thinks the new relationship between USAID and the State Department, in which the agency's administrator comes under the authority and foreign policy direction of the secretary of state, is better than what existed earlier. "My authorities now flow from the president through the secretary to me. Legally, there was more independence before. But as a practical matter, foreign policy is under the purview of the secretary of state." He points out that, unlike the former arms control agency and USIA, USAID is not a bureau of the State Department but a statutorily independent agency. Although he reports to the secretary, "it's healthy that we maintain an independence because our mission is a bit different than State's." USAID takes the longer view—democracy building, long-term program implementation—while State "is often more driven by crisis, a little more oriented to the short term." The relationship between the two is "really close," especially in the field, but State "is the 800-pound gorilla we're in bed with so we have to be nimble on our feet."

Working that out, he says, is in some senses the biggest issue he faces, "to ensure that everyone in the agency is focused in the right direction," the direction set by his seniors in the Oval Office and on the seventh floor at State. Within USAID, the world divides into several bureaus "and they naturally compete with one another for resources and for my time." That competition is healthy, he adds, and at the same time "it's important that we speak and act with one voice" that is consistent with what the rest of the foreign policy community is doing and saying.

A second particular challenge for USAID is the complex humanitarian emergencies arising from war. The agency answers the call when U.S. military forces are not involved, as in East Timor, and when they are, as in Kosovo. Describing the typical sequence, Anderson says it begins with a military engagement "where there has been death and, often, a lot of rape, and women and children who have been traumatized." There may be huge flows of refugees into neighboring countries. While the diplomats seek to halt the conflict, "you have to start feeding and treating the refugees." Later comes the transition from crisis to an intermediate stage of rebuilding and development that can take years. This kind of cycle, Anderson notes, is new in the world, and the U.S. and other governments are answering with new systems to deal with it. USAID, for example, set up an Office of Transition Initiatives within its Bureau of Humanitarian Response.

Addressing these contingencies, Anderson says, "is going to be something the United States, no matter who's in the White House, is going to have do more and more of. We have to be quick, we have to have the resources, we have to cooperate with other countries, we really have to know what we're doing."

Of all the diverse efforts in which USAID is involved around the world, it is the humanitarian crises—floods in Venezuela, Hurricane Mitch, earthquakes in Turkey—that inevitably capture most media interest. Anderson wishes the other issues on the agency's agenda got more coverage: for example, the development of democracy in Central America and such specific matters in that region as promoting bilingual education and micro enterprises. "Those things are really important," he says. "The problem is, does the press think it's important? Not so long ago there was civil war in El Salvador and Guatemala and we're trying to help them build." He thinks the press has an obligation to inform Americans about such ongoing struggles, beyond the understandable interest in earthquakes and "people buried in rubble." Nature, meanwhile, marches relentlessly on. In 1999 floods, earthquakes, and other natural calamities overran some 315 million people around the world. In 1998 USAID responded to sixty-five such catastrophes, up from twenty-seven the previous year. And that's only the natural disasters.

The agency works with a broad range of partners and collaborators—more than 300 U.S. private voluntary organizations and 3,500 American companies, universities, international agencies, other federal agencies, and other governments. USAID's requested budget for 2001 is $7.5 billion, some $200 million lower than what it operated on in 2000. The budget covers USAID's own programs and those it administers with other agencies. The total sought for 2001 includes operating expenses of $519 million.

"This agency is primarily individuals committed to improving the lives of others around the world," Anderson says. "For most of the people who work here, it's not just a job."

PROFILE

Current Administrator Agency for International Development
J. Brady Anderson, 1999–

Career summary
U.S. ambassador to Tanzania, 1994–97
Sociolinguistic surveyor, Wycliffe Bible Translators, Tanzania and Kenya,
    1989–94
Assistant to Bill Clinton as Arkansas attorney general and governor, 1977–81
Private law practice, Arkansas

Education
Rhodes College, Memphis; University of Arkansas School of Law; All Nations
    Christian College (United Kingdom)

Administrators of the Agency for International Development since 1989

Clinton administration
J. Brian Atwood, 1993–99 (currently executive vice president, Citizens Energy)

Bush administration
Ronald W. Roskens, 1989–93 (currently president, Global Connection)

Department of Defense

▨ Secretaries of the Army, Air Force, and Navy

EXECUTIVE LEVEL II—Presidential appointments with
Senate confirmation

RECOMMENDED SKILLS AND EXPERIENCE ■ All three current
service secretaries have strong backgrounds in legal schooling and the
practice of law. Early in their careers, two served multiyear tours of active
duty in one of the services; one of them is a West Point graduate. Two
were previously under secretaries in the military departments they now
head. Their resumes also variously reflect advanced training in business
or economics, teaching experience, tenure in elected office, and extensive
community service.

"As a lawyer, my stock in trade is trying to figure out what to do in
complex situations," says F. Whitten Peters, secretary of the air force since
1999. He thinks that background—putting the facts together, making
arguments, designing practical solutions, trying to move people toward
them—was helpful preparation for what he is now doing. Army secretary
Louis Caldera, in his job since 1998, comments along similar lines.
"You've got to be able to ask the right questions, send the answers you
get back if they don't make sense, and make decisions when presented
with alternatives." Caldera, who represented a downtown district of Los
Angeles in the California state legislature, also points to the value of "people, media, public relations, and political skills," since "you want to bring
your influence to bear, but in a constructive, nonconfrontational way."

Ideally, says navy secretary Richard Danzig, a service secretary would
offer a range of skills "that exceed anything any one of us would ever really have. There is almost nothing that isn't relevant to this job"—whether
it's physics, biology, international military affairs, diplomacy, domestic
politics, management of a large organization, economics, race relations,
or the character of young people as the country changes. Danzig, who
took on his position in 1998, says it is therefore inevitable that service secretaries have areas of strengths and of weakness. "If you had a stronger
technology background, you'd be a better service secretary. But on the
other hand, if you had a stronger people background, you'd also be a better secretary. Whatever the cards you have, the trick is to play that hand
the best you can, recognizing that you don't have all the aces." He does

think the "most vital competency is an ability to elicit from the organization information about how things are, and also how they could be if various changes were made—and get honest views about that and forge the best possible consensus about where to go. It relates to managing a big organization that has both rich traditions and urgent imperatives to adapt and change."

Is a military background essential to these positions? "Helpful, but not essential," Caldera says.

He and Peters both stress the need to be "a very quick study." And it goes without saying, Caldera says, "that you need an enormous capacity for work. You're going ninety miles an hour every day." Being able to figure out what's important in "a constant fire hose of information coming in," Peters adds, "is really pretty critical."

INSIGHT ■ Arguably, these three jobs best embody that fundamental tenet about the station of uniformed military services in this particular democratic society: that they operate at all times under the control of civilians appointed by and responsible to the president. Within the Department of Defense, of course, civilian control is vested in the secretary of defense. But that authority extends to the secretaries of the army, navy, and air force, a level at which civilian control is directly and tangibly expressed.

Beyond that, says Caldera, the Defense Department is so complex "that the scope of command and control necessary for the secretary of defense to be effective would be very difficult to achieve without service secretaries." Civilian oversight and control is required, he says, if there is to be coherent, administration-led policy on developing the country's national security capability and how to use it in the world. "And the span of control required is just too broad for the secretary of defense alone." Civilian authority is easily eroded, he adds. "You have to work at strengthening it."

In the comments of the three civilian secretaries about their jobs, deep respect for the people in uniform whom they oversee—their achievement, skill, and commitment—is never in doubt. Caldera asserts, however, that "it would be a mistake to put people in the civilian secretary jobs who will just basically rubber stamp everything that the uniformed side wants to do." He makes a further point: "Soldiers want to see their secretaries. Communities where our installations are located want to see them." Part of his job, he says, is functioning as "the civilian face of the American people for the soldier: What does the country think of the job the military is doing for them? I'm also the face of the army to the American people: what is the army doing for the country today?"

Danzig makes a similar point. "Service secretaries play an important role in mediating between the larger society and the military department. The values of that larger society need to be conveyed to the department." As examples of values, he cites Americans' views about improprieties on the part of members of the services, about who should be promoted, the role of women in the military, and "the emphasis we place on recruiting from different segments of society." All these, he says, involve larger judgments from society as a whole "that need to be constantly updated in the military. It can't remain unchanged as society changes."

In the other direction, Danzig says, "things are happening within the military that society needs to understand." For instance, where military service was the norm for most American men in World War II and the early decades of the cold war, "we have moved to a professional military including women and men" that represents only 5 percent of the total population. He also believes that military secretaries have a "critical agenda-setting role" in questioning accepted beliefs about what works and will work in the future and in setting priorities in terms of organizational energy and money. "It's the strength," he says, "of bringing in somebody from the outside to run an organization rather than simply promoting internally."

The mediating and agenda-setting functions that Caldera and Danzig describe bear on another dimension of these jobs—ensuring the flow of adequate resources—that, if anything, is even more important. A very large investment of time in budget development, advocacy, and defense is, quite simply, an imperative for the service secretaries. Peters calls the air force budget, and explaining it to the Congress, his primary responsibility. Especially in the eyes of the Congress, the secretaries must justify what their departments do, and how, and why they need continued support. After a decade and more of downsized budgets and personnel rosters in the wake of the cold war's end, the Pentagon saw the first real increase in authorized spending in its fiscal 2000 budget. "It's good we have that," says Peters, "but we have a lot of equipment that's now fourteen years older than it was the last time we had any money." Not only that, he adds, but the air force is deploying its equipment four times as often today as ten years ago. "It's time to start rebuilding. There's a major budget problem down the road about that. Americans need to understand, among other things, what the air force does and why we need money."

And while the army's Caldera predicts modest defense budget hikes in the next few years, "it's still a tremendous resource allocation challenge because you have much more need than you have resources." A central part of the service secretary's task, as he describes it, "is truly being the decisionmaker about what kinds of forces and equipment we will need in the future." Yet, on arrival in the job, "there is already a five-year defense program in place, with assumptions about what we will fund over the next five, six, seven years." A newly minted service secretary who wants to change that is "trying to pivot an organization that is already committed—rhetorically and in terms of budget projections, dollars, and vested interests and defenders of the program, from Congress to contractors to internal advocates." An important debate is under way in the country, he says, about whether the services are investing too much in assets that were important in the cold war but don't carry the capabilities necessary in the twenty-first century.

"Someone has to rationalize this giant wish list of all the things we used to do well and new things we want to do well," Caldera argues. If one of the desired objectives is to "build goodwill for the United States" through engagement in the world differently than in the past, then it's a completely different set of capabilities and tools.

"One of the unique things about being a service secretary," he says, "is that it's not your budget. It's the Defense Department's budget." Each secretary is "crowded out a little" by the growth in programs that is Pentagon-wide, in such areas as health care. "And you have each service saying, 'this is what we can do, but this is what we would like to do.' We all have our lists of unfunded requirements. Within that, we all battle for our share of the budget." While resource allocation decisions are best made within the department, Caldera says, they are often made by the Congress.

Three other factors common to these positions deserve mention. First is the central part service secretaries play in a multitude of personnel issues. Among the more consequential of these are the continued reform of in-service attitudes toward equal opportunity and uniformed female personnel at all levels; the selection of officers to be elevated to flag rank; and the proper positioning of talented people to do the work of the services and advance upward in rank and responsibility. Second are the congressional committees and other power points with which the service secretaries regularly deal: the Armed Services and Appropriations committees of Senate and House, the Joint Chiefs of Staff and other senior military leaders within the department and in the field, the Office of the Secretary of Defense, the White House, and the Office of Management and Budget. The third shared point of reference is the Pentagon-wide exercise known as the Quadrennial Defense Review, next scheduled for 2001. "It was tough last time," Peters recalls, "and it will be tough this time. The army is fundamentally changing the way it operates. We in the air force have fundamentally changed the way we operate (with a restructuring plan called Expeditionary Aerospace Force Reorganization). The navy is looking to make its ships much less personnel intensive. There are a lot of changes taking place. And I think this QDR is going to be a fundamental relook."

Finally, the central question for a service secretary as Danzig sees it is "whether an organization can survive for two centuries and more and adapt to the twenty-first century. Can you figure that out to some degree and also bring the organization as a whole to embrace the solution? I don't think a good secretary necessarily comes in with a solution, but with the ability to develop the organization's capacity to find it and rally around it. And succeeding secretaries need to do it for their time."

▨ Secretary of the Army

Short term, Secretary of the Army Caldera thinks the first priority of his job is "getting the best and brightest kids into the enlisted and officer ranks of the army." He calls it a readiness challenge. To respond to it, he has attacked recruiting "with a personal, hands-on approach." That has meant revamping the marketing and advertising programs, travel around the country, "community summit meetings" in key cities, and a dozen other projects to get desired recruits to enlist in army careers and attract them into the Reserve Officer Training Corps and West Point.

Long term, the priority is on improving the understanding among members of the Congress and opinion makers about the importance of ground forces to national security and the need for equipment upgrade. The latter is an issue Caldera is trying to frame for the next administration, one about which he is insistent. The army's acquisition programs—research, development, and procurement—"are in the worst shape of any of the three services," he says. "People don't see army divisions in the news much. They see and think about jets, submarines, and aircraft carriers a lot and don't think about the equipment the soldier needs to do his or her job." The army is trying to transform itself from the era of the seventy-ton tank designed to fight Soviet ground forces on the plains of central and northern Europe to "a much lighter, agile, deployable force that can flow anywhere in the world in a matter of hours or days and provide tremendous capability regardless of the mission we're called on to do."

But to transform, Caldera says, "requires resources." When the steep Pentagon budget declines of the late 1980s and 1990s began—40 percent cuts in resources and force structure—"we didn't know how busy we would be in the post–cold war world. Now the question is whether we need to put back some of the people and resources that we took away." He also mentions such new missions as missile defense, protection from weapons of mass destruction, and cyberwar that are making further demands on the budget. In sum, it's a matter of replacing aging equipment, using technology to upgrade it, and tending to such areas as a growing bill for environmental remediation. Despite a $70 billion army budget, "we feel as if we've tightened our belts because we've got a good $5 billion to $20 billion more we could spend in the army alone." The army has a uniformed work force of just over a million active duty, National Guard, and reserve personnel and 270,000 civilian employees. It manages 25 million acres of land.

In addition, Caldera notes a significant foreign policy role for the secretary of the army. He has been involved in hurricane relief in Central America, the probe of Korean War atrocities that may have been the work of American soldiers, U.S. support for Colombia in its narcopolitical wars, and conversations with Saudis, Kuwaitis, Israelis, Greeks, and Turks about the U.S. commitment to their defense.

About relations with the Congress, Caldera says the army is "pretty widely acknowledged as the most flat-footed service on the Hill. We don't do as good a job as the others in selling our programs" (although the Army Corps of Engineers, as related below, may have been a temporary exception). The selling problem is rooted, Caldera says, in a service ethic of playing the role of the "good Boy Scout who goes by the rules—puts the needs of the country first, the needs of the army as a service second." That hurts the army's ability to compete effectively for dollars. To counter this, "we've been working on getting much more sophisticated help: telling members we need their assistance, getting some of our retired officers to advocate for the army, and getting some of the think tanks and others who are focused on defense issues to look more closely at the challenges that are facing the army." A harder case to make, Caldera says, and one which the secretary must lead, is reminding people that "no shooting war was ever won except on the ground," that terrain can't be held without soldiers to take and hold it. "We don't use soldiers to enforce no-fly zones, steam through the Strait of Taiwan, or fire cruise missiles. But if you're going to defend South Korea, eject the Iraqis from Kuwait," defend the United States itself—"anything that is a shooting war"—the army is going to be involved.

The recent battle over control over the Army Corps of Engineers is one of the more interesting variations on the theme of a service secretary's many-faceted engagement with the Congress. In March 2000 Caldera instituted management changes designed to strengthen civilian control of the corps.

His move followed reports that the corps had doctored studies of the Mississippi and Illinois rivers to secure approval of big civil works projects for itself and had designed a secret effort to increase its budget by $2 billion. Two months later, the Senate Appropriations Committee voted to bar any management changes for the corps. Some senators said they hadn't been consulted about Caldera's actions, which included forbidding military leaders of the corps from independent lobbying of the Congress. The Clinton administration then delayed the proposed changes pending discussions on the subject with the Congress. (When this was written, the full Senate had not voted on the Appropriations Committee measure.)

Thinking overall about the nature of his responsibilities, Caldera points to the fact that uniformed leaders bring "very different skills" to charting the army's course than those of their civilian overseers. "The secretary is the one with a better sense for the many kinds of roles the military will play in the future. That's a political decision," quite separate from military expertise about the best way to train soldiers to perform those roles or what kinds of equipment are necessary. Diversity is another issue— "very important in our society" and something to which the military must pay constant attention in order to enjoy the continued support of the people. The military view that "we're strictly a merit-oriented organization and that any need for diversity will take care of itself," he states, "is not the best answer" for Americans who "expect opportunities for women and minorities to be available." Therefore, the secretary must reach out as a mentor, thinking about the "unique problems faced by young minority and women officers," encouraging them to make careers in the service, and seeing that they are getting the mentoring and grooming that will help them compete for promotion at the highest levels.

Nor can the secretary "be intimidated by the number of stars people are wearing," Caldera says, or by the illustrative experience of being handed for the first time a proposal "that everyone below you has staffed up and signed off on and is due in the Office of the Secretary of Defense in a couple of hours." This kind of thing will happen, "not because they're malicious but because that's the way the bureaucracy works. There's this theory that service secretaries should be treated like beloved and rich old uncles. Treated with great respect, but not listened to. You can fall into that trap very quickly if you don't assert yourself: out of the loop on key decisions."

The secretary must therefore make it clear "what issues must come to you before a decision is final—and where and when. You've got to lay out what your priorities are so that they are clearly understood. Remember that you're working against 225 years of service tradition."

Secretary of the Air Force

Air force secretary Peters sees several major upcoming challenges facing the leadership of his service. First, he says, the service needs 1 or 2 percent real budget growth a year "to accommodate the retirement of a number of older airframes and replace them with modern airframes." There are numerous other requirements for additional resources as well. For example, in its fiscal 2001 budget proposal, the air force stripped $500 million from infrastructure accounts, Peters says, "to fund critical modernization needed to close some gaps we saw in Kosovo in the way we operated there."

As this was written, the air force annual budget was about $71 billion. It had 365,000 personnel on active duty and a civilian work force of 165,000, plus 180,000 members of the Air National Guard and the Air Force Reserve.

Another immediate issue, Peters says, is people. "We haven't been retaining and recruiting as many as we need to keep the air force together and the reasons have been inadequate pay, inadequate retirement benefits, too much work, and too many deployments." With the retirement issue resolved and the pay problem "on the glide path to being fixed with the Congress," the other personnel issues are one focus of the Expeditionary Aerospace Force Reorganization, a restructuring program announced in mid-1998. "A very high proportion of those who join and stay in the air force ultimately get married," Peters notes. The result is that the military services, once 70 percent staffed by single individuals, are now a 70 percent married force. The restructuring plan "is intended to make life much more predictable and stable and ultimately cut workloads, both on deployment and at home, so that people can spend more time at home."

Next are "some real fork-in-the-road issues the next administration's going to have to deal with," such as how to use various kinds of unmanned vehicles that will play an increasing part in air force operations and for which "we need both money and doctrine;" how to improve the performance of satellite launch vehicles, whose failures in the last two years have been more numerous than usual; and, related to that, making sure that the Titan IVB program comes to a successful conclusion in the next three to four years (the Titan IVB is a heavy-lift vehicle that carries government payloads, typically earth satellites, into space).

Questions like these relate to very basic force structure considerations that will be on the table in the context of the Quadrennial Defense Review in 2001. "The quality and quantity of our various forces will be a real issue," Peters says. "Key decisions are going to have to be made as early as March and April. There are some real cross-cutting questions of how much airlift we need and whether we trade off airlift for fighter forces, or vice versa. Our bombers are getting very old: do we start a new bomber program?" All this is tied, of course, to what the Defense Department's resources will be—how much money the next administration can reasonably ask for such purposes as national missile defense or space. Then there's the matter of the country's aging strategic nuclear force and how, or whether, negotiations with Russia will affect its size and future.

Peters also discusses the concern that the air force develop the "kinds of leaders the current world environment requires." The service, he says, has had many people "who only fly, or who only do space, or only do weather, or intelligence. What we've seen in places like Kosovo is that the really effective commander knows about and feels comfortable in many different kinds of systems. The commander we want is able to take those tools and put them together in a suite or ensemble that wins wars." That means more cross training and particularly "integration of the space part with the air part." Currently, the air force has many specialty tracks that tend to finish at the level of colonel or brigadier general. Peters says "the trick is to get people comfortable in several specialties so that they can be credibly viewed as generalists" and be eligible for promotion to the general officer level.

He puts considerable emphasis on his job's responsibilities as a principal internal and external spokesman of the air force—as mentioned earlier, a role shared by all three service secretaries. As he outlines it, the secretary must articulate to external audiences the reasons "why the air force is of value to the American people." Internally, it's "going out and explaining to the 800,000 people who work for the air force what the air force is doing, where it wants to go, what the problems are, and what solutions we have." In particular, that currently includes "why people should stay in the air force. We are trying to be effective advocates for the men and women in uniform, and the civilians, National Guard, and reservists who also work with us, to make the air force the kind of institution they want it to be."

The external-internal communications task is especially vital, Peters believes, "in an era when most Americans have not served in the military." Some people may dislike the circuit of "Rotary clubs, media events, editorial boards, and back to the internal audience," he says, "but it really is a very important part of what we do."

What has been information technology's impact on air force business and personnel systems? "Not as great as I would like on the basic business systems," Peters says. Many such systems are still of the "archaic main-frame" type, or derivatives. While acquisition procedures are under way to improve this in areas such as air force depot operations and accounting, changing other major systems, like those for personnel management, takes great amounts of time, he adds. That contrasts sharply with the use of technology on the air force's command, control, and war fighting side. "Information technology is the way the world is going," Peters says. "It's all very net centric and we're spending a lot of time and energy getting our command, control, intelligence, surveillance, and reconnaissance computers working together." Overall, he says he wants to leave behind a new chief information officer structure. "We must pull a lot of things together much more than we have. What's there is fairly good, but we now recognize that all this data needs to integrate with itself. We need a better structure with more people to do that. It's another challenge for somebody."

"Whoever has this job," Peters thinks, "has got to decide what he or she is interested in and good at, and what kind of help is required. Because it's far more than you can do in twenty-four hours a day, seven days a week." Areas in which there is talented, experienced help—in this case, such as acquisition and financial management—are areas in which he thinks the secretary does not need to invest significant time. On another front, he has "pushed and tugged" people into agreeing to a complete restructuring of air force headquarters. Begun in 1999, this program aims at "making life tolerable for the very smart people we bring in by alleviating the needless administrative burdens of working here." It involves centralizing of staff functions and a range of decisions on roles and missions across the board: "what we should be doing, who should be doing it, whether it should be done here or in the field, whether we send certain functions to the field and take back certain others." The reorganization will be about half complete when the new administration takes power in 2001.

The air force works best when it works as a team, Peters observes. That "key culture trait" on the uniformed side spills over to the civilian side as well. In his own office, he says, it manifests itself in his working relationship with the service's chief of staff. "I think we've achieved more by worrying less about turf and more about presenting a common, joint program, and by respecting each other's strong points. And I hope the next person who comes in here has that same mind-set—that it's important to forge a strong bond with the uniformed leadership. That doesn't mean surrendering civilian oversight; it just means there's a lot to be done. And it's much easier if you have everybody pulling together than pulling apart."

Secretary of the Navy

"The navy and the Marine Corps," notes Navy Secretary Danzig, "are older than the Republic." And no organization in the country, other than the army, has lasted as long as the U.S. government. Even the mature industrial giants of this country are relatively young, he says.

As stated in the "Insight" section of this triple profile, Danzig defines the main concern of service secretaries as finding ways to keep their centuries-old military institutions abreast of the contemporary world and bringing them to adopt and pursue that objective. Within that framework, and in addition to the secretary's mediating and agenda-setting roles also outlined earlier, he mentions a third: integrative leadership. "You're dealing with an extremely complex, $90 billion organization," he says. "The navy and Marine Corps together employ almost 900,000 people, including civilians and reservists. There are many stove pipes—separate channels, in which submariners, aviators, marines, and people on the communications and high technology sides think in different ways about certain things. This organization very much needs leadership that can balance the different parts against one another, that can see where more is needed here, less there, and where opportunities exist for synergy."

One of the major issues facing Danzig on a regular basis is the need to make judgments on promotion among the top hierarchy of officers— three- and four-star admirals and Marine Corps generals. At bottom, this involves decisions on "who, among the very good people who have spent three decades in the military, are the ones who really deserve to rise to the very highest levels." To a lesser degree, the secretary is involved in decisions affecting more junior people, with greater emphasis on getting the right people into the right jobs. "Showing what the institution values is important," Danzig says. "For example, I've placed considerable stress on the fact that this isn't a zero-defect environment—that the best leaders are sometimes people who have made mistakes and that you can learn from that and move forward." This is particularly complicated, because "different people match in different ways for different jobs in different times. It's difficult to try to treasure people as individuals, yet at the same time make it work for the organization."

Decisions on the investment of resources present another continuous challenge "because," Danzig says, they're "multidimensional." The navy, for example, could develop a new weapons system that might yield great benefits ten years from now. But to make that judgment, several kinds of knowledge are necessary. "You have to understand the nature of your vision of the world ten years from now. You have to have some grasp of the basic physics or chemistry of the program and of whether it is likely to work. On the business side, you have to know the cost and estimate the likelihood that the system can actually be delivered. You have to have some sense of the military utility." There is also the consideration of trade-off: investing in the new system might mean, as an example, giving up funding educational opportunities for officers that could be provided right now. "That's a very tough set of judgments, because you're trading today against ten years from now and trading things of one kind for things of another kind."

Danzig points to another principal dimension of the job: the many constituencies that are deeply interested in these issues. "Each has a part of the puzzle," he says. What has to be done here, on any given question, is to "figure out how to talk honestly and coherently with them, learn what each has to say, make a judgment and spend enough time to explain it to them, try to persuade them to come together on it."

On the technology front, Danzig calls the navy a "very proficient service." Because the navy works all over the globe, "we're extremely involved with communications, including satellite communications." Most observers, he says, "would say we are leaders in the information technology revolution within the government." Among the examples he mentions in the navy's "rich technology flow" is planning for a combined navy and Marine Corps intranet "that will connect up all our technology."

Every week, he says, the navy and Marine Corps recruit a thousand high school graduates. "That's a big challenge in an economy that obviously gives them many alternatives and when 70 percent of high school graduates go to college." Danzig thinks this success has its roots, at least partly, in a sense of camaraderie. "It's special because they train together, deploy together, spend six months out there, traversing the globe in a carrier battle group or a marine amphibious ready group. It's an amazing way to spend six months and an amazing experience for those who participate in it."

PROFILE

Current Secretary of the Army
Louis Caldera, 1998–

Career summary
Managing director and chief operating officer, Corporation for National
    Service, 1997–98
Representative, California Legislature (46th Assembly District), 1992–97
Deputy counsel, Los Angeles County, 1991–92

Private law practice, O'Melveny and Myers and Buchalter, Nemer, Fields and
Younger, 1987–91
Commissioned officer, U.S. Army, 1978–83

Education
Graduate, U.S. Military Academy, 1978; J.D., Harvard Law School and MBA,
Harvard Business School, 1987

Secretaries of the Army since 1989

Clinton administration
Togo D. West Jr., 1993–98 (currently secretary, Department of Veterans Affairs)

Bush administration
Michael P. W. Stone, 1989–93 (deceased)

PROFILE

Current Secretary of the Air Force
F. Whitten Peters, 1999–

Career summary
Under secretary of the air force, 1997–99
Principal deputy general counsel, Department of Defense, 1995–97
Associate, then partner, Williams and Connolly, 1978–95
Law clerk to Associate Justice William J. Brennan Jr., U.S. Supreme Court,
1977–78
Law clerk to Judge J. Skelly Wright, U.S. Court of Appeals for the District of
Columbia, 1976–77

Education
B.A., Harvard University, 1968; M.S. in economics, London School of
Economics, 1973; J.D. Harvard Law School, 1976

Secretaries of the Air Force since 1989

Clinton administration
Sheila E. Widnall, 1993–97 (currently Abby R. Mauze professor of aeronautics,
Massachusetts Institute of Technology)
Michael B. Donley (acting), 1993 (currently commissioner, U.S. Commission on
National Security/21st Century)

Bush administration
Donald B. Rice, 1989–93 (currently president and CEO, UroGenesys)

PROFILE

Current Secretary of the Navy
Richard Danzig, 1998–

Career summary
Adjunct professor, Maxwell School of Citizenship and Public Affairs,
    Syracuse University, 1997–98
Under secretary of the navy, 1993–97
Partner, Latham and Watkins, 1981–93.
Principal deputy assistant secretary of defense for manpower, reserve affairs,
    and logistics, 1979–81; deputy assistant secretary, 1978–79
Taught contract law, Stanford and Harvard Universities, 1972–77
Law clerk, Associate Justice Byron White, U.S. Supreme Court

Education
B.A., Reed College; J.D., Yale Law School; Rhodes Scholar, Ph.B. and Ph.D.,
    Oxford University

Secretaries of the Navy since 1989

Clinton administration
John H. Dalton, 1993–98 (currently chairman and CEO, Metal Technology)
Frank B. Kelso III (acting), 1993 (retired)

Bush administration
Sean O'Keefe (acting), 1992 (currently Louis A. Bantle professor of business
    and government policy and director, national security studies, Maxwell
    School, Syracuse University)
Lawrence Garrett III, 1989–91(current position not available)

▨ Under Secretary for Acquisition, Technology, and Logistics

EXECUTIVE LEVEL II—Presidential appointment with
Senate confirmation

RECOMMENDED SKILLS AND EXPERIENCE ■ Individuals considered for the job need sound, extensive defense-related management experience. That might be in private-sector defense contracting and R&D
or—at the Pentagon itself—in technology development and application.
Even better would be a background in the private and public sectors. An
engineering and scientific background with a research component is valu-

able. Most essential, however, is a high comfort level within the operational culture of the Defense Department. If that includes a wide range of working relationships and personal associations, so much the better. All this is even more critical than in the past, given the changing nature of the demands placed on U.S. defense capacity, its evolving role in American national security policy around the world, and the impact of defense technology on American business and industry.

INSIGHT ■ This is one of the two or three most critical positions in the U.S. defense establishment. It serves not just today's military commanders in the field, but those who will be there ten or fifteen years from now. Activities it oversees currently account for about 64 percent of the Pentagon's annual spending, or $170 billion of a total defense budget of $276.8 billion in fiscal year 2000.

That's more than the national budgets of most countries. It pays for everything the Department of Defense buys and supports to sustain U.S. military power—and, when necessary, to project it anywhere in the world—plus the extensive research and evaluation required to keep it technologically predominant.

That broad definition covers many important specific responsibilities. The acquisition function embraces procurement—contracting for and purchasing defense-related items in a huge range—and acquisition itself, which covers the full range from research and development to logistics. Then there are nuclear, chemical, and biological programs; international technology transfer programs; environmental protection; military construction; public-sector depots, arsenals, and shipyards; further progress in acquisition reform; and the viability of vital private-sector technology and manufacturing industries. Among the senior decisionmaking groups the acquisition and technology chief chairs or sits with are the Defense Science Board, the Defense Acquisition Board, the advisory board of the Defense Threat Reduction Agency, the Aeronautics and Astronautics Coordinating Board, the Nuclear Weapons Council, and the Department of Defense Ethics Council.

Within the $170 billion current annual outlay managed by this position are procurement costs of $60 billion and $38 billion for research and development. Jacques Gansler, who took over the job in late 1997, estimates the logistics component in the $80 billion range; the figure is approximate, he acknowledges, "because of our poor bookkeeping system." Still plagued by "lots of inertia and need for change," it is the department's vast logistics operation that gets people, machines, weapons systems, technology, communications, medical supplies, food, fuel, and munitions wherever in the world, and whenever, they must be. Getting that job done depends on a number of interlocking systems—such as inventory, planning, storage, transport—some of which are viewed as World War II vintage. In any case, "they're not up to world class like Wal-Mart or FedEx," Gansler says. Among the major lacks are "modern information technology and rapid transportation." He says logistics is undergoing a transformation aimed at bringing it into the twenty-first century. (Two of the many activities under his supervision are offices for logistics reinvention and logistics systems modernization.)

"The first thing about the job is its breadth," says Gansler. He keeps a twenty-four-hours-a-day, seven-days-a-week schedule, a lot of which is "going from meeting to meeting." The pace and workload can force big decisions into cramped time frames—"you have an hour to figure out if you want to buy a nuclear aircraft carrier. The next hour is whether you want to allow this industrial company to merge with that one."

Decisions like the latter, where the very future of private-sector defense contractors can be in play, exemplify the measure of responsibility this job carries. The top companies that compete for defense contracts once numbered about fifty. Consolidation within the industry has reduced these to five; in some product categories, Gansler says, it is down to two. "If you have eight companies competing in a sector, no problem. When you have only two and one of them wins two contracts in a row, the other one disappears. Then you have a monopoly situation that you don't want." So monitoring the health of the defense industrial base, a long-standing concern of this job, now also involves decisions on whether to allow mergers between competing contractors—decisions made in coordination with the antitrust regulators of the Department of Justice.

The job requires a similar kind of decisionmaking in the transfer of technology to other countries, where it can also affect industrial structures in those places. Typical questions here, says Gansler—"do we allow country A to get some advanced technology, should Stealth be transferred to country A and, of course, to company X within country A"—are matters that take a good deal of his time.

This position gets support from various senior officials under its authority. Their areas are advanced technology, logistics, environmental security, industrial affairs and installations, international and commercial programs, and all acquisition matters related to command and control, communications, computing, intelligence, and space. The under secretary has authority, direct or through deputies, over the Ballistic Missile Defense Organization, the Defense Advanced Research Projects Agency, the Defense Logistics Agency, the Defense Threat Reduction Agency, Chemical and Biological Defense Programs, the On-Site Inspection Agency, the Office of Economic Adjustment, and the Defense Acquisition University.

From that extended list, it's easy to see why few committees on Capitol Hill lack interest in some aspect of what this under secretary is responsible for. Beyond the appropriations committees of both houses, Gansler deals mainly with the armed services committees. But the impact of the functions he manages on such other sectors as the environment, housing, small business, and transportation bring him into steady contact with the relevant committees of jurisdiction.

Of the many entities the job supervises, two—the Office of Defense Research and Engineering and, within it, the Defense Advanced Research Projects Agency—are fundamental in taking advanced weaponry that works from the idea stage to combat. A good example is the F-22 Raptor, the air force's upcoming stealth fighter, whose development was a contentious, billion-dollar line item in the fiscal year 2000 budget. Both of these positions are examined elsewhere in this book.

As suggested above, information technology figures conspicuously in the areas of this position's concerns. In its information transactions with industry, for example, the Defense Department in a major undertaking has established common digital formats that permit each side to use common data, not separate data sets, with mutual access to the computers of both parties.

Second, because of the primacy of good communications in any military operation, the acquisition team must ensure that American commanders have the latest and the best in communications technology. "When we went into Kosovo," Gansler recalls, "we found our radios didn't talk to those of our allies in a secure fashion. We had to talk in the open." This is the long-standing issue of interoperability, without which a Marine pilot in an F-18 can't talk to an army tank unit commander on the ground. Gansler says "each service has its responsibilities but in a communications system it has to be interservice." The problem gets worse when other nations are involved.

Those charged with the extensive acquisition and technology mission must expect to deal on a regular basis with continuing rivalry between the military services in the development and use of equipment and systems. "There's sometimes a conflict," says Gansler, "between what the services would like to do and what we think might be good for the country—which may not be exactly the same."

PROFILE

Current Under Secretary for Acquisition, Technology, and Logistics
Jacques S. Gansler, 1997–

Career summary
Executive vice president and director, TASC
Deputy assistant secretary of defense, material acquisition
Assistant director, defense research and engineering (electronics)
Vice president, ITT
Program management, Singer Corporation
Engineering management, Raytheon Corporation
Adjunct professor, Harvard University and the University of Virginia

Education
B.E., Yale University; M.S./EE, Northeastern University; M.A., political economy,
    New School for Social Research; Ph.D., economics, American University

Under Secretaries for Acquisition and Technology since 1989*

Clinton administration
Paul G. Kaminski, 1994–97 (currently chairman and CEO, Technovation)
John M. Deutsch, 1993–94 (currently faculty, Massachusetts Institute of
    Technology)

Clinton and Bush administrations
Donald J. Yockey, 1991–93 (deceased)

Bush administration
John A. Betti, 1989–91 (current position not available)
*Title assigned to this position prior to the tenure of the incumbent.

▨ Director, Defense Research and Engineering

EXECUTIVE LEVEL IV—Presidential appointment with
Senate confirmation

RECOMMENDED SKILLS AND EXPERIENCE ■ "Looking back,
the really good people in this job have come out of the defense industry or
one of the laboratories that work on defense projects," says Hans Mark,
who became director in 1998. His own background is illustrative. As a
University of Texas professor, he taught aerospace engineering and engineering mechanics for ten years and also held an endowed chair in engi-

neering for six years (he was chancellor of the university for eight years during this period). Previously, he was under secretary of the air force, moved up to the post of secretary, and later became deputy administrator of the National Aeronautics and Space Administration. Still earlier, Mark was a professor of nuclear engineering and department chairman at the University of California and a research scientist at the university's Lawrence Livermore National Laboratory. In these positions, he was involved with a very wide range of advanced technological endeavors, from space shuttle flights and satellite reconnaissance to distant space flight, tilt rotor aircraft, and nuclear weapons testing.

As with the under secretary position to which this job reports, candidates should understand the connections between defense technology, American industry, and U.S. foreign policy. They have a distinct leg up if they also know how to survive and achieve within the U.S. defense culture.

INSIGHT ■ The disintegration of the Soviet Union in 1991 may have lessened to some degree the risk of world nuclear conflict. But it left behind— and in some cases helped unleash—the proliferation of regional conflicts that present a collective security problem of almost equal gravity. Tensions like those between India and Pakistan, and their emergence as overt nuclear powers, aggravate and complicate the job of defense planners. Nor can they ignore the continued existence of a Russian nuclear arsenal or the danger it could conceivably present in the control of the wrong people. In this scenario of multiple moving parts, decisions on where today's threats to American national security are likely to come from remain fundamental for all those who, like the director of DR&E, must make the right choices for the defense technology of the future.

This post is an advisory one, not a line position. As officially described, the director of DR&E is the chief technical adviser to the secretary of defense and the under secretary for acquisition and technology. More accurately, the director advises and reports directly to the under secretary; it is the under secretary who advises the secretary in this area. In that sense, Mark says, the official language is "a slight exaggeration." The job has oversight of—official language again—"defense research, development, test, and evaluation."

Put more meaningfully, the position is closely concerned with the quality of defense technology—how to move it forward, keep it virtually unmatched over time, and bring it on line constantly in specific weapons systems of the future. Former director Charles Herzfeld once described this as "making sure the United States will continue to have technical superiority over any other power, available in a form the military can use."

Pursuit of those goals must deal with limited resources for research and development and the habitual preference of the military services (noted elsewhere in this volume) for competing, rather than complementary, weapons systems. A key requirement of the position, therefore, is skill in evaluation, negotiation, and supplying the right advice on investing the Pentagon's current $38 billion R&D budget. "I review the programs," Mark says, "the big dollar items, the F-22 fighter and Crusader artillery piece and some of the missile programs. I write reports on them. I directly influence the Defense Advance Research Projects Agency (DARPA—examined separately in this book) and the Defense Threat Reduction Agency. Those are the two things I have direct jurisdiction over."

He has about six staff people in his immediate office, and some 150 in the various offices under his supervision. "What's important in any job like this and I learned this twenty years ago, when I was secretary of the air force, is that there are some really very good people in the Pentagon," Mark says. "And for almost everything you rely on them. You decide two or three projects that you want to really do and forget about the rest. Just let the machine work. Just a few things that I really push. You cannot master it all." If capable people are there to help, "then what you really do is manage at the margins." For instance, he thinks he has "probably influenced five or six million" of DARPA's $1.8 billion annual budget.

Another example of managing at the margin was the restructuring of the airborne laser weapon system. Despite a decision to delay the weapon's actual deployment for several years, the need to test it remained. The question was what kind of testing would be more productive—airborne testing, involving costs for the aircraft involved, or testing on the ground. Mark argued the case for airborne testing, which he believed would yield much more technical information. His view prevailed. "So that's the kind of thing I do on big programs," he says.

What were some of his priorities? In addition to the airborne laser project, Mark says a reliable, safe nuclear weapons stockpile has been very high on his list. "I spent the first thirteen years of my technical career helping to design and test nuclear weapons," he says, adding that he worked on ballistic missiles for forty years. "It's probably one of the reasons they brought me in, because that's getting serious."

Mark says a healthy dose of modesty is important in this work. "You can't do everything. Listen to the folks that work for you. Because nine times out of ten, they're honest and trying to do a good job. Hang in there. You're going to lose some battles and be prepared to do so. If you come out 51 percent ahead, be satisfied with that."

PROFILE

Current Director or Defense Research and Engineering
Hans Mark, July 1998–

Career summary
Professor, aerospace engineering and engineering mechanics, University of
    Texas, 1988–98
John J. McKetta Centennial Energy chair, University of Texas,1992–98
Senior research engineer, Institute for Advanced Technology, University of
    Texas, 1990–98
Chancellor, University of Texas System, 1984–92
Deputy administrator, National Aeronautics and Space Agency, 1981–84
Secretary of the air force, 1979–81
Under secretary of the air force, 1977–79
Director, NASA-Ames Research Center, Mountain View, California, 1969–77
Professor of nuclear engineering and department chairman, University of
    California at Berkeley, and research scientist and division leader, Lawrence
    Livermore National Laboratory, 1955–69

Education
B.A., physics, University of California at Berkeley, 1951; Ph.D., physics,
    Massachusetts Institute of Technology, 1954

Directors of Defense Research and Engineering since 1989

Clinton administration
Anita K. Jones, 1993–97 (currently Lawrence R. Quarles professor of
    engineering and applied science, University of Virginia)

Bush administration
Victor H. Reis, 1991–93 (currently director, Center for Nuclear Strategies,
    Science Applications International Corporation)
Charles M. Herzfeld, 1990–91 (currently senior associate, Center for Strategic
    and International Studies)

Reagan administration
Robert C. Duncan, 1987–89 (currently chairman, Hicks and Associates)

Assistant Secretary for Command, Control, Communications, and Intelligence and Chief Information Officer

EXECUTIVE LEVEL IV—Presidential appointment with Senate confirmation

RECOMMENDED SKILLS AND EXPERIENCE ■ According to the current assistant secretary, this position needs an engineer with a strong business background—probably someone who has been a CEO in the private sector—and military experience. Within those general areas, however, are important specifics. In the engineering category, the right candidate should know electronics, including computers, and communications. In business, the best qualifications are a strong capacity to manage, with an emphasis on research and development. In the military, the desired background is a close understanding of the military services and their individual cultures, usually through previous service in the Defense Department. Underlying all these, look for an individual who relates as easily to people as to technology. Technocrats will not do well here.

People who combine these qualifications don't come along every day, of course. A former Pentagon executive who held similar responsibilities at the military service level may have best summed up the proper mix. The job's proper occupant, he suggested, is someone who is used to wielding authority, knows the services, has a "systems approach," and can handle technical matters with facility.

INSIGHT ■ "Everything I do," says Arthur Money, who came to this position in 1998, "is at the policy oversight guidance level for communications, command and control, and intelligence functions"—universally called C3I—"for the Department of Defense across its entirety." He is also the Pentagon's chief information officer, a position created by the Information Technology Management Reform Act that later became the Clinger-Cohen Act of 1996.

The C3I functions are designed, in the Pentagon's own language, to provide "information superiority"—the ability to gather and make use of an unbroken stream of information and at the same time deny (or take advantage of) an adversary's ability to do the same, enabling U.S. military forces "to survive and succeed on every mission." Within the broad C3I designation are such subsets as information policy and management, information security, counterintelligence, security countermeasures, space systems and policy, surveillance, and reconnaissance.

Money calls information superiority "the mainstay of how the revolution in military affairs is proceeding in the department." Taking his chief information officer, or CIO, duties into consideration as well, he sees his job as squarely in the center of this change. "I'm responsible," he says, "for the flow of information end to end, whether it's war fighting information or business-related information."

A major hurdle here, like that found elsewhere in the Defense Department, continues to be the standardization between the three military services of certain kinds of weapons, equipment, and systems used by all three. That includes the information technology systems at the core of the C3I/CIO operation. Using C3I systems, military commanders in the field get information they need to see how their forces and those of the adversary are deployed, to know what targets are available at a given moment, to communicate with one another, and to give orders, direct their forces, and watch the unfolding of combat. This is more difficult—and success is less assured—when, say, a tank unit commander, a navy destroyer captain, and missile-equipped ground attack planes are using different communication systems. Eliminating these divergences and achieving the utopia the Pentagon calls "interoperability" is a goal that has engaged Money's predecessors, confronts him, and will challenge his successors. "Getting this department to work in an end-to-end, seamless, uninterrupted flow of information," he says, "and then getting everybody on the same page of music is the largest management issue."

The problem, however, does not lie only with the familiar, stubborn instinct of the military services to design, use, and control their own systems. It is also the ceaseless march of technology. Money recognizes that "we have legacy systems that were never designed to interoperate in an end-to-end situation. How do you modernize, move toward interoperability, when we'll have legacy systems around for thirty or forty more years? We're probably inventing a legacy system every day as we sit here. Some vulnerabilities are being buttoned up, but others are being created." Looking at the future, he depicts this struggle as a "continuum."

Meanwhile, a parallel effort is going on with U.S. military allies. Even if the Pentagon should somehow gain total interoperability, Money points out, "it does us no good to have systems that only we can talk to. I don't mean just in war, but anywhere along the spectrum, from conditions of peace to humanitarian operations to noncombatant evacuations to actual combat." There is "a constant, ongoing pressure for interoperability" that can handle different combinations of partners and systems—"very much an evolving, ever-changing environment."

Money thinks the global reach of the C3I function will only expand. "On a given day, the Department of Defense isn't in one place. We're in thirty or forty or fifty locations. Today, we have an operation going on in Sierra Leone, where some United Nations people were killed last night. Or Rwanda, East Timor—there are operations taking place constantly. It's a constant churn."

He says about a third of the Defense Department's budget each year— "$75 billion to $100 billion, I'd say"—falls into the areas of his responsibility. His direct staff numbers 250 and his office works with 500-plus contractors. The wider scope of his authority touches several hundred thousand civilian and uniformed employees. On Capitol Hill, he normally interacts with six committees, in formal hearings six to twelve times a year, and in more frequent, informal in-person contacts. With the press, "I'm probably in front of a camera or microphone once a month and there are a fair number of interviews in the office or over the phone."

Wearing the chief information officer hat, Money has a range of assignments. Major among them are:

—Deciding whether potential Pentagon acquisition of information technology justifies the investment risks involved, selecting the technology to be acquired, and getting maximum value from it—all in coordination with the department's planning and budgeting system

—Installing performance- and results-based management of the department's information technology. Among other tasks, this entails setting goals for information technology efficiency and effectiveness in defense operations and in delivery of the department's services to the public, and an annual report on progress that is part of the Pentagon's budget submission.

—Making certain that information technology acquisitions are interoperable across the Pentagon

—Developing integrated IT architecture for the department

—Managing IT training

As this suggests, the Defense Department does not develop most of the information technology it uses. "We're using what's coming out of the commercial marketplace," Money says. "It's the only way we can keep up, or in fact gain the advantage we want." This has its own difficulties, he adds. For example, he must "keep the budget line here compatible with buying technology that's obsolete within eighteen months, yet we're programming money that's two to five years out."

Has there been adequate progress within the Department of Defense in integrating information technology with policymaking? "We're doing better," Money says, "but it's a new feature that in a cultural sense will take some time to be accepted." The department created its planning, programming, and budgeting system long before this, he notes (in fact, it goes back to the 1960s), and "a lot of the IT stuff is additive and different. There are some incompatibilities with some of the congressional budgeting processes. But we're working through those."

PROFILE

Current Assistant Secretary for Command, Control, Communications, and Intelligence and Chief Information Officer
Arthur L. Money, 1998–

Career summary
Assistant secretary of the air force for acquisition, 1996–98
Vice president and deputy general manager, TRW Avionics and Surveillance Group, 1995
President of ESL (a subsidiary of TRW before incorporation into its Avionics and Surveillance Group), 1990–94
Various positions with ESL 1972–90, including vice president, advanced programs and development; and vice president, Studies, Analysis and Systems Division

Education
B.S., San Jose State University, 1965; M.S., University of Santa Clara, 1970

Assistant Secretaries for Command, Control, Communications, and Intelligence since 1989*

Clinton administration
Anthony M. Valgita (acting), 1996–97 (currently vice president, Federal Systems, SRA International)
Joan Dempsey (acting), 1997 (currently deputy director, central intelligence for community management, Central Intelligence Agency)

Bush administration
Emmett Paige Jr., 1993–96 (currently president and COO, OAO Corporation)

Duane P. Andrews, 1989–92 (currently corporate executive vice president, Science Applications International Corporation)

*Note that "chief information officer" was added to the title with the incumbent.

Comptroller

EXECUTIVE LEVEL III—Presidential appointment with Senate confirmation

RECOMMENDED SKILLS AND EXPERIENCE ▪ In a very real sense, this job compares to that of financial manager in a $268 billion business. Therefore, extensive experience in finance, budget management, accounting, or another related specialty is important. Yet the current comptroller, William J. Lynn III, thinks that, while that kind of background is helpful, the position requires a broader range of experience and skills, among them program analysis and particularly congressional budget formulation. He notes that most recent occupants of the job were congressional staffers. Lynn himself served in Defense Department program analysis and budget jobs, was a Senate staff member working on defense and arms control questions, and focused on defense analysis and strategy in a couple of think tank contexts.

INSIGHT ▪ Officially, the comptroller is the principal adviser to the secretary of defense for budgetary and fiscal matters and serves as the department's chief financial officer. The position is really three jobs. It's responsible for overseeing development of the Pentagon budget and its justification and defense on Capitol Hill. It supervises the department's internal programming and planning, such as multiyear defense plans and the accompanying tradeoffs and cost analyses. And it manages the department's finances and accounting.

This tripartite assignment began to emerge during the Bush administration, which brought finance and accounting under the oversight of the comptroller—then an assistant secretary-level job with mostly budget responsibilities. The third piece, program evaluation and analysis, was added by the Clinton administration, which also retitled the position as an under secretary. "The biggest challenge is trying to balance between the three," Lynn says. "You can't spend as much time on any one as was the case earlier, so it's more trying to integrate the three, sort through the most important issues, and deal with them."

Was it a change for the better or did it bring additional problems? Lynn thinks it's a far better way to do things. "First, it's narrowed the secretary's span of control. So basically, for anything involved with money, he has only one button to hit. And that makes it easier for him to manage the building." More important, he continues, integration of the three sides of financial management links the particulars of the internal program budget and the congressional budget justification in ways in which they weren't completely connected before. "That's a linkage that has to be made," he says. "So putting this together has been a little bit of wear and tear on the occupant of this office, but it's definitely worth it in terms of the integration we get."

The change was also part of a more extensive decision by the transition team of the first Clinton administration to structure the department's organization in four main cones, each led by an under secretary reporting to the secretary. These are budgeting, programs, and financial management (the comptroller's domain); manpower, readiness, and medical services; acquisition and technology; and policy. The two major organizations under comptroller oversight are the Defense Contract Audit Agency and the Defense Finance and Accounting Service.

Lynn sees the management of priorities as his job's biggest challenge. "The key is to spend the money on the highest priorities so that you end up with a strategy-driven budget. So the right allocation of the resources is the big issue." In that context, he adds, "most of the Pentagon has advocates of one particular function or another, whether it's strategic nuclear forces or air forces or ground forces or health issues. And all of them will argue cogently that they can do their jobs better if they have more money. The problem is, we don't have more money. So we try to help the secretary make trade-offs between more health care and more force structure, or between buying weapons faster and a smaller structure." Balanced, objective advice is hard to come by, because everyone in the system is an advocate. His role is to provide that advice. Is a proposed project realistic? Is it really going to cost what they say it's going to cost?

According to Lynn, his budget and program analysis staff is "extraordinarily good—probably the best in the Pentagon." People in both operations generally combine considerable experience in the department with advanced degrees. "It's a high degree of professionalism, and an extremely talented staff." The third area of his responsibility—the Defense Finance and Accounting Service—has a staff of 20,000 around the country that runs interactive financial systems across the department. That unit was created in 1991 from the staffs of the individual military services. "Over time, we've built up a cadre of very good people at DFAS," Lynn says, "and we've just instituted a departmentwide process in which people will be trained and certified as defense financial managers."

Future under secretaries in this job will have to deal with an increasing number of challenges, he believes, "most likely with a relatively constant budget"—he doesn't foresee major increases. Among the challenges he points to the need "to recapitalize the equipment as well as to continue to attract and train the best people within a relatively constant level of resources."

PROFILE

Current Under Secretary and Comptroller of the Department of Defense
William J. Lynn III, November 1997–

Career summary
Director, program analysis and evaluation, Office of the Secretary of Defense, 1993–97
Assistant to the secretary of defense for budget, 1993
Legislative counsel to Sen. Edward Kennedy (D-Mass.) (defense and arms control) and staff representative on the Senate Armed Services Committee, 1987–93
Senior fellow, Strategic Concepts Development Center, National Defense University, 1985–87
Professional staff, Institute for Defense Analysis, 1985–87
Executive director, Defense Organization Project, Center for Strategic and International Studies, 1982–85

Education
B.A., Dartmouth College, 1976; J.D., Cornell University Law School, 1980; M.P.A., Woodrow Wilson School, Princeton University, 1982

Comptrollers of the Department of Defense since 1989

Clinton administration
John J. Hamre, 1993–97 (currently president and CEO, Center for Strategic and International Studies)

Bush administration
Sean O'Keefe, 1989–92 (currently Louis A. Bantle professor of business and government policy and director, National Security Studies, Maxwell School, Syracuse University)

Department of State

■ Permanent U.S. Representative to the United Nations

Presidential appointment with Senate confirmation

RECOMMENDED SKILLS AND EXPERIENCE ■ Substantial seasoning in the vineyards of diplomacy, particularly of the multilateral kind at a senior level, is the single best preparation for this job. In fact, Richard Holbrooke, U.S. permanent representative to the UN since mid-1999, is emphatic that extended experience in the multilateral arena—at NATO, for example, or in an extended international negotiating setting—is the only kind that really counts. Holbrooke's own career, summarized at the end of this profile, is a case in point. "Multilateral diplomacy is very rare in the world and most practitioners have had little experience with it," he says, adding that a previous "normal" ambassadorship or two overseas is of "very limited value."

But a background in the Congress, or in working with legislators and legislation, is a significant advantage: the coalition-building skills acquired there are equally useful in New York. Poise and resourcefulness in a variety of public speaking and media arenas are also essential to effectiveness in the job. Finally, it hardly needs stating that anyone considered for this position should be deeply conversant with the particulars, goals, and history of U.S. foreign policy, its UN dimension in particular.

INSIGHT ■ As the chief representative of a country that for more than half a century has been the key leader and catalyst at the United Nations—and remains its single biggest financial supporter—the individual in this job manages a portfolio like no other in current American diplomacy.

First is the UN itself. Few would deny its achievements over time, whether on the broad front of international stability and peacekeeping or in such individual areas as world health, trade, humanitarian assistance, and human rights. But UN history is also one of antagonism, dispute, crisis, and doubt. Member nations small and large, including the United States, have on occasion ignored their obligations to the UN when their own interests of the moment seemed paramount. Despite virtually level budgets in recent years, accompanied by a cut of more than a thousand jobs and moves to increase efficiency and accountability, the UN Secretariat in New York has drawn reproach as a complacent, inflated bureaucracy. Until 1999, the U.S. Congress, driven by those who wanted a reduced U.S. membership assessment and internal UN reform, had declined for a time to authorize full dues payments to the UN and other international organizations.

Yet the United Nations, in most views, remains a singularly valuable world institution. The Congress as a whole, including members who are most critical of the UN, supports continued U.S. membership. Polls show that most Americans recognize the constructive, useful role the UN is designed to play. And, as has been the case since 1945, Americans support UN goals—and U.S. membership—as a means of advancing U.S. national interests. The UN has never been the answer to every problem of U.S. foreign policy. But with its breath of membership, it is an instrument through which nations can broadly share the workload and costs of trying to maintain basic global stability, peace, and progress. Not least, the UN in a very real sense is the most effective court of world opinion. On all these grounds, the UN is, to quote the Department of State, "the preferred vehicle for pursuing U.S. foreign policy objectives."

That gives the chief U.S. representative in New York a number of standard tasks and special concerns. Among these, as outlined by Holbrooke, are to work with the permanent representatives of all 188 other member countries and to speak for the United States in the UN General Assembly and particularly in the Security Council, which he calls "the premier decisionmaking body of its kind in the world." Less standard, and critical, is "to get better performance out of the UN Secretariat," especially the Department of Peacekeeping Operations. Here, reflecting on experience in places like Bosnia, Kosovo, and Sierra Leone, Holbrooke thinks the fundamental problem is that "the UN peacekeeping operation does not seem well structured or equipped to conduct military operations. It's just not there. Military operations are the province of serious military structures, not an ad hoc, gerrymandered, multinational organization cobbled together on a voluntary basis." It's vital, of course, to resolve such inherent handicaps, given the close parallel between UN peacekeeping (some seventeen missions around the world at this writing) and U.S. objectives.

Second in the U.S. permanent representative's portfolio are responsibilities outside the immediate UN framework. Here, relationships with the U.S. Congress are prime, for reasons not limited to the U.S. dues-UN reform question discussed in more detail below. "In my view," Holbrooke says, "the next ambassador should understand that he or she should spend a lot of time with Congress, as much as in New York or in the executive branch." When he goes to Washington, he says, he usually heads directly to the Congress. While much of his liaison and consultation work with the Department of State—also an important responsibility—can be done by telephone, "the Congress has to be one-on-one, individual discussions with members. And the ambassador to the UN must be the main spear-carrier for congressional support of whatever the administration wants from the UN." Discussing a further assignment beyond the UN itself, Holbrooke says the public education task is key. In particular, "the first ambassador of a new administration has a very substantial role" here and should spend "a very good chunk of time" in it. This outreach should extend to a variety of public and private audiences, including an array of nongovernmental organizations whose work significantly supplements, and sometimes replaces, that of the UN.

Asked what will head the agenda of the U.S. representative to the UN after the 2000 presidential election, Holbrooke says "it's incumbent on whatever administration is in power to make the case for the value of the UN in American foreign policy and the need for the United States to pay its fair share of the cost." Not surprisingly, the latter issue has been a special thorn in the side of recent U.S. ambassadors in New York, including Holbrooke. Depending on whether U.S. or UN calculations are used, this country by 1999 owed the UN about a billion dollars or more in back dues—a situation that sparked hostility from other members, lost the United States a seat on an important budget committee, and posed a theoretical threat to its vote in the General Assembly. A 1999 agreement between the president and the Congress broke that impasse, making possible a federal budget provision to repay $926 to the UN in three slices. Each is conditional on certification by the administration that the UN has met a range of a range of required reforms. "We've made huge progress on reform," Holbrooke says, "but we've still got a long way to go."

Apart from the question of its back dues, the United States annually contributes nearly $2.5 billion to the United Nations system, including the World Bank and the International Monetary Fund—more than any other country. Although this figure represents 25 percent of the regular budgets of the UN and UN-system organizations, according to the U.S. Mission to the UN, it amounts to less than a quarter of 1 percent of the U.S. federal budget. Included in the $2.5 billion are assessed contributions of $500 million; monetary and in-kind food assistance of about $700 million; about $800 million in voluntary contributions to other UN programs; and $460 million in support of UN specialized and affiliated agencies like the World Health Organization, the International Labor

Organization, and the Food and Agricultural Organization. Beyond this are U.S. contributions to UN peacekeeping operations, currently assessed by the UN at 30.5 percent of the total cost; a 1995 U.S. law, however, restricts U.S. peacekeeping support to 25 percent.

The UN assesses regular dues according to each member nation's share of the world economy. Since the U.S. economy constitutes 26 percent of the global total, the U.S. Mission points out, the U.S. benefits from its 25 percent dues assessment. Moreover, U.S. support will in effect be cut by some of the conditions on which payment of U.S. arrears is based. They place assessment rate caps of 22 percent on contributions to several large UN-system bodies like those listed just above. More significant, the conditions would reduce assessments for the UN regular budget first to 22 percent and ultimately to 20 percent, and cap peacekeeping contributions at 25 percent.

In 2001 Holbrooke thinks the primary early issue in which the chief U.S. representative will be centrally involved is determining "what the role of the UN should be in American foreign policy." The decision, he says, is one for the "next president and his entire foreign policy team, with the support of the Congress." Should the U.S. ambassador in New York be a cabinet-level member of that team? Holbrooke doesn't think so, but if the president wants it that way, "that's fine." With or without cabinet rank, he says, the high profile of the job will require close understanding between the secretary of state and the national security adviser. "That's not to say that these people will always agree. There have to be differences of opinion. That's healthy. The important thing is to keep the differences within the system."

His advice to successors? "Listen carefully to the members of the UN community. Try to close the gap between the UN and the Congress. Don't waste a lot of time on bureaucratic minutiae. You have a very solid staff for the routine. Focus on the big, sweeping issues. Be innovative."

PROFILE

Current Permanent U.S. Representative to the United Nations
Richard C. Holbrooke, 1999–

Career summary
Vice chairman, Credit Suisse First Boston, 1996–99 (during this period, served also as special presidential envoy to Cyprus and Special Envoy in Bosnia and Kosovo)
Assistant secretary of state for European and Canadian affairs, 1994–96

U.S. ambassador to Germany, 1993–94

Managing director, Lehman Brothers, 1985–93

Vice president, Public Strategies, 1981–85

Assistant secretary of state for East Asian and Pacific affairs, 1977–81

Managing Editor, *Foreign Policy,* 1972–76

Various assignments, U.S. Foreign Service, 1962–72, including director, Peace Corps in Morocco; member, American Delegation to the Paris Peace Talks on Vietnam; special assistant to the under secretary of state; and several posts in Vietnam.

Education

B.A., Brown University, 1962

U.S. Permanent Representatives to the United Nations since 1989

Clinton administration

Bill Richardson, 1997–98 (currently secretary of energy)

Madeleine Albright, 1993–97 (currently secretary of state)

Bush administration

Edward J. Perkins, 1992–93 (currently William J. Crowe professor of geopolitical studies, University of Oklahoma)

Thomas R. Pickering, 1989–92 (currently under secretary of state for political affairs)

▓ Under Secretary for Arms Control and International Security Affairs

EXECUTIVE LEVEL III—Presidential appointment with Senate confirmation

RECOMMENDED SKILLS AND EXPERIENCE ■ While a grounding in mathematics and science is useful, negotiating experience and the ability to communicate are essential. "I'm comfortable dealing with scientific concepts—and they loom large," says John Holum, who directed the former Arms Control and Disarmament Agency and, on its integration into the Department of State, was nominated to this under secretary position in late 1999. He took his undergraduate degree in math and physical sciences. People without that background can always learn enough to handle the issues, especially with the deep expertise of the bureau's career staff; still, it is a clear advantage if you bring it in with you. Perhaps the dominant feature of the job is what Holum calls "a continuous process of negotiating," both within the U.S. government and with other governments. "Before we go overseas, we have a complex internal process, with all the relevant players weighing in, to settle what the U.S. position is." That requires extensive negotiation with the defense and intelligence communities, the Departments of Commerce and Energy, and the National Security Council. Overall, he says, the position basically requires "persuasion, negotiation, patience, and energy."

INSIGHT ■ As a start, it's important to understand the recent restructuring of this job, which now includes the mission and responsibilities of the former U.S. Arms Control and Disarmament Agency. ACDA was an independent entity whose director reported directly to the president. When it was folded into the Department of State in 1999, Holum—who had headed the agency since 1993—was the clear choice for the new under secretary of state post and received a recess appointment to the job in the summer of 200. He had meanwhile served as a senior adviser to the president and secretary of state for arms control, nonproliferation, and disarmament. Today, in a policy and oversight context, he's responsible for four functions, some of which came into the new structure with him:

—Preventing the spread of weapons of mass destruction—nuclear, chemical, biological, and missile systems. Nonproliferation, as this long, tenacious, hard-fought effort is known, takes place mostly in a bilateral context, where the United States goes after countries selling missile or nuclear technology, for example, to governments it judges might make the wrong use of it.

—Arms control. This involves not only negotiating further strategic arms reductions with Russia in a bilateral framework or new agreements with numbers of other countries, such as the comprehensive nuclear test ban treaty (which the U.S. Senate failed to ratify), but implementing existing treaties. Implementation is a major, often overlooked dimension of arms control. As more agreements have come into being, making them work and resolving disputes is more complicated and consumes increasing time. Commissions have been established to facilitate this work; Holum provides policy leadership here and sometimes participates, at senior or subcabinet levels.

—International security relationships. This involves managing defense trade control issues, about $6 billion in annual international military assistance, plus foreign military sales, economic support funds, and such other matters as peacekeeping operations overseas or land mine removal in a number of countries savaged by recent wars.

—Verification and compliance activities required by U.S. participation in arms control and nonproliferation agreements.

Has the switch from running an independent agency to operating within the State Department affected the nature or outlook of the job? One result is that Holum has fewer internal administrative duties, but the overall scope of his work has broadened. Perhaps more critical for him is future preservation of the job's independent voice within government arms control and foreign policy councils. The old ACDA was created with the idea that its judgments and recommendations on arms control and related issues would not be colored by worries about relations with individual countries. Such worries might properly influence the State Department's own approach to arms control. As Holum explains it, State wouldn't necessarily want to raise unpleasant subjects like nonproliferation or sanctions at the expense of good relations with the country concerned. He acknowledges that may be an oversimplification—that State routinely tries to advance U.S. interests with other countries on a range of issues like drugs, terrorism, arms control, and nonproliferation. "But the bias in the State Department," he says, "is toward maintaining relationships."

He therefore feels it is vital "to have independent advocacy for things like preventing the spread of nuclear weapons, even if it would ruffle feathers internationally" and adds that "we had an independent agency doing that." In negotiating and agreeing with the secretary of state to eliminate ACDA, he made it a condition that independent advocacy would continue under the new arrangement. Alone within the State Department, therefore, his position has a direct reporting line to the president, through the secretary. This means that "when arms control and similar issues are on the agenda, I still have a seat at the table at National Security Council meetings (chaired by the president) or at the principals and deputies committee levels" where foreign and defense policy decisions are shaped and finalized.

In practice, Holum notes, the new reporting line through the secretary to the president doesn't differ greatly from his own earlier situation at ACDA, because, "as ACDA director, I always told the secretary of state what I was telling the president." But he knows this reporting relationship is an unusual one, and his particular hope and expectation is that it will be continued by the next administration. "I'm very anxious that the unique features we established to preserve the independent voice for arms control and nonproliferation are protected." It will be important, he thinks, not only to be aware of the increased authorities of the under secretary position but also to use them as required.

Holum defines three major operational challenges for this job. One of them is controls on defense trade—a system that developed in an era of large defense budgets, a marked American lead in most technologies, and government as the biggest spur to the advance of those technologies. All that has changed. Now most new technology comes from the private sector and government is incorporating it for its own needs. Defense budgets have been declining, and the United States shares its technological leadership with a number of other countries. This has put pressure on the U.S. defense trade control system to modernize, among other reasons, "so we don't delay uncontroversial transfers to close allies or stand in the way of further consolidation within the U.S. defense industry or across borders." Design of a new system is under way, "but there's an enormous amount of work ahead to finish this, continue to update it, and put it in place internationally."

The second challenge relates to Senate rejection of the Comprehensive Test Ban Treaty in October 1999. While Holum thinks there was "a considerable political element" involved, he also sees a signal that the existing "bipartisan consensus favoring arms control as a national security instrument" is in danger. His department has work to do, he says, in rebuilding the consensus. "Whoever has this job in the future will have that burden, both to keep the rebuilding task on the administration's agenda and in dealing with the Hill and the public—public education as well as more visible political persuasion."

Pertinent to this is a new group of senators from relevant committees called the National Security Working Group, successor to an old arms control observer group from the days of the SALT II treaty. It emerged from the belief of a number of senators in the value of continuous engagement with the administration as treaties are being negotiated. This can help avoid the extensive international complications that ensue when something like the test ban treaty goes down to defeat. "Regardless of beginning positions," Holum comments, "it's important for senators to be fully informed of what we're doing. The more they know, the better off we'll be, even if they end up opposing what we do."

As for public education on these complicated issues, Holum thinks the media is one channel. Staying in contact with nongovernment organizations and keeping them informed is another. He himself does a good deal of speaking—a major speech every two weeks is not uncommon—to a variety of audiences. Examples are town hall meetings or academic experts on arms control and nonproliferation.

Challenge number three is the growth in the technology of weapons of mass destruction. Twenty countries currently pursue chemical weapons. A similar number are seeking biological weapons. "Scores of countries, maybe as many as forty, are pursuing missile capability," Holum says. The situation calls for more intense diplomacy using "all the levers"—sanctions, inducements, assistance, and the like. Limiting weapons spread can't be done with export controls or supplier regimes alone. What's also needed is stronger, better use of what he calls the "demand-side tools: the treaties by which countries voluntarily agree to give up these capabilities."

The four bureaus Holum runs are staffed by about 600 people. Almost all work in the United States. There is also a resident delegation in Geneva. He has a personal staff of sixteen.

"When I leave," he says, "and whoever my successor is, I hope to be able to sit down and talk about the recent history of this job, and the merger with State, and explain why we did what we did. With somebody that's knowledgeable on the subject, that probably won't be hard. There's also a lot of knowledge on the Hill about what we've done and a lot of support for it. I think it's important to preserve it."

PROFILE

Current Under Secretary for Arms Control and International Security Affairs
John D. Holum (served as senior adviser while awaiting confirmation),
April 1999–

Career summary
Director, U.S. Arms Control and Disarmament Agency, 1993–99
Law practice, O'Melveny and Myers, Washington, D.C., 1981–92
Policy planning staff, Department of State, 1979–81
Staff member, Sen. George McGovern (D-S.D.), 1965–79

Education
B.S., mathematics and physical sciences, Northern State Teachers College;
J.D. with honors, George Washington University School of Law

Directors of the Arms Control and Disarmament Agency since 1989*

Clinton and Bush administrations
Ronald F. Lehman II, 1989–93 (currently director, Center for Global Security
 Research, Lawrence Livermore National Laboratory)

Bush and Reagan administrations
William F. Burns, 1988–89 (U.S. Army, retired)
*Position title changed during the current incumbency.

Under Secretary for Political Affairs

EXECUTIVE LEVEL III—Presidential appointment with
Senate confirmation

RECOMMENDED SKILLS AND EXPERIENCE ■ The major require-
ment is solid, lengthy exposure to foreign policy and international affairs.
While that kind of background is not exclusively acquired in official U.S.
diplomacy, it's a simple fact that career U.S. Foreign Service professionals have held the post in nine of the twelve appointments to it over the
past three decades. In any case, there is little room for on-the-job learning here. Wherever they come from, candidates should be closely schooled
in the recent history and current directions of the United States in a global
context, preferably with a record of substantial on-site engagement in that
arena.

Effective service in this job also rests on a well-developed sense of the
Congress and the politics of foreign policy; and of how American and foreign publics view the U.S. role in the world. The more widely the under secretary has traveled or lived overseas and the broader the relationships and
contacts throughout the international foreign policy community, the better
served the position will be. Familiarity with the culture of the career foreign
service at home and abroad—including the accumulating burden imposed
by years of severe shortages of resources—is just about mandatory.

INSIGHT ■ In some ways, this job carries the real key to day-by-day
policymaking and implementation at the Department of State. At first
glance, State is a stovepiped agency—regional and functional bureaus
grouped under individual under secretaries, working much of the time only
with others in their own groups. According to Under Secretary Thomas
Pickering, however, State has also been trying to create a task-oriented

capability that allows any of those under secretaries to reach department-wide for the means to handle a specific issue or crisis. The under secretary for political affairs has the best leverage to make that happen, because alone among other senior officials, the individual in this job has a running, detailed overview of what's happening substantively everywhere in the building and around the world.

Further, this under secretary—whom some think of as the department's chief operating officer—presides at the crossroads where State's senior career professionals and its political leadership connect. Through this job flow many of the main currents of department decisionmaking: information, recommendations, specialized expertise in one direction; choices, command, guidance in the other.

Third, the under secretary remains the department's chief political crisis manager, a troubleshooter on call for urgent special assignments like the near civil war in Colombia, the emergency evacuation of Americans from crisis situations, or North Korea's on-and-off flirtation with nuclear power status. Action of a different kind was necessary in April 2000, while the votes were still being counted in Peru's close presidential election. As President Fujimori pondered whether to accept a second-round run-off vote in the presidential election or claim outright victory in the first round, Under Secretary Thomas Pickering and other senior U.S. officials made strategic telephone calls to Lima, underlining the dangers of ignoring the actual electoral result and the will of the people.

Even when one of the department's four other under secretaries takes the lead on a given crisis, the political affairs under secretary is never far from the action. As the third-ranking official and chief policy manager at State, Pickering can be found in the middle of the fray as policy is debated, set, refined, cleared, and carried out.

In addition, half a dozen geographic and international organization bureaus fall under the oversight of this position. The job also engages closely with the interagency consultative process where so much of the scut work of developing U.S. foreign policy positions takes place. At deputy-level meetings of U.S. foreign affairs agencies, one of the last stops in shaping foreign policy recommendations, the under secretary is often tapped to represent the department. Likewise, as the third-ranking official at State, Pickering when necessary replaces the deputy secretary, and occasionally the secretary, as the department's acting chief.

The portfolio goes on—U.S. political planner for the annual Group of Eight summit meeting, liaison with the new Department of State bureaus that are the former Arms Control and Disarmament and U.S. Information Agencies, member of the secretary's inner circle, unofficial representative of the views and interests of the career foreign service. Someone once described this job as State's utility infielder but, in reality, it ranges far toward the outfield fences as well.

Pickering, a career diplomat and seven times a U.S. ambassador, has also focused particularly on four countries considered central in the process of "transition to democracy." Besides Colombia, they are Nigeria, Indonesia, and the Ukraine. Given the preeminent place in the world that history has bequeathed to this country, "people increasingly look to us to take the lead," he says. The situation is complicated by the "jealousies, uncertainties, unhappiness, and sometimes real antagonism" that inevitably accompany that role. "So the style of how we work and the ways in which we carry our responsibilities forward can be very important." The result, says Pickering, who became under secretary in 1997, is that the job has gained in responsibility. "If, in fact, we're called on to take the lead and we don't, then inevitably we are going to pay a serious price."

Media relations are a significant dimension of his job. He deals with journalists directly and—as one of the officials who clear press guidance for the department spokesman—indirectly as well. He travels to Capitol Hill regularly for testimony and consultation and does "a reasonably large amount" of public speaking. "A certain part of the job," he also points out, "is getting to know and work with the Washington diplomatic community, the academic institutions, and the think tanks."

One of Pickering's predecessors, Robert M. Kimmitt, recommended that any new arrival in this job put as much energy and outreach into it at the beginning as possible. A "narrow window of opportunity" exists at that moment, he said, and recommended seizing it early, "before people get stale and before you are overrun by external exigencies."

PROFILE

Current Under Secretary for Political Affairs
Thomas R. Pickering, 1997–

Career summary
President, Eurasia Foundation, 1996–97
U.S. ambassador to Russia, 1993–96
U.S. ambassador to India, 1992–93
Permanent U.S. representative to the United Nations,1989–92

U.S. ambassador to Israel, 1985–88

U.S. ambassador to El Salvador, 1983–85

U.S. ambassador to Nigeria, 1981–83.

Assistant secretary for oceans and international environmental and scientific affairs, 1978–81

U.S. ambassador to Jordan, 1974–78

Education

B.A., Bowdoin College, 1953; M.A., Tufts University, 1954; M.A., University of Melbourne (Australia), 1956

Under Secretaries for Political Affairs since 1989

Clinton administration

Peter Tarnoff, 1993–96 (currently president, International Advisory Corporation)

Bush administration

Arnold Lee Kanter, 1991–93 (currently senior fellow, Forum for International Policy)

Robert M. Kimmitt, 1989–91 (currently partner, Wilmer, Cutler, and Pickering)

6

Positions in Health, Safety, and Environmental Policy

Consumer Product Safety Commission

▨ Chairman

EXECUTIVE LEVEL III—Presidential appointment with
Senate confirmation

RECOMMENDED SKILLS AND EXPERIENCE ■ A background in
consumer affairs or advocacy, or in the practice of law—preferably, legal
experience in the area of federal administrative or regulatory decisions—
are clearly the first attributes to look for. Training or a work history in science or engineering is helpful, though not required. But the chair of this
agency should have the potential to analyze a variety of data in these sectors. The current chair emphasizes commitment to the objectives of the
commission, a balanced approach to its consumer and industry constituents,
and communication and media savvy—"very important," she says, "for an
agency with a small budget to get the media on your side and use them in
creative ways."

INSIGHT ■ "We're on the side of the angels here," says Ann Brown,
who has led the U.S. Consumer Product Safety Commission since 1994.
"Our mission is to protect families, especially children." The staff of the
CPSC, she adds, "is extremely mission oriented" and she sees herself as
"basically a cheerleader making sure they keep their eyes on the sparrow."
Selling a product or satisfying stockholders is not this organization's job.
"It's selling safety, making people familiar with what we do and how they
can find us."

Established in 1972 by the Consumer Product Safety Act, the commission is an independent regulatory agency charged with protecting Americans from undue risks of injury and death related to consumer products. But
when Brown took over, the agency itself had been crossing rough terrain.
In the 1980s, it sustained cumulative cuts of 50 percent in staff and 60 percent in budget; between 1981 and 1989, its leadership passed through the
hands of four chairman and five acting chairman. For the last half of that
decade, although the CPSC's establishing legislation set the commission's
membership at five, appointed by the president for seven-year terms, the
agency operated under only three. No nominees were put forward for the
other two seats and the Congress responded by not appropriating funding
for them—a situation that remains unchanged today.

Today, with the exception of food, drugs, cars, boats, cosmetics, tobacco, and guns, the CPSC covers a range of 15,000 categories of consumer products that run from aquariums to zippers. These are products that collectively are involved in 29 million injuries and 22,000 deaths each year. Information that allows the commission to track them comes in through various channels—a toll-free hotline with nearly a hundred telephone lines, a web site where people can file reports online, a system for collecting injury information from hospital emergency rooms, and the commission's own investigation and research into potential product hazards. To reduce risks to consumers, the agency can take one of several approaches. It can order or arrange the recall of a product, develop voluntary or mandatory standards for the manufacture and use of a product and enforce compliance, ban products where no practical standard is possible, or inform the public about potential hazards and recommended safe uses.

"We've worked cooperatively with industry on many ventures," Brown says. "Most of the time, we don't have to regulate. More than 99 percent of our recalls are voluntary." As an example, she describes the agency's campaign to eliminate drawstrings in the necks of children's clothing that presented a danger of strangulation on playground equipment, escalators, and other objects that children regularly encounter. "I brought the industry in, gave them good data, worked with a mother whose child had died when the string in the hood of her sweatshirt got caught on a playground slide. By the next school season, the industry had voluntarily removed the strings from the necks of kids' garments." "The baseball bat is always in the closet," she points out. "Regulation is always a possibility." But moving voluntarily and quickly to the solution of a safety problem is far more preferable.

In practice, CPSC activity is a mix of all the measures cited above. Recommendations about a product's safety and what to do about it are developed by a staff limited to a ceiling of 480—slightly smaller than it was in 1992. Most of its members are engineers, chemists, behavioral scientists, statisticians, physicists, epidemiologists, and other technical experts. Just over half work in the agency's headquarters in a Maryland office building about two miles outside Washington and in a second location where the CPSC has its own health sciences and engineering laboratory. The rest operate out of the commission's field offices across the country or telecommute.

A random glance at CPSC product recalls illustrates the breadth of the agency's focus. Some 26,000 fire extinguishers with a risk of explosion caused by contents under high pressure. More than 200,000 alternating-current adapters for notebook computers, carrying a fire hazard from overheating. A third of a million bottles of windshield washer fluid, not sealed with child-resistant closures as required by law. Nearly 10 million battery-powered ride-on toys that overheat and can cause fire. More than 10 million toy basketball nets that can tangle around children's necks. About 3,000 front-suspension forks installed on mountain bikes that can break off and cause loss of control. More than 2.5 million weed trimmer heads with metal chains whose end link can detach and fly through the air at high speed. More than 9 million playpens whose rivets present a strangulation danger.

Decisions on CPSC actions, such as rule making, are the main work of the commissioners. As with other federal regulatory bodies, the rules governing their proceedings leave little room for inconsistency or irregularity. A quorum must be present for meetings, which are announced in advance, are open to the public, and are recorded electronically. Commission consideration of a case for potential rule making moves through a three-stage procedure that can be canceled at any given point if the hazard is otherwise resolved. Public notices of any meetings of commissioners with outside parties appear on a calendar ahead of time.

Brown considers her chief responsibilities to be:

—Setting an agenda for the commission. "I had an agenda before I came," she says, "and it wasn't hidden. It was very much up front."

—"Making sure that not a penny is wasted." Although the agency's budget has risen by 25 percent during her tenure (it asked for a fiscal 2001 appropriation of $52.5 million), its funding is still "minuscule," she says, given the size of the CPSC mission. "Our budget is half the size it was in 1981, in real dollars." The agency's fiscal 2000 appropriation ($49 million) was "the amount of money the Pentagon spends in an hour and a half."

—Being effective on Capitol Hill. "We have to show Congress that the commission is an exceptional value and that our work is bipartisan. Protecting families and children is not a partisan mission."

—Using the media as a principal channel for educating Americans about product hazards and about the commission's work and its importance to them. In Brown's view, success with the media enhances respect for the CSPC as well as congressional, industry, and public recognition of what it does. "The press finds our work interesting," she says with a sense of pleased surprise, noting that she appears regularly on morning television and radio programs and makes a point of speaking in plain, non-bureaucratic English.

—Creating the best possible working environment for the staff. "The career staff is our most valuable asset here," Brown observes. The agency does as much as it can, she says, to recognize achievement and provide training and career advancement. She says she has "opened up the agency. I want ideas from the bottom up. When we won an innovations award, it was for an idea that came from the staff, not from the top." Conferred in 1998 by the Ford Foundation's Innovations in American Government program, the award recognized the CPSC's Fast-Track Product Recall initiative, begun as a pilot project in 1995. Reducing from months to days the time between discovery of a potential hazard and the actual recall of the product, fast track represents a negotiated deal between the commission and industry. When a company volunteers for fast track, the commission bypasses most of the normally time-consuming recall process, including the preliminary determination made by the commission to justify the recall. Companies fear—and often fight—this determination, because it can imply guilt and attract liability suits. Avoiding it greatly speeds the process. Today, about half of all recalls are fast-tracked.

As for current challenges and those to come, Brown mentions three. "Keeping pace with technology is a huge issue. Every day there are more technically complex consumer problems. We need to ensure that product safety standards keep pace with that." She says the agency has asked the Congress for a research budget that would allow it to give its mission more sophisticated technical leadership. Second is the sale of hazardous and illegal products via the Internet, to which the CPSC has responded so far with Safe Online Shopping, "an undercover group of trained staff members, working with clean computers and nongovernment credit cards." The Internet's role being what it is, this is something the commission will have to continue chasing down for the foreseeable future. Third is "the globalization of the market place." While most of U.S. industry knows CPSC rules, "this is not the case with manufacturers abroad." The agency therefore collaborates with the U.S. Customs Service "to be certain that globalization doesn't bring fresh dangers to American families."

Brown advises successor chairmen to "arrive with an agenda, know what you want to accomplish." Her first nomination process (she has been appointed to this job twice) took nine months, giving her a lengthy opportunity "to talk with everybody before I came on board." Once in the job, she says, "you have to take risks, be innovative, deal with the tough issues. If you deal only with the safe, piddling things, you'll go nowhere. Take on the risks—but be politically smart about it."

PROFILE

Current Chair of the Consumer Products Safety Commission
Ann W. Brown, 1994–

Career summary
Vice president, Consumer Federation of America, 1980–93
Chairman of the board, Public Voice, 1983–93

Education
B.A, George Washington University, 1959

Chairmen of the Consumer Product Safety Commission since 1989

Bush administration
Jacqueline Jones-Smith, 1989–94 (currently associated with the
    Maxima Corporation)

Department of Agriculture

▓ Under Secretary for Food Safety

**EXECUTIVE LEVEL III—Presidential appointment with
Senate confirmation**

RECOMMENDED SKILLS AND EXPERIENCE ■ A strong background in public health and food safety—a requirement set out by the Congress—is the first. This position oversees the Food Safety and Inspection Service, a science-based public health agency responsible for the safety of meat, poultry, and egg products; part of its responsibility is to advise the secretary of agriculture on these and other issues that go beyond food safety itself.

Second is good connections into the U.S. science and health community. That's because, in addition to this agency's reliance on scientific research and other units within the Department of Agriculture, it looks for external advice and assistance on many occasions in its regulatory activities. Tapping into outside scientific sources for advice, as the current under secretary's earlier career permitted her to do, added to and helped to broaden her perspective.

Finally, the Food Safety and Inspection Service must engage the Congress on specific issues that in 2001 will continue to include protecting, and preferably increasing, the number of its inspectors. As a veteran of a prior stint with the former Office of Technology Assessment, a congressional agency, the current under secretary is convinced that experience in the legislative branch is a clear advantage.

INSIGHT ▪ In one of those seeming eccentricities in the division of regulatory authority among federal agencies, the FSIS is responsible for seeing to the safety, wholesomeness, and accurate labeling of meat, poultry, and meat and poultry products moving in interstate and foreign commerce—except for eggs in the shell. Processed egg products, yes. But shell eggs come under the jurisdiction of the Food and Drug Administration. Actually, while the FSIS carries the main responsibility for food safety, it works regularly with the FDA and others, like the Environmental Protection Agency, whose activities complement or affect its duties under the federal government's food safety mandate.

Beyond leading the FSIS itself, this under secretary oversees the federal role in Codex Alimentarius, an international program of two United Nations bodies—the World Health Organization and the Food and Agriculture Organization. Codex sets international standards for food, most related to food safety. The U.S. Codex office manages the development of U.S. positions on these questions, consulting with other government agencies as well as with industry and the health-care, academic, and consumer communities.

Catherine E. Woteki, who became under secretary in July 1997, also coordinates the Agriculture Department's several other activities related to food safety, scattered among six offices and services. Part of the information the FSIS needs in order to regulate comes from economic and agricultural research performed within the department or coordinated by the department with the states. Part of it emerges from risk assessment and cost-benefit analysis. From the Animal and Plant Health Inspection Service comes data on diseases that can also cause human illness. And the Agricultural Marketing Service conducts tests—for aflatoxin, for example, in commodities being purchased for government programs—that Woteki says also have implications for human health.

Woteki leads U.S. delegations to various international meetings on food safety issues. She says her work involves her with the Organization for Economic Cooperation and Development and the World Trade Organization.

She is, in addition, the Agriculture Department's emergency planner against the possibility of major catastrophe in which the continued operation of the federal government would be critical. She is vice chair of a department antiterrorism council, established by the secretary, that works with the National Security Council.

With a work force of about 8,100, the FSIS inspects 6,500 meat and poultry plants nationwide and monitors food coming from foreign countries. Its ranks include inspectors, compliance officers, scientists, and veterinarians.

When the Congress reorganized the Agriculture Department in 1994 legislation, it created this position, gave it oversight of the FSIS, and made food safety the agency's only function. In part, the move was spurred by congressional recognition, after a West Coast outbreak of *E.coli* bacteria the previous year, that a better food safety approach was urgent. In part, the reorganization was the product of a related awareness that the goals of food safety and food marketing—once combined in the old department structure—were in basic conflict.

One of the regulatory changes since 1994 requires the labeling of meat and poultry products with information for consumers on safe handling and proper preparation. But the most significant was adoption by the FSIS of an entirely new strategy for the inspection of food. The Hazard Analysis and Critical Control Point system uses science-based measures to reduce contamination and improve inspection performance. Where the old approach relied on after-the-fact visual identification of problems at food processing locations, HACCP aims at prevention—in processing plants, in transit, in storage, and at the places where food is sold. It places greater responsibility on the industry for controlling and monitoring its operations. And it transformed the FSIS into a science-based agency.

"The whole HACCP approach," Woteki says, "is premised on industry taking responsibility for the safety of its product. Each plant is required to develop and have in place a HACCP plan to follow every day it is in production. The role of the Department of Agriculture inspector or state inspector changes to oversight and verification that the plant is meeting its responsibilities."

In January 2000 the HACCP program entered its final implementation phase. About its results to date, Woteki says "we have a very good story to tell." When the last phase began, every meat and poultry slaughter and processing plant in the country, whether inspected by the federal government or by one of the twenty-five state programs, was meeting the requirements of HACCP. "We have excellent data on the performance testing required under HACCP for salmonella, which is one of the major causes of food-borne disease," she says. "Our data indicate that salmonella levels have decreased a quarter to a half, depending on the product." The biggest drops occurred in poultry products, where salmonella levels had been the highest.

The country's 300 largest food processing plants produce three quarters of all U.S. meat and poultry products. They were required to begin the HACCP program in its first year. Data collected over a three-year period by a food-borne disease surveillance system of the Centers for Disease Control showed "a very substantial and significant decrease in salmonella illnesses in people," Woteki notes. "And CDC attributes part of that decline to implementation of HACCP in meat and poultry plants. So from the process standpoint, the product standpoint, and the human illness standpoint, all the indicators are going in the same direction and showing that we're making a difference."

But there are apparent problems with administering food safety, some imbedded in law and politics, others in the scope of coverage and the degree of bite in FSIS regulations. The *Washington Post* reported early in 2000, for example, that, unlike the case for numbers of other faulty products, no recall authority exists for impure meat because the Congress—despite the efforts of the Department of Agriculture—has refused to grant it. Withdrawal of bad meat continues to depend on volunteer action by the company involved. Likewise, the Congress has not established penalties for violations of food safety rules.

A case in point is the announcement in May 2000 that the government for the first time would require meat processing plants to test for contamination by listeria, a bacterium that has been killing about 500 people a year. Although the action pleased consumer groups, it did not allow the mandatory recall of listeria-contaminated food that may still escape from the processor onto food store shelves or provide punishment for violators of the new rule. The only recourse for FSIS in these cases, the *Post* article said, is to close a plant down. Until the listeria decision, no microbial testing took place in food processing plants, only in slaughterhouses. It was not clear whether testing for other contamination would also now include processing plants.

With HACCP implementation complete, the budget requested by the FSIS for fiscal 2001 in some respects marked what Woteki sees as the agency's transition to the future. At the same time, she says, "HACCP is not static. It is dynamic, and has to change in response to emerging problems." The program was in fact designed to do just that. The FSIS in 2000 announced the development of new inspection models for plants that slaughter only young, healthy animals and that would be tested in about twenty-five volunteer plants. These experiments, Woteki explains, will determine whether inspectors are performing functions not related to food safety that could be turned over to the plants. Without any reduction in product safety, she says, the findings potentially will free more time for inspectors to focus on safety. The tests of the models, which were to run through 2000, would identify which elements of them work and can be reflected in budget development.

Woteki is convinced that the creation of her job "really separated our public health mission for food safety from the marketing function of the department." It has, she adds, "put to bed the criticism about conflict of interest." She points out that the position is the only one in the 1994 reorganization for which Congress specified that its occupant should have professional credentials in public health and food safety.

PROFILE

Current Under Secretary for Food Safety
Catherine E. Woteki, 1997–

Career summary
Acting under secretary for research, education, and economics, Department of
　Agriculture, 1995–97
Deputy to the associate director of science, White House Office of Science and
　Technology Policy, 1994–95
Director, Food and Nutrition Board, National Academy of Sciences, 1990–94
Deputy director, health examination statistics, Department of Health and
　Human Services, 1983–90
Director, Food and Diet Appraisal Research Group, and associate
　administrator, Human Nutrition Information Service, Department of
　Agriculture, 1980–83
Nutrition project director, Congressional Office of Technology Assessment,
　1977–80
Assistant professor, Department of Nutrition and Food Science, Drexel
　University, 1975–77
Clinical researcher, University of Texas Medical School at San Antonio,
　1973–75

Education
B.S., Mary Washington College, 1969; Ph.D., Virginia Polytechnic Institute
and State University, 1974

Under Secretaries for Food Safety since 1989*

Clinton administration
Michael R. Taylor (acting), 1994–97 (currently professor of law, Georgetown
University Law Center, and consultant on public policy involving food,
agriculture, and environment)

Clinton and Bush administrations
H. Russel Cross, 1992–94 (currently CEO, Future Beef Operations)**

Bush and Reagan administrations
Lester M. Crawford, 1987–91 (currently research professor and director, Public
Policy Institute and Center for Food Nutrition, Georgetown University)**
*The under secretary position was established in 1994
**Served as administrator, Food Safety and Inspection Service

Department of Energy

▓ Assistant Secretary for Environmental Management

EXECUTIVE LEVEL IV—Presidential appointment with
Senate confirmation

RECOMMENDED SKILLS AND EXPERIENCE ∎ In the words of the
most recent assistant secretary for environmental management, Carolyn
Huntoon, "the interest in meeting a terrific challenge has to be there—you
have to be excited about doing this." A difficult assignment like this one,
with many people and many billions of dollars engaged in a complicated,
long-range effort, needs experience in managing large projects. But it also
takes the kind of leadership that knows how to give a geographically dis-
persed work force around the country the support it requires while letting
it do its job. As is evident from Huntoon's own career, solid and relevant
scientific or technical competence based on significant working experience
is beneficial. Specifically, that might have been developed in one or more
such fields as nuclear engineering, the technology involved in cleaning up

waste sites, environmental protection, or health care associated with radiation injury.

INSIGHT ■ Environmental management, Huntoon says, does not exactly describe what this position and the office under its supervision really do. The Office of Environmental Management "does not just manage the waste left behind by the cold war. We are working hard to clean it up." What she's referring to is stockpiled waste and contaminated ground, water, and structures left behind in the unsafeguarded, unprotected manufacture of nuclear weapons that began in World War II and continued well into the 1980s.

That was when the Department of Energy and the administration of the time, pushed by lawsuits and the application of environmental statutes, finally decided to tackle what was clearly a high-risk and potentially dangerous environmental problem. The decision transformed the department itself. Created in 1989, the Office of Environmental Management became and remains one of the department's largest (with about a third of the total department budget and 2,700 employees), although at the beginning it had neither the resources nor the people to get much done.

Today, EM's requested budget for fiscal 2001 is $6.3 billion. "It's the largest environmental cleanup program in the United States," Huntoon says, "and probably the largest of its kind in the world." That only begins to tell the story. EM's list of designated cleanup sites in thirty states numbered 113 in the spring of 2000, and new sites may be added. The biggest are in South Carolina, Tennessee, Washington, Ohio, Colorado, Idaho, and New Mexico. Most of the EM budget goes toward cleanup at these sites. On a much larger list are 4,000 facilities of differing kinds that EM is tasked with deactivating, decontaminating, and disposing of in various ways. Also involved are 1.7 trillion gallons of contaminated groundwater throughout the EM complex. Many firms and more than 100,000 individuals are doing this work under contract with EM.

It will take decades to complete the entire cleanup. "And by complete," Huntoon makes clear, "I don't mean putting things back the way they were, but just stabilizing, processing, and storing radioactive waste and materials in order to reduce the risk. We're talking about a $150 billion cost for the estimated remaining life costs of completing the program." The need to make this effort at such a cost in resources and time is "something that the administration and the Congress acknowledges," she says. "It's a responsibility of the federal government. We created this as part of our defense program, and now we need to clean it up."

Describing a top priority, she says EM has put a lot of emphasis on the 177 underground tanks containing 55 million gallons of high-level radioactive waste at the Hanford (Washington) site near the Columbia River. Built to hold high-level radioactive waste for twenty years, they've been there nearly forty. Some have leaked. "We have pumped the liquid out of the leading tanks into safer tanks, but we cannot just let these tanks sit there forever," Huntoon says. "So EM is monitoring them carefully." At the same time, it plans to build a processing plant that would stabilize the waste so that it can be stored safely for a very long time—"a multiyear and multibillion dollar effort."

Many sites that were contaminated will eventually be turned over to the communities near which they are located for various uses. Sometimes these sites have buildings or other facilities that can't be cleaned up and must be torn down and destroyed and the rubble treated as radioactive material.

At this point, one dimension of this position needs special attention. To continue making progress on its mission into the long-distance future, EM must support the development of science and technology that wouldn't otherwise be available. This is a unique undertaking, roughly comparable to the Defense Department's need to keep certain industries alive, healthy, and competitive to provide the sometimes rarefied but indispensable equipment and technology it will need in the years ahead. The techniques and procedures used to clean up radioactive material and sites "aren't necessarily the ones people would be developing if they weren't needed for our work," Huntoon explains. "We have to make sure the right technologies are being developed. We are sponsoring basic science research in certain areas and, in others, we're sponsoring technology deployment by testing new and innovative technologies." Further, handling a large lifecycle price tag means trying to drive down costs with more efficient, technically advanced, safe operations. "We have challenges today at many of our sites for which there are no answers yet. That's why we're managing a program in science and technology as well," she says. "It's well worth the investment."

How does EM collaborate with the states in which its work takes place? What relationships does it have with other environmental authorities? What is its approach to the public on the issues its work raises?

In most cases, advisory boards representing the communities around or near cleanup operations look at every aspect of the work being done. EM site managers meet regularly with the boards; Huntoon does so whenever she can. "We are being open with local leaders and residents about the risks and hazards that exist and how we're trying to deal with them," she says. For years, the sites were operated under tight security. During that period, while the production of nuclear weapons was casting off hot waste materials into air, buildings, ground, and water, few questions were asked, even by the Congress, about their disposition. Even fewer were answered.

After the end of the cold war, Huntoon says even officials responsible for the cleanup weren't completely aware of the entire situation at each of the Energy Department's weapons production facilities. "We're now trying to deal with it by being as open and inclusive as we can to any groups interested in the cleanup," especially people living close to the sites "who are concerned about their safety, the health of their families, and protecting their drinking water and their environment." Huntoon's senior staff meets frequently with these groups, showing them waste treatment and disposal plans and budgets and sharing other details.

EM cleanup operations in the states are regulated by state environmental authorities and by the federal Environmental Protection Agency. That's because many sites have "mixed" wastes—hazardous chemicals as well as radioactive material. Beyond this, EM has entered into legally enforceable agreements with many states, as Huntoon says, "to carry out certain activities by specified times. We approach each of these projects with definite start and end dates, and confirmable milestone dates along the way. As in most complex projects, it's critical to prioritize"—in Huntoon's case, to tackle the situations with the most immediate risk first, "the things you can't put off." Exploring this job before she took it, she adds, she quickly learned how essential effective management is when it comes to "resources, people, contracting, and the budgets we were asking for." Given the importance of the work EM is doing, Huntoon says, contacts within the states are not limited to the regulatory level and sometimes involve governors and their staffs.

Because the problem EM is addressing originated in the U.S. defense effort, a good portion of its funding is overseen by the congressional armed services committees. The issue here goes beyond the usual competition for resources among agencies and programs. Actual cleanup is such a long and often drawn-out process, Huntoon observes, that it's hard to show enough progress at any given point. While the strongest support comes from members representing districts containing cleanup sites, congressional acceptance of the cleanup as a cold war legacy is helpful. "We have to be sure," Huntoon says, "that, when we ask them for money, we know what we're going to do with it and can support the request. Then, as we accomplish things, we need to make sure we show them to the Congress and get the good news out to the public, too."

What's the biggest challenge in all this? "Just the enormity of the job," she replies. One piece of advice she would give successors concerns honoring EM's commitments. When they aren't met, she cautions, "the Environmental Management program gets hurt and the entire cleanup suffers." She is emphatic in her praise for EM's professional work force across the complex and at headquarters—people, she says, "who are responsible for our continuing success."

PROFILE

Current Assistant Secretary for Environmental Management
Carolyn Huntoon, July 1999–

Career summary
Special assistant to the administrator, National Space and Aeronautics Agency
Program coordinator, Office of Science and Technology Policy, Executive Office
   of the President
Director, Johnson Space Center, NASA, 1994–96; various other assignments,
   1968–94

Education
B.S., Northwestern State College; M.S. and Ph.D., Baylor College of Medicine

Assistant Secretaries for Environmental Management since 1989

Clinton administration
Alvin L. Alm, 1996–98(currently professor emeritus, Cloquet Forestry Center,
   University of Minnesota)
Thomas P. Grumbly, 1993–96 (currently president, Environment and Facilities
   Management Group, Kaiser Group International)

Bush administration
Leo P. Duffy, 1989–93 (currently president, Duffy Group)

Department of Health and Human Services

Commissioner, Food and Drug Administration

EXECUTIVE LEVEL IV—Presidential appointment with
Senate confirmation

RECOMMENDED SKILLS AND EXPERIENCE ■ Choose from a
mix of these qualifications: a degree in medicine or at least a strong, relevant technical background; exposure to the legislative process; managerial and communication skills; a degree of confidence in dealing with
political Washington and the media; credibility with the pharmaceutical
industry and among scientific professionals; and proven talent for distinguishing the forest amid multitudes of trees.

Jane Henney, a physician with an earlier stint at this agency under her
belt before taking the commissioner's job in 1998, has a special slant on
preparation for the position. "If the new commissioner walks in here from
the outside, even with the technical skill, ability, and background and a high
desire to do well, the first year will be frightening," she says. "There are just
so many unknowns." While prior experience at the Food and Drug Administration is not a requisite, she felt "particularly blessed" to have learned
in her previous tour many of the ropes that she thinks someone new needs
a year to grasp.

Whatever the choice, she adds, "25 percent of the economy is under the
purview of this agency. It will always get a great deal of scrutiny, no matter what administration or Congress you're talking about. They're going
to want to be sure they've got somebody in this position that can do the
job in as apolitical a fashion as possible. Because once an organization like
this begins to be perceived as political in its decisionmaking, it can only
be damaging."

INSIGHT ■ The facts about the Food and Drug Administration's scope
of responsibility remain as staggering as ever. It regulates 95,000 business
and manufacturing firms for the health and safety of what they produce
and the accuracy of product labeling. Each year its 1,050 inspectors and
investigators look at 15,000 establishments and collect about 30,000 sam-
ples of domestic and imported products for investigation. Each year the
FDA finds 3,700 of these unsuitable for consumption and engineers their

voluntary or mandatory recall and stops another 42,000 foreign products before they enter the United States.

Essentially, the FDA's mission in protecting public health is to make judgments about risk. If its inspectors find pesticide residues in food, are they significant enough to endanger health? Will an implanted medical device, expected to deteriorate over time, do so too quickly on average to be safe? Can DNA analysis kits foresee actual illness or merely indicate its possibility? Is a prescription or over-the-counter drug capable of delivering the benefits its manufacturer claims for it without damaging side effects? For all drugs and medical devices, what is the right balance between risk and benefit?

Encompassed in the sweep of FDA scrutiny are food, medicines, vaccines, blood and blood products, medical devices, cosmetics, products that emit radiation, and feed and drugs for farm animals and pets. From manufacture through transport and storage to sale, the agency every year monitors such products whose collective value is a trillion dollars. When its finds a product unsuitable, the FDA encourages its manufacturer to correct or withdraw it. If a manufacturer cannot do that, or won't, the FDA can take it to court to enforce its authority and confiscate the product. When appropriate, it can seek criminal penalties against manufacturers and distributors. It says it performs all of these tasks at a cost of $4 per American taxpayer per year.

Each year the agency certifies about a thousand new medical products, including about 500 pharmaceuticals, for marketing after careful review of the research data submitted in manufacturers' applications. It then pursues their history in the actual marketplace, collecting and analyzing reports on their use. As one of Henney's predecessors, David Kessler, explained to us four years ago, the speed of the review process must be weighed against its safety in assessing any drug application. Speed may be crucial in getting a product on the market that fights life-threatening or major disease for which no alternative treatment exists. It's less important when the drug under review is designed for minor maladies, especially if patients have a choice of other medications already available. In those cases, it is far more urgent to be certain the drug is safe, since many more consumers will be using it.

In 1992 the Congress enacted the Prescription Drug User Fee Act, essentially requiring manufacturers to pay the costs of reviewing new drug and biologics applications. It was an attempt to give the FDA greater resources for its review process, thereby responding to complaints from the industry and other groups that lengthy FDA review was putting research investments at risk while costing markets and lives. In return, the FDA undertook to speed its decisions on new drug applications; to that end, based on its projected fee income, it soon augmented its review staff by several hundred employees.

"We were greatly helped by the user fee program," Henney says, noting that it provided "for reviews, not approvals—companies aren't buying approvals." At the same time, she points out the stipulation that the fee program was to be considered "additive"—separate from the regular FDA appropriation. Thus, she says, the fee revenue might make the FDA budget appear to be increasing, but "many other programs have not benefited." Other "fundamental and core programs," which must undergo the annual struggle for appropriations, "are at real risk when it comes to the coverage in other areas, particularly the postmarket arena."

Indeed, Henney is strongly concerned by the looming resource problem. The number of products regulated by the FDA, she continues, has not decreased, while "the complexity of science is increasing." She thinks the FDA is staying even so far, but its continued ability to do so will be "highly dependent on the resource base that we have. And that has been eroding over time." For fiscal 2001, the agency requested an appropriation of $1.4 billion, an increase of about 4 percent from the previous year. Its request included funds for such objectives as halting the illegal sale of drugs over the Internet and reducing annual deaths from medical errors, estimated at 100,000. The agency's budget statement said its ability to assure safety is "directly linked to maintaining a strong science base that keeps pace with accelerating technology." It framed the situation with these points:

—Expenditures for drug research are seven times what they were twenty years ago.

—The drug discovery process is being fueled by major breakthroughs in biomedical and information technology.

—Medical device technology has shifted from X-rays and CAT scans to include robotics, miniaturization, and biomaterials.

—Trade and trade standards are being globalized.

—Consumer purchases are being shaped increasingly by the Internet, not the print and electronic media.

"There are programs," Henney says, "where we have been the world leader but where, because of major resource shifts, we almost don't have a presence any more. The agency's priorities have had to change, sometimes because of the new things authorized by Congress without accompanying appropriations." Private-sector investment in research and development plus that supported by the National Institutes of Health together total $50 billion annually, she says, and many of the products of this R&D come to the FDA for review at a time when the agency's ability to perform is dwindling. "So there's a tremendous disconnect between providing the continuum of scientific thinking on the front end, where you do discovery, and scientific judgments about whether something should come to the marketplace."

Related to this problem is the nature of the review process, something Henney says she has raised with the Congress. "People often think the review of an application is just looking at a bunch of papers. You make a decision on the fly, take up the next one—a sweatshop kind of activity." In reality, a review depends significantly "on what you've had time to put in your head." Scientists who make review decisions need time to stay current in their fields, learn new ones, get training and education time, be able to present papers at professional meetings, and earn respect in their areas. To do that, Henney says, "you're talking about time away from the review process."

The fact is, she adds, that both the FDA and industry are troubled by reviewers who are "not current with today's science" and are therefore sometimes wrong, or slow, or reluctant to take risks. A considerable turnover among reviewers makes this problem worse.

Henney thinks the FDA must adjust its thinking about its scientific reviewer ranks. They should be considered "not as full-time employees on salary" but in a salary-plus situation. "We're talking about an employee who is funded at 110 percent up to 150 percent, in order to bring to the table the kind of professional expertise we really need."

When she took over as FDA commissioner, Henney had a number of priorities that have actual (or, in the case of tobacco, potential) relevance for the agency's future leadership. There was the need, already discussed, to maintain and enhance the FDA's scientific base. There is the Food Safety Initiative, which involves a national alert system for food-borne illness, more seafood safety inspections, and increased food-safety research, training, and education. There is the FDA's 1996 move to begin regulating the nicotine in cigarettes as a drug and restrict sales and advertising to young people (later halted by the Supreme Court's decision that the FDA lacked authority over tobacco).

And there was the full implementation of the FDA Modernization Act of 1997, a strategic plan for the future direction of the agency designed to take into account the increasing complexity of the technological, trade, and public health environment in which it operates. "It touched practically everything within the agency," Henney says of the legislation, and is "really sweeping" in what it has meant for drugs, biologics, and devices. A "huge amount of legwork" went into its implementation. The modernization measure "put into law many things the agency had already been doing in the area of reinvention, trying to work more efficiently," she says. It also reauthorized the Prescription Drug User Fee Act, an affirmation that, in Henney's view, "said the program worked."

She sees other important aspects of the modernization legislation. First, it requires the FDA to report to the Congress "about where we are and where we are not in meeting our statutory obligations. Frankly, that gives us the formal opportunity to say we aren't meeting this or that, and why. And usually, the 'why' is tied to resource issues." Second, the modernization act explicitly called for the FDA "to engage regularly with the individuals and organizations who have a stake in how this agency works." Included in that are consumers, consumer and patient advocacy groups, scientists, individual companies, and trade associations. The agency reaches out to them in forums like stakeholder meetings and interactive television conversations, fanning its senior staff out across the country to participate. "We're asking them for ideas about what we're doing and about what we should be considering," says Henney. "This year the topic was how to leverage resources—ours and theirs."

Information technology has helped this outreach, Henney says. Beyond videoconferencing (the FDA operates a television studio), the agency has made extensive use of the Internet with its web site, one of whose features is devoted to bioengineered foods. Using it, consumers could not only read transcripts of the three public meetings on this topic that the FDA convened in the fall of 1999, they also were able to comment on FDA policies in this area. Henney says also that the agency is moving toward electronic submission of new drug applications and the conduct of reviews simultaneously instead of sequentially.

She characterizes FDA relations with the Congress as "friendly and strong, in terms of the agency's mission and the desire that it do well." While "we get criticized from time to time," she comments, "what regulatory agency doesn't? Where there's a mismatch is providing the kind of financial support the agency needs." In the structure of the appropriations process, the FDA is grouped with the Department of Agriculture on

Senate and House agriculture appropriations subcommittees, where it competes for discretionary funding dollars. "We've held our own in percentage of dollars," Henney says. "There's just not a lot of dollars there. We get up against that year after year, and it's become a very intense struggle." On the media front, Henney recognizes that the FDA will always be of great interest. Within the constraints binding a regulatory agency, she says the organization strives for openness and transparency with journalists and thinks it has paid off in a sustained level of respect from the public.

How does Henney view her own responsibility as the FDA chief? "To analyze the capacity of the organization and focus on capacity-building initiatives," she answers. The FDA deals with controversial issues where there are few rights and wrongs. "It's a matter of making the right judgments. No matter what the issue is, if you have strong capacity, the organization can deal with it." She says she has tried to emphasize that most of what the agency does must rely not only on its basic statute but also on science. "Are we prepared, both individually and collectively as an agency, to bring the best science to bear on our decisions, whether the decision relates to review, policy, or enforcement? That's where I've invested a great deal of my time and effort."

She thinks the nature of what consumers expect is changing. Where traditionally they have wanted protection, they now look for a high level of information and guidance on how to interpret it. "While we still need to be sure products meet a certain standard and that the regulated industry is compliant, the agency will have to adjust to who consumers are and what they desire from an agency like this." With the Internet, the need for openness and transparency will grow. How the FDA meets that requirement, accelerating and widening openness, will need to be thought through carefully.

Meanwhile, the "revolution in genetics" and how it may change products from medicine to food, will strongly challenge the review process. It is also altering the businesses the FDA regulates. "We've been geared to thinking of bricks-and-mortar plants we go into and inspect," Henney says, "and we know the retailers, the buyers, and where the raw materials come from. The Internet changes all that. It's going to add a churn and swirl to our world. How do we approach that? How do we make sure standards remain high? Those are the kinds of things that will face us in the next ten to fifteen years."

PROFILE

Current Commissioner of the Food and Drug Administration
Jane E. Henney, 1998–

Career summary
Vice president, University of New Mexico Health Sciences, 1994–98
Deputy commissioner for operations, Food and Drug Administration, 1992–94
Vice chancellor for health programs and policy and acting director,
  Mid America Cancer Center, University of Kansas, 1985–92
Various positions at the National Cancer Institute, National Institutes of
  Health, 1976–85, including deputy director, 1980–85

Education
B.A., Manchester College, 1969; M.D., Indiana University School of
  Medicine, 1973

Commissioners of the Food and Drug Administration since 1989

Clinton administration
Michael Friedman (acting), 1997–98 (currently senior vice president,
  government affairs, G. D. Searle)

Clinton and Bush administrations
David A. Kessler, 1990–97 (currently dean, School of Medicine,
  Yale University)

Bush administration
James A. Benson (acting), 1989–90 (currently affiliated with Advanced Medical
  Technology Association)

Director, National Institutes of Health

EXECUTIVE LEVEL IV—Presidential appointment with
Senate confirmation

RECOMMENDED SKILLS AND EXPERIENCE ■ Strong credibility, a
reasonably persuasive manner, and a lack of narrow, vested interests are the
first qualifications suggested by Dr. Harold Varmus, the Nobel Prize laure-
ate who led the National Institutes of Health from 1993 to late 1999. When
he held the job, Varmus says, he was seen as being there "to promote science and speak with as much integrity as possible. No one perceived me as
having personal ambitions or conflicts of interest."

Credibility, he makes clear, also includes the credentials that have always been mandatory for this job, among them a wide-ranging knowledge of medicine or biology and up-to-date familiarity with the advance of research in a number of fields at the core of National Institutes of Health concern. Formal training at least through the doctoral level is also on this list, although a medical degree is not a must in the view of some who know the job well.

An ability to manage and a solid scientific reputation are essential. As we pointed out in this space four years ago, however, the selection of a director should avoid two extremes: first, a great manager with no particular affinity for science or medicine and, second, a highly capable scientist without significant regard for running things or for taking the public interest into account.

INSIGHT ▪ Every NIH director, Varmus believes, should strongly champion basic scientific research as the best hope for truly revolutionary progress in medicine.

But many well-meaning stakeholders in the work of the National Institutes of Health, don't go quite as far. They range from members of the Congress to the pharmaceutical industry to advocates for the disabled and those with life-threatening diseases. These groups prefer that the NIH invest its core efforts in applied research, fueled by a comparable percentage of its budget, that will solve high-visibility diseases like cancer—ailments for which the chances for a quick breakthrough are slight.

Varmus is in no sense slighting this concern or the need for applied research. "The easy job is advocating clinical and translational research," he says. "That is the research that clearly leads to therapeutic products. And we should be advocating it." In fact, he adds, clinical research is under a variety of stresses, some controllable by the NIH, some not. "We have to pay attention to that part of the research enterprise because it has fallen on some hard times."

Nonetheless, he says, "we can't lose sight of the need to sustain the deeper and more complicated argument" for basic science. Given the multiplying and exciting examples of the results that investments in this kind of research will produce in ten, twenty, and thirty years, he doesn't think the argument will be hard to sustain. "They are paying off faster and faster," he says. "I see more and more advances that are applicable to the clinic, based on the results of a logical process of research findings, not simply good luck."

Fundamental to basic research is the impossibility of predicting where it will take you or how significant it will turn out to be. Varmus has said that the most useful results are frequently not those that basic researchers think they will produce. As the *New Yorker* magazine reported in a June 1999 profile of Varmus, he is fascinated by the far-reaching changes in medicine that research into "cellular-level functions and especially genetics" is creating. And as the *Prune Book* on science and technology jobs suggested in 1992, it was the NIH's work on genetics, especially as related to cancer, as well as its accumulated insights in the fields of virology and immunology, that equipped it to understand and take on the AIDS retrovirus in the 1980s. That example of basic research saved years of time in organizing medicine's response to AIDS and, later, boosted the survival rate among the disease's victims.

In the Congress, in any event, Varmus managed to do what all NIH directors must: create and sustain support for both kinds of research. "My view," he says, "was that you should treat everybody as someone who is going to be interested in NIH goals—namely, improving health through research. And that everyone is interested in helping once they learn what the NIH does." He tried to approach the "persuasion process" by "exposing members of Congress to scientists doing good work. That's what turns people on."

The Congress has been turned on by the NIH for years. Legislators of both parties, while they may divide sharply on such issues as stem cell research, have since the 1960s been generous with NIH budgets, consistently giving the agency more than it requested even in times of severe federal deficit and fierce battles for available funds. Varmus says he tried to deal with the stem cell and other policy issues in as straightforward a way as possible. "I think some of the ethical issues are legitimate subjects of debate and, in a pluralistic society, we come at them from different points of view. People have to understand that there are arguments on both sides of some of these questions. They simply have to weigh the arguments and consider what is most obviously in the public interest."

To get an overall picture of the NIH, consider its formal mission and some facts and statistics. It leads the world in biomedical and behavioral research. As the central federal health research institution, it develops new, fundamental learning about the nature and behavior of living systems and how that knowledge can be used to improve human health, extend human life, and detect, diagnose, and treat disease and disability of every kind.

Most of the NIH budget (almost $19 billion requested for fiscal 2001) supports research directed toward those objectives. Some of this activity is designed and conducted at the NIH itself. This intramural program, absorbing about 10 percent of the budget, encompasses more than 2,000 investigations run by a scientific work force of 16,000 doctors, nurses, dentists, veterinarians, researchers on training stints, and laboratory staff. They work in the twenty-five specialized, individual institutes and centers that compose the seventy-building, 322-acre NIH campus outside of Washington, D.C. About 25 percent of the professional staff members are at the doctorate level.

A total of 82 percent of the budget goes into extramural research projects via grants and contracts to just over 50,000 nonfederal scientists in every state and elsewhere in the world. Their bases are some 2,000 hospitals, medical, dental, nursing, and pharmacy schools, schools of public health, universities, nonprofit research institutions, and private research laboratories.

Integral to the NIH complex is a 350-bed research hospital and laboratory, whose 10,000 inpatients and 70,000 outpatients each year provide an opportunity for clinical studies by the NIH's intramural scientific staff. The NIH also operates the National Library of Medicine, one of the world's top sources of biomedical information and a leading communicator of that information around the globe. Among the many thousands who have conducted research at the NIH or received NIH support, five won Nobel Prizes for their work in NIH laboratories. Some ninety others are Nobelists with accomplishments that range from discovering the cause of hepatitis to unraveling the genetic code. Harold Varmus was one of them.

Asked about other concerns that will head the agenda of the NIH director in 2001 and the years that follow, Varmus begins with stem cell research, one of the most contentious. The subject here is what are called human pluripotent cells that can give rise to all of the various kinds of specialized cells in the body. As this is being written, the first issue in this area is the use of federal money for research into uses of preexisting human pluripotent cells that can spectacularly advance medical understanding and treatment of resistant maladies like diabetes and heart disease. "preexisting" cells are those that have been derived—in private research not supported by federal funding—from nonliving fetuses or living embryos. Federally supported research that damages or destroys embryos is currently banned by law. But a legal opinion developed by the Department of Health and Human Services and announced in early 1999 found that this prohibition does not apply to stem cells because they are not embryos. It said the use of stem cells derived with the use of nonfederal funds is legitimate. The second issue involving stem cell research is whether actually to permit federally funded derivation of stem cells from embryos.

Varmus favors legislation covering both these bases, not only authorizing the NIH to perform or support research using preexisting stem cells but allowing federal funding of stem cell derivation. "Many of us are increasingly convinced, day by day, that this is an incredibly important avenue of research," he says. But there is another equally important reason why he wants the federal government fully in this particular picture. "The whole point of the NIH role is obviously so that the research is not done completely in the private sector—so that there is public scrutiny." Further, as he told a Senate appropriations subcommittee in January 1999, "federal involvement creates a more open research environment, with better exchange of ideas and data among scientists, more public engagement, and more oversight." Federal support, he added, "increases the fiscal resources and expands the pool of talented investigators." In our conversation with him, Varmus also pointed out that the private sector is moving more quickly in stem cell research than the public sector.

After the Department of Health and Human Services issued its legal opinion, the NIH published guidelines in the *Federal Register* for public comment. In the spring of 2000, it was studying the comments and revising the guidelines, with the expectation of completing them by the summer.

Meanwhile, Varmus says, "some members of the Senate and, I assume, from the House are interested in promoting that kind of legislation." At the same time, he takes care to add, "the task for NIH is to work out a means to do what the law allows it to do and not inject its opinion on the matter."

Another question for the incoming NIH director concerns electronic publishing, an objective that engaged Varmus during his last year in the job. In 1999 he proposed establishment of a system that would put the products of research by the worldwide life sciences community on the Internet. It would cover results in biology, medicine, and plant and animal research. As Varmus outlined it, the first site in the envisaged international system is an NIH repository—PubMed Central—for what he called "barrier-free access to primary reports in the life sciences." Available at the site are peer-reviewed reports from journals. In the future, there could also be reports that have been screened but not peer reviewed, coming into the site from organizations independent of the NIH. Varmus thinks electronic distribution "will over the next few years dramatically change the way scientists gain access to the primary research literature."

He mentions two further issues for the future. First, "how we're going to deal with increasing pressure to consider raw data as a commodity to be sold in various forms by the private sector," a new phenomenon that he says lies at the heart of the current dispute over the use of products from fast-advancing human genome research. Second, "what are the proper criteria for patenting in the biomedical arena? How do we encourage the free distribution of research tools and modulate the push by academic investigators to seek patent protection?"

Another issue in this category is worth mentioning. Related to congressional concern with reducing drug prices, it gained some election-year prominence in June 2000. Members of the Congress on both sides of the aisle proposed that pharmaceutical companies pay a return-on-investment-fee from their profits on drugs developed with government-funded research. Despite the practical and other difficulties that make such a fee unlikely in the near term, this is a debate in which the NIH director will play a central role.

What should be considered in hiring the leadership of the NIH's individual institutes? "The successful people I brought in were mostly very closely connected to active science," Varmus says. "Sometimes they were running their own labs very competently; sometimes they were fully involved in research management. Frequently, they were basic scientists who knew enough about disease to lead an institute with a clear, disease-related mission." He would not exclude candidates for these senior posts who don't have medical degrees. "What you're looking for is people who are willing to work hard and have a strong command of current research activity in the area they're responsible for."

Finally, Varmus expresses a personal view of the job of leading the NIH. One of the things that became less interesting for him as time went on, he says, was the lack of real opportunity for "science management." It is the director's responsibility to set directions, deal with policy disputes, and work with the Congress and the administration. "But when an idea was formulated, even by me, advocated successfully, and the money was there, then it was necessary to turn over the actual management of it—the interesting part, the doing of the science—to institute directors and their close colleagues. Basically, there are no programs managed from the director's office."

He thinks that's the way it has to be, since in any case the director would not have time to manage all the programs. "But," he thinks, "it does make the job ultimately a little less satisfying than it might be if there were some domain in which the director actually had a hands-on role. That's a frustration in the job that is not apparent at first glance.

PROFILE

Last Appointed Director of the National Institutes of Health
Harold E. Varmus, 1993–99*

Career summary
Professor of microbiology, biochemistry, and biophysics, University of
  California at San Francisco, 1979–93
Associate professor (1974–79), assistant professor (1972–74), and post-doctoral
  fellow (1970–72), UCSF Clinical associate, NIH, 1968–70
Internship and residency, internal medicine, Columbia-Presbyterian Hospital,
  1966–68

Education
Amherst College, B.A., 1961; Harvard University, M.A., 1962; Columbia
  University, M.D., 1966
*Left the position in late 1999 to become president of the Memorial Sloan-
  Kettering Cancer Center. In January 2000, Ruth Kirschstein, a thirty-
  eight-year career veteran of the NIH, became acting director, a slot she had
  also filled for four months in 1993. Between late 1993 and January 2000,
  she had served as NIH deputy director.

Directors of the National Institutes of Health since 1989

Clinton administration
Ruth Kirschstein (acting), July–November 1993 (currently again acting
  director, NIH)
Bernadine Healy, 1991–93 (currently chairman, Research Institute, Cleveland
  Clinic Foundation, and director, American Red Cross)

Bush administration
William F. Raub (acting), 1989–91 (currently deputy assistant secretary,
  Office of Science Policy, Department of Health and Human Services)

▓ Administrator, Health Care Financing Administration

**EXECUTIVE LEVEL IV—Presidential appointment with
Senate confirmation**

RECOMMENDED SKILLS AND EXPERIENCE ■ This agency cur-
rently lays out several hundred billion dollars of public money every year to
help provide one of the most intensely debated commodities in public pol-

icy and in the country generally—health care. Leading such an effort takes, first, a detailed grasp of that debate. More than that, it requires a deep understanding of health-care financing as a field, as a major operational challenge, and as a mission and issue with lasting impact on millions of citizens in an aging America. That kind of knowledge is developed in various ways: substantial service at senior levels with a relevant congressional committee, for example, or with a large health-care provider organization, or within the executive branch of government itself in closely related work. For four years before becoming administrator in 1997, Nancy-Ann DeParle handled the health and personnel portfolio as an associate director of the Office of Management and Budget.

Personally, the administrator should be able to deal patiently and constantly with people; reach decisions quickly; bring tested public communications skills to the job; and manage a continuous relationship with the Congress that is laden with oversight. The environment is not one of contemplation, but of action. You can get up every morning, DeParle says, and be excited about helping millions of people get better health care. "If you like writing your own analyses or sitting down and debating health policy, this isn't the job for you."

INSIGHT ■ The Health Care Financing Administration has 75 million customers, or something approaching 30 percent of the U.S. population. Mostly, they are the old, the poor, the disabled, and the young uninsured. Through its Medicare, Medicaid, and children's health insurance programs, HCFA assists in the cost of their care at an annual level of $360 billion. That represents about a third of the total outlay in the United States for health care and somewhere between 15 and 20 percent of the federal budget. The figure is up nearly a third over its 1995 total.

Medicare covers 39 million people who are age sixty-five or above, are disabled, or suffer from permanent kidney failure. Its payments go directly to about seventy contractors around the country that pay the billion or so annual claims of care providers and individuals. Medicaid, assisting 34 million people, is a state-based, state-administered program for which HCFA supplies matching funds. It helps low-income families and individuals, including pregnant women and those with high medical bills. A third, newer project—the Children's Health Insurance Program, begun in 1997 and managed by HCFA with the Health Resources and Services Administration—gives matching funds to states to extend coverage to up to 5 million uninsured children.

HCFA, with a work force of 4,200, also oversees the proper management of these three programs by state agencies and contractors. It sets out the policies for paying health-care providers. Its own inspectors and surveyors enforce federal safety and quality standards for hospitals, clinics, nursing homes, and similar facilities. It researches the effectiveness of health-care methods and treatments. With the exception of research, the agency regulates all laboratory testing in the country; nearly 160,000 facilities are involved. With a much-used web site and a national toll-free telephone number, HCFA launched a national Medicare education program for all beneficiaries that goes well beyond the booklet it mails to newly eligible recipients.

It is not exactly news that an agency handling as much information as this one, with two major claims operations responsible for hundreds of billions of dollars a year, needs technology that can do the job. Both of DeParle's immediate predecessors recognized the problems and costs typically inherent in a multiplicity of information systems—in HCFA's case, fourteen of them—that are often incompatible with one another. In 1991 the agency embarked on a plan to build a Medicare transaction system, a single, integrated process that would handle all HCFA programs. In its April 2000 issue, *Government Executive* magazine traced what then happened. During the next six years, HCFA spent some $50 million to bring the new system into being. But a number of factors intervened. They ranged from cloudily defined objectives, inadequate contracting procedures, underestimated costs, and a Congress lukewarm to differences in procurement approach between the agency and the administration. Plans for the new system were canceled in 1997, a few months before DeParle arrived in the administrator's post.

Today, most observers say the effort was not a total loss. According to *Government Executive,* for example, HCFA did merge its fourteen processing systems into six and cut back on the contractors and sites that were managing them. "The goal—to simplify a Byzantine Medicare claims-processing system—was the right one," DeParle says, "but the new design didn't do that. The good thing is that, a year into it, the plug was pulled. That meant we did not waste hundreds of millions of dollars on a system that wasn't going to work." One of her first steps was to hire a chief information officer, the first HCFA had ever had. Unhappily for the creation of a new claims-processing system, this expert then spent the next two years preparing the agency for Y2K, leading the contractors in improving and testing the processing systems at sixty sites around the country. In the end, the HCFA met the test; the Y2K crisis didn't occur.

DeParle likens her job to that of a ship's captain, "trying to keep it going, steering it in the right direction." Just as a captain must also see to the comfort of passengers or the quality of the food, she says, the HCFA administrator is concerned with the Congress, the providers whom HCFA reimburses, the beneficiaries of Medicare, and the states who are partners in Medicaid—"lots of different audiences that you have to satisfy."

When she took over the job, HCFA had just undergone the first functional reorganization since its establishment in 1977. It had taken about two years. Among other changes, it moved the agency away from a rather hierarchical, stovepipe structure to a flatter design that would allow greater collaboration between its operational and policy divisions. It installed a greater degree of customer focus. And, like most such exercises, the reorganization was physically and psychologically disrupting. Thousands of offices and people moved; egos were hurt; some employees didn't understand the new parameters of their jobs. "And right on top of that," DeParle recalls, before she was confirmed in the job, "Congress passed the Balanced Budget Act of 1997, which included the most significant changes in Medicare and Medicaid in thirty years"—and represented a "massive" shift in the U.S. healthcare economy. "All those people who were a bit shell-shocked from being moved around and reorganized were those who now had to implement the new legislation."

To protect the Medicare trust fund from long-foreseen bankruptcy— revenue from the Medicare payroll tax flows into the fund, payments to beneficiaries flow out—the 1997 act reduced Medicare's reimbursement rates to care providers. Little changed from the standpoint of beneficiaries, but providers didn't like it. DeParle says inquiries flooded in from members of the Congress on behalf of providers: Why is HCFA doing this? Some legislators who enacted the changes in the first place seemed to have forgotten they had done so, she adds, "which added to HCFA's burden in implementing the changes."

Footnote: In June 2000 several health-maintenance organizations announced they would shortly withdraw from Medicare or limit their participation. Their decisions, which would end coverage for about 170,000 people across the country, was part of what the White House foresaw as a growing trend. Although Medicare is expected to raise payments to HMOs in 2001, this is not seen as sufficient for providers facing costs that are rising faster.

During her tenure, DeParle says, the agency has received a good deal of congressional scrutiny. Without making a comparison with the experience of her predecessors on this score, she thinks it has been "a lot." By and large, she also thinks it has been appropriate. "This is one of the most important programs the federal government operates—certainly one of the largest in terms of the taxpayer and beneficiary dollars that we are stewards of. Not only do we have an impact on the lives of people directly covered by our insurance, but I'm seeing more and more the impact we have on their families." The HCFA web site is a particularly good example. Even before the agency could announce and publicize the site after it went on line, "people started finding and using it." The web site responds to a demand for information not only from seniors but also from people seeking to work out health care on behalf of seniors.

For DeParle, the critical HCFA role, illustrated by the "massive" use of its web site, justifies the extensive congressional interest in what the agency does and how it does it. "To me, it says the oversight is appropriate," DeParle says. "Most of it has been fair. We've had to make some tough decisions together, the administration and the Congress, to ensure that the Medicare trust fund will be solvent. It is now in the best financial shape in years, and that gives us the breathing room to make the changes for our generation."

PROFILE

Current Administrator of the Health Care Financing Administration
Nancy-Ann DeParle, 1997–

Career summary
Associate director, health and personnel, Office of Management and Budget,
   1993–97
Attorney, Covington and Burling, 1991–93
Partner, Bass, Berry, and Sims, Nashville, 1989–91; associate, 1984–87
Commissioner, Department of Human Services, State of Tennessee, 1987–89
Clerk to chief judge, U.S. Court of Appeals, Sixth Circuit, 1983–84

Education
B.A., University of Tennessee, Knoxville, 1978; B.A., M.A., Balliol College,
   Oxford University, 1981

Administrators of the Health Care Financing Administration since 1989

Clinton administration
Bruce Vladeck, 1993–97 (currently director, Mount Sinai School of Medicine,
   and senior vice president for policy)

Bush administration
Gail R. Wilensky, 1990–92 (currently chair, Medicare Payment Advisory
   Commission (MedPAC), and senior fellow, Project Hope)

Bush and Reagan administrations
William L. Roper, 1986–90 (currently dean, School of Public Health,
   University of North Carolina, Chapel Hill)

Department of Labor

▓ Assistant Secretary for Occupational Safety and Health

EXECUTIVE LEVEL IV—Presidential appointment with
Senate confirmation

RECOMMENDED SKILLS AND EXPERIENCE ■ "I was in this field
for five years, directing OSHA at a state level, before coming here," says
Assistant Secretary Charles Jeffress. "That's an advantage. It helped me
enormously in gaining the confidence of the staff here." It also meant that
Jeffress, who had spent twenty years engaged with workplace and labor
issues, was able to get a running start on a tough job. He points out that
the average tenure in his position had short. "So if you don't come here
prepared, you're leaving by the time you've learned."

Without such a background, however, candidates should have some of
the other relevant credentials. They include a knowledge of the regulatory
environment, experience in developing operational or performance standards, and management and motivational skills. Also recommended is a
feel for the context in which the Occupational Safety and Health Administration pursues its mission—an environment where those being regulated
and those who benefit scrutinize OSHA constantly, sometimes with equal
dissatisfaction.

INSIGHT ■ "One of the things about this job that I've never kidded my-
self on," Jeffress reflects, "is that OSHA and the assistant secretary simply
saying things doesn't make workplaces safer. It's what employers and employees do at their work sites that makes the difference." That view shapes
his own approach: "Our job is to find ways to motivate those people to
evaluate their own situations and invest in the changes necessary."

Therefore, while this small agency (2,260 employees, $380 million budget) must be "a cop on the beat," Jeffress also sees a big role for "sales and marketing." A regulatory agency cannot survive just by issuing regulations, he asserts. "We've got to talk to people about why health and safety is important, about how it's to their own benefit."

For the record, OSHA is almost thirty years old. Since its establishment, the agency says, workplace fatalities have declined by half and on-the-job illness and injury rates have dropped 40 percent. In the same period, employment in the United States almost doubled, to 105 million, and the places where people work climbed in number from 3.5 million to 6 million. At private-sector companies in 1998, the 5.9 million figure for injuries and illness—93 percent of them were injuries—was the lowest yet recorded and the injury and illness rate per 100 workers, at 6.7 percent, was on a six-year down curve.

OSHA's founding legislation allows states the choice of handling their own work-site safety and health responsibilities with OSHA approval. Twenty-one states currently do so, covering private- and public-sector work sites, consulting with federal OSHA, and getting as much as half their costs from Washington. In the twenty-nine that elected OSHA jurisdiction, OSHA runs and funds everything.

Although OSHA's 1,250 inspectors in 1999 spent almost 80 percent of their time at manufacturing and construction sites (the percentage of state-run inspections was comparable), Jeffress says that 70 percent of American employees don't work in those industries. And while manufacturing and construction are historically thought to be the most dangerous, Jeffress says that 70 percent of injuries occur elsewhere. From his earlier experience as occupational safety and health director in North Carolina, he remembers that grocery and department stores and nursing homes were among the top ten most hazardous workplaces. "A lot of people are mobile, going from place to place, doing repairs or selling things. They're working in retail stores, warehouses, delivering health care to people with blood-borne pathogens, lifting patients." The pattern is the same on a national scale, where he adds hospitals to the list of industries with high numbers of injuries.

"We've only just begun to collect the data that have opened our eyes to this," Jeffress says. He notes also that most of the standards OSHA writes focus on manufacturing and construction and "most of our experience with compliance is in those areas." Breaking free of this traditional emphasis, he says, is the agency's biggest task. So far, he acknowledges, "we've merely touched the tip."

At the same time, however, OSHA has moved toward better use of what it has. Based on surveys, it sends its inspectors to workplaces identified as the most dangerous. Before that, it dispatched inspectors at random—Jeffress calls it a lottery and "not a particularly effective way to get where we needed to go." The agency has taken similar steps with its compliance assistance and consultation resources, communicating with dangerous workplaces it hasn't the resources to inspect.

It is using the Internet as a communications tool, with 25,000 pages of documents and a database available at its web site. "If you want the results of any inspections ever made, they're up there," Jeffress says. "If you want to see the interpretations we've made on applying a particular standard, they're up there. If you want to look at the educational materials on new standards we're developing, like ergonomics, they're up there." An OSHA critic, the National Federation of Independent Businesses, has linked its site to OSHA's, encouraging searchers to go there for information on worker protection—"a good sign," says Jeffress. OSHA's web site gets 18 million hits a month.

During 2000 OSHA was readying a test case on another critical issue—writing more performance-based, as opposed to procedural, standards. Ergonomics was the framework, an area in which the Congress several years earlier had forbidden OSHA to spend any development money. But in the spring of 2000, hearings took place on an OSHA ergonomics proposal for which it hoped to issue a final standard before the end of the year. The proposal, however, was later killed in the House of Representatives. "It's creating huge amounts of controversy," Jeffress said at the time. "Within the agency, there are concerns about a performance standard that doesn't say exactly what someone has to do, because it's difficult to enforce. Outside, they're afraid OSHA would have too much discretion—if the standard doesn't say exactly what we mean, a compliance officer might interpret it to demand things that are excessive by someone else's interpretation." For example, the standard might not specify how much weight an individual is allowed to lift, but require instead that the force used to perform a job be reduced.

Employers have urged the development of performance-based standards. But the basic question they pose is probably the one Jeffress frames: "Can we apply them reasonably?" Therefore, he says, "be careful what you ask for because we're now delivering it and people are very worried about it." OSHA's enforcement mentality in the past, he says, was, here's a rule, go apply it. "Now we're saying, here's a principle, go see if someone is doing it well. That's a very different kind of approach. Our lawyers are nervous about it. Our compliance offices are uncertain about it. I think it's the right thing to do. The jury is out."

Along with changing the basis of the standards OSHA sets out has come the parallel need to reorient the agency's inspection corps. Jeffress encourages inspectors to move from "just being cops" to being safety and health professionals, to concentrate on assisting employers to create safer workplaces "and not worry quite so much about whether this or that rule is being violated." The OSHA training institute has added a course to ingrain that philosophy.

Asked whether the size of his agency's work force is adequate, Jeffress answers that he had ten times the resources when he ran the North Carolina program as he does in Washington, "on a per-work site or a per-person-covered basis." More pointedly, he says European countries invest six to ten times as much per worker on health and safety as the United States. He also questions the gap between spending on worker protection and on environmental protection in this country, noting that the Environmental Protection Agency "spends more money in one year than OSHA has spent in its entire thirty years." But Jeffress says also that the president has proposed and the Congress has appropriated "significant increases"—14 percent—for OSHA over the last two years. For fiscal 2001, the administration requested another 11 percent. If the agency should thus receive a 25 percent boost over three years, Jeffress wouldn't complain. "But when you start from a very small base, even a relatively high rate of growth doesn't get the job done."

More frustrating, perhaps, is what he identifies as the remoteness of the business and labor representatives he deals with in Washington, from their constituencies around the country. In North Carolina, he dealt directly with plant managers and union presidents. In Washington, it's trade associations, who Jeffress says tend to conceive their missions as opposing regulation per se, and international union officials who may or may not know "exactly what's going on in the plants." One of the most challenging dimensions to the job, therefore, is "to figure out a way to work with people whose knowledge is not based on what's happening in the workplace and still achieve my substantive objectives."

Jeffress has followed the initiative of his predecessor, Joseph Dear, in placing particular importance on the role of the agency's front line—its inspectors. Because they are in the country's workplaces every day, he sees them as the prime channel for the advice that can change behavior. "These are the people who have to motivate others, who have to feel responsibility and some ownership of what we do." Each of the agency's area offices operates in response and strategic teams. It is their mission to ask what OSHA can do to make a difference. "Which industries can they work with? Where are the key people in business, labor, and the public sector who can help OSHA build some partnership to achieve our objective?" He wants the regional teams to develop strategic plans that make sense for their areas and not limit themselves to inspections. Jeffress reports that this empowerment of the frontline worker "has had significant consequences in terms of stronger relationships between our inspectors and the people they regulate. Now we've got hundreds of local partnerships around the country. They're not made with a cookie cutter, either. There are different partnerships doing different things in different ways."

It is not surprising that he thinks a key part of OSHA's future direction is "keeping it local. Give local people the authority and discretion to design local programs that work."

At the end of our conversation, Jeffress elaborated on a point he made earlier. OSHA's continued progress in worker safety depends on researching new ideas, finding more effective ways to pursue worker safety and health, continuing to take risks in untried directions. Successor assistant secretaries should "expect to spend a lot of time pushing people beyond the limits they might set for themselves." Second, they should understand the importance of being the "public spokesperson," representing the agency and its goals, calling public attention to safety and health requirements, helping frame the public debate. More than he had anticipated, he says, OSHA itself and other related agencies of government take careful note of what the individual in this job says.

Those two assignments, Jeffress says—leading the agency past the perceived limits of what it can do and getting more Americans to grasp and participate in its mission—are "the most important ones to take on and the most important to be prepared to take on."

PROFILE

Current Assistant Secretary for Occupational Safety and Health
Charles N. Jeffress, 1997–

Career summary
Deputy commissioner and director, Occupational Safety and Health
  Administration, North Carolina U.S. Department of Labor

Education

B.A., University of North Carolina; Program for Senior Executives in Government, John F. Kennedy School of Government, Harvard University, 1990

Assistant Secretaries for Occupational Safety and Health since 1989

Clinton administration

Joseph A. Dear, 1993–97 (currently chief of staff, Office of the Governor, Washington State)

Bush administration

Dorothy Strunk (acting), 1992 (currently consultant, United Parcel Service)
Gerald F. Scannell, 1989–92 (currently president, National Safety Council)

Department of Transportation

■ Administrator, National Highway Traffic Safety Administration

EXECUTIVE LEVEL IV—Presidential appointment with Senate confirmation

RECOMMENDED SKILLS AND EXPERIENCE ■ "This is a public health agency, whose leader has to understand that," says Ricardo Martinez, who as the most recent appointed administrator, headed the National Highway Transportation Safety Administration—NHTSA—from 1994 to 1999. He says the position should be filled by a physician or other health-care provider who brings expertise in motor vehicle crashes and knows how to make policy. Some who have held the job put priority on an understanding of the federal regulatory environment and its impact on private industry. A knowledge of the industry and consumer associations who are stakeholders in what this agency does is useful. A legal or engineering background gives the administrator extra credibility, but is not regarded as essential.

INSIGHT ■ In 1970 the Congress created NHTSA in an attempt to cut the death and injury, to say nothing of the economic loss, resulting from motor vehicle highway accidents. The death rate was then running at almost

52,000 a year—nearly 95 percent of the total American deaths that the then-current war in Vietnam would eventually produce. The yearly fatality rate was 4.7 per million miles of travel.

By 1997, according to figures cited by Martinez in a preface to his agency's fiscal 2000 budget request, the yearly death rate stood at 40,000, or 1.6 per 100 million miles of travel. That's progress, especially considering the increase in the number of vehicles on the highways; changing national demographics; rising driver, passenger, and pedestrian populations; a growing number of younger and older drivers; and a number of other factors. But the 1997 statistics used by Martinez showed that more than 6.8 million motor vehicle collisions were still occurring each year on the country's highways, at an economic cost of $150 billion. Traffic accidents were still the leading cause of death for people age six to twenty-seven.

NHTSA's mission is constant positive change in these figures over time and in many other associated statistics, such as proper use of safety belts and child seats, air bag effectiveness, alcohol- and drugs-related crashes, driver education, and safety-oriented vehicle construction. The agency—with about 700 employees and a requested fiscal 2001 budget of just under $500 million—works toward these objectives with a range of regulations and programs. It conducts high-speed crash tests on passenger vehicles; sets and enforces safety performance standards for motor vehicles and vehicle equipment; investigates safety defects, seeking recall and remedy as necessary; encourages the use of seat belts, child safety seats, and air bags; supports states and localities with matching grants to assist their highway safety and drunk driver programs; researches driver behavior and traffic safety; and issues consumer information on a variety of vehicle safety subjects. The agency has a number of additional, related responsibilities—issuing and enforcing fuel economy standards, investigating odometer fraud in the sale of used vehicles, and enforcing vehicle antitheft regulations.

When he took over the administrator's job, Martinez recalls, it was clear that people over time had forgotten that safety is a public health issue. They tended to think that regulating industry was NHTSA's only responsibility. "That's simply not true," he says. "It's not all about regulation. Issues like drunk driving are issues in which relationships with the states and communities, and with organizations that can help carry out solutions, are critically important." He tried to make certain "that we kept the broader picture in mind: that motor vehicle injury is a public health matter, that we need a larger number of partners to implement it, and that the tools we use depend on who the partners are."

Because the motor vehicle is "so ubiquitous in society," he says, this position's big challenge, therefore, "is to balance all the different stakeholders' wishes, to craft a middle-ground solution that meets the needs of the various constituents and puts public health first." Again, he points out, this was "not the norm" when he arrived. "The norm was more about cost and liability, and less about focusing on how things perform in the real world and how we solve problems in the real world." Most of the stakeholders in vehicle safety were inside the Washington beltway—"insurers, car companies, and safety groups"—among whom he often encountered polarized positions. "What we did," says Martinez, "was to add medical, public health, nursing, and law enforcement people and state and local policymakers to the debate. And that expanded our opportunities dramatically."

This illustrates what an earlier administrator also saw as a necessity for success in this work: keeping the safety issue before the largest possible public while justifying the agency's actions to obvious constituents like the automakers. In something of a parallel to this external outreach, Martinez worked to broaden the NHTSA work force and turn its focus outward, saying "I basically tried to reconfigure, restructure, reengineer, and retrain the agency." To a staff heavy in engineers and lawyers, he added "a lot of people with medicine and public health backgrounds and tried to balance our approach to focus on both the vehicle and the social issues." In turn, that relates to the belief expressed by another of Martinez's predecessors. She suggested that effectiveness in improving highway safety requires cultural change in society, in addition to regulation and enforcement. "Is it really possible to solve the drunk driving problem with a new device on the car?" she asked. "No, you have to change people's behavior."

With the Congress, Martinez says, he sought to use a proactive and bipartisan approach. After all, he notes, with highway crashes a leading cause of death and with a mission of seeking to reduce them, "you can reach essentially everyone." He visited the Hill regularly, also offering to take part with members of the Congress in events in their home communities that put a focus on traffic safety. He also made himself "very available and approachable" to the media. Worried that reporters and editors were tiring of topics like drunk driving or child safety seats, he says, "we really tried to put a human face on the issues." Eventually, "we got to where the media began to appreciate us as a source of information, as opposed to yet another bureaucracy they needed to expose." As a result, he says, "we got a tremendous amount of media. The joke was that, where we used to count our press clips, we were now weighing them."

PROFILE

Current Administrator of the National Highway Transportation
Safety Administration
Position vacant

Administrators of the National Highway Transportation
Safety Administration since 1989

Clinton administration
Ricardo Martinez, 1994–99 (currently senior vice president, WebMD)
Marion Blakley, 1993–94 (current position unavailable)

Bush administration
Jerry Ralph Curry, 1989–92 (general, retired, U.S. Army)

Nuclear Regulatory Commission

▨ Chairman

EXECUTIVE LEVEL II—Presidential appointment with
Senate confirmation

RECOMMENDED SKILLS AND EXPERIENCE ▪ "Somebody who is
totally unfamiliar with the nuclear power industry and nuclear power regulation could conceivably do this job," says Chairman Richard Meserve,
"but would have to work very hard early on just to get on top of things."
A predecessor in the job expressed the same view a decade ago: "You
wouldn't want to come in here totally ignorant of anything nuclear." But
the choice should not go to the other extreme, either. Another earlier chairman, warning against too much technical background, believed a prominent, accomplished nuclear researcher "would not only be unhappy but not
be a specially good commissioner."
   Meserve is a lawyer who also describes himself as a "technical person."
In fact, he holds an applied physics degree, has clerked at the U.S. Supreme
Court, and has chaired or sat on a number of National Academy of Science
committees. One such group, under his chairmanship, sought ways to
strengthen Russia's protection of weapons-grade nuclear material. He also
points to the chairman's bilateral relationships with regulators from other

countries, "in which you try to strengthen regulatory capacity abroad." He believes it is in U.S. interests to try to ensure nuclear safety everywhere and thinks it helps to have experience relevant to this international dimension of the job.

Several personal qualities are valuable. Because the Nuclear Regulatory Commission's five members operate in a give-and-take decisionmaking environment, the chairman usually needs skill, including negotiating skill, to reach agreement. "That's a very different kind of responsibility than the technical one," Meserve says, "but in its personal relations side, perhaps equally as challenging." A law background is helpful in this context as well as with the complicated administrative law issues the commission deals with. Last but hardly least, the chairman should have sufficient independence and objectivity to see what's wrong with the industry the commission regulates as well as its benefits.

INSIGHT ■ The NRC sets broad policy for the regulation of the civilian nuclear power industry, with the mandate of protecting human safety, human health, and the environment. This is a sensitive and technically complicated activity. It is carried out with very sophisticated regulatory tools—detailed requirements for licensing and inspection of nuclear power plants that the NRC develops and enforces. One task for the chairman, Meserve says, is the substantial one of mastering the regulatory system well enough to be able to decide how it should be modified. "That's probably a more substantial job at this agency than at any other," he says, "just because of the highly technical, very advanced nature of the regulatory system we have for reactors in this country."

Regulating by commission is a second major element of the job. The NRC is an independent body, its five members appointed by the president. It sets the broad policy for the agency. At no time can more than three represent one political party. Commissioners serve five-year terms that are not concurrent among themselves or with the life of an administration. One member rotates off the commission each year unless reappointed. In selecting a chairman, a president can choose from among the existing membership or go outside.

With the chairman needing majority agreement to get a decision on a given issue, Meserve says, "there's a fair amount of work you need to do in accommodating others. It's a collegial process, but one that imposes constraints and delays that might not arise or be typical of, say, the job of running the Environmental Protection Agency." Lando Zech, who chaired the NRC in the late 1980s, had a phrase describing the job's policy-level challenge: "How to get things done with a five-headed body." Normally, the chairman can vote first or last on a decision. Voting first is a means of leading the way to agreement, but voting last may be useful if the commission appears divided. None of this, of course, is very different from the situation in other federal entities of this kind. But in any case, Meserve says, developing effective relationships with other commissioners "does take some time."

What about the old debate on the merits of running the commission with a single administrator instead of five commissioners? When we talked with him, Meserve was too new in the job to have developed strong views. There would be some efficiency gains with a single commissioner, he believes. But "there are benefits to the commission structure because you must articulate your reasoning and persuade others. Viewpoints come to the fore because others are participating in the decisions." He also thinks the staggered terms of commissioners give the agency stability. "You don't have any radical changes at the top. For a regulated industry, that continuity is valuable." By contrast, with a single administrator serving a term that ran parallel to that of an administration, NRC policy might veer sharply with every presidential election.

A few facts: In 2000, there were 103 operating nuclear reactors in the United States, producing about 20 percent of the country's electrical power. The NRC licenses reactors for forty years; the first ones issued were due to expire in 2000. Four years ago, Meserve thinks, many people expected most plants to be decommissioned at the expiration of their licenses. "All of a sudden, however, there's great interest in getting into the business. Companies are trying to buy nuclear power plants." He thinks it likely, therefore, that most plants—not the handful that were predicted—will file amendments seeking license extension.

What's the explanation? "I think it reflects something of the changed economic climate for electricity in the United States. There has basically been a deregulation of electricity markets and a lot of restructuring." That has perhaps opened opportunities that didn't previously exist, leading Meserve to predict that "nuclear power will be with us for a while." But no utility would choose to build a new nuclear power plant today, he adds. "It doesn't make economic sense. Natural gas at the moment is cheap. Typically, if they have access to a natural gas supply, utilities would build combined cycle natural gas turbines, which are very efficient."

On the safety of nuclear power reactors, Meserve notes there has never been a significant release of radioactive substance from a nuclear power reactor in the United States. "And although there are concerns about how to deal with spent fuel," he says, "I believe that is ultimately going to prove to be a manageable problem." Compared with the amount of electricity reactors are currently generating, the costs of used fuel disposal will not be overwhelming. "So there are environmental benefits from nuclear power, especially if we get serious about greenhouse gases in this country and about global warming." The economics of electric power production could change, he suggests, if fossil fuels become costlier. It's therefore conceivable that nuclear generation over time will be seen as more acceptable, though right now a substantial percentage of Americans would prefer not to have it. Should that day come, Meserve thinks—and this is something for his successors to ponder—"there are lots of ideas" for the design of even safer reactors than those now in use.

The NRC chairman is also its chief executive officer, carrying the administrative duties of the agency, including budget and personnel matters, and setting its agenda and schedule. Until very recently, the NRC had to earn virtually all its costs from licensing fees and, in the 1990s, its budget in real terms and its staffing level—currently at about 2,800—declined. Among other impacts, this has significantly cut the agency's research resources. "We need to make sure we are funding research in areas that relate to our mission," Meserve says. "I'm worried about that." For fiscal year 2001, the agency requested budget authority of $488.1 million, $18.2 more than for 2000. And beginning with that fiscal 2001 request, the NRC persuaded the Office of Management and Budget that an increasing part of its budget—starting at 2 percent and leveling off at about 10 percent after five years—should be appropriated from the general fund, not from fees.

At this writing, there was no indication how this idea would play on Capitol Hill. Although in 1998 Congress had the NRC under "very stringent examination," Meserve says the agency now has support from all sides on Capitol Hill. That required "a fair amount of effort," including monthly reports, "to respond to congressional concerns and make sure the Congress appreciates what we do and why we do it the way we do it. That's something we will continue, because once you build support you don't want to lose it."

As the NRC's public spokesman, Meserve thinks its credibility depends on its openness. "You don't want people to think you're a captive of the nuclear power industry or of antinuclear groups and their views. The only way you can navigate between those poles is to be completely aboveboard about what you're doing and why." After his visits to power plants, he customarily schedules a press conference, whose purpose among others is to allay any notions that his presence was occasioned by something amiss at the plant.

An earlier chairman once described this position as "one of the toughest, most lonely jobs in the federal government," one that brings "zero friends, no well-dones from the White House or the Hill," and "no reward except personal satisfaction." Meserve is inclined to agree. "You're focusing on an important but narrow segment of the world. It's not one that the general public is particularly attuned to at the moment. There's no great public interest in what we're doing." That would, of course, change, if major problems arose. "But you can't take this job with the idea that it's a stepping stone to public visibility." In fact, he adds, the NRC is an agency where one has to hope "that fame is not the result of being here."

PROFILE

Current Chairman of the Nuclear Regulatory Commission
Richard A. Meserve, October 1999–

Career summary
Partner, Covington and Burling, 1981–99; legal counsel to president's science and technology adviser, 1977–81
Law clerk to Supreme Court Justice Harry Blackmun
Law clerk to Judge Benjamin Kaplan, Massachusetts Supreme Judicial Court

Education
B.A., Tufts University, 1969; J.D., Harvard Law School, 1975; Ph.D., Stanford University, 1976

Chairmen of the Nuclear Regulatory Commission since 1989

Clinton administration
Greta Joy Dicus, 1999, currently NRC commissioner
Shirley Ann Jackson, 1995–99 (currently president, Rensselaer Polytechnic Institute)

Bush administration
Ivan Selin, 1991–95 (currently affiliated with the Phoenix Group)
Kenneth M. Carr, 1989–91 (vice admiral, retired, U.S. Navy)

7

Positions in Employment Policy, Income Security, and Welfare

Department of Agriculture

▓ **Under Secretary for Food, Nutrition, and Consumer Services**

▓ **Executive Level III—Presidential appointment with Senate confirmation**

RECOMMENDED SKILLS AND EXPERIENCE ■ Candidates need a background in nutrition assistance. That could be in one or more such areas as infant and child nutrition, food stamps, food distribution, or school lunch programs. It's interesting to note that Shirley Watkins, who took the position in mid-1997, is the first person to come to it with that kind of experience. Besides the substantive advantages this gave her, she didn't have to spend time learning the job from the career people working with her. Particularly because of the sizeable annual budget on which the Food, Nutrition, and Consumer Services operates—$35 billion, or two-thirds of the Department of Agriculture's total—this under secretary should have training or background that can provide sound financial management oversight. A high comfort level with information technology would be helpful in achieving more online capacity for the customers of these programs, like the possibility of filing food stamp applications from such locations as public libraries. Watkins also points to the usefulness of ability in a second or even third language beyond English.

INSIGHT ■ "Building coalitions and a strong consensus, and being able to listen to people, is very, very critical for this position," says Watkins. Take food stamps, for example. This program has served effectively and for a long time as the federal government's main weapon against hunger, allowing low-income families to buy healthy, nourishing food with coupons and with cards that transfer this benefit electronically at stores and other outlets. It's the largest of the programs, Watkins says, for which her office has policy development responsibility—and one of fifteen operated by the Food and Nutrition Service, a major program division under her supervision. When it comes to building coalitions and consensus in the food stamp program, Watkins is talking about stamp recipients, of course, but also about governors and other state officials, mayors, and advocacy groups.

In an earlier time, she says, the FNCS had not worked with all of the stakeholders in programs like food stamps to pull them together as a core constituency group. In the area of child nutrition, for instance, the targeted stakeholder group broadens to include not only those typically involved with food stamps but also school districts, school nutrition officials, food producers, processors, and marketers; local YWCA's, YMCAs, and other youth organizations; and summer camp directors. Watkins says the FNCS has sought, particularly through its seven regional offices, to "go in and actually listen to what people are saying about these programs and what they'd like to see changed. We brought people to the table and asked, what does it take?"

For the child nutrition programs administered by the Food and Nutrition Service—the National School Lunch Program, the School Breakfast Program, the Summer Food Service Program, the Special Milk Program, the Child and Adult Care Food Program—such feedback was valuable. Some of what Watkins and her people heard about these programs was also cranked into legislative language when the time came to request their reauthorization. Watkins says it was the first time in twenty years that any administration had sent language of this kind to the Hill. Another beneficiary was the Special Supplemental Nutrition Program for Women, Infants, and Children—WIC.

"We took the changes people recommended and put them in those (legislative) packages," Watkins says. It's a good reason, she believes, why this under secretary should avoid the mistake of concentrating on only one initiative and putting aside all the others. "You can't just look at one aspect, because you have fifteen programs and each one is critical to somebody in this country." It's probably useful, therefore, to sketch in capsule form the program domain overseen by this job. First, the Food and Nutrition Service, whose programs extend a nutritional safety net to families and individuals needing it. Though some of these efforts seem almost identical, each is directed at a population segment with specific requirements. Here's the full spectrum:

—Food Stamps. The centerpiece of Department of Agriculture nutrition assistance programs. It distributes monthly allotments of benefits determined by such factors as the household size and income of recipients. These take the form of coupons for use at retail stores and electronic transfers, using plastic cards that transfer funds from a food stamp benefit account to a retailer's account. State food stamp agencies handle the authorization and monitoring of recipients. Welfare reform legislation in 1996 required states to switch to electronic benefit transfer by 2002.

—Women, Infants, and Children. Aimed at improving the health of low-income pregnant and postpregancy women and infants less than five years old. The program provides supplemental foods rich in nutrients that these individuals often don't have, plus nutrition education and access to health services. According to a 1990 study cited by the FNCS, women in the program during their pregnancies incurred lower Medicaid costs for themselves and their babies than women not participating.

—The WIC Farmers' Market Nutrition Program. Increases the access of WIC participants to fresh produce.

—National School Lunch Program. Supplies cash reimbursements and commodity foods to nonprofit food services in elementary and secondary schools and in residential child care institutions. Serves nearly 30 million children every day. More than half eat free or pay a reduced price.

—School Breakfast Program. Assists about 7 million children each day with a system and nutrition standards similar to those of the school lunch program.

—Summer Food Service Program. Some 2 million low-income children receive free meals during school vacation periods. Local sponsors of the program receive federal reimbursement.

—Emergency Food Assistance Program. Provides commodity foods to states for distribution to households, and to soup kitchens and food banks. The program was designed to reduce inventories and storage costs of surplus commodities. Since 1989, Congress has appropriated funds for additional commodities.

—Child and Adult Care Food Program. About 3 million children and 60,000 adults receive meals in child and adult day-care centers, made possible by cash reimbursements and commodities.

—Commodity Supplemental Food Program. Designed for a population similar to that of the WIC program, this is direct food distribution that also serves the elderly. As in WIC, it is shaped for the nutritional requirements of its approximately 375,000 recipients.

—Special Milk Program. Supplies about 150 million half pints to children in schools, summer camps and child-care institutions that lack a federally supported meal program.

—Food Distribution on Native American Reservations. Provides commodity foods to low-income families living on and near reservations. About 125,000 people participate in the program each month.

—Nutrition Program for the Elderly. Provides cash and commodity foods to states for about 20 million meals per month for the elderly, served in centers for the elderly or delivered by meals-on-wheels programs.

—Nutrition Assistance Program in Puerto Rico, American Samoa, and the Northern Marianas Islands. Block grants totaling about $1.3 billion to these territories to pay for cash and coupons distributed to participants.

—Homeless Children Nutrition Program. Reimburses providers for meals they serve in emergency shelters to homeless children of preschool age.

—Nutrition Education. Supports nutrition education in the food assistance programs for children noted above, providing materials, other support, and technical assistance for food service professional staffs. This program also supplies education materials to such other programs as food stamps and WIC.

The Center for Nutrition Policy and Promotion represents the other major FNCS program area under the authority of this under secretary. Described by the FNCS as the Agriculture Department's central connection between science and the nutritional requirements of the public, the center was established in 1994. It assesses the nutrient content of this country's food supply, continuing an effort that began almost a century ago; and examines the cost-effectiveness of the government-sponsored nutrition programs cited above. The center, staffed mostly by nutrition scientists, nutritionists, and economists, also develops nutrition policy in the department, issues periodic updates on the cost of family food plans and of raising children, and explores effective ways to communicate nutrition information to the public. Among its publications is *Dietary Guidelines for Americans,* prepared jointly with the Department of Health and Human Services.

Watkins says the FNCS staff and administrative (but not program) budget have been declining steadily and, in the last six years, dramatically. In response, she and her leadership colleagues have challenged the programs, especially at the regional office level, "to look at every area of the operation and find out what needed to be reinvented."

One result was the identification of outdated functions that could be dropped and others that could be done with technology, not by people. The FNCS also asked the regions what they would be focusing on in the next five or six years and required them to develop one combined business plan instead of several. "Those are the kinds of things this office can and should provide leadership for," Watkins says. A further example is the encouragement of the regional operations to expand their local working relationships beyond state and city authorities to businesses, advocacy organizations, and farmers who'd like to sell their products directly to schools.

She reports "a wonderful working relationship" with leadership on both sides of the aisle in the Senate and House agriculture committees. "These programs have received bipartisan support over the years. There is something in here for everybody in this country and we look at it as working with the committees to improve programs for people."

Overall, Watkins defines two elements of the job's mission. First, to bring leadership and vision to both main areas of its responsibility—"not only policy development but overseeing the two businesses, as I call them." Second, to "look at what makes the two of them work effectively for the employees as well as the customers they serve." For the future, the big task will be "putting forth nutrition as a major focus for programs and people in this country. Now we give lip service to it. But we don't really think in terms of the importance of nutrition and how it relates to the amount of money being spent on various high-cost diseases related to eating and nutrition."

There's another issue here. Watkins strongly believes that FNCS programs must be positioned as a nutrition safety net, not as welfare programs. She looks at nutrition as the preventive approach, as opposed to treatment of malnutrition. "Putting the N-word in the agency" is how she frames this challenge—to which the FNCS has already been responding via the materials it develops, the speeches its leadership gives, and the testimony it puts before congressional committees.

PROFILE

Current Under Secretary for Food Nutrition, and Consumer Services
Shirley Watkins, 1997–

Career summary
Deputy assistant secretary, Marketing and Regulatory Programs, Department of Agriculture, 1995–97
Deputy under secretary, food, nutrition, and consumer services, 1993–95
Director, nutrition services, City of Memphis Public Schools
Earlier positions as food service supervisor, home economics teacher, elementary school teacher, and (with the University of Arkansas Extension Service) home demonstration agent

Education
B.S., University of Arkansas at Pine Bluff; M.Ed., University of Memphis

Under Secretaries for Food, Nutrition, and Consumer Services since 1989

Clinton administration
Mary Ann Keefe (acting), 1997 (currently deputy administrator for international cooperation and development, Farm and Foreign Agricultural Services, USDA)
Ellen Haas, 1993–97 (currently president and CEO, Food Fit.com)

Bush administration

Ann Chadwick (acting), 1992–93 (currently executive director, American
    Association of Family and Consumer Services)*
Catherine A. Bertini, 1990–91 (currently executive director, World Food
    Program)* Position vacant, 1989
*Served as assistant secretary for food and consumer services

Department of Health and Human Services

▨ Assistant Secretary for Children and Families
▨ Executive Level IV—Presidential appointment
with Senate confirmation

RECOMMENDED SKILLS AND EXPERIENCE ▪ Two credentials
are important here. The first is an extensive substantive background in social services at the federal or state level, plus a detailed knowledge of current federal welfare policy and its recent history. Second is management
experience; this could be supplied by the deputy to this position, but that's
a less preferable arrangement. At the very least, the individual who runs
the Administration for Children and Families—ACF, established a decade
ago—needs leadership skill in addition to the expertise on substance.
Olivia Golden, who took over as assistant secretary in 1997, feels she has
drawn on all her earlier experience in the job: budget director in state government human services; programs and policy director at the Children's
Defense Fund; commissioner for children, youth, and families within ACF
itself; and lecturer in public policy at Harvard.

It's helpful, she says, to have seen human services issues from several
different points of view in order to grasp their complexity in the intergovernmental framework. She wouldn't insist on every feature of the
broad background she herself brought to the job. "But if you've only been
in one place, I think it is hard. Creating a pathway to getting something
done does require a sense of the wide variety of people who are involved,
or potentially involved, if you can figure out how to draw them in."

INSIGHT ▪ This job deals with what Golden calls "highly visible agendas all moving at once." ACF incorporates some sixty federal programs
directed at helping families and children beset by any of a multitude of dis-
advantages to move toward more economic security and healthier lives.
It's a long list and a broad waterfront—Head Start (now covering a million

children), enforcement of child support, child care, foster care and adoption, child abuse and neglect, low-income energy assistance, Native Americans, developmental disability programs, temporary help for destitute families, community services, family preservation, social services, refugees (ACF resettled the ethnic Albanians the U.S. admitted during and after the Kosovo crisis in 1998). ACF's work in these areas ranks high in the attention of the Congress and state governments, among others.

"It's been very clear that getting results in these areas means using a lot of bully pulpit and public affairs strategies with states and communities," Golden says. Accordingly, she has invested considerable time with officials of state social services agencies, state legislators, and employers, and in focus groups with parents, "trying to build motion in states." The job has involved her in policymaking and regulatory rule making, as well as a far-reaching internal reorganization.

"We're an agency that has lost about 25 percent in staff," Golden says— the level is about 1,500—"at the same time that our program dollars have massively increased and our responsibilities expanded." The agency, which has ten regional offices, worked from a budget of about $42 billion in fiscal 2000. That is up from about $30 billion, which was the ACF budget in 1996 when reform legislation sharply altered the nature and operation of welfare services in the United States, mainly by giving the states a much more prominent role and increasing accountability.

At the same time ACF has moved to adjust to this fundamental change, its budget history has been one of "a striking increase in program resources and decrease in administrative resources," Golden says. "We have dramatically changed the character of our work with states and communities. We've brought the Head Start and child-care communities together. Our changing role in welfare reform has added agencies to the list of those with which we need good working connections." Traditionally, education was ACF's most important emphasis in assisting children, and some of its youth and child welfare programs had links to the Department of Justice. Now, she says, "relationships with Justice have become front and center and housing and transportation are also important." With ACF's partners in the states and communities now doing much of the work of helping people to move from welfare to work and to rise within organizations once they have jobs, "that requires a different set of connections." At ACF, while it is "really a different world than it was five or six years ago," Golden says, "there is still a ton of things to do."

She sees her job's core responsibility as selecting a few areas of intense personal attention while building a close-knit leadership team that can keep the overall focus broad. "You can try to get ten things done instead of responding to a hundred," she says, "but the areas are so important that you need a strong and serious team." Golden thinks she has done that. "I've spent quite a lot of time on recruitment and coaching development with my senior team, both career and political. And I've been here long enough to be able to make selections for positions on both sides."

In Golden's outlook, the next stages of welfare reform will concern giving people the kind of support they need to hold onto their first jobs, improve in them, and move up. "There's no way," she says, "that we've adjusted yet, either in policy or on investment, to the number of parents in this country who are not working. That remains an enormous issue." She also sees a challenge in assisting people "whom no state has ever really served before"—those who remain part of the social services caseload, those who still face barriers to employment. "We now have the dollars. And I feel a real urgency in getting them invested in useful ways that can shape the next round of national policy."

Her agency, she says, will also have to find a way to stop the "drastic slide in our administrative resources." It has gone a considerable distance in adjusting to this—figuring out how to restructure for greater efficiency. But the ACF staff is "very heavily retirement age. When employees leave and you can't replace them, you may lose a huge amount of experience and knowledge. It means we risk very big gaps in particular areas. I think we've gone about as far as we can." She sees this as a "big issue" for her successor. With the federal budget in surplus, a time "when the big-picture questions play out," Golden thinks it is "very much a time to take some of the next ambitious steps and fight for the resources to accomplish them."

She is concerned about keeping the momentum she feels ACF has achieved. "What I'm afraid of is that things will grind to a halt. It's taken huge energy to keep movement going with an administration and Congress of different parties. There is huge promise, but everything could easily stop. If you combine the reduced staffing resources, the fact that lots of these issues have conflict around them, and the possibility that we could have a new administration figuring out its agenda and a Congress that wasn't very sympathetic, you could easily have zilch happening. I think these are the biggest worries."

PROFILE

Current Assistant Secretary for Children and Families
Olivia Golden, 1997–

Career summary

Commissioner for children, youth, and families, Department of Health and
 Human Services, 1993–96

Director, programs and policy, Children's Defense Fund, 1991–93

Chair, Advisory Committee on Children and Youth, City of Cambridge, Mass.,
 1990–91

Lecturer in public policy, Kennedy School of Government, Harvard University,
 1987–91

Candidate, Commonwealth of Massachusetts Senate, 1986

Budget director, Massachusetts Executive Office of Human Services, 1983–85

Education

B.A., Harvard University, 1976; M.A., 1981, and Ph.D., 1983, both in public
 policy, Kennedy School of Government, Harvard University

Assistant Secretaries for Children and Families since 1989

Clinton administration

Mary Jo Bane, 1993–97 (currently professor, Kennedy School of Government,
 Harvard University)

Bush administration

Jo Anne B. Barnhart, 1990–93 (currently president, JAB and Associates)*
Eunice Thomas (acting), 1989–90 (current position unavailable)**
Catherine Bertini (acting), 1989 (currently executive director,
 World Food Program)**

*Held position as administrator, Family Support Administration, 1990–91.
**Held position as assistant secretary, Family Support Administration.

Department of Labor

▓ Assistant Secretary for Pension and Welfare Benefits
▓ Executive Level IV—Presidential appointment
with Senate confirmation

RECOMMENDED SKILLS AND EXPERIENCE ■ A broad back-
ground in the administration of private sector pension and health plans
serves this job well. Candidates familiar with the statute basic to the operations of the Pension and Welfare Benefits Administration—PWBA—have

a clear advantage going in. An understanding of the marked evolution in retirement coverage over the past generation is also useful, as is experience with investment management. "There's no perfect background," says Richard McGahey, an economist by training, who held this position in 1999. He thinks a background in economics or business helps, also stressing the value of "a healthy humility about what you don't know."

INSIGHT ■ The primary name of the game in this job and agency is ERISA—the Employee Retirement Income and Security Act. It is the chief federal statute protecting the pension and health benefits of 150 million participants and stakeholders in the benefit plans of private-sector employers. How many plans? About 6 million. Their collective assets? About $4.9 trillion.

Two generations ago, only the privileged well-to-do could expect a comfortable retirement, Acting Assistant Secretary Leslie Kramerich reminded a House subcommittee in April 2000. "Today," she said, "eight and a half million retirees are receiving monthly checks from private pension funds of employers." Another 4 million received a lump sum on retirement. These benefits amount to more than a quarter of the total income of retirees age sixty-five or above and more than a third that of people age fifty-five to sixty-four. Kramerich, who succeeded McGahey at the helm of PWBA in late 1999, recited further eye-catching statistics. Some 47 million Americans were earning pension benefits in 1998, more than four times the number half a century ago and almost twice that of the late 1960s. The $4.9 trillion in assets of the U.S. private pension system, up from $260 billion in 1975, "represents nearly one-sixth of the financial assets in the U.S. economy and far exceeds the gross domestic product of most other nations."

Private pension system assets are also this country's biggest single source of investment funds. But investment structures and benefit plans themselves depend on proper fund administration and careful investment decisions. Those are responsibilities that can only be undertaken in the interests of pension fund participants and beneficiaries. That's where ERISA comes in. "It was designed," Kramerich said, "to protect plans, and ultimately the participants in the plans, from the self-interested conduct of trustees and other persons in a position to influence the operation of the plans." While PWBA manages the application of ERISA with two other federal agencies (the Pension Benefit Guaranty Corporation and the Internal Revenue Service), it carries most of the law's out-front regulatory duties. These are set out in Title I, which contains rules for pension plan reporting and disclosure, vesting, participation, funding, fiduciary conduct, and civil enforcement. To administer these, PWBA has set itself a four-part mission:

—Find and correct violations of the relevant statutes

—Help pension plan officials meet their legal responsibilities through the fullest possible understanding of the statutes

—Design policies and laws that spur the growth of employment-based benefits

—Help employees get the information necessary to protect their benefit rights

When he ran PWBA, McGahey put priority on "making sure the regulatory framework in ERISA was adequate, both to meet the changing economic needs of business and to protect the rights of workers covered by it." That may sound simplistic, he says, "but I think there's a considerable tension there that goes to virtually everything that happens in the agency. ERISA covers both pension and health plans, which are of enormous importance to people—and as the population ages, it just gets more and more significant. Striking an adequate balance between those goals is pretty challenging." He identifies a third factor in the balance: the obligation to carry out administration policy. It's a matter, he sums up, of "being involved in something that almost necessarily has a lot of partisan aspects to it and still doing a professional job."

Discussing the issues he dealt with as assistant secretary, McGahey refers first to patients' rights with respect to health maintenance organizations. "In my last year, and continuing now, that question and patient relationships to other forms of managed care are obviously a very significant issue in the public dialogue," he says. Second is the question of "trade-off between the kinds of incentives you give to businesses to establish pension plans and the extent of coverage you get for workers." Here, the operative fact is the extremely complex regulatory and financial testing that ERISA requires of companies that want to establish pension plans. This causes some observers to argue that the qualifying requirements for employers are too onerous and should be eased, because, as currently written, they tend to limit the extension of employment-based pension and health benefits to greater numbers of people. Others say that ERISA protections are there for goods reason: to safeguard workers' benefits. "If you relax the rules too much," McGahey says, "you disproportionately reward wealthy business owners." Since employers who adopt ERISA-qualified plans get tax breaks, he points out, "the idea is that you should get a broader public benefit in return." It comes down to deciding "whether you are, in effect, trading off fewer people with pension plans to get better protection for those who have them. It's a pretty tough call," with no real scientific testing for it and vocal advocates on both sides.

"The other thing that people need to understand about this job," he adds, "is that there is now so much money in retirement accounts that a lot of attention is being paid to these issues. There is a lot of lobbying, a lot of people who work them pretty hard. People should be aware of that and careful and responsible in how they deal with it."

Because ERISA is "an extremely dense, complicated law," McGahey finds comparatively few people who understand it, including "relatively few substantial congressional actors. You have to really care not just about the outcomes of issues, but how these things work. There are few members on the Hill who have the time and energy and jurisdiction to do that." The upside of this, however, is that "you can actually have a pretty professional conversation with a small number of staff who care about it. And that's bipartisan. There really is no partisan aspect to it. There are Republicans and Democrats who have become really expert on these issues." One exception to the nonpartisan tenor of this dialogue, he recalls, is the patients' rights question with HMOs. But it was so "broadly important politically that it drew a lot more people into the debate than one would normally see on an ERISA issue."

To comply with ERISA regulations requires "a fair amount of paperwork," McGahey says. All pension plans, for example, must file an annual report. "While I was there, we went to full electronic filing of that form." The choice of the information technology for this, and of the vendor, was a careful, extended, highly competitive one. The agency, he notes, "is not scared of technology" but, like everyone, has a funding issue. "The federal government in general has trouble keeping up with the cutting edge in terms of hardware but, more importantly, in terms of staff" and top-level programmers are hard to hold in a very competitive job market. Further, "as a public system, you've got to be accessible to everybody. You can't just skim off those who are most technologically sophisticated." Thinking about the nature of the agency and the recordkeeping that is necessary, McGahey believes that PWBA's many information technology challenges will grow. But harnessed correctly, he says, information technology "can actually reduce the paperwork and regulatory burden for people."

His perceptions about the PWBA staff can be useful clues for the agency's leadership to come. "They are very good about not trying to overstep their roles," he says. "I generally found it good to let the professionals do what they do as long as they kept you informed about the broad directions they're pursuing and you didn't interfere with or direct their fact-finding or recommendations to you." He also found a tendency "to be a bit protective of the existing regulatory structure and ways of doing business. That's true of any organization—you get into habits." How that affects such matters as the willingness of business companies to establish new pension plans, however, are questions on which "there's a little less sensitivity within the agency."

What's ahead for PWBA as a new administration takes office in 2001? "I think the issue of pension coverage and advising about it is important," McGahey says. "Pension coverage in the United States has actually been sort of static, if you consider people covered by an employer-provided pension plan." Here he touches on some critical facts. "ERISA was really written for a different era, at a time twenty-five years ago when you thought of pension plans as defined benefit plans—the employer promised you would work a certain amount of time and you would get a certain amount of money when you left." In contrast and more recently, the "huge explosion in retirement coverage has come in defined contribution plans, mainly 401Ks, where an employer may or may not make a contribution, but makes no explicit promise. It's up to you or your investment managers what your retirement income is going to be."

Second is "the seismic change in the way health care is delivered in this country." He mentions some numbers: in the late 1980s, about 25 percent of people with health insurance through an employer received it via some form of managed care arrangement, usually an HMO or a preferred provider arrangement. By the late 1990s, the figure was close to 80 percent. "This is a massive change in the way employers deliver health care," McGahey says, "so it's not surprising that we now have a vigorous debate about how to regulate it. It's going to continue. The question is how it gets regulated to get both the economic efficiencies and still provide the rights."

Finally, beyond the need to find and acquire the right information technology and staff, he points to the probable retirement of many knowledgeable and experienced senior people in the next five years. "There's a huge amount of valuable expertise there that could be lost without some really conscious way of capturing it."

McGahey says he is happy with what he is doing now, but wishes he was still at PWBA. "The people were great, the issues were interesting even when they were tough. I've never worked with a more dedicated or smarter group of professional people, many of whom could be making a lot more money than they make now." One also discovers in dealing with ERISA issues "how hard it is to move the system," he says. "The American system's not designed to move very fast, which has its virtues. Whoever gets this job will find that out. But it was a great experience."

PROFILE

Current Assistant Secretary for Pension and Welfare Benefits
Leslie B. Kramerich (acting), 1999–*

Career summary
Deputy assistant secretary for policy, pension, and welfare benefits
    administration, Department of Labor, 1998–present* *
Attorney-adviser to the chief negotiator, Pension Benefits Guaranty
    Corporation, Department of Labor, 1993–98
Attorney, Verner, Liipfert, Bernhard, McPherson, and Hand, 1989–93
Various staff and advisory positions, U.S. Congress, 1982–89

Education
B.S., Case Western Reserve University, 1981; J.D., Ohio State University
    College of Law, 1984
*Not interviewed for this profile
* *Continues to hold this position while serving as acting assistant secretary

Assistant Secretaries for Pension and Welfare Benefits since 1989

Clinton administration
Richard McGahey, 1999 (currently managing vice president, education
    and family support, ABT Associates)
Olena Berg, 1994–97 (currently senior adviser and board member,
    Financial Engines)
Position vacant, 1993–94

Bush administration
Donald G. Ball, 1989–93 (currently of counsel, Williams, Mullen, Clark,
    and Dobbins)

Social Security Administration

▨ Commissioner
▨ Executive Level I—Presidential appointment with Senate confirmation

RECOMMENDED SKILLS AND EXPERIENCE ▪ No one can run this
agency without a strong grounding in both Social Security policy and the
statistics and economics that drive it. That expertise is more essential than

ever, given the need eventually to design a response to the problem of Social Security's future insolvency and the alternative proposals being advanced meanwhile to give contributors to the system a better return on their investment or to build supplemental retirement accounts. While those processes slowly nudge the long-term solvency question toward some definitive answers, the commissioner will be at the center of internal policy deliberation, public discussion—and public education.

This is a cabinet-level job, with the difference that it carries a six-year appointment. Kenneth Apfel, who came to it in 1997, says that gives the position a somewhat independent quality. It adds to the importance of choosing a commissioner "with legitimacy as an educator, as someone who can articulate the pros and cons of various options." Apfel also points out that "understanding the give-and-take of Washington is critical" to handling the post effectively. His own experience was relevant and extensive: service in the Congress and as a senior official of the Office of Management and Budget and the Department of Health and Human Services.

INSIGHT ■ The debate about how to deal with Social Security's still-distant but problematical solvency crisis did not begin or end with the presidential election campaign of 2000. Neither did debate about whether to supplement the system or privatize it to some degree. But the campaign did intensify the discussion about these alternate ideas. It brought before a much wider public various proposals that their advocates said were basically aimed at helping people protect their retirement income.

This is not, in any case, the place to review those ideas. Apfel does say, however, that "virtually no one on the Washington scene wants to fully privatize the Social Security function" and thinks that outcome is unlikely. But he thinks that "some limited form of privatization," such as a private savings component, is "a major debatable issue" that will be at the core of continuing discussion within the Social Security Administration and in the Congress. It is, Apfel says, "clearly one of the things the new commissioner will have to deal with." Still, he reminds us, "it is only one option of many. Whether non–Social Security budget surpluses should be transferred to the SSA to help strengthen the system, or whether the Social Security portfolio needs diversifying to get higher rates of return, whether the retirement age should be changed or the wage cap should go up—there's a whole series of choices on the table."

What the SSA manages is the world's largest income security plan and the country's biggest entitlement program. The system comprises retirement, survivors, and disability insurance programs—collectively known as Social Security—as well as the Supplemental Security Income program for old, blind, and disabled individuals who are financially needy. In addition, the SSA studies the problems of poverty and economic insecurity in the United States and recommends solutions through social insurance. Nearly all Americans are protected by SSA programs. About 20 percent currently are receiving benefits: 98 percent of the $461 billion requested by the agency for fiscal year 2001 will go out in monthly payments to 50 million people.

The remainder will fund the SSA's delivery of services. Each workday, for example, there are 100,000 visits to the agency's 1,300 field offices and 240,000 daily calls to its 1-800 telephone number. Each day the SSA processes 20,000 claims for benefits and takes part in 2,400 hearings before administrative law judges. Each year it issues 16 million new or replacement Social Security cards; credits 250 million pieces of earnings data to the accounts of American workers in order to calculate their eventual retirement benefits; and sends about 125 million statements to them. The agency's computers maintain more than 200 million of these records in a secure, separate, bombproof bunker protected by guard dogs and barbed wire.

Apfel, the first Social Security chief to be confirmed in the position since the agency became independent in 1995, lists three key roles for the commissioner. Internal management and service delivery—"ensuring that we're providing service to the American public"—is a significant, sizeable management task that is the commissioner's "premiere responsibility." Second is the new policy dimension of the job. The legislation that moved the SSA out of the Department of Health and Human Services and made it an independent agency elevated the status and responsibilities of the commissioner. As a cabinet-level official, Apfel says, he attends cabinet meetings and deals directly with the president and the White House economic team in discussions on long-term Social Security reform and changes in policy and programs. The same is true with the Office of Management and Budget. On Capitol Hill, he is far busier than his predecessors were under the old setup—committee hearings and individual meetings with legislators there and in their home districts.

Third, Apfel says, is "the public side of the job," which has grown as Social Security issues have taken on greater visibility. "There's a lot more time in media interviews" across the country; over the past year, by his estimate, he has taken part in at least 200 meetings with editorial boards and with individual interviewers on radio and television talk shows.

This public affairs schedule also included town meetings with members of the Congress, other public discussions on Social Security reform, and "intergenerational" sessions on the future of the system.

Among the issues facing the SSA, he says, is a "very sizeable increase" in workload as growing numbers of baby boomers retire and also move toward the disability-prone years. Apfel expects a significant rise in the number of disability filings, an area that, according to him, already represents half the work of the agency. "The disability program is very hard to administer," he says. "Ensuring the legitimacy of its decisionmaking process is important. It had big backlogs that we've been working down through management improvements." In addition to the agency's 65,000 employees, another 15,000 work at the state level through the disability determination system," he says. Even though they are state employees, "we provide 100 percent of the resources to the states to do the initial adjudication of disability cases." Adding to the impact of a higher agency workload will be a big wave of internal retirements at the SSA between 2003 and 2006.

What these inevitabilities mean, Apfel says, is "real stresses on the organization in the next five to eight years and a major need for new technology. We provide good service, but there are weaknesses now. They will be exacerbated if we can't continue to invest heavily in technology." In 1993 the agency got presidential approval of more than a billion dollars to install local area computer networks in its field offices and lessen dependence on its mainframe computer. Today Apfel says that was an important step. "But the reality is that the system is already relatively obsolete." The agency not only needs new internal information technology, but it also must move into Internet use "in a very aggressive way over the next few years. We won't be able to handle the volume of work coming through the door unless we provide a greater service option through the Internet." As a first step, the SSA during 2000 moved toward handling some simple initial claims for retirement benefits via the web. "But moving forward on technology through the Internet will be a major task for the new commissioner," Apfel says. These service delivery issues, he emphasizes, "are challenge number one, and it's a real one and it's big and it's tough."

The agency's policymaking competence has been another priority. When the SSA was part of the Department of Health and Human Services, much policymaking took place at the department level on its behalf. At independence, the new entity was not geared to take this on, and the urgency of putting capable policy machinery in place was apparent. "We've created an office of policy," says Apfel, "and we're about halfway along in fully strengthening that function as a service both to the president and the

Congress." The commissioner now also sits on the Board of Trustees for Social Security and Medicare, which meets twice yearly to review the agency's work, look at long-term projections by SSA actuaries, and make appropriate recommendations. Also serving on the board are the secretaries of the treasury, health and human services, and labor, and two public members. Further, the independence legislation established a bipartisan advisory board for the SSA, which reports periodically on issues surrounding Social Security and the operations of the agency and works with the commissioner, the agency, and the Congress. While it does not have decisionmaking authority, Apfel says, the board "has clearly become an important part of the Social Security framework in Washington."

He sees a third main challenge in public information and education. "The solvency issue is major," he says. "The only way we're going to be able to tackle it is with a citizenry that has a much greater understanding of how Social Security works, the issues it faces, and the choices we face as a country. So we have very significantly escalated our public education activities here"—as exemplified in part by his own crowded public outreach agenda. "In an agency as visible as the Social Security Administration, there's a need for the commissioner as spokesperson, to use the role almost as a teacher." In light of the extensive public education that he believes is required, he views his role, which is "somewhat different" than other senior administration officials, "as more an educator with the public than as taking a particular political positioning."

Noting that he has been in a number of different roles at several federal agencies, Apfel says the SSA is a "special place, a special program, and a special culture—a remarkable can-do agency. Some of its greatest strengths are its people and its commitment. Whoever takes this position will find, inside the agency, that it is extraordinarily rewarding."

PROFILE

Current Commissioner of the Social Security Administration
Kenneth S. Apfel, 1997–

Career summary

Associate director for human resources, Office of Management and Budget, 1995–97

Assistant secretary for management and budget, Department of Health and Human Services, 1993–95

Legislative director for Sen. Bill Bradley (D-N.J.), 1989–93

Member of the staff of Sen. Bill Bradley, 1982–89

Staff member, Senate Budget Committee, 1980–82

Presidential management intern, Department of Labor, 1978–80

College administrator, Newbury College, 1973–76

Education

B.A., University of Massachusetts, 1970; M.A., Northeastern University, 1973;
M.P.A., Lyndon B. Johnson School of Public Affairs, University of Texas, 1978

Commissioners of the Social Security Administration since 1989

Clinton administration

John J. Callahan (acting), 1997 (currently assistant secretary for management,
Department of Health and Human Services)

Shirley S. Chater, 1993–97 (currently associated with University of California,
Institute of Health and Aging)

Lawrence H. Thompson (acting), 1993 (currently fellow, Urban Institute)*

Clinton and Bush administrations

Louis D. Enoff (acting), 1992–93 (president, Enoff Associates)*

Bush administration

Gwendolyn S. King, 1989–92 (retired)*

Dorcas R. Hardy, 1986–89 (currently chairman and CEO, Work Recovery)*

*Served when the Social Security Administration was an agency of the
Department of Health and Human Services

8

Positions in Education, Training, and Lifelong Learning

Department of Education

▦ **Assistant Secretary for Elementary and Secondary Education**

▦ **Assistant Secretary for Postsecondary Education**

▦ **Assistant Secretary for Special Education and Rehabilitative Services**

▦ **Assistant Secretary for Vocational and Adult Education**

▦ **Assistant Secretary for Educational Research and Improvement**

EXECUTIVE LEVEL IV—Presidential appointments with Senate confirmation (except where indicated that occupant is in an acting status)

RECOMMENDED SKILLS AND EXPERIENCE ▪ Certain skills—like the ability to work with diverse groups amid contention and differences of opinion—are common to all of the Department of Education assistant secretary positions being surveyed here. Judith Johnson, acting assistant secretary for elementary and secondary education since 1997, adds to that the ability "to live and work in ambiguity and controlled chaos." Understandably, she thinks a background in consensus building is essential in her job and places high value on "problem-solving, critical-thinking, analyzing, and communications skills." This assistant secretary should be able to understand "what it means for constituents to carry out whatever policy you are crafting or promoting." No one should expect serious consideration for the job who lacks a solid background in teaching, school administration, or a closely related area.

Candidates for the postsecondary education post should know the U.S. higher education system and, preferably, have direct administrative or grant management experience at a college or university. The key is understanding how higher education institutions work—where they require help in general efforts to reform and improve, what they need to increase access for disadvantaged students, how (and whether) they plan strategically, how their sharing of information can be enhanced.

Judith Heumann, who became assistant secretary for special education and rehabilitative services in 1993, lists management and political skills, "an ability to be collaborative," and budget and legislative experience as general requirements. Specifically, she thinks the individual in the job should bring or quickly acquire an in-depth knowledge of the legislation directly governing the job's responsibilities as well as of other laws that affect disability, such as the Social Security statutes.

"You should know a lot about your subject matter," says Patricia McNeil, who was deputy assistant secretary and acting assistant secretary for vocational and adult education for three years before her appointment to the position in 1996. She did, in fact, know a lot. Before coming to the Department of Education, she headed policy and strategic planning in the Labor Department's employment and training office, led the National Commission for Employment Policy, and was legislative director to a member of the House of Representatives. "I've been in Washington a long time," McNeil says, and in this position she has used both the knowledge and contacts accumulated in thirty years of work in closely relevant areas. Beyond those kinds of professional credentials, she thinks the individual in her job must be skilled at working productively with people and know how to be "proactive in a government environment."

An ability to work with diverse groups and viewpoints has come up in the interview comments of several previous assistant secretaries for educational research and improvement with whom we have talked. One of them also underscored the value of good political instincts. Candidates for the job should have a background in performing or managing education research. Experience in the classroom or school administration should be seen as near essential, and advanced-degree schooling in education is a strong asset. A former appointee to the job stressed that it requires a sophisticated grasp of the realities of the American school system and where and how decisions are made. And, says Assistant Secretary C. Kent McGuire, who came to the job in 1998 from the nonprofit sector, "there's no question about having to adapt. This is a very different animal."

INSIGHT ■ These five positions run programs that will spend just over two-thirds of the $40.1 billion the Department of Education requested as its discretionary budget for fiscal year 2001. If that sounds like a lot of money, consider that the department's figure is less than 7 percent of the more than $600 billion this country spends each year on education. Educational spending by a handful of other federal agencies accounts for another 3 percent. The remaining 91 percent of U.S. outlays on education comes from state, local, and private sources.

Given that education is predominantly a state and local function in the United States, the vigorous, long-running debate over the small federal role at first glance can seem out of proportion. But federal programs are instrumental at key places in the lumbering, problematical American educational machine. Perhaps their greatest impact is on the education of disadvantaged and disabled children and increasing their access to higher education. Federal education programs are also critical, however, in

—assisting college students to meet tuition bills;

—supporting local programs that train teachers in core subjects;

—helping renovate school buildings and moving toward better school discipline;

—promoting innovation at the college and university level;

—strengthening vocational and adult education and literacy, as well as their integration into mainline secondary and postsecondary schooling and, generally, education reform;

—producing a range of research findings and statistics for the benefit of all parties involved in improving American education.

Since these activities touch a spectrum of issues important to various of this country's education constituencies—local versus federal control of how federal education funds are spent, teacher competence, class size, school vouchers are examples—it's not surprising that they have been the topics of spirited, sometimes acrimonious debate. It is a discussion that has sometimes engaged the American public as a whole. It is also a discourse that reflects the evolving nature of American public education and of the demographics of those to be educated. It even questions the future of public education itself.

But the most divisive issue, says Judith Johnson, the acting assistant secretary for elementary and secondary education, is the question of what should be the role of the federal government itself. She adds that this is "never a direct question. But it plays itself out in debates over legislation, over budget appropriations." She makes a further, and important, point: "There is probably very little disagreement on where we all want to end up, but lots of disagreement on how you get there. Maybe disagreement isn't the best word—lots of opportunity for differing perspectives on how to get to the same goal."

She says the fact that education is "a national priority" defines the federal role to some degree. "But we always have to be careful that, as we craft policy, we're doing it with the greatest potential for flexibility at the state and local levels, yet be very clear on what we hope to accomplish." In all of this, she values the role of the critics of education policy, who "offer two or three options." Either they're wrong, which "allows you to reaffirm that you're on the right track." Or they "cause you to pause and rethink, or modify your decisions." The department has its critics, she says, inside and outside "and it's around this notion of who controls the policy."

(When this was written, Senate and House appropriations subcommittees had just taken action on the department's 2001 budget requests that the secretary of education said would "do little to allow or encourage real progress for students, teachers and schools, and in the case of the House bill, actually turn back the clock on education reform.")

▨ Assistant Secretary for Elementary and Secondary Education

When she arrived in this job as acting assistant secretary, Johnson says, she was "stunned" by the size of the annual budget of the Office of Elementary and Secondary Education—OESE. But she no longer is. "It's a minuscule investment," she says. "It could be doubled and we still wouldn't really be providing the kind of support I think we could provide. It's an uphill battle to get the kind of money into public education from the federal government and Congress that we feel ought to be there."

Still, the discretionary OESE budget of $17.2 billion requested for fiscal 2001 reflected the largest year-to-year increase—19.5 percent—since the start of the Clinton administration. Under its operating authority, the 1965 Elementary and Secondary Education Act, the OESE, with its staff of about 250, delivers the funds to 15,000 school districts and 51 million students via half a dozen major grant programs. Of these, Title I is the biggest, aimed at high-poverty schools, where children test at far lower levels than their low-poverty peers; it focuses on reversing the direction of failing schools, raising teacher quality, and seeing that students get the required grades at each level before moving up. (But Title I, which affects 11 million children, "doesn't reach every poor child in this country," Johnson says. "There aren't enough dollars.").

The Goals 2000 program, begun in 1994, is designed to help local communities boost academic standards, attract and train better teachers, raise the engagement of parents, and work on problems of safety and discipline. Other parts of the OESE effort target the objectives of school renovation, class size reduction, extended learning opportunities, teachers' professional development, safety, and a drug-free school environment. A program also exists for special assistance to school districts adversely affected by federal activities that reduce the property tax base on which local school funding largely depends.

"The biggest battle we've had is over reducing class size," says Johnson. Viewing the issue as "an educational challenge," not a political struggle, she says it's frustrating when educators must push something they know is educationally sound through political hurdles. The disagreement is not about whether all children should be able to read when they finish third grade, she says, but on how to achieve that objective. Over the coming four years, she foresees another conflict over what to do about failing schools and the children in them. "How do you hold schools accountable and what are the options when they fail to meet the needs of their children?" She's not an advocate of vouchers—basically, a means for students to choose private schools as alternatives—"because there isn't enough room in private schools for every child in the country."

Johnson sees less disagreement over a third issue: the quality of the teaching force. "But it's another challenge," she says. "I think everybody agrees we haven't a clue as to how we're really going to bring 2 million new teachers into the country's educational system in ten years." In any event, she has come to think that may not be the answer to the teaching need, that people are still thinking too much in terms of traditional school structure. She suggests that technology—notably, the Internet—could change things so dramatically that "maybe we won't need the teachers. Maybe 2 million of something else, but it may not be teachers."

At this writing, some doubt existed that the Elementary and Secondary Education Act, probably the biggest molder of the federal role in public schools, would win congressional reauthorization in 2000 as scheduled. The chief obstacle was a difference of views about whether local school authorities should get greater freedom from federal rules to set their own priorities for spending the money the legislation would provide. Another issue threatening to hang up any reauthorization by the 106th Congress was gun control—specifically, a proposal to include in a juvenile justice bill such measures as mandatory trigger locks and background checks at gun shows. Failure to reauthorize the Elementary and Secondary Education Act means that the programs it covers continue operating under the act as last reauthorized in 1994.

Meanwhile, the OESE has begun developing what Johnson calls the "accountability agenda." Part of it is "figuring out how to hold states and districts accountable for performing to high levels." High performance, she says, currently means "closing the achievement gap," and it might be encouraged with a Baldrige-type award program. Another segment of the agenda addresses the condition of school buildings. "We believe that you give them some time and some resources," she says, "and if they don't turn themselves around, you either radically reconstitute the school or you close it." While this is beginning to happen in some parts of the country, "there's not a lot of evidence yet that it's working, but no evidence to say we shouldn't keep trying it."

A third agenda item—and it's a sensitive one—centers on student performance. It would substitute benchmarks and performance indicators for what Johnson calls "the practice of social promotion and retention." It means "you need to think differently about the kinds of supports and services provided to children who need extra help so that you can get them before they're in trouble." The idea of high performing districts, benchmarks, performance measures, and monitoring and reporting it all "is new in public education," she says. "It's still taking hold. I'm sure it's a legacy we will leave, although I don't know how it will play out over the next few years."

Future occupants of this job should not only work with educational organizations in Washington, she says, but "be sure they are reaching out to people beyond the beltway." Her office has convened practitioners from around the country in a number of forums—"people who work and live in this field on a daily basis"—who offer guidance and comment on OESE proposals that have been "incredibly helpful." Going in the other direction, she has been a frequent public speaker, with "many opportunities to articulate the policies of the administration."

She thinks public education "is sitting on the edge of something. And while many people are pointing to its demise, I think it's pointing to restructuring and reinventing. I'm not one of those predicting the end of public education. But I'm not sure we can define what it's going to look like in ten years."

▪ Assistant Secretary for Postsecondary Education

When the Congress in 1998 reauthorized the Higher Education Programs segment of the Office of Postsecondary Education—OPE—it established the Office of Student Financial Assistance as a separate, semiautonomous entity within the Department of Education. The new unit became the federal government's first "performance-based organization." (The only other to date is the Commerce Department's Office of Patents and Trademarks, discussed in the "Economy, Technology, and Trade" chapter of this book.)

The change left the OPE with an annual budget of about $200 million and two principal operations through which it develops policy and directs programs that assist all institutions offering education after the high school level, as well as students in those institutions. Included in the post-secondary category are colleges and universities (public and private, two-year and four-year), nonprofit technical and business schools, employers, unions, professional associations, community groups, student organizations, and others.

Through its Higher Education Programs unit, the OPE manages projects that increase the access of disadvantaged students to post–high school education and strengthen the capabilities of colleges, universities, and other institutions that serve high numbers of such students. Notable among these efforts on the student side are the outreach and support programs, known as TRIO, that help disadvantaged students from middle school through postgraduate study. On the institutional side, several Title III programs aim at improving academic programs and administrative capacity. The office also oversees the U.S. end of international education activities established by the Fulbright-Hays Act and serves African American, Hispanic, Native American, and Native Hawaiian educational constituencies. All of this, says Claudio Prieto, the deputy assistant secretary for higher education programs, "is directed to assist institutions in meeting felt needs in serving the new student population." That population began increasing "exponentially" in 1972 with enactment of the Federal Pell Grant program (for students of families earning less than $20,000 a year) and other legislation.

The other major OPE element, the Fund for the Improvement of Post-secondary Education, works mostly through the seed grants of its Comprehensive Program to support innovative reform projects that will raise the quality of higher education, will improve access to it, and can become national models for the overall effort to advance education at this level. Among the objectives on the program's "agenda for improvement" are curriculum and teaching reform, more productive use of resources, higher retention and completion rates among disadvantaged students, a more civil environment for learning, teacher education and faculty development, and dissemination of best practices so that higher education can learn from its own achievements.

▓ Assistant Secretary for Special Education and Rehabilitative Services

Judith Heumann defines the mission of her office (OSERS, for short) as giving disabled people the capacity to be fully integrated adults in the national community.

To do this, the OSERS, which requested appropriations of about $9.3 billion for fiscal 2001, helps to educate children with special needs, rehabilitate disabled young people and adults, and—with research—enhance the lives of disabled individuals. Three main OSERS units carry out this work, coordinating and funding programs that affect 49 million people.

"One of our challenges is that disability is still an area people don't understand," Heumann comments. "They understand it better, but it isn't something most people pay attention to, in the way they think about race, or women, or even learners of English. So you have all the stereotypical notions to deal with in getting people to really take these issues on." For example, the OSERS deals with issues such as the expulsion or suspension of disabled students from school. "We've advocated very strongly that this population of kids is one on which a lot of time must be spent," she says, "despite the fact that many would prefer just to get them out of school."

With this kind of problem in mind, her office seeks to work in as integrated way as possible with the Education Department's other elements, including those covered in this discussion. "It's a big enough challenge as it is," she says, "because they all have their own day-to-day work. We're trying to get people to think about the message of the department—that 'all means all'—and look at how to carry that out." Her intent here has been to show her colleagues that integrating OSERS issues into their own agendas doesn't take them off track, that "they have a responsibility to deal with our population. We're also there to help them figure out ways to do it more efficiently."

Aware that information technology is a huge potential resource for its mission, the OSERS has looked for access for the disabled and learning disabled. "We've been trying to address the question of industry moving forward without taking these needs into consideration," says Heumann. She sees technology as a phenomenon that can either "open doors never possible for people with all kinds of disabilities or close them." To tackle the problem, she started with the Department of Education itself—its telephones and web sites—"because what we've argued is that the federal government must be a model. We can't expect others to do what we're not doing ourselves." As a result, the department adopted accessibility standards that must be met when it purchases new hardware and software and other federal agencies then adopted them.

In the area of relations with the Congress, Heumann says, "disability has been reasonably bipartisan. There are ebbs and flows." She regards working with the Hill as critical, and the OSERS, she says, has tried to be proactive. For recent reauthorizations of both the special education and rehabilitation legislation, for instance, "we were trying to think about what needed to be done. We really started the ball rolling—invited the Hill and others to participate in our thinking." Much of the office's work involves interaction with members of Congress and congressional staff, either in developing legislation or carrying it out.

What should those who take over this office in 2001 give special attention to? Heumann lists several concerns:

—Being certain that "well-trained people, both general education and special education," are serving disabled children to get the maximum out of professional development funds the OSERS provides.

—Applying good monitoring and enforcement to "make sure that the states are in compliance with the law." This, she says, "is an area that I spend a substantial amount of time on, because there is criticism from every direction." But it has to be done in a positive way, she adds—saying that "we believe the states need to exert the authority the law intended them to exert."

—In the area of rehabilitation, "making sure we are providing a level of qualifications that the employment market needs." This means "staying on top of what employers are looking for and seeing that our rehab counselors (state employees who are 80 percent federally funded) are doing effective work."

—Keeping in mind that "not all disabled individuals are born with their disabilities," a fact that requires extra focus on what it takes for such people to adjust, stabilize their lives, and move ahead.

▒ Assistant Secretary for Vocational and Adult Education

With annual budget authority of $1.7 billion and a work force of about 120, the Office of Vocational and Adult Education leads the Education Department's work and grant making in the areas of vocational and technical education, adult education and literacy, high school reform, community colleges, and correctional education.

Assistant Secretary McNeil also heads such additional programs as the White House initiative on tribal colleges and universities, Enterprise Zones-Enterprise Communities, and Community Technology Centers. She represents the secretary of education on the National Skills Standards Board. The National Institute for Literacy Board, and the vice president's Leadership Council on 21st Century Skills for 21st Century Jobs.

"When I came here, there was a very traditional vision of vocational education," says McNeil. "It really grew out of a manufacturing-based economy and was still fairly rooted in a 1960s version of vocational education." From her point of view, however, this no longer responded to the needs of the workplace or of young people going through programs supported by the Office of Vocational and Adult Education.

McNeil has therefore pushed a broader vision, one that "makes vocational education at the secondary level integral to education reform efforts." She was able, she adds, to have a substantial part of this new approach reflected in amendments to the Carl D. Perkins Vocational and Applied Technology Education Act of 1998. "We decided we were no longer going to have regulations in the management structure of our programs. We don't have regulations; we have guidance." Her office established partnerships with the states in both vocational and adult education to carry out the new law, which among other objectives calls for integrating academic and vocational education, providing students with experience in all aspects of an industry, responding to the needs of people who are members of special populations, engaging parents and employers, supplying strong linkages between secondary and postsecondary education, and expanding the use of technology.

From this flowed what McNeil calls "a need to rethink what the American high school looks like." With no money, but a strong notion of the goal, her office launched the New American High Schools Initiative in 1995 and, she says, the secretary of education "took high school reform on as a key objective." By focusing on high schools, "we help the vocational educational community to see that they can't be a stand-alone entity any more—that at least at the high school level they must be part of a high school reform agenda." High schools involved in the initiative use new teaching techniques, technology, smaller learning communities, community service, and work-based experience to boost classroom learning and cultivate better relationships with employers, the campuses, and parents.

Until recently, the federal government provided very little money for adult education, McNeil notes. "This country had an attitude that, once you get out of school, you're on your own. We've been reluctant to give real help in upgrading skills to any but the very, very needy—and then not very much." Now, she says "we've almost managed to double that budget and the White House has adopted a forward-looking presidential initiative on adult education." Because "we'll never have enough federal money to solve the problems in this area," however, what's really needed is the involvement of other partners. The goal: "get communities excited about having an agenda at the local level to really raise the educational levels of all individuals, youths and adults." To energize this mobilization of additional resources, the OVAE has "used the bully pulpit" and also secured some "strategic investments from our research and national activities budgets."

With such shifts on both the vocational and adult education fronts came the need to get OVAE staff members to do some fresh thinking about how their roles would and should change. "At least since1980, our job had been the cop, the librarian, and the banker," McNeil says. "That was how we viewed it and what a lot of our activities were. A lot of staff time went into it. Now we see ourselves much more as leaders and experts in the field, brokers of information and technical assistance. It takes a different kind of thinking, and in some cases a different set of skills and knowledge. We're in that transition right now."

One of the benefits of working in vocational and adult education at this particular time, McNeil says candidly, has been that "it was not a focal point for the Hill or the administration." She and her colleagues had some leeway to think about the changes outlined above "without others trying to think about it for us." What helped, too, were her own personal contacts in both places. "It was just long-term pushing, making information available, helping people see the value of what we were suggesting." Another factor was the strategic plan and performance reports mandated by the 1993 Government Performance and Results Act, for which the Department of Education was a pilot agency. The House Appropriations Committee took that very seriously, she says, "and so did we. We began using it to drive changes in behavior and focus our activities and budget requests around the act's objectives." That changed the focus of OVAE programs to results—student outcomes—and away from a sole focus on states and other organizations who receive its grants.

Consistent with her efforts to date, McNeil believes the future of vocational education at the secondary level "lies in becoming an integral part of high school reform efforts." Historically, the U.S. student population has been characterized by "kids on the academic track and kids on the vocational track." That's no longer very relevant to the twenty-first-century American economy, in which "knowledge and skills are the key to personal economic success and on economic success as a country." She asserts that "all students should be educated to the same challenging academic levels." They need the employability skills of communications, problem solving, analyzing information effectively, and working well with others. She says further that they ought to understand computers "and, depending on what careers they pursue, have a set of other technical skills that may not all be the same but are definitely necessary" in a variety of positions.

"I also think all students need to be prepared to go to college and to be life-long learners," she continues. "Whether you concentrate on technical course work or academic course work, you should come out of high school with a strong academic foundation and be ready to go on to the post-secondary level." Whether or not you subscribe to that view, "that's the way the labor market is going. And this is now actually reflected strongly in the accountability provisions of our legislation." McNeil hopes future legislation will bring additional changes, "at least to link us much more closely into secondary school activities." As for the postsecondary level, "we should be linked both back into the high schools and forward into the four-year universities and the graduate schools as well as out into the workplace and into the issue of retraining for adults."

In partnership with the states, she says, the OVAE has designed a set of sixteen "broad, career clusters" covering jobs in the labor market that range from lawyer, teacher, architect, and engineer "all the way down to the paraprofessional jobs in those areas." The career clusters are already in use in certain communities. McNeil sees potential applications to adult education and job training programs.

What's the future path for adult education? "We have a huge population that needs services and is not getting them," she says. "We have a lot of quality issues in adult education—how to get people to stay longer, how to boost the learning curve" so that someone reading at the fourth-grade level, for example, doesn't have to wade through eight years of adult education to read at the twelfth-grade level. "That's where we're hoping technology can make a big difference, in terms both of access and of improving the quality of the education via distance learning that comes right into the home." It is also her hope that technology can help resolve problems of language differences, as in the case of some kindergarten-to-twelfth-grade schools where twenty languages are spoken.

The adult program "right now serves a little over 4 million people a year," says McNeil. "We have to figure a way to help all Americans get the knowledge and skills to work, raise children, and be good citizens in the twenty-first century. I'm talking about 44 million people who don't have them."

In this job, she comments, "you can get an awful lot done. Sometimes I'm amazed at how much we've been able to do through the power of good information, persuasion, partnership—using the limited authorities we have, not by command and control, but in a persuasive, nudging, leadership way." The main test is to make vocational and adult education more visible to the public and change public perceptions of what they are. "I think we've laid a good foundation for change," says McNeil, "and there's a lot more work to do."

▨ Assistant Secretary for Educational Research and Improvement

Guiding research and development that will expand the country's understanding of what education is, where it's going, and what it needs is this assistant secretary's primary assignment. The Office of Educational Research and Improvement—OERI—both conducts and supports education-related research, tracks the quality of education through analyzing statistical data it collects, encourages the application of its findings to improve classroom instruction, and distributes all this information to the broad American professional education community. The office's National Center for Education Statistics is a national and international clearinghouse for information about education that also promotes standardized definitions for statistics and terminology and compares U.S. and foreign education data.

Identifying his major specific responsibilities in overseeing these operations, Assistant Secretary McGuire begins with the role of "spokesperson for the department on matters of education research." This is a task that matters, now and for the future, "given that the idea of backing up what we believe should happen in schools and universities with research and evidence has become really important." Political affiliations don't matter here, he points out. "The demand for evidence, and the ability to ground our ideas with knowledge, is as strong as it's ever been." Anyone who comes to this job should assume an out-front role on this issue, he says.

Second, the OERI has historically housed most of the department's competitive grants in research, demonstration programs, and dissemination activities. A "real premium" exists on the quality of peer review that goes into the making and oversight of the grants and into designing the competitions for them. "Looking out for the public interest and exercising intellectual leadership in that work is a big role, and I think the person in the assistant secretary's office should act as the chief steward."

Third, the job carries "a sort of managerial imperative." This is the need to be "as clear as possible about the ideas driving the work and to lead by example, to set a tone and discourse inside the organization about what's important and relate that to the work people do and how the place runs itself."

But some, including McGuire, think the OERI has a substantial problem in pursuing its real mission—a situation that is not easy to change. "The challenge right now," he asserts—"and I argue that it will continue to be a challenge—is not to do everything, but to get much more organized around doing a relatively limited number of really important things really well." In his view, the OERI, with a staff of 350 and a budget of nearly a billion dollars, "should be much more focused on its research and development mission and about how we mobilize and use the knowledge we already have." Not that the OERI isn't focused, he adds. "It's just that we are asked to do quite a number of other things. I think the challenge here is to figure out how to get a better fit between mission and activity. We need to rule a few things out."

As an example of "other things," McGuire offers the 21st Century Community Learning Centers program, which, for a variety of "predictable reasons," is a politically popular initiative. It aims at increasing learning opportunities in a secure, supervised setting free of drugs through such strategies as schools that stay open longer, intensive mentoring in basic skills, and antiviolence counseling. The program began as a million-dollar demonstration project, he says, grew in a year's time to $40 million and then to $200 million. Effective as it is—"a large competitive program that purchases good services all over the country"—it is not what the OERI should be doing, McGuire argues. Instead, "we should be generating evidence about how particular strategies before or after school work across a range of settings. We shouldn't be running competitions that have to do with making 200 or 300 awards a year. I'm talking about building knowledge about the nature of these interventions."

This thinking eventually led him to move the program out of his domain and into the Office of Elementary and Secondary Education. There, he says, the learning centers program is in a part of the department "that can, through its own technical assistance, outreach, monitoring, and guidance, look for synergies across programs." The program is part of "a family of things" that can be led and managed together, "which in my opinion makes a lot of sense. That's what I mean by making careful judgments about which program is really best suited to this kind of office and which are very possibly better done elsewhere."

McGuire cites another example—a $20 million program that gives schools funds to hire and provide professional development to guidance counselors. "I'm all for it," he says. But, again, he argued that the program would be better placed in the Office of Elementary and Secondary Education. "They said, 'You're right, we'll take it.'" In this case, he notes, it would have been easy to have kept the program, added the $20 million to his office's budget, and acquired five to ten additional staff members. It would have added to his "quiver of programs" and given the OERI greater visibility and constituency. "There are powerful incentives to think in those terms," he says. "But I believe the viability of this office and its credibility in the Congress and in the field is ultimately associated with being seen as a first-rate research and development operation, in much the same way that organizations like the National Institutes of Health or the National Science Foundation are perceived."

A predecessor in this job in the early 1990s, Diane Ravitch, expressed similar views in a later interview. "There are a lot of interesting and important things happening in the country that the federal educational research program has nothing to do with and isn't looking at," she said in 1996. She endorsed the type of research done at the National Science Foundation which, she said, supports "both basic and applied research with multiyear funding." She also questioned congressional reauthorization of the dozen OERI regional research centers without looking at "their role, quality, and achievements" and thinking about making them more "service oriented and entrepreneurial."

In truth, says McGuire, only $140 million to $150 million of the office's budget "has anything to do with our mission. The rest has to do with our legislative authority." He has been trying to get more funding directed at what he sees as OERI's central mission: "research, development, and dissemination." Doing that makes it much harder to raise dollars, he says, and to explain why they are needed. "But it's very consistent with the historical federal role. So I've been trying to make those assessments, been willing to have the place get a little smaller, instead of bigger, in order to make it less confusing to the policy community."

He voices the hope that "whoever comes here next will agree that, though it's hard, the much more essential part of organizing and managing federal education research and development resources is to articulate clearly the three or four things that it's important to try to do at this point in time." In the course of that, McGuire foresees "a really interesting challenge" for his successor in "trying to educate a number of publics." First, leadership is required among researchers. Right now, "that's not a community, and communities need to be built." Second, appreciation needs to be developed in the practitioner community for "the power and leverage associated with using knowledge to inform policy." Whoever can be "really thoughtful" about accomplishing these goals, McGuire says, "will go down in history."

PROFILE

Current Assistant Secretary for Elementary and Secondary Education
Judith Johnson (acting), 1997–

Career summary
Assistant superintendent for curriculum and Instruction, White Plains (N.Y.)
     Public School District
Director of instructional services, Southern Westchester regional education
     center
Service as an administrator, Mamaroneck and Nyack (N.Y.) school districts
Classroom teacher, guidance counselor, and alternative high school
     administrator, New York City public schools

Education
B.A., Brooklyn College; M.A., New York University; professional diploma,
     State University of New York at New Paltz; completed doctoral course
     work, Columbia University Teachers College

Assistant Secretaries for Elementary and Secondary Education since 1989

Clinton administration
Gerald N. Tirozzi, 1996–97 (currently executive director, National Association
     of Secondary School Principals)
Thomas W. Payzant, 1994–96 (currently superintendent of schools, Boston)
Position vacant, 1993–94

Clinton and Bush administrations
John T. MacDonald, 1990–93 (currently senior adviser, Council of Chief State
     School Officers)

Bush administration
Beryl Dorsett, 1989 (currently assistant professor, Fordham University)

PROFILE

Current Assistant Secretary for Postsecondary Education
A. Lee Fritschler, 1999–*

Career summary
President, Dickinson College, 1987–99
Director, Center for Public Policy, Brookings Institution, 1981–87
Chairman, U.S. Postal Rate Commission, 1979–81
Dean, College of Public and International Affairs, American University,
   1977–79
Academic and administrative positions, American University, 1964–79

Education
B.A., Union College, 1959; M.P.A., 1960, and Ph.D., 1965, Syracuse University
*Not interviewed for this profile

Assistant Secretaries for Postsecondary Education since 1989

Clinton administration
David A. Longanecker, 1993–99 (currently executive director, Western
   Interstate Commission for Higher Education)

Bush administration
Carolyn Reid-Wallace, 1991–93 (former senior vice president, Corporation for
   Public Broadcasting)
Michael Farrell (acting), 1991 (current position not available)
Leonard Haynes, 1989–91 (currently adviser to the superintendent, District of
   Columbia Public Schools)

P R O F I L E

Current Assistant Secretary for Special Education and Rehabilitative Services
Judith E. Heumann, 1993–

Career summary
Vice president, World Institute on Disability, 1983–93
Special assistant to the executive director, California State Department of
   Rehabilitation, 1982–83
Deputy director, Center for Independent Living, 1975–82
Legislative assistant to chairman, Senate Committee on Labor and Public
   Welfare, 1974–75

Education
B.A., Long Island University, 1969; M.A., University of California at
   Berkeley, 1975

Assistant Secretaries for Special Education and Rehabilitative Services since 1989

Bush administration
Robert R. Davila, 1989–93 (currently vice president, National Technical
Institute for the Deaf, Rochester Institute of Technology)

P R O F I L E

Current Assistant Secretary for Vocational and Adult Education
Patricia W. McNeil, 1996 (acting 1993–96)

Career summary
President, Workforce Policy Associates
Director, Office of Strategic Planning and Policy Development, Employment
and Training Administration, Department of Labor
Executive director, National Commission for Employment Policy

Education
B.A., University of Massachusetts, 1963

Assistant Secretaries for Adult and Vocational Educational since 1989

Clinton administration
Augusta S. Kappner, 1994–96 (current position not available)
Betsy Brand, 1990–92 (currently codirector, American Youth Policy Forum)

Bush administration
D. Kay Wright (acting), 1989–90 (currently commissioner, Office of Basic
Education, Commonwealth of Pennsylvania)

P R O F I L E

Current Assistant Secretary for Educational Research and Improvement
C. Kent McGuire, 1998–

Career summary
Program officer, education portfolio, Pew Charitable Trusts, 1995–98
Program director for education, Lilly Endowment, 1991–95
Policy analyst, then director, School Finance Collaborative, Education
Commission of the States, 1980–89

Education
B.A., University of Michigan; M.A., Columbia University; Ph.D.,
University of Colorado

Assistant Secretaries for Educational Research and Improvement since 1989

Clinton administration
Sharon Porter Robinson, 1993–98 (currently senior vice president and COO, Educational Testing)

Bush administration
Diane S. Ravitch, 1991–92 (currently senior fellow, Brookings Institution; research professor, New York University; adjunct fellow, Manhattan Institute; and senior fellow, Progressive Policy Institute)
Christopher T. Cross, 1989–91 (currently president, Council for Basic Education)

Department of Labor

▒ Assistant Secretary for Employment and Training

EXECUTIVE LEVEL IV—Presidential appointment with Senate confirmation

RECOMMENDED SKILLS AND EXPERIENCE ■ A strong understanding of the evolving U.S. employment and labor markets is just about mandatory, preferably acquired in administering public-sector employment and worker education programs at the state level. Knowing the recent history of federal-state relationships in operating these programs is an asset. On another level, this position also needs someone who grasps the impact of globalization and its international trade dimension on jobs and job skills in this country. A teaching or scholarly background in the field—as a labor economist, for example—could be useful. But "an academic in this job who carried it out as an academic wouldn't accomplish anything," says Raymond Bramucci, whose experience included service as a union official and state labor commissioner before he took this position in 1998.

INSIGHT ■ Bramucci describes his topmost priority in this position as "sparking an effort to ensure that American workers are competitive in a world that doesn't pay anything for noncompetitive people. While our economy can no longer afford to exclude any workers, the global economy is ruthless," he adds. "And the only people who have a chance to succeed are those armed with knowledge and lifelong training."

The Employment and Training Administration, or ETA, supports the emergence of a more efficient, more effective U.S. labor market, primarily by assisting state and local work force development programs. It supplies those efforts with job training, employment, and income maintenance services as well as labor market information. Most ETA work is now propelled by the Workforce Investment Act of 1998, which in July 2000 replaced the Job Training Partnership Act that had been ETA's legislative mandate since the early 1980s. The WIA is designed to consolidate and improve ETA programs in partnership with states and localities.

In particular, the WIA brings to ETA operations a new emphasis on investing in the creation of more robust local labor markets and on strengthening working relationships with the state and local programs that ETA helps to support. As the organization's mission statement puts it, ETA under the new law becomes more of a market developing than a grant-making entity. That requires a switch from a command-and-control style to one of greater flexibility where frontline staff have more decision authority. Internally, it means shaping a staff with the additional training and skills to take that on. The ETA fiscal 2001 budget request was the second since the restructuring of the agency began under the Workforce Investment Act. It asked for an appropriation of $11 billion, about 8.6 percent more than in the previous year. Of the total budget, discretionary programs constituted more than 90 percent.

Under the new act, each governor must set up a state work force investment board, divide the state into what Bramucci calls "intelligent entities" that reflect regional populations and economies, and form local boards for each of these on which employers are 51 percent of the membership. "We're talking billions of dollars," he says, "basically distributed on a population basis, on a need basis. The governors and local boards use the money to act on the economies of their regions." The first funds under the new law were dispensed in July 2000.

"My task here is to put the new Workforce Investment Act into place," Bramucci says. It will allow ETA to deploy people who are "empowered locally to participate in decisionmaking on how you allocate resources. Without it, the marketplace will not yield the workers that employers need or allow people to become independent and self-supporting. That's a first. We never had that kind of an economy before." What does it take to achieve this? "Hard work," he replies, and "inspiration, exhortation, and understanding." One obstacle to overcome, he adds, is the duplication and lack of coordination in government programs aimed at the same goals. "Government funds similar things with dissimilar revenue streams," Bramucci asserts. "It promotes parallel programs. So we're always trying to coordinate with one another. Government is like a heavily laden ship going into battle—hard to steer. But if you master that, it can deliver a real blow."

Where ETA is concerned, cutting through that confusion of multiple programs and responsibilities is one of the improvements the Workforce Investment Act is intended to make. "The whole theory of the new investment system is one-stop shopping," Bramucci says. The vehicles for this are called career centers—places, he says, where customers can get the information they need without being told "that's not the right form, this is not the right place, you've got to go over there, we only take care of this, we don't take care of that."

Who are the key partners in the WIA? "Employers, number one," says Bramucci. "Poor people, people who train, community-based organizations, community colleges, trade unions, technical schools. Some are clients, some are customers. We have to meld." While ETA has sustained good relationships with these colleagues, he points out, "it's not just one big happy family. There are real issues to resolve and a natural animus between the locals and the governors, and the community-based organizations perceive themselves as getting squeezed out of the picture."

Various bones of contention are at work here. Of the funds made available through ETA, for example, governors' offices get 15 percent off the top for training funds and have discretion on how they are used. Again, disagreements arise over how to draw the map of state investment regions. "We have to keep everybody engaged," says Bramucci, "and try to decide these issues fairly. But basically we let them evolve and try to get people to talk to one another and come to accommodation. Shotgun weddings don't work. If we can get people on these boards who really work easily with others in the community, we can make a difference."

Information technology, he says, "is an incredible part of our arsenal." The centerpiece is a web-based service called America's Job Bank. As a partnership of federal, state, and local governments and other groups, it helps working Americans find the training they need to advance and gives employers nationwide access to the skilled employees they seek. "It's probably the most successful job network, public or private, in the country," Bramucci says, "with nearly 1.5 million jobs and almost 2.2 million job seekers." On another front, the Joint Employment and Training Technology Conference, an ETA program, is a major annual showcase for the applications of information technology to job and work force development.

The most important relationships in his work, Bramucci believes, "are between the levels of government that we work with. I'd say the least understood issue is getting people to respect one another and form collegial bonds. That will let them share information and resolve problems in a spirit of collegiality, rather than with accusations and lawsuits. I've probably made a thousand speeches since I've been here and that's the theme every time, including when I testify before Congress."

Despite the mandatory nature of the WIA, Bramucci says "we're trying to get people to implement the law without ordering them to. We're the coach. You don't have to have people moving at the crack of a whip." He already sees signs of a change among the agency's partners. "I think people grasp the difference," he says. "We're trying to change the way we treat our partners and I think it's beginning to succeed. I have now gone coast to coast, trying to spread the gospel and I hear people repeating phrases I started using eighteen months ago. Once you plant the seed, if you're true to your principles and keep pushing, you can grow and harvest a lot of great things."

PROFILE

Current Assistant Secretary for Employment and Training
Raymond L. Bramucci, 1998–

Career summary
Commissioner, New Jersey Department of Labor, 1990–94
Director, New Jersey operations, Sen. Bill Bradley (D-N.J.), 1979–90
Various positions, International Ladies' Garment Workers' Union, 1957–79

Education
Not available

Assistant Secretaries for Employment and Training since 1989

Clinton administration
Tim Barnicle, 1995–97 (currently executive director, National Center on
   Education and the Economy)
Doug Ross, 1994–95 (currently president, Small Business Association
   of Michigan)
Position vacant, 1993–94

Bush administration
Roberts T. Jones, 1989–93 (currently president and CEO, National Alliance
   of Business)

9

Positions in
Law Enforcement

Department of Justice

▓ Solicitor General

EXECUTIVE LEVEL III—Presidential appointment with
Senate confirmation

RECOMMENDED SKILLS AND EXPERIENCE ■ Some people familiar with this position think it requires a professional background on the bench or in the teaching of law. Seth Waxman, solicitor general since November 1997, doesn't see it that way. He points out that nearly everyone who has held the post since the 1950s has had that background. The only exception is Waxman himself—who also notes that he is the first person in the job since Thurgood Marshall to have been a trial lawyer. "I view it as a great advantage that I grew up in the law trying and arguing cases and writing briefs," he explains. Ultimately, the responsibility of the solicitor general—determining and advancing the interests of the United States in litigation—requires "the perspective of representing a client." The special challenge lies in the kind of client the solicitor general serves: not a person or a company, but the United States. As will be seen, that challenge—and the independence that are essential to an SG's effectiveness—are the key features of this distinctive position.

An ability to make decisions quickly and efficiently across the entire spectrum of federal law is a prime requirement of the position. So is skill in presenting oral arguments that are exceptionally clear. That's because the solicitor general personally appears before the Supreme Court when it hears the most important and difficult cases in which the SG has a role. Quick thinking and clear presentation here are critical, often decisive assets. At the same time, a great deal of the SG's advocacy on behalf of the United States is written advocacy. The SG must therefore be able to write and edit with equal speed and precision—work that must be of unquestionably superior quality. Finally, the office and the SG personally must enjoy a high level of confidence from the president and the attorney general. "Otherwise," Waxman says, "they won't trust the SG to make important judgments. That would be quite harmful to the interests of the United States, the president, the judiciary, and certainly the SG's office."

INSIGHT ■ Ask almost any nonlawyer for an opinion about the position of solicitor general, says Waxman, and you'll get a blank stare. "Solicitor general of what?" will be the reply, or "Which branch of the military is the job in?" But ask any lawyer the same question and the answers will often be that it's "the greatest job in the world," or "the best lawyer's job in the country," or "every lawyer's dream." You can also get an idea of the unusual nature of this post from another Waxman anecdote. When cabinet officers who differ on a particular point of policy or law that is to be presented to a court in litigation learn that the final decision will be made by the SG, "their instant reaction is likely to be, 'Who on earth is the solicitor general?'"

The solicitor general position dates back to the post–Civil War era. Before 1870 the attorney general had the statutory duty to defend U.S. interests in the Supreme Court and advise the president and cabinet on questions involving federal law. But the attorney general lacked the staff, time, authority—and sometimes the substantive knowledge—to do that or to tell U.S. attorneys how to interpret laws. As a result, federal lawyers often took inconsistent positions in court on principles of federal law. Further, the attorney general had to hire private lawyers to represent U.S. interests in the Supreme Court and around the country. That meant courts were hearing varying positions presented as the U.S. position. Together with the crush of litigation that followed the Civil War and the need to enforce the civil rights mandates of Reconstruction, this kind of confusion persuaded the Congress to create both the SG job and the Department of Justice.

Specific sections of the Judiciary Act of 1870 laid out the SG's purpose. As Waxman outlines it, the idea was "that there should be one person responsible for providing a strategic vision about the litigation interests of the United States across the country, to make sure that the government speaks with one voice on questions concerning the constitutionality of acts of Congress, how legislation should be interpreted, and how particular disputes should be resolved." The underlying theory is that "there be one person who sees the whole field and can make decisions about what the substantive position of the United States should be and by what strategy that position should be advocated."

During the next 80 years, as the government grew larger and demands on the SG's time rose, the SG was generally freed from the early responsibilities to assist in managing the Department of Justice and to provide legal advice. "What was left was a pure litigation job," Waxman comments. Fixed by law and unchanged for decades, these are the SG's existing responsibilities:

—Represent the interests of the United States in the Supreme Court. That is, identify the cases in which to petition for review, decide what position to take in response to petitions filed by third parties, brief and argue all cases accepted by the court for review in which the United States has an interest, and respond to invitations from the court to express the view of the United States in particular cases.

—Decide when the United States will appeal any case or ruling it has lost in any court. (The United States is a party in many thousands of cases at any given time.)

—Determine whether the United States should intervene in any case where the constitutionality of an act of the Congress is in question.

—Decide when the United States should participate as an *amicus curiae*— friend of the court—in any appellate court, and approve the U.S. position taken in the brief.

The SG is the only officer in government required by statute to be "learned in the law." It is one of only two positions with offices and responsibilities in two branches of the government (the vice president is the other). In addition to offices at the Department of Justice, the SG has an office in the Supreme Court. The special relationship with the court—a relationship, Waxman stresses, that is characterized by special responsibilities, not perquisites—has led many observers to call the SG the "tenth justice."

One measure of that relationship is evident in the court's longstanding practice of inviting the SG to explain the views of the United States in cases in which the government is not a party. A recent example came in a case brought by HIV-positive Alabama prison inmates seeking to end their segregation from other inmates. At the invitation of the court, Waxman circulated the lower-court opinions and briefs to the Civil, Civil Rights, and Criminal divisions in the Justice Department, to the Bureau of Prisons, the Department of Health and Human Services, and to other interested federal agencies. After getting their views and those of his staff, he filed a brief advising the court that, while the United States didn't necessarily agree with the resolution by lower courts of every question in the case, "the legal test applied by the Court of Appeals was not incorrect." Interpretation: the brief suggested the Supreme Court not hear the case because its function is generally not to correct errors but "to resolve conflicts in the interpretations of the law." Agreeing, the court declined to hear the case and the appeals court decision stood.

Nothing in the Constitution requires the SG to be independent. And technically, as an official of the executive branch reporting to the president and the attorney general, the SG is not independent. But solicitors general over the years have, de facto, built a solid and critical tradition of independence—a tradition that benefits all three branches of government.

Among many other factors, according the SG a measure of independence gives confidence to the judiciary in general, and the Supreme Court in particular, that (1) the SG presents the views of all the interests of the United States, including the Congress, and (2) the SG's briefs and arguments are based scrupulously on the rule of law, not on partisan political considerations.

"I'm certain," Waxman says, "that most if not all SGs would have been unwilling to serve absent a measure of independence, because that would be forsaking an attribute of the office that's critical to the overall interests of the United States." The entire system of government, and of checks and balances, gains strength when courts are confident the SG is advocating positions on behalf of a client—the United States—whose interest is not in partisan advantage or achieving a particular result at all costs, but in seeing that justice is done.

What happens if the court does not view the SG that way? In the early 1990s, the Supreme Court declined to overrule its earlier *Roe v. Wade* decision on abortion rights. The decision to decline was not on the merits of *Roe v. Wade* but on the *stare decisis* principle, which in effect holds that settled law—in this case, a law that has offered a certain protection to a generation of women—should not be lightly overturned. In a separate opinion concurring with the decision to decline, three justices criticized several earlier interventions by the SG of the time who, despite *stare decisis*, had suggested the court overrule *Roe v. Wade*.

The SG's job is not a proactive one. "We don't roam around looking for interesting issues to champion or litigate," Waxman says. "Agencies or departments come to the SG because they have lost a case or want to appeal, or want to intervene or file an *amicus* brief. Or the Supreme Court agrees to hear a case in which the United States is a party and we have to file. Or we're asked to petition the court for a hearing." In all such cases, the SG's office assigns the case to an appropriate litigating division of the Justice Department and solicits the views of every other executive branch agency with a stake in the issues involved. Each agency sees the recommendations of all of the others. Further recommendations come from two members of the SG's staff and the entire package then hits the desk of the SG. On average, says Waxman, he gets recommendation packages in six to twelve cases every day.

In a small number of cases, where issues of overriding importance are at stake, or where the attorney general or president has a personal interest in the issue, the solicitor general makes certain that the president and the attorney general are comfortable with his decision. His responsibility,

Waxman says, is "to make decisions, not recommendations." At the same time, however, he must be "sensitive to those cases where either the president or the attorney general might conceivably want to overrule me." In his own experience, Waxman says, this is a very rare occurrence.

PROFILE

Current Solicitor General
Seth P. Waxman, November 1997–

Career summary
Various positions in the Department of Justice, 1994–97, including acting solicitor general and acting deputy attorney general
Before 1994, private law practice with Miller, Cassidy, Laroca, and Lewin, specializing in criminal, civil, and appellate litigation
Law clerk to the late Gerhard Gesell, U.S. District Judge for the District of Columbia

Education
B.A., summa cum laude, Harvard University, 1973; J.D., managing editor of the law journal, Yale Law School, 1977

Solicitor Generals since 1989

Clinton administration
Walter E. Dellinger III (acting), 1996–97 (currently professor, Duke University School of Law)
Drew S. Days III, 1993–96 (currently Alfred M. Rankin professor of law, Yale Law School)

Bush administration
Kenneth W. Starr, 1989–93 (currently professor of law, New York University School of Law)

■ Administrator, Drug Enforcement Administration

EXECUTIVE LEVEL III—Presidential appointment with
Senate confirmation

RECOMMENDED SKILLS AND EXPERIENCE ■ Substantial work in law enforcement—as a police official, investigative agent, or prosecutor, for example—is a requisite. It should include some time in more senior positions of command in enforcement organizations. Such a background assumes an understanding of this country's criminal justice system. Considerable additional advantages accrue to administrators who understand economics, are familiar with international trade, or have lived or traveled extensively overseas.

INSIGHT ■ In 1998 a federally conducted survey estimated that 13.5 million Americans had used illicit drugs within the thirty days before being interviewed. About ten of every hundred people between the ages of twelve and seventeen were among those users. Both of those statistics represented declines from the peak year, 1979, when an estimated 25 million-plus people in this country used illegal drugs, including more than sixteen of every hundred in their teens. But in 1998 the survey found that heroin users (130,000) had nearly doubled from five years earlier, with their average age rapidly dropping from the twenties into the teens.

Further, the Drug Enforcement Administration in the same year made 37,322 drug arrests in the United States. That figure had risen steadily, year to year, and doubled between 1988 and 1998. And the DEA in 1998 seized illegal stashes of marijuana, cocaine, crack, heroin, and methadone worth $86 million, the highest ever. Incomplete data showed that the 1999 figures would be comparable. Drugs remain the foremost source of criminal activity in the United States.

The DEA is the lead federal agency in the enforcement of U.S. laws governing narcotics and controlled substances. Operating in the United States and fifty-two other countries, it makes arrests for interstate or international violations of the laws, seizes the assets of those caught manufacturing or trafficking in drugs, develops cases against them, and puts these in the hands of appropriate U.S. or foreign authorities. It does this in collaboration with other federal as well as state and foreign enforcement agencies. The agency manages a number of other activities in support of its responsibility—a national narcotics intelligence collection system, training, research, information exchange. To give further support to international narcotics control, it liaises with the United Nations and Interpol. Beyond its far-ranging contest with this world of illegal substances, the DEA also enforces the regulations covering the legal production and dispensing of controlled prescription drugs.

Donnie R. Marshall has spent his career with the DEA, becoming the agency's administrator in June 2000, after serving in the position in an acting capacity. "The biggest change I want to bring about," Marshall says, "is to enhance our ability to use intelligence information to assess the threat, identify the groups that are creating it, understand the way they do business, and what their vulnerabilities may be. And then set about systematically attacking those vulnerabilities and dismantling the major drug organizations. We can and should do a better job of collecting and analyzing the information and getting it out to the people who use it to do their jobs."

Another major focus for Marshall is the DEA work force. He believes fundamentally that individual employees are the greatest strength of his agency—"more than cars or badges or guns or technical equipment." Within the framework and ethical bounds of the profession, he says, people should be allowed to display their initiative, use their skills, get the right training, "and show what they can do."

A glance at the DEA's list of programs suggests the intricate, diversified, sometimes exotic nature of its work—asset forfeiture, demand reduction, forensic science, intelligence, money laundering, mobile enforcement teams, and more. For fiscal year 2001, the agency requested a budget of $1.47 billion, approximately 8 percent of the funding requested for the federal government's total drug effort and about $60 million more than the actual DEA budget in 2000. Of its 9,000 employees, well over half are special agents; about 940 are intelligence specialists and chemists. While both the dollars and the number of people have grown over the last few years, Marshall expects this growth to slow somewhat in the next two budget years.

He says the agency works in every major and many medium-sized cities in this country and has 500 people overseas. Since almost all of this country's flow of major narcotics like heroin and cocaine comes from abroad, foreign-based DEA agents operate mostly in countries that are sources or pipelines. The federal government's responsibility for combating drugs is shared—some would say loosely shared—among a dozen agencies. As the point organization in this group, the DEA is supposed to lead the way, not just for a colleague organization like the FBI within its parent Department of Justice, but for elements of the Treasury, State, Transportation, and Agriculture departments and for regional and state agencies as well.

History shows, however, that among the federal entities involved in the drug wars, collaborative harmony and agreement on policy have been difficult objectives. The White House Office of National Drug Control Policy, established by the Congress, was intended to improve this situation. But the jury remains firmly out on how effective this has been. And despite many examples of effective coordination between agencies, opinion still divides on whether drug control policy should reside at a single or at multiple locations.

Marshall thinks of his major leadership responsibility at the DEA in terms of "providing a set of core values, a vision, and goals for the DEA, and attaining those goals in an ethical manner that maintains public trust." He identifies a wide audience for what he says, inside the agency as well as among those outside with an interest in the problem of drugs and related issues. "They listen to everything I say, the statements I make, the messages I put out even in informal settings." For him, therefore, communication is really the key—"communicating the vision, the direction, the messages we want to get out, sticking with it, and recognizing where the message isn't well understood."

P R O F I L E

Current Administrator of the Drug Enforcement Administration
Donnie R. Marshall (acting), 1999–

Career summary
Various positions with the Drug Enforcement Administration, 1969–present,
   including deputy administrator; chief of operations; chief of domestic
   operations; senior inspector, office of professional responsibility; country
   attaché, Brazil; and special agent in Dallas and Houston

Education
B.S., Austin State University, 1969

Administrators of the Drug Enforcement Administration since 1989

Clinton administration
Thomas A. Constantine, 1994–99 (currently professor, State University of New
   York, Albany)

Clinton and Bush administrations
Robert C. Bonner, 1990–94 (currently partner, Dunn and Crutcher)

Bush administration
Terrence M. Burke (acting), 1990 (currently director, International Operations,
   IGI International)

Bush and Reagan administrations
Jack Lawn, 1985–90 (currently chairman and CEO, Century Council)

10

Positions Influencing the National Infrastructure

Department of Commerce

▓ Director, Bureau of the Census

EXECUTIVE LEVEL IV—Presidential appointment with
Senate confirmation

RECOMMENDED SKILLS AND EXPERIENCE ■ An active partisan
political background should be considered disqualifying for this job.
That's not to say that the director of the Bureau of the Census should be
a novice to the political environment that surrounds the bureau's work,
especially the decennial census. But at the bureau, detachment, objectivity, and political neutrality on the job are especially serious watchwords.
Apart from that, the director needs good management, personal, and public affairs skills, plus training and experience in one or more such pursuits
as statistical analysis, survey methodology, or the practical uses of census
data. Familiarity with the federal government is valuable, as is a solid reputation among statisticians, demographers, and other professionals for
whom this position has special interest.

INSIGHT ■ As 2001 begins, the Bureau of the Census will still be de-
celerating from the peak activity of its most visible and consequential
program—the ten-year census. It will still have much to do, however, before the work of the 2000 census is complete. Among the most important
will be the release in April 2001 of the enumerated census results—the
actual population head count. By statute, those results must be published
before April 1, 2001.

But that may not be the whole story. Also in the picture, as this is written, is the hotly debated question whether the final census numbers will or
should be adjusted to reflect the results of a sample survey of 314,000
households carried out by the bureau in the late spring and summer of 2000.
The sampling is designed to show the extent to which hard-to-locate elements of the population—such as inner-city racial minorities, people living
in nontraditional households, and children—were miscounted in the actual
census. Historically, traditional census taking has undercounted some parts
of the population. In the 1990 census, 8 million people were not counted at
all and 4 million were counted twice.

Although the bureau has studied statistical sampling for many years, the
technique has never been used to improve the results of a decennial census.

In 1980 the bureau concluded that sampling was not a reliable enough method; in 1990 the bureau director's recommendation that it be used was rejected. In June 2000 the secretary of commerce announced a proposed regulation giving the Bureau of the Census the authority to decide whether the sample survey conducted during the summer improves the accuracy of the 2000 census. Within the bureau, a committee of senior career professionals would review the results of the sample, called the Accuracy and Coverage Evaluation, which was to include more than twice the number of households it covered in the 1990 census. From its review, the committee would make a recommendation to the director, who would make the final decision. Published in the Federal Register in mid-June, the regulation issued by the secretary was available for public comment for forty-five days.

It's not hard to see why the results of the decennial census—and lately, how they are arrived at—are the focus of keen and widespread attention. Billions of federal grant dollars, not to mention the potential redrawing of congressional and state legislative districts, are at stake in every decennial census. In 1999 the Supreme Court said that census results cannot be used to divide seats in the Congress among the states. But it left open the question of including sampling results in determining whether the boundaries of congressional and state legislative districts must be redrawn, how federal dollars should be distributed, and much else. Political parties, of course, are intently interested in the redistricting impact, especially when control of the Congress could hang on whether and how the count is adjusted.

Kenneth Prewitt, who has headed the bureau since 1998, sees this as "a big political question that has still not been fully resolved. We've resolved it operationally, technically. But it will still be fought out politically and in the courts." What used to be a politics of census results, he says, is now a "politics of census methods." He calls it "a very bad place to be, because it makes for bad science and bad politics." He believes all stakeholders in this issue "need to have an important conversation about how to save the science—not by taking politics away from the census, because you never do that, but by allowing politics to play a role in how the numbers are used, not in how they're collected." Meanwhile, when we interviewed him in April 2000, he thought much of his census 2000 work in the ensuing five months would center on "making sure we have done what we can do as an agency to prepare ourselves to give the Congress and the administration what they need."

Decennial censuses are the major events in the life of the bureau. Year in and year out, however, the bureau performs hundreds of other surveys and studies of varying size and timing, whose results serve to augment and elaborate the basic picture of the country outlined by the decennial's emphasis on people and housing. Among these are every-five-years censuses of agriculture and such other sectors as manufacturing, construction, minerals, and transportation. The bureau issues monthly and quarterly studies in a wide range, statistical compendia of housing and commerce data, population estimates, and a variety of other reports. In all, it engages in some 150 operations of this kind each year. It hardly needs to be said that these products have many users.

For Prewitt, the decennial census "is the moment when the bureau becomes most publicly visible and disproportionately huge numbers of people take their measure of how well the bureau can do this job." The decennial also produces what one of Prewitt's predecessors called the bureau's "two-pronged budget," covering a ten-year cycle. "It's not just a single-year budget," he says, but one that builds as the decennial approaches, then winds down afterward toward the next buildup a few years later. Through fiscal year 2000, the bureau spent $6.2 billion in planning and conducting the 2000 census. In its budget submission for 2001, it requested $719.2 million, including nearly $393 million—more than half—for close-down activities related to the 2000 decennial. "When we're fully staffed for the decennial, we have somewhere between 500,000 and 600,000 employees," Prewitt says, in addition to the 7,000 or 8,000 professionals who normally staff the bureau and will remain behind when the 2000 census is history. "In this sense," he comments, "it's a big challenge, because of the huge spike every ten years. It's a management issue, how you ramp up and ramp down with minimum disruption to the rest of the agency. Because you can't do the decennial as a separate function. You need your statisticians, your geography department, your information technology people, all of whom are still doing bureau projects apart from the decennial."

He calls the operational issues involved in the census "vast and difficult. There really is no easy way—if there's any way at all—to count 275 million Americans on a given day." To do it, the bureau printed eighty-three different questionnaires, totaling 485 million pages, and mailed 98 million of them. In the eight months up to April 2000, bureau personnel drove 61 million miles to deliver 24 million more. Prewitt notes the "very, very big impact" of information technology in the bureau's data-scanning operation. After all, we get 120 million pieces of paper and have to take information off those and put them into a reasonable format." In 2000 all of this was optically scanned at four sites around the country—the bureau's own permanent existing operation, plus three sites "built from scratch." In the middle of 1999, a substantial part of Prewitt's job became one of mobile "cheerleader for the census," taking him from Puerto Rico to Hawaii, from Alaska to the Mexican border, and to inner cities, homeless shelters, and migrant worker farms. There were sessions with many minority groups, mayors, and governors. "It was a salesman's job," he says, "trying to sell the importance of the census and make sure that we (census employees) were all roughly doing the same thing."

The 2000 census is the most scrutinized in history, Prewitt said at the time of our interview. "We're doing it in a fish bowl. We have the Census Monitoring Board, which has a big staff and budget and tracks everything we're doing. We have between seven and ten major standing advisory committees, who don't just give us advice but actually help us do it." He also mentions the Commerce Department's inspector general, the Congress's General Accounting Office, and "two or three dozen" journalists whose beat is the census—"a lot of very knowledgeable people paying attention." He adds two other facts: a good 99 percent of the American public "can give you some elementary facts about the census" and the mail-back response rate for questionnaires, after dropping for three decennials, reversed course in 2000 to register 66 percent. "We stopped that drop," he points out, "despite public attitudes toward government, which have hardly improved at all in the last decade."

Commenting on the long form and short form questionnaires used in 2000, Prewitt recalls that this split practice began in 1940, mainly to reduce the burden on respondents. That turns out to have been "prescient," because in 2000, "there's a lot of concern about respondent burden." Nonetheless, he thinks that 2000 will be the last census to use the short form-long form method. "We actually believe we ought to get the long form data on a continuous basis—a sample of about a quarter of a million a month, or three million a year. After five years, we've interviewed 15 million households, roughly equivalent to the number we get from the long form in a one-out-of-six sample." What this means is that "the country would have the equivalent of long-form data every year, not every ten years. It's a much more powerful design." In fact, the bureau has already been preparing to do this on the assumption that the 2000 decennial would be the last to use the current approach. "Then, if you've already done the long form, in 2010 you basically are doing only the elementary count. It's a much simpler exercise."

Reflecting on the work he oversees, Prewitt takes note of this country's entry into the information economy—the "knowledge economy." In exactly the same way that canals, railroads, and highways are infrastructure to an industrial economy, "information is infrastructure to a knowledge economy." And the decennial," he says, "is basic to the quality of that information infrastructure."

PROFILE

Current Director of the Bureau of the Census
Kenneth Prewitt, 1998–

Career summary
President, Social Science Research Council, 1995–98
Senior vice president, Rockefeller Foundation, 1985–95
President, Social Science Research Council, 1979–85
Director, National Opinion Research Center, University of Chicago, 1975–79
Teaching at the University of Chicago, Stanford University, Columbia
  University, Washington University, and the University of Nairobi, 1963–79

Education
B.A., Southern Methodist University, 1958; M.A. Washington University, 1960;
  Ph.D., Stanford University, 1963

Directors of Bureau of the Census since 1989

Clinton administration
James F. Holmes (acting), 1998 (currently regional director, Atlanta, Bureau of
  the Census)
Martha Farnsworth Riche, 1994–98 (currently affiliated with Farnsworth Riche
  Associates)
Harry A. Scarr (acting), 1993–94 (deceased)

Bush administration
Barbara E. Bryant, 1989–93 (current position unavailable)
C. Louis Kincannon (acting), 1989 (currently deputy secretary general and
  director, statistics, OECD Secretariat)

▨ Under Secretary for Oceans and Atmosphere

EXECUTIVE LEVEL III—Presidential appointment with
Senate confirmation

RECOMMENDED SKILLS AND EXPERIENCE ■ Advanced-degree training and a professional background in science or technology are prerequisites for this job. D. James Baker, under secretary and administrator since 1993, also recommends experience in an area of this agency's concern. Otherwise, "it's too easy to be fooled or not understand what's really happening," in which case "other people drive the agenda." He himself was a National Oceanographic and Atmosphere Administration scientist in the 1970s, with previous experience in "satellites, weather, and oceans," and a state university dean in ocean and fishery sciences. These credentials also make a big difference in the national and global scientific communities where NOAA's chief must work with confidence and respect.

INSIGHT ■ NOAA (as this agency is universally known) has two broad missions: (1) analyzing and predicting the atmospheric environment and (2) protecting it in its marine and ocean dimensions. With a work force of 12,500 at 400 sites around the world, NOAA does this work in several specific ways:

—Operates the country's weather forecasting at more than a hundred stations nationwide, providing data from two polar orbiting and two geostationary earth satellites.

—Provides long-term forecasting—on the El Niño ocean current, for example—and longer-range prediction on global warming and other climate change, plus archived weather and climate data for the United States.

—Manages all U.S. salt-water commercial and recreational fisheries. This is NOAA's biggest commercial component, dating from the agency's formation in 1970.

—Protects marine mammals and assists endangered marine species to recover.

—Administers the U.S. coastal zone management program, a federal-state partnership in which states that adopt federally set standards get NOAA funding to do their planning.

—Maps and charts all U.S. coastal waters (the navy does this for waters outside the U.S. coastal zone) and manages the National Marine Sanctuary Program.

Two concerns have recently demanded large amounts of the NOAA administrator's time. The first relates to the modernization of the National Weather Service, one of the agency's five primary components. Over the last ten years, weather stations have dropped in number from 300 to 120, new kinds of weather satellites have come on line, and a single program combining civilian and military satellites has replaced former separate systems. Providing the technology for "the best possible observations and forecasting of the environment" continues to be "one of the major things we do," Baker says.

Second is the stewardship of the marine environment, increasingly complicated by the growth of the U.S. population. "As population grows," Baker explains, "there is more stress on all of the resources in the environment—the fish, the mammals, the coastal environment." Ever more people live in areas that are fish habitats, for instance. This is putting increasing pressure on the habitat, resulting in declining numbers of fish. The commercial fishing industry is feeling the strain, Baker says. A continuous struggle takes place between the industry, which is reluctant to scale back its fishing; the Congress, which tends to support the industry; and the conservation community, which wants to slow down use of the resource.

Baker's job here is "to find a middle way so that we can make this work." That's not really a science or technology problem, he adds. "It's dealing with many different constituents, and a changing way of life, to find a solution." With individual fishermen and the industry as a whole, that means reaching eventual agreement on a sustainable fish population that will be lower than it was a generation ago. And "nobody is happy about that," he says. NOAA is trying various solutions, meanwhile, to provide alternatives for those who fish for a living—buying back boats, providing some family assistance, suggesting other occupations.

But fishermen have a special life-style, are notably independent, and love what they do. "I have lots of books about the science and ecology of fisheries," Baker comments. "None of them tells me how to deal with unhappy fishermen and members of Congress who see a resource declining and don't know how to solve it." So far, he acknowledges, neither does NOAA. "When we take tough measures, we have seen some stocks begin to recover. Our major challenge is to convince our constituencies that tough management approaches are needed to ensure a sustainable level of harvest."

Since 1993 NOAA's budget has risen about 6 percent annually. In fiscal 2000 it was $2.35 billion, an increase of just under 6 percent, but less than what the agency asked for. According to Baker, the Congress has always liked NOAA, which is why it "put back most of the money that was cut in the early 1980s."

In the process, NOAA developed and has retained a strong relationship with Congress, including bipartisan support, "which has been very valuable to us." He says NOAA probably gets as much oversight from the Hill as any agency in Washington. Committees with main jurisdiction are the House committees on Resources and on Science and the Senate Commerce, Science, and Transportation Committee.

"We're mostly an environmental agency," Baker points out, "inside a department that is oriented to business, science, and technology. That brings some conflicts and some very positive things for us." His comment is a reminder of the view, once expressed by a former NOAA administrator among others, that the agency was misplaced and perhaps ought to move under a more compatible roof, or even into independent status. That might be awkward, since NOAA is the biggest of the Commerce Department's several agencies and accounted for just over half its fiscal 2000 budget (excluding a special appropriation for the 2000 census).

But Baker sees strong reasons for his agency to stay where it is. "Being in Commerce gives us a very good link with the business community," he says. "As we look at issues for the future, it is important that the voice of the private sector be there." The modernization of the weather service, for example, has given the private sector a "key role" in delivering weather information to the public. Where once government did it all, NOAA's weather people today provide a basic forecast on which private weather services produce tailored forecasts for their consumers. "Most of what you see is really a private-sector product built on what the government is doing," Baker says. He calls it "an important public-private partnership between the two."

Similarly, NOAA's connection to business and industry as an agency within Commerce is significant for the health of marine sanctuaries. Sanctuaries have a variety of purposes, such as the sheltering of humpback whales or protection from the effects of offshore oil drilling. At the same time, Baker says, "as the digital world becomes more important," communications companies want to lay fiber optic cable through some sanctuaries. NOAA has therefore been negotiating a way to permit this to happen while still protecting marine resources.

Baker thinks this kind of activity with the business community will grow. Through round-table discussions and other forms of dialogue, "they're getting a better understanding of the conservation issues, while our people gain a better sense of what the business community is doing."

He also believes NOAA is better off in a cabinet department, with a secretary who can represent the agency's interests at the highest levels, than as an independent agency whose chief would get less attention. That view is valid, one of Baker's predecessors said a decade ago, so long as the secretary keeps NOAA's objectives clearly in mind and gives it sufficient support and autonomy. Part of the administrator's job, he believed, is therefore to educate the secretary and the department about NOAA.

In any case, as another of Baker's predecessors once observed, the Department of Commerce may be misnamed. In addition to NOAA, the department contains the National Institute of Standards and the Bureau of the Census. It's easily as much a technical agency as one focused on business and trade. NOAA, it can be argued, should feel quite at home.

PROFILE

Current Under Secretary for Oceans and Atmosphere
D. James Baker, 1993–

Career summary
President, Joint Oceanographic Institutions
Dean, College of Ocean and Fishery Sciences, University of Washington
Group leader, deep sea physics, NOAA's Pacific Marine Environmental
   Laboratory
Associate professor, Harvard University
Research associate, University of Rhode Island

Education
B.S., Stanford University, 1958; Ph.D., Cornell University, 1962

Under Secretaries for Ocean and Atmosphere since 1989

Bush administration
John A. Knauss, 1989–93 (currently professor and dean emeritus, University of
   Rhode Island School of Oceanography)

Department of Housing and Urban Development

▨ Assistant Secretary for Housing and Federal Housing Commissioner

EXECUTIVE LEVEL IV—Presidential appointment with Senate confirmation

RECOMMENDED SKILLS AND EXPERIENCE ▪ Assistant Secretary for Housing and Federal Housing Administration Commissioner William Apgar was associated with Harvard's Joint Center for Housing Studies for twenty years before taking this position in late 1998. There, he says, "we had extensive contacts with the whole range of the housing industry." He talked regularly with tenant-based organizations, housing advocacy groups, home builders, realtors, mortgage bankers, and business people. All of them saw that, as an academic, "I didn't have any money in play; I was not in it for any self-interested purposes." He thus came to the FHA job "with a high degree of respect from a wide range of players. I think that's helped me to bring people together, to find common ground on legislation." As a credential for this position, that background of course makes logical good sense. Extensive experience in one or more of the housing-related areas that Apgar mentions, such as housing finance, qualifies equally well.

At the same time, as in every federal job with responsibility for big budget numbers, large work forces, and—in this case—significant risk imposed by a huge loan structure, management skills are prime. Apgar's predecessors also underscore the value of familiarity with financial markets and of knowing something about the nature and history of FHA's holdings as a loan insurer and guarantor.

INSIGHT ■ At the Department of Housing and Urban Development— HUD—the Office of Housing is the major party at the table. With two related missions, it commands a third of the department's operating budget and employs 3,300 people. As assistant secretary, this position's occupant has regulatory supervision of programs that (1) directly assist low-income families to live in single- and multifamily housing they couldn't otherwise afford and (2) furnish loans to developers of housing for such families and for the handicapped and elderly.

In the FHA role, which normally soaks up the lion's share of attention and effort, this job manages an organization responsible for half a trillion dollars of mortgage insurance. The insurance guarantees mortgage loans covering nearly 7 million single-family homes ($450 billion) and of some 1.6 million units of multifamily housing ($50 billion).

"We operate through thousands of partners," Apgar says, "all of whom have the capacity to do a lot of good or set the government up for a lot of problems if they don't abide by the rules." One of the job's big concerns, in fact, is maintaining the "very delicate balance" between the need to monitor the FHA's business partners—lenders, developers, builders—and a continued outreach to home loan borrowers of low and moderate incomes.

In managing its portfolio, the FHA is required by the Congress to maintain a specified capital adequacy ratio in its Mutual Mortgage Insurance Fund (the ratio is the economic value of the fund divided by the total insurance in force). That's because the fund was just about broke in the late 1980s and early 1990s, getting less cash from new business than obligations coming due. Corrective steps, including better management, have since reversed that situation. "In the last several years, we've been able to expand the amount of mortgage lending and also increase the health of the fund," Apgar says. As a result, while the mandated capital adequacy ratio by 2000 was supposed to be 2 percent, a report by a leading independent accounting firm in March 2000 showed that it actually achieved 3.66 percent—almost exactly what Apgar predicted when we talked with him several months earlier.

The report also found the mortgage fund itself to be in what the FHA called its strongest condition since its creation in 1934 (and stirred new opposition from national banking, building, realtors', and mayors' associations to a congressional proposal to privatize the FHA and its colleague HUD agency, Ginnie Mae).

Apgar says the FHA's regained health reflects a good economy but also an expansion of FHA lending. One reason for that is automated underwriting, a gift of the age of information technology. For a would-be borrower, a mortgage lender can go on line to put the key information about the borrower into the automated underwriting system. The system makes a loan decision then and there—in two minutes, according to Apgar. If it is an approval, the borrower can make the housing purchase immediately, picking up the paperwork when it comes through later, also electronically, at one of the FHA's home ownership centers. "We can now close a loan from beginning to end in as little as seven days," Apgar says. "And most of that time is waiting for the appraisal"—a requirement the FHA still applies and one that, Apgar points out, "slows us down relative to a private lender."

The FHA has in fact come a long way in information technology from the day, a bit more than a decade ago, when it was carrying a $330 billion insurance portfolio and, according to a previous commissioner, owned only a hundred computers. "Actually," says Apgar, I think we benefited from that lag, because we just basically moved to the top. We didn't have a lot of heavy investment in old systems we needed to protect and defend like other agencies." When it comes to mortgage processing, he relates, "some might have criticized us for not developing our own underlying system. But we managed instead to go into partnership with Fannie Mae and Freddie Mac and get access to state of the art processing. We process 4,000 homeowner mortgage applications a day, virtually all on line. We've moved light years in four years."

(Fannie Mae and Freddie Mac operate in the secondary mortgage market, buying mortgages from primary lenders and thereby freeing up capital for further loans to homebuyers. Unlike them, the FHA does not invest directly in mortgages. The mortgages it insures are packaged by lenders and sold to Ginnie Mae, a government corporation that serves as a guaranteed secondary-market mechanism to link federal housing markets with the capital markets. The *Washington Post* reported in a March 2000 article that the FHA was conducting an inquiry into Fannie Mae and Freddie Mac lending policies that might be forcing minority borrowers to pay higher mortgage rates. It quoted Apgar as saying that the "absence of active involvement" by the two institutions in buying mortgages to African Americans "limits the opportunity" for such families to get conventional mortgages. The article said spokesman for Fannie Mae and Freddie Mac acknowledged that their organizations' purchase of mortgages to African Americans has dropped below the national average.)

"We're rapidly approaching the time when all our business will be done over the Internet," Apgar says. Much business is already being done that way. Starting in 2000, FHA began using handheld computers in inspections of its multifamily properties. The information collected—defects to be fixed, critical health and safety matters that need attention, and the like—go back to FHA field offices electronically. "Next year," Apgar adds, "we'll electronically distribute that information right back to the owners or managers of the buildings." The FHA has also started electronic collection of the audited financial statements that owners of multifamily housing are required to submit each year.

What about the potential risk of a $500 billion insurance portfolio backed by the federal government? Apgar points to agency computers that monitor auditing and compliance issues relating to FHA housing and scan various indicators for indications of financial stress. In addition, FHA field offices use a ranking system for the housing units under their jurisdictions to spot those with particular risk on the financial or compliance fronts. "Our early warning systems have improved so we can get ahead of the curve in looking for areas of stress," Apgar says.

But on another level he describes a potentially "tricky" situation on the single-family side. Private mortgage lenders are increasingly ready to lower their payment percentages to make mortgages more affordable to low- and moderate-income borrowers. "Some of our better customers (borrowers of FHA-insured loans) are going to the private sector. In a sense, that's not a new story. When we started off in the 1930s, private lenders would only make 50 percent down payment loans for five years and thought we were nuts doing 20 percent down for thirty years." Gradually, private lenders began attracting borrowers who no longer needed the FHA advantage to afford a mortgage. "And so we went to 10 percent, to 5, to 3, and in some instances to 0 percent. And the industry has been following us as they see that the risk of some of these borrowers is not as great as perceived. But that leaves us with greater risk"

The FHA, Apgar says, thus expects to lose more money on its lending than a private company does. "That's why we created it. But people fear we'll go too far, that as the quality of our buyers gets too low we'll expose the government to big risk. Maybe down the line that will happen. But now, when the actuarial people look at our portfolio, they say we're rock solid."

In 1996 former FHA commissioner C. Austin Fitts expressed to us the view that, in the information age, many of the country's domestic problems "can be addressed over time through access to education, job retraining, and job opportunity. But it's got to go through housing." Housing will be either "a prison that traps people in isolation" or, if hooked into the Internet, "the door to access and opportunity." The FHA portfolio should not be "Internet redlined," she said, but remain what it is intended to be—a platform for access. It must serve those whose chances for employment are increasingly limited by the progress of technology and the productivity of those who do have jobs. The FHA, with a huge portfolio in underserved neighborhoods, has "two risk profiles," she said. "Those neighborhoods can go down and, with them, all your money. Or they can lift, because your housing is part of the solution."

Apgar agrees. Many assisted housing organizations, public and private, have realized that they are also investors in these neighborhoods—that "the capacity of residents in their buildings even to pay subsidized rents is only as good as their capacity to earn some minimal income." The system works best, he says, when the income of such people rises, because their skills grow and they can move on to nonsubsidized housing. "HUD is obviously a housing agency, but many of our most significant recent initiatives have been in the economic development arena." Nor is the problem being targeted confined to neighborhoods. "Whole cities have been left behind," he says. A lot of HUD's economic development energy is going into the effort to give appropriate assistance to cities like Gary, East St. Louis, and Syracuse, "where they're still trying to find their way in the information age."

The FHA's operating budget—salaries, expenses, information technology, procurement—runs about $700 million a year, approaching two-thirds of the HUD total. It gets very little money via the appropriations route. "We actually make money for the government," Apgar says. "Last year we contributed about $2.5 billion of revenues over expenses that go into the consolidated (HUD) budget." The FHA pays for its own staff and systems costs and for 40 percent of HUD salaries and expenses as a whole. Through attrition, it is losing some of its most valuable staffers, but at least as retirements occur, "we're able to hire replacements."

Apgar calls dealing with the Congress "a full time job." Despite Washington's "major budget food fights," he says HUD has fared reasonably well. "Large parts of the government ended up in an omnibus bill last time (fiscal 2000), but we managed to have a budget that went through the committees and did it the old-fashioned way." Speaking of HUD generally, he thinks it has been blessed with Republican committee chairs who were "very strong advocates for housing." No matter what the outcome of the 2000 congressional elections, he advises, "you've got to remind folks of the importance of housing as a bipartisan issue and just keep pushing."

An increasing number of FHA-insured loans are going to first-time homebuyers and minority families. Between 1992 and 1997, according to FHA figures, first-time buyers with FHA loans jumped from 64 percent of total buyers to nearly 81 percent. Minority families rose from 22 percent of the total to almost 38 percent.

The FHA, Apgar says, is launching "a new automation of our multifamily processes," similar to the automatic underwriting system described earlier—"an online, paperless application system for multifamily lending. We're going to create a new, expanded role for the lenders in terms of sharing some of the underwriting responsibilities, where we do less on the underwriting and provide more of a quality assurance function."

This new operation was scheduled to begin in August 2000. It will be in its infancy when the new administration takes over, Apgar points out, and "like all change, this is going to be particularly disruptive." He foresees "a lot of temptation, in the early phases, to say this isn't working, to go back to the old way. But we can't continue to deal with a world in which the private sector can approve an application on a multifamily deal three and four times faster than we can." He hopes his successors will stay with the new system. "I think this has to be the way of the future."

PROFILE

Current Assistant Secretary for Housing and Federal Housing Commissioner
William C. Apgar, 1998–

Career summary
Lecturer in public policy, Kennedy School of Government, Harvard University,
and executive director, Joint Center for Housing Studies, 1978–98

Education
B.A., Williams College, 1968; Ph.D., Harvard University, 1978

Assistant Secretaries for Housing and Federal Housing Commissioners since 1989

Clinton administration
Nicholas P. Retsinas, 1993–98 (currently director, Harvard Joint Center for
    Housing Studies, Harvard University)

Bush administration
Arthur Hill, 1990–92 (deceased)
C. Austin Fitts, 1989–90 (currently chairman, Solari)

Department of the Interior

▧ Director, National Park Service
SENIOR EXECUTIVE SERVICE

RECOMMENDED SKILLS AND EXPERIENCE ■ Substantial experi-
ence in land management at the federal or state level and general management skills are the obvious requisites. Beyond them, however, the choice for
this position should have a demonstrated sense of the national park system's
role and place in American society—not just its history, variety, purpose,
and use, but the need to stay abreast of the evolving public that it serves.
The current director spent almost twenty-five years in the National Park
Service in positions of steadily increasing responsibility.

INSIGHT ■ This position has policy and administrative oversight for the
nearly 380 separate natural, recreational, and cultural areas and trails—
some 83 million acres—that make up the domain of the National Park Service. They range from the ancient (pre-Colombian dwellings) to the historic
(Revolutionary and Civil War battlefields) and the monumental (Vietnam
and Korean War memorials)—and from celebration of human achievement
and determination (the Lincoln and FDR memorials, Ellis Island) to exal-
tation of the works of nature (Yellowstone and Redwood national parks).
    In 2001, about 290 million people—a number greater than the popula-
tion of the United States—are expected to visit the areas operated by the
National Park Service, or NPS. They will do so not only in forty-nine states

and the District of Columbia, but also in Puerto Rico, the Virgin Islands, American Samoa, Guam, and the Northern Mariana Islands. To accommodate and instruct these visitors, sustain the resources they will walk or drive through and camp in, protect historic and cultural sites, and do the maintenance, construction, and acquisition that all this requires, the NPS asked for a fiscal 2001 appropriation of $2.3 billion. The agency has 20,000 full-time and seasonal employees, working in Washington and six regional offices.

Speaking about one of the priorities of his job, NPS director Robert Stanton said preservation of the system's resources isn't limited to its natural assets. It also embraces the manmade ones: roads, bridges, visitor stations, and other structures, all of which the service nurtures with a $150 million annual construction program. Traffic management, for example, is "a key to preservation and public enjoyment." The example he cites is the south rim of the Grand Canyon, the most visited NPS location in the American West. "We have on the drawing table a major alternate transportation system," he says, "so we can physically separate people from their cars and still allow them to come in and enjoy the park." The NPS is eyeing the same solution for Yosemite Valley National Park and in the spring of 2000 inaugurated one at Utah's Zion National Park.

To protect water resources, the service in 1999 issued regulations on the use of watercraft. And shortly after we talked with Stanton, the NPS banned off-road snowmobiles from most of the park system, pointing to evidence that they were damaging its environment. The order applied to twenty-five parks and recreation areas where snowmobiles had been part of the scene for years.

Stanton's other chief concern is that all Americans have "the opportunity to experience their parks." In this, he recognizes that many people, for lack of resources or time, will never physically get to the Yorktown or Fredericksburg battlefields, the Grand Tetons, the Statue of Liberty, or any number of other locations. "But with today's technology," he says, "there are ways to impart the value of these resources. The Internet has given us a great opportunity to reach out." While the NPS operates general web sites, individual parks operate their own sites as well. Stanton says many parks "are experiencing visitors via the electronic media that they would not otherwise have." There are also special online services—for example, a tour of parks and other facilities related to the history of the U.S. civil rights movement. Another centers on recreational resources. It tells boating enthusiasts, for instance, where they can find the water areas that suit them and is operated with other federal agencies, for example, the U.S. Forest Service, to make it as comprehensive as possible.

The Forest Service, in the Department of Agriculture, is one of several other federal agencies with which the NPS has shared responsibilities. Inside the Interior Department, one of these is the U.S. Fish and Wildlife Service, which, like the NPS, operates under the authority of the assistant secretary for fish and wildlife and parks. The others at Interior are the Bureau of Land Management, the U.S. Geological Service, and the Bureau of Reclamation. Stanton also points out that, "in addition to managing those areas directly entrusted to us, we also provide technical and financial assistance to states and their political jurisdictions." The NPS administers those services through the Land and Water Conservation Fund, the Historic Preservation Fund, and other legislation. Further, there is the international dimension of NPS work. "I would say that in the eighty-plus years of our history we have assisted, at their request, no less than 100 other countries in establishing their national parks or equivalent preserves," Stanton notes.

Because needs of the NPS exceed the agency's appropriation by the Congress, it is authorized to accept donations in cash and in kind. "We are very fortunate," Stanton says, "that Americans care a great deal about parks and our programs. We get outstanding private-sector contributions." As he explains, the Congress created the National Park Foundation about thirty years ago "principally to provide resources to us from the private sector." The foundation is the agency's "principal liaison with commercial enterprises and has done a great job assisting us on a number of fronts." He says the NPS is seeing an increase of between 5 and 15 percent annually in donations.

The kind of private contribution that Stanton says pleases him most, however, comes from individual volunteers. More than 100,000 of them have signed up for the NPS's Volunteer in the Park program, in which they maintain trails, provide computer services, groom horses, clean artifacts, serve as guides at the Vietnam War Memorial or the former home of nineteenth-century abolitionist Frederick Douglass—"the whole gamut of park operational activities," he says.

Other NPS revenue derives from several sources. One of them is entrance fees at parks and campgrounds. The service is now authorized to retain 100 percent of these, giving it $140 million, Stanton says, to invest in facilities upgrades and resource management. From the Transportation Act for the 21st Century comes about $160 million for improvements to roads and bridges (the NPS system according to Stanton, has 8,000 miles of primary roads). A third source is franchise fees from concessions granted by the NPS, mostly for food, lodging, and transportation services, of which the service also now keeps 100 percent.

What kinds of problems are prominent in NPS operations (other than the occasional mistake of the kind that produced the extensive wildfire near Los Alamos, New Mexico, in May 2000)? "Our organic legislation of 1916 is very clear," Stanton comments, "that we are to preserve these resources, unimpaired, for future generations, but also to provide for public use and enjoyment. That's a management challenge—and that's the beauty of it, to test our ability to do both." It would be no problem just to use the resources, or just to preserve them. "But when you have to do both, that's the challenge." Besides the traffic management problem, which is major, he mentions the concern with invasive species, both animal and plant, "that are really taking over the habitat of native species" in some areas. It's an issue that confronts other agencies in its impact on grazing and food production. There are also the threats to parks and their resources presented by urban encroachment, air pollution, and the toxic agents in runoff from agricultural activity.

"If I have a passion," Stanton reflects, "it is a substantial increase in the involvement of young people in the programs of the National Park Service." The service is trying to do that in several ways—principally through its Parks and Classrooms program, which links students in their school environment with the resources available to them in the parks. It also has the authority to hire people as early as age fifteen via the Youth Conservation Corps program and another called the Public Lands Corps.

It will be "incumbent" on future park service leadership to continue seeking the resources the NPS needs, Stanton says. The route to this lies not only through the Congress, where the director must "continue to argue the case," but through other sources beyond fees and the private sector.

The NPS should also continue to work with "our many partners who really want to join us in caring for these special places."

The service, he emphasizes, needs to "continue to be relevant to contemporary society, recognizing and appreciating the change in the demographics of the country." And, repeating a thought expressed earlier, Stanton asserts that "every person, born here or a new citizen from elsewhere, should have some familiarity and, I hope, a deep appreciation of the national parks that are their heritage."

P R O F I L E

Current Director of the National Park Service
Robert G. Stanton, 1997–

Career summary
Various positions with the National Park Service, 1966–96, including director,
National Capital Region, 1988–96; associate director for operations, 1987;
deputy regional director, 1978–86; assistant director, park operations,
1976–78; deputy regional director, Southeast Region, 1974–76;
superintendent, Virgin Islands National Park, 1971–74; superintendent,
National Capital Parks-East, 1970–71

Education
B.S., Huston-Tillotson College, 1963; graduate work at Boston University and
George Washington University

Directors of the National Park Service since 1989

Clinton administration
Roger G. Kennedy, 1993–97 (retired, author)

Bush administration
James M. Ridenour, 1989–93 (currently director, Eppley Institute for Parks and
Public Lands)

Department of Transportation

▨ Administrator, Federal Aviation Administration

EXECUTIVE LEVEL II—Presidential appointment with
Senate confirmation

RECOMMENDED SKILLS AND EXPERIENCE ■ If the chief of the
Federal Aviation Administration comes to the job with a strong management and strong technical background, "that's a perfect world," says
Jane Garvey, who became FAA administrator in 1997. But if that's not
the case, "this is an agency with very strong technical expertise" to support the boss, and the aviation industry it regulates is generous in collaborating to find the right technological solutions to given problems.

"It's great to have a technical background," she says. But what is more important is "the ability to bring in the right people and ask tough questions." From her perspective, sound management experience—the kind that teaches an executive to "set benchmarks, lay out deadlines, and stick with them"—is almost a prerequisite.

Many who have held this job had significant exposure to civil or military aviation, or to the aviation industry. But there is no clear consensus on whether personal experience as a pilot is the kind of high-profile asset it was once thought to be. On another front, however, no one should be considered who cannot equably handle a large volume of congressional and media attention and operate often and with confidence in public and media environments.

INSIGHT ■ Modernization has always been a watchword for the Federal Aviation Administration, and never more so than now. As air passenger traffic continues to grow, and with an excellent safety record as backdrop, the agency's leadership is focused on improved technology in aircraft, and especially in air traffic control, as a key resource for the FAA's primary mission: safety.

Always in the spotlight, regularly the target of criticism, periodically mentioned as a candidate for privatization, the FAA is at the same time an operational, a regulatory, and a technical agency—and an essential element of the country's economic and social infrastructure. It develops rules for air traffic, assigns the use of airspace, and runs airport towers and control centers to direct air traffic safely. It builds or installs visual and electronic air navigation aids and sees to the security control of air traffic as required by national defense. For the U.S. commercial space transportation industry, which it regulates (and encourages), the FAA licenses commercial space launches and launch facilities.

The agency, with a work force of 49,000, oversees the safety of civil aviation, issuing and enforcing regulations and standards concerning the manufacture, operation, certification and maintenance of aircraft. It rates pilots, certifies airports that serve air carriers, allocates grant money for airport improvement, protects the security of civil aviation, regulates the shipment by air of hazardous materials, and runs its own technical research center.

Garvey calls this country's civil air safety history "an extraordinary record in aviation." That makes the FAA's task even more straightforward, if hardly simple: "keep advancing safety in an industry that is growing." The agency's primary safety instrument is, of course, the routing and control of civil air traffic, an area in which, Garvey says, "the technology's very challenging." Here, in the newest phase of modernization, the FAA is taking on the use of satellite-provided global positioning information. While Garvey guesses that "there are probably a handful of people in the world who understand it," global positioning systems are the wave of the future for air traffic control—"much less reliant on fixed routes in the sky and much more reliant on global navigation." The United States is a leader in many sectors like this one, she says, and other countries benefit. Rather than develop and test the technology themselves, they depend on this country to do it, then they buy the technology off the shelf once the system is perfected. "We'll take on some enormous tasks, maybe take some hits along the way, but we'll get it done."

How exactly does something like setting up global positioning unfold? Discussing the process, Garvey also provides useful insight into the management of a complex project. Government has a tendency to set out toward objectives so ambitious that it often never sees the light of day, she says. "In my view, the best way to achieve the grand and glorious visions we all have for modernization is to do it incrementally." With air traffic control modernization, the task was "first, get the consensus with industry and a very clear agreement." The FAA sat down with the airlines and air traffic controllers in 1997 to "figure out what the benchmarks are, what the building blocks are, what we want to put in place now that may not be the full solution but will get us there incrementally." That is what is happening. "We've got six technologies we're working on with industry right now," Garvey says. "We deploy the systems and they help us measure to see how well they're doing. That is paying off. We've started to see some of the platforms over the last year and a half. We're not waiting for the whole thing; we're getting them out there."

But just as vital as technology, Garvey takes care to point out, are the "human factors issues," which she calls "the key piece that sometimes we've missed at the FAA, which is seeing how the technology works in an operating environment." For that, bringing in the air traffic controllers has been "absolutely critical." Where the FAA has succeeded in the last two or three years is "in those programs we've brought them into and said we need them on the team, need them to be part of the solution with us." That helps the agency to a much greater understanding of what the human factors are and where the right solutions to problems lie.

Looking at safety from the standpoint of its regulatory mandate—and recognizing that it had already dealt with many of the easier issues—the

FAA under Garvey organized an agenda called Safer Skies. It directs agency resources to actions that safety data and analysis show can make the biggest difference in lowering the accident rate. "We said, let's really look at the data," Garvey recounts. "We have data now that we didn't have ten or fifteen years ago." As she relates it, the historical data for commercial aviation points to two situations "where we've got some difficulties."

One of these is "controlled flight into terrain"—for example, into a mountain. The answer devised by the FAA is collision avoidance technology: an audible flight deck alarm signal that the agency believes can reduce this kind of accident by 80 percent. As the FAA's proposal for installation of the technology went through the customary rule-making procedure in which comment is invited from interested parties, "the airlines got out ahead of us," Garvey says. They agreed the technology was necessary and liked the proposal. "So they're actually putting collision avoidance into the planes."

The second safety problem highlighted by the data—uncontrolled engine failure—spurred the FAA to issue nine proposed airworthiness directives in 1999. It got them out quickly, went into the rule-making period, and received very little comment. That was because, Garvey says, "we had worked with the industry, worked together with the data, and we all said this is what we need to do." In 2001 she thinks the agency should fix its sights on approach and landing procedures and runway incursions "because that's what the data is telling us." The agency has also begun to look not just at data, but at trends. "That's how we're going to make this safety record, which is so strong now, even better, by identifying precursors and trends."

What is most important in moving forward all these elements for which this job is responsible? "A collaborative, constructive partnership with the aviation community in its broadest sense," Garvey says. "We won't modernize the system unless we have the users, which includes the controllers and the industry, going in the same direction with us. So establishing a kind of consensus with them on what it means to modernize, what elements we want to put in place, is really crucial. With the safety agenda, we all own a piece of it, even recognizing that we're the regulator and have to call the shots when there's noncompliance. But determining together the most important priorities is something you can do in useful collaboration with the partners, whether they are flight attendants, pilots, the airlines, the aircraft industry, or consumer groups. Partnership has been the guiding theme I've tried to instill here."

In the late 1980s, support grew for the idea that the FAA should be an agency independent of the Department of Transportation (the move was recommended in 1988 by the Aviation Safety Commission, established by the Congress) and, alternatively, that the air traffic control system be broken out of the FAA. At several points, legislation was introduced into both houses of the Congress. At least part of this sentiment derived from the feeling that less-than-expert Department of Transportation staffers were micromanaging the FAA's operational duties and endangering the safety level of the air traffic control system.

While nothing obviously came of those proposals, more recent discussion has centered on privatizing air traffic control. Garvey believes that the post-2000 election period will see more debate on this subject. In 1994, she says, the Clinton administration proposed making the FAA a "quasi-government corporation" and, later, making it a performance-based organization (like the Commerce Department's Office of Patents and Trademarks, examined in this book). Neither of those ideas found much of a reception on the Hill, she says. But she thinks the issue raised—is there a better way to operate—is a valid one. "We're pretty unique in the civilian government. We're around twenty-four hours a day, 365 days a year. This is a service entity. Is there a better way to do it?"

The FAA, she continues, is looking at what it can do to move more to a performance-based organization "within the legislative framework that we have. I want to be able to say that we have taken advantage of every administrative flexibility we have." In the aviation world, she adds, the United States is just about the only industrial country without "some form of quasi-private or government type of corporation."

What the FAA did get, in 1996, were new procurement and personnel systems—the result of the administration's perception that current law was keeping the agency from timely acquisition of both equipment and people. With the help of the Senate Appropriations Committee, a provision went into the FAA 1996 budget freeing it from existing personnel and procurement regulations and exempting it from the control of both the Office of Management and Budget and the Merit Systems Protection Board.

Have these radical changes made a difference? "Two wonderful tools," Garvey answers. "On acquisition, our procedures are much more streamlined. We've cut the time it takes to award a contract in half." She also thinks, although it's still too early to know definitely, that the new process has reduced costs for some contractors. Personnel reform, though it presents a tougher challenge, has also benefited the agency. It can attract people from private industry that it could not attract earlier and made it possible to offer slightly higher salaries and, in some cases, bonuses. "We've hired some scientists and technology specialists at a higher level than I think we could have before," says Garvey, "and, again, streamlined the process to greatly reduce the time it takes to get people on board."

But she thinks the agency will realize the full promise of personnel reform "only when we completely shift from what is now a tenured system—with which we're all familiar in government—to pay for performance. And that's a very hard shift for people." While employees like pay for performance in principle, its implementation raises such concerns as how performance tied to pay is defined and who does evaluations. Garvey expresses satisfaction at the contract the FAA negotiated with air traffic controllers, a negotiation the agency entered with some fundamental objectives in mind. It wanted, for example, to freeze the number of controllers. Garvey personally wanted "recognition that they would buy into modernization and help us get it done." The negotiation succeeded. Controllers are very well paid, Garvey says, "but if you ask people here who have been around contracts a long time, they would say that we in management got an enormous amount in return. I don't think we've ever had a better working relationship with the controllers than we have today."

She describes the agency's and her own relationship with the Congress as positive, commenting that "I'm not sure you can do these jobs if you don't have a degree of support from the Hill." With the media, "it's tough because of the nature of their jobs. I like to be as responsive as I can. I remind my people all the time, we need to get back as quickly and as forthrightly as possible. We have a core group of reporters in aviation that I think are extraordinary—seven or eight who really know the issues. You can tell when the pros are on the scene, particularly when they are reporting a crash, because they present it in a very balanced way." On the whole, she sums up, she's sometimes pleased with what's happening vis-à-vis the media, and "some days I just feel discouraged."

Looking ahead, Garvey identifies three concerns on the administrator's agenda. First is modernization—"a great, great challenge" for the FAA that "in a sense is never finished because there is so much technology." Second is the structure of the agency: is it organized correctly to carry out modernization truly effectively? Third is "keeping that bar of safety high and raising it higher, especially in an industry that is growing by leaps and bounds."

The FAA is in a period of change, Garvey points out. "And that's going to be true for several more years."

PROFILE

Current Administrator of the Federal Aviation Agency
Jane F. Garvey, 1997–

Career summary

Acting administrator, Federal Highway Administration, 1997; deputy
administrator, 1993–97
Director, Logan International Airport, Boston, 1991–93
Commissioner, Massachusetts Department of Public Works, 1988–91

Education

B.A., Mount Saint Mary College, 1965; M.A., Mount Holyoke College, 1969

Administrators of the Federal Aviation Administration since 1989

Clinton administration

Linda Hall Daschle (acting), 1996–97 (currently senior public policy adviser,
Baker Donelson)
David R. Hinson, 1993–96 (currently businessman and aviation professional)
Thomas C. Richards (acting), 1992–93 (currently corporate consultant)

Bush administration

James B. Busey, 1989–93 (admiral, retired), U.S. Navy

11

Positions in Central Management

Executive Office of the President

▧ Director, Office of Management and Budget

EXECUTIVE LEVEL I—Presidential appointment
with Senate confirmation

RECOMMENDED SKILLS AND EXPERIENCE ■ Perhaps no perfect model exists for the credentials that best serve a position with the great range, depth, and staggering workload of this one. Business, economics, the law, and politics are all relevant backgrounds—but a mix of one or more of them is more helpful still. The indispensable elements are a strong grasp of the federal budget process, a significant degree of comfort with budgeting practice, institutional familiarity with the executive branch and the Congress, and experience at the intersection of political power and the disposition of public resources. Success in enforcing the president's policy and budget plans throughout the administration requires personal qualities of versatility, intellectual agility and stamina, and poise at the highest levels of executive branch authority.

Finally, and most vital, a director cannot hope to operate effectively without close personal links to the president and the White House chief of staff. For Jacob J. Lew, OMB's chief since 1998, good relationships in that quarter mean that OMB "will be well integrated into the White House decisionmaking process." Without that relationship, the director and his staff would lack the authority and credibility essential to their policy, financial, and management oversight of the federal executive.

INSIGHT ■ One new and key feature of the federal budget landscape—the surplus—will clearly affect the way future directors approach this job. Not that the mission of the position itself will change: the director's major task will always be to use the discipline of limited resources to make the right choices for the president among many competing priorities across the executive branch.

But in framing the job that way, Lew explains why the era of surplus makes a difference in how he sees the job. When distinguishing between programs for which strong cases can be made, he says, "it's more of a challenge when the perception is that there's no natural constraint"—that is, no budget deficit. "With a surplus, when everyone looking around sees little pots of gold that might be theirs, it's up to the president and budget director to set a tone where rigorous review is still the order of the day." That is true also because the federal budget is also a macroeconomic tool of considerable heft: fiscal policy can encourage low interest, strong investment, and growth—or just the opposite.

He adds a thought: OMB has come through such a long period of deficits that there's some confusion about what it takes to reduce the deficit and what it takes to do the job well. "Even when fiscal policy permits additional spending, you still need the discipline a budget provides. You still want to ask if programs work, if we're getting what we want to get out of them, if agencies are doing the jobs they're supposed to be doing. All those kinds of questions are important in terms of doing an effective job."

Does the surplus offer a better opportunity to be effective than a period of constraint? "This year," Lew answers, "we were very conscious of the fact that we were putting together a budget in a time of very good fiscal health. And we still made a bunch of very tough decisions." In a period where natural constraint gradually falls away, good budget making requires ever tougher policy argument and analysis. "It's no less important a function. Whoever becomes OMB director will inherit what we now face—the need to maintain discipline in a time of surplus. It's a great challenge."

Three characteristics mark OMB's distinctive role within the federal community. First, this experienced, dedicated agency is an omnipresent force in the central functions of governing—resource allocation, policy implementation, budget development, regulation, financial management, information systems, procurement. Second, because of its management responsibilities, OMB has governmentwide clients. But third and most important, if less immediately apparent, its principle client is the president.

The responsibility to assist the chief executive in deciding the allocation of public resources spent by the federal government has many complex moving parts. To inform those decisions fully, OMB frames the policy and resource issues for the president in five primary areas (each headed by a program associate director). It then develops the president's decisions as the framework of an annual budget, directing dozens of cabinet departments and independent agencies in shaping their individual components. OMB supervises the agencies as they subsequently propose and defend their budget requests to the Congress. It works closely and constantly with legislators around the calendar to support those legislative requests and seek enactment of the administration program they embody. In the process, of course, an administration's goals can and do regularly clash with the different notions developed and nourished in the Congress, regardless of which party is in charge. Not surprisingly, OMB usually spearheads the work to negotiate the countless adjustments and agreements—sometimes right up to final budget deals at the summit—that are necessary to reach overall policy, program, and budget concord between the administration and the Congress.

Within the administration itself, beyond the central budget portfolio, lies another entire set of OMB mandates. "We have coordinating functions on a wide range of issues that sometimes rise to the president's attention, sometimes don't," Lew says. They range from making sure all government agencies adhere to administration policy, to clearance of documents, congressional testimony, and public speaking. OMB's deputy director for management oversees the Office of Federal Procurement Policy, the Office of Federal Financial Management, and the Office of Information and Regulatory Affairs—all three administering management responsibilities based on statute.

What about the proposal to put the federal budget on a two-year cycle, which the Clinton administration supported? A little history is useful here. Once upon a time, OMB spent only part of each year preparing the budget and working with the Congress to enact it. Most of the remaining time could be invested in the agency's other tasks. Today, as Lew notes, funding issues dominate year-round. In the fall, the Congress is often still finishing appropriations for the fiscal year about to begin, while OMB meantime has started work on the next year's budget, to be presented in midwinter. That means a continuous focus between September and February either on negotiating the current budget (for the year just begun) or developing the next one. Then, in early spring, comes the administration's midyear supplemental budget request for the year in progress. When that is complete, the appropriations cycle for the coming year is already well under way and continues into the fall. Full circle, nonstop.

With a two-year budget cycle, Lew believes, "you'd have a break. When Congress finished its work in one of the years, you'd be looking at changes, management questions, longer-term issues. And then the supplemental would be much bigger—because unlike the current supplemental, it would be kind of a midcycle correction." Opponents of biennial budgeting think the supplemental would become too big, almost a new budget by itself, and the whole process would be back where it started. But Lew thinks there's reason to hope that things would, in fact, be different. "It's not a good situation," he says, "to have no break where you can step back and take a longer view." In any case, he believes enactment of a two-year cycle in 2000 (legislation to that effect was under consideration at this writing) would not affect his successor immediately, but in phases.

How do congressionally set caps on federal spending affect the state of the budget? In fiscal 2000, Lew says, the Congress exceeded its own caps, but "because of revised economics, we did better than had been projected and there was a surplus, no matter how you measure it." For fiscal 2001, OMB proposed new caps at what it considered reasonable levels. "In a time of surplus, it's critically important to be realistic about what the discretionary (nonentitlement) spending requirements are," he says. "You have to project the surplus based on a reasonable and enforceable set of limits—not come back year after year and have to bust the caps." If the Congress elects lower limits that exaggerate the size of the surplus, he notes, it will create a continued need to circumvent those caps. "And you won't have the surplus that's projected." Part of the OMB director's job is to keep these kinds of large budgetary questions in perspective, Lew believes. He thinks the choices made on them "are consequential for many years" and that "whoever takes my place will have to balance those judgments."

In 1994 an exercise called OMB 2000 sought to blend the agency's management functions more closely into the work of its budget side. The five budget areas run by program associate directors became Resource Management Offices, charged not just as policy developers and enforcers, appropriations managers, and budget examiners, but with integrating the full gamut of management concerns into their agency oversight duties. In 1996 people who had observed the results of this move to date were divided about the degree of its success. For his part, Lew thinks the result has been "more cohesion and unity." No matter what the organizational structure, he says, the pressures of the funding cycle keep the demand for work on the pure budget issues at formidable levels. Nonetheless, "if you look at the priority management objectives in the president's budget, they are highly integrated with our budget objectives." That was not an accident, he adds. "It was a deliberate attempt to put concentrated senior time into advancing management initiatives that support our budgetary priorities."

Is there any life left in the old argument by some that management deserves its own place within OMB or, perhaps, a separate identity outside OMB? Hardly any. "I don't see much push for it," says Lew, who also thinks it's a bad idea. In any case, says Barry White, a thirty-year OMB veteran, who was deputy associate director for education, income, and labor, the value is not in an isolated focus on management per se, but on using those tools to improve program performance. "You can get good program results with lousy financial management, bad procurement practice, obsolete information systems," White says. "But there is always a much better chance for great performance if those elements work effectively and can be brought to bear on making a program perform the way it is supposed to. That's what is possible when the management and budget focus is in the same organization."

OMB's staffing level is fairly stable, at about 500. Lew thinks the organization, with a very high workload, "needs to grow a little bit overall"; it has asked the Congress for some additional positions. The agency has long been known for the talent, expertise, and consistently superior performance of its career staff. Even at the senior level, there are relatively few politically appointed jobs. "We manage with a thin layer of political or policy staff and a large career staff," Lew says. "The key is to get the synergy between the two." The "unique" value that OMB adds to the executive office of the president, in his view, is a "very strong career staff that can be marshaled from the first day a president walks in the door. It doesn't take six months for people to learn their way around. If you can get political leadership in place quickly, that leadership will be briefed, staffed, and ready to hit the ground and run."

That brings up again the connection that runs between the president, the chief of staff, and the OMB director. It is crucial, Lew explains, because "it takes the support of the president in order to be able to say no on a credible basis. If everything can be run up the flag pole and perhaps reversed, OMB can't filter for the president and make decisions."

He elaborates on that point. When an agency wants to challenge an OMB decision, there are only two ways to go around the OMB director—through the president and through the chief of staff. It's not that OMB or its director has to win every round, because inevitably that won't happen. What's important is that the right decisions get made to carry out the president's objectives. This is not done by end running anybody, but by including everyone in an agreed solution.

Lew emphasizes that the ability to say no shouldn't be equated with the obligation to say no. "OMB directors who come in thinking that it's a 'no' job don't understand the job. An OMB director who has the confidence of the president and chief of staff will be able to work with the departments to make a real difference in terms of budgetary and substantive policy. The job is to help get to 'yes'—the policy that works, that fits overall as a comprehensive administration policy."

PROFILE

Current Director of the Office of Management and Budget
Jacob J. Lew, 1998–

Career summary

Deputy director, OMB, 1995–98

Executive associate director and associate director for legislative affairs, OMB, 1994–95

Special assistant to the president, 1993–94

Executive director, Center for Middle East Research, 1992

Attorney, Van Ness, Feldman, and Curtis, 1987–92

Assistant director, then executive director, House Democratic Steering and Policy Committee, 1979–87

Education

B.A., Harvard University, 1978; J.D., Georgetown University Law School, 1983

Directors of the Office of Management and Budget since 1989

Clinton administration

Franklin D. Raines, 1996–98 (currently president and CEO, Fannie Mae)

Alice M. Rivlin, 1994–96 (currently member, Financial Control Board of the District of Columbia; senior fellow, Brookings Institution)

Leon Panetta, 1993–94 (currently president, Panetta Institute)

Bush administration

Richard G. Darman, 1989–93 (currently partner and managing director, Carlyle Group)

Appendix A

Chapter 1 Sources

The women and men listed below took part as panelists or speakers in one or more of three leadership conferences for presidential appointees and nominees that took place in 1997, 1998, and 1999 under the joint sponsorship of the White House and the Council for Excellence in Government. Excerpts of their comments and counsel, offered in plenary sessions of the conferences, appear in chapter 1 of this book. The affiliations shown for these individuals were current as of June 30, 2000.

Paul Begala, assistant and counselor to the president

Mike Berman, president, Duberstein Group; former legal counsel and deputy chief of staff to the vice president

Ann Brown, chair, U.S. Consumer Product Safety Commission

Jack Buechner, partner, Manatt, Phelps, and Phillips; former member of Congress (R-Mo.)

Kay Casstevens, deputy counsel and director of legislative affairs for the vice president; former chief of staff to U.S. Sen. Tom Harkin (D-Iowa)

Joseph Dear, chief of staff to the governor, Washington State; former assistant secretary, Occupational Safety and Health Administration, U.S. Department of Labor

Jack Donahue, Raymond Vernon lecturer in public policy, John F. Kennedy School of Government, Harvard University

Mortimer Downey, deputy secretary, U.S. Department of Transportation

Jack Ebeler, Robert Wood Johnson Foundation; former deputy assistant secretary and acting assistant secretary for policy, U.S. Department of Health and Human Services

Mickey Edwards, lecturer in public policy, John F. Kennedy School of Government, Harvard University; former member of Congress (R-Okla.)

Dan Glickman, secretary of agriculture; former member of Congress (D-Kans.)

Daniel S. Goldin, administrator, U.S. National Aeronautics and Space Administration

Pat Griffin, president of Pangaea and senior adviser, Johnson Smith; former assistant to the president for legislative affairs

Lee Hamilton, director, Woodrow Wilson International Center for Scholars; former member of Congress (D-Ind.)

Peter Hart, chief executive officer and senior president, Peter D. Hart and Associates

Karen Hostler, congressional correspondent, the *Baltimore Sun*

Kathleen Hall Jamieson, dean, Annenberg School of Communications, University of Pennsylvania

Steven N. Kelman, Weatherhead professor of public management, John F. Kennedy School of Government, Harvard University

Susan King, vice president for public affairs, Carnegie Corporation of New York; former special adviser to the secretary, U.S. Department of Housing and Urban Development

Andy Kohut, director, Pew Research Center for the People and the Press

Mel Levine, partner, Gibson, Dunn, and Crutcher; former member of Congress (D-Calif.)

Ann F. Lewis, assistant to the president and White House Communications Director

Tom Mann, director, Governmental Studies Program, Brookings Institution

Barry R. McCaffrey, director, U.S. Office of National Drug Control Policy

Patricia McGinnis, president and CEO, Council for Excellence in Government

Howard Metzenbaum, chairman, Consumer Federation of America; former U.S. senator (D-Ohio)

Cheryl Mills, deputy counsel to the president

Mark Moore, professor of criminal justice policy and management, John F. Kennedy School of Government, Harvard University

Bob Nash, assistant to the president and director of the Office of Presidential Personnel

Constance Berry Newman, under secretary, Smithsonian Institution; former director, Office of Personnel Management

Norman Ornstein, resident scholar, American Enterprise Institute for Public Policy Research

Franklin Raines, chairman, Fannie Mae; former director, Office of Management and Budget

Gene Randall, news anchor, CNN

Bill Richardson, secretary of energy; former U.S. permanent representative to the United Nations; former member of Congress (D-N.M.)

Carol Rasko, senior adviser to the secretary of education; director, America Reads Challenge

Phil Sharp, lecturer in public policy, Kennedy School of Government; former member of Congress (D-Ind.)

Hannah Sistare, staff director, Committee on Government Affairs, U.S. Senate

Gene Sperling, assistant to the president for economic policy and director of the National Economic Council

Pete Williams, legal correspondent, NBC News; former assistant secretary of public affairs, U.S. Department of Defense

James R. Whittinghill, senior vice president, American Trucking Association; former deputy chief of staff to U.S. Sen. Bob Dole (R-Kans.)

Morley Winograd, senior policy adviser to the vice president and director, National Partnership for Reinventing Government

James Lee Witt, director, U.S. Federal Emergency Management Agency

Janet Woodcock, director, Center for Drug Evaluation and Research, U.S. Federal Drug Administration

Additional Positions Meriting Attention

This book examines sixty-one positions, twenty of them in group profiles. Almost all of them are Executive Schedule jobs filled by presidential appointment and confirmed by the Senate. Another eleven such positions, though selected for the book, are not discussed because their occupants were not available for interview.* All selections of positions were made by a committee of Principals of the Council for Excellence in Government. They began with a list of nearly 150 positions, a number distilled in several stages from the more than 1,100 in the presidentially appointed, Senate-confirmed category.

Refining the 150 down to a number manageable for the book often involved difficult choices between jobs that were of almost equal importance in the eyes of the committee. Those that did not make the list are shown below by category and by department or agency. Some have been discussed in earlier *Prune Books*.

Economy, Technology, and Trade

▨ Department of Agriculture

Under Secretary for Farm and Foreign Agricultural Services

▨ Department of Commerce

Assistant Secretary for U.S. Foreign and Commercial Service
Under Secretary for International Trade
Under Secretary for Technology

▨ Department of Energy

Assistant Secretary for Energy Efficiency and Renewable Energy
Assistant Secretary for Political and International Affairs
Under Secretary

*Director of the Central Intelligence Agency, Chairman of the Board of Governors of the Federal Reserve System, Chairman of the Council of Economic Advisers, Director of the Federal Bureau of Investigation, Commissioner of the Immigration and Naturalization Service, Chairman of the Federal Communications Commission, Surgeon General of the United States, Administrator of the Environmental Protection Agency, Administrator of the National Aeronautics and Space Administration, Assistant Secretary of the Treasury for International Affairs, and Assistant Secretary of Commerce for Import Administration.

Department of State

Under Secretary for Economic, Business, and Agricultural Affairs

Department of the Treasury

Commissioner, U.S. Customs Service
Under Secretary for Domestic Finance
Under Secretary for International Affairs

Independent Agencies

President, U.S. Import-Export Bank
Vice Chairman, Federal Reserve System

Foreign Policy, National Security, and Defense

Department of Defense

Assistant Secretary for Special Operations/Low Intensity Conflict
Chairman, Joint Chiefs of Staff
Director, Operational Test and Evaluation
Under Secretary for Personnel and Readiness
Under Secretary for Policy

Department of State

Regional Assistant Secretaries of State (Europe, Africa, Near East,
   South Asia, East Asia and Pacific, Western Hemisphere)
Under Secretary for Global Affairs
Under Secretary for Public Diplomacy

Health, Safety, and Environment

Department of Health and Human Services

Administrator, Substance Abuse and Mental Health Services
   Administration
Assistant Secretary for Planning and Evaluation

Department of Labor

Assistant Secretary for Mine Safety and Health

Environment Protection Agency

Assistant Administrator, Air and Radiation
Assistant Administrator, Enforcement and Compliance Assurance
Assistant Administrator, Policy and Planning
Assistant Administrator, Prevention, Pesticides, and Toxic Substances
Assistant Administrator, Research and Development
Assistant Administrator, Solid Waste and Emergency Response
Assistant Administrator, Water

Jobs, Income Security, and Welfare

Department of Housing and Urban Development

Assistant Secretary for Fair Housing and Equal Opportunity
Director, Federal Housing Enterprise and Oversight
Director, Multifamily Housing Assistance Restructuring

Department of the Interior

Assistant Secretary for Indian Affairs
Chairman, National Indian Gaming Commission

Department of Labor

Assistant Secretary for Employment Standards
Administrator, Wage and Hour Division
Director, Women's Bureau
Solicitor

Department of Veterans Affairs

Under Secretary for Veterans Benefits Administration

Education, Training, and Lifelong Learning

Department of Education

Under Secretary

Law Enforcement

Department of Justice

Assistant Attorney General, Civil Division
Assistant Attorney General, Civil Rights
Assistant Attorney General, Criminal Division
Assistant Attorney General, Environment and Natural Resources
Assistant Attorney General, Office of Justice Programs
Assistant Attorney General, Office of Legal Affairs
Assistant Attorney General, Tax Division
Director, Bureau of Justice Assistance

Department of State

Assistant Secretary for International Narcotics and Law Enforcement Affairs

Department of the Treasury

Under Secretary for Enforcement

Independent Agencies

Director, Office of National Drug Control Policy

National Infrastructure

Department of Housing and Urban Development

Assistant Secretary for Community Planning and Development

Department of the Interior

Assistant Secretary for Fish and Wildlife and Parks
Assistant Secretary for Land and Minerals Management
Assistant Secretary for Water and Science
Director, Bureau of Reclamation
Director, Fish and Wildlife Service
Director, U.S. Geological Survey

Department of Transportation

Administrator, Federal Highway Administration
Administrator, Federal Transit Administration
Assistant Secretary for Aviation and International Affairs
Assistant Secretary for Transportation Policy
Associate Deputy Secretary

Independent Agencies

Director, Office of Government Ethics

Central Management

General Services Administration

Administrator

Office of Personnel Management

Director